HAP ARNOLD

AND THE EVOLUTION OF AMERICAN AIRPOWER

DIK ALAN DASO

SMITHSONIAN INSTITUTION PRESS
Washington and London

COPY EDITOR: Anne Collier Rehill
PRODUCTION EDITOR: Robert A. Poarch
DESIGNER: Janice Wheeler

Library of Congress Cataloging-in-Publication Data
Daso, Dik A., 1959–
    Hap Arnold and the evolution of American airpower / Dik Alan Daso.
       p.   c.—(Smithsonian history of aviation series)
    Includes bibliographical references and index.
    ISBN 1-56098-824-X (alk. paper)
    1. Arnold, Henry Harley, 1886–1950. 2. World War, 1939–1945—Aerial
operations, American. 3. Generals—United States—Biography. 4. United
States. Army Air Forces—Biography. 5. Air power—United States. I. Title.
II. Series.
  D790.A925   2000
  940.54'4973—dc21   99-048037

British Library Cataloguing-in-Publication Data is available

Manufactured in the United States of America
06 05 04 03 02 01 00 5 4 3 2 1

⅘The paper used in this publication meets the minimum requirements of the
American National Standard for Information Sciences—Permanence of Paper
for Printed Library Materials ANSI Z39.48-1984.

On pages i and xxi: Henry Harley "Hap" Arnold's handwritten initials, included on
hundreds of Air Force documents during his military career.

We damned airmen were "too cocky, too big for our boots, undisciplined, too damned free all around!" My answer to that is one which I feel more strongly to-day than I did then: . . . Of all the Air Force's faults, its greatest has always been the fact that it has made its work seem too easy.

Henry Harley "Hap" Arnold

CONTENTS

FOREWORD BY RICHARD OVERY   ix

PREFACE   xv

INTRODUCTION   1

1   HENRY HARLEY ARNOLD (1886–1903)   7

2   CADET "PEWT" ARNOLD, WEST POINT CLASS OF '07 (1903–7)   13

3   SECOND LIEUTENANT HENRY H. ARNOLD, INFANTRY (1907–11)   32

4   "THEY ARE HERE TO LEARN TO FLY" (1911–12)   44

5   "A CUSHION-CHAIR OFFICER" (1912–16)   61

6   CAPTAIN TO COLONEL: THE GREAT WAR (1916–18)   80

7   INTERWAR YEARS, A DIFFICULT EDUCATION (1918–29)   101

8   INTERWAR YEARS, COMMAND EXPERIENCE (1929–38)   121

9   CHIEF OF THE ARMY AIR CORPS (1938–41)   151

10 COMMANDING GENERAL, ARMY AIR FORCES (1941–44)   169

11 GENERAL OF THE ARMY: FIVE STARS FOR AIRPOWER (1944–46)   198

12 HASTEN THE CAISSON (1946–50)   215

EPILOGUE: "THE SPIRIT OF A MAN"   226

APPENDIX 1: CADET RECORD, CAREER ASSIGNMENTS,
AND MILITARY RANK PROGRESSION   235

APPENDIX 2: ARMY AIR CORPS AND AIR FORCES
ORGANIZATIONAL CHARTS   239

NOTES   247

SELECTED BIBLIOGRAPHY   295

INDEX   307

FOREWORD

The memoirs of Gen. Hastings Ismay, Churchill's representative on the British Chiefs of Staff Committee during World War II, contain one of the few profiles of Gen. Henry "Hap" Arnold written by those who had regular contact with him during that conflict. Ismay recalled that Arnold possessed "an unlimited belief in air power," which he sustained with an unusually friendly disposition. Arnold "was always cheerful and smiling," commented Ismay, who thought "Hap" must be an abbreviation of "happy," which it was. When it mattered though, Arnold could also be tough. The British chiefs of staff respected him, in words sent on the occasion of his retirement in 1946, as a "staunch and generous friend."[1]

This was a fitting tribute to a man who had championed airpower in the United States all his life and who, more than any other airman, had helped to persuade Roosevelt and the U.S. Congress that war would only be won by mobilizing that power on the very largest scale. The British chiefs perhaps recognized just how much the Allies had depended on the Unites States's vast air effort to achieve final victory. For all this, Arnold never became a household name like Billy Mitchell or Charles Lindbergh.

In other memoirs he features very little. Eisenhower mentions him only three times; Churchill's great multivolume history of the war gives Arnold scarcely more than a dozen brief entries.[2] This can be explained by the general's unusual diffidence at the great summit meetings and in Combined Chiefs of Staff conferences where, according to Ismay, he spoke little if General Marshall, his immediate superior, was present.

The great inter-Allied meetings were not to Arnold's taste. He did, in Ismay's very British phrase, "splendid work behind the scenes." In this he was very like

Gen. George C. Marshall, whom Arnold first met in the Philippines in 1914 on military exercise and with whom he subsequently formed a firm friendship. Arnold, like Marshall—or Eisenhower for that matter—was not a commander with combat experience. Dik Daso reminds us that by the time Arnold took over command of the Air Corps in 1938, he had never fired a shot in war, nor dropped a bomb, though he was to cause thousands of others to do so. Arnold was a military manager who recognized that the building of any military service, particularly one as expensive and technically complex as an air force, needed a balance between all the elements of airpower: technology and science, personnel selection and training, production and doctrine.

Military management never grabbed the headlines, but it is the essence of the modern military machine. Though Arnold chafed at the bit as a young officer when he was not in a cockpit, his strengths were recognized from the start as those of an organizer, planner, and manager of men. The evolution of the American air arm under the wing of the much more powerful U.S. Army also required airmen to be politicians, and Arnold had to rise to that challenge. It is evident that the administrative structure of the air forces encouraged U.S. airmen to be managerial in style. Chief of the Air Corps was a modest job when Arnold took it over in 1938 at the height of American disarmament, but it embraced all aspects of the air service, from combat to logistics, training, production, research and development. When the job changed to that of commander of the Army Air Forces in 1941, the task became a colossal one. Only Hermann Goering, the former fighter pilot who became overlord of the German air force in 1935, had an equivalent set of responsibilities.

Here, of course, the resemblance ended. Goering was never equal to those responsibilities; he squandered German airpower because of it. Where Goering was indolent or poorly informed, Dik Daso shows that Arnold was a whirlwind of work who relied on being a clear thinker, fully in command of the facts. A less charitable critic might argue that Arnold tried to do too much, perhaps from a Napoleonic fear of delegation to men who did not share his clarity of thought or his work ethic. Certainly when he finally handed his job over to Gen. Carl Spaatz in 1946, he passed on a long memorandum setting out guidelines for his successor to follow. Arnold was an ambitious man, in the best sense of the word. He believed that his dedication to airpower was necessary for the infant service, and he clearly liked to be at the center of things. Later in life he gave up the reins of command with great reluctance, despite the terrible toll that work had taken on his own health and on the happiness and unity of his family.

Any assessment of Arnold's contribution to the development of American airpower must take into account the many roles in which he found himself. He was above all a crusader for aviation, who saw earlier than many how important aircraft were going to be for the development of modern, industrialized warfare. He did not indulge, as many did, in the idea of a fully independent air force, relegating navies and armies to the sidelines (though he had copies of Douhet's work in his files).[3] But he was committed to the idea that in an age of total war, bomber aircraft were peculiarly suited to bringing pressure directly to bear on the enemy's economy and military infrastructure, and to defeating the enemy's air force.[4] He was an unswerving advocate of the heavy bomber during the long fight in the 1930s to get the B-17 accepted for volume production. He did not write airpower doctrine, but he knew what he wanted it to say.

At times, Arnold's advocacy of offensive aviation—"real air power," as he described it in his memoir—was critical. He played an important part in swinging Roosevelt behind large-scale air rearmament at a memorable White House meeting on 14 November 1938. This saved the heavy bomber and laid the foundation for massive American air forces.[5] Arnold was the central player later in the war at the Casablanca Conference in persuading Roosevelt and Churchill to endorse American daylight bombing and make possible the Combined Bomber Offensive.

Arnold was committed with perhaps equal passion to the idea of organizational unity rather than independence. He was an enthusiast for proper systems of training and personnel selection, without which the quality of commanders—from the most junior to the most senior—could not be secured. This explains his willingness to allow commanders in the field a good deal of independence from top-level interference in the actual conduct of operations. These proved to be important priorities when Arnold found himself overseeing the mushrooming of the American Air Service in 1941. Training and logistics were not the glamorous side of war, but without adequate trained manpower and systems of supply, air combat after 1941 would have withered on the vine.

Dik Daso's biography of Arnold focuses not on his strategic grasp nor on his organizational skill, but on what was arguably his most significant attribute: his recognition that the exercise of airpower relied critically on the mobilization of modern science and technology. Few leading airmen would have dissented, but few seem to have shared Arnold's breadth of vision or powerful conviction that airpower was entirely hostage to what scientists and engineers could develop. He formed close links with the scientific community and was constantly alive to what those working at the scientific threshold might supply.

Arnold himself in his memoirs gives a typical example when he discusses the origin of napalm. On a visit to Britain in 1941, he saw for himself the new incendiary bombs that had been used by the Germans and the British with devastating effort. He returned to Washington aware that there was a deficiency to make up. He called together representatives of the Ordnance Department, the Chemical Warfare Service, and Dr. Vannevar Bush, the MIT scientist who became chief scientific adviser to the Roosevelt administration as director of the Office of Scientific Research and Development. Bush told Arnold about an incendiary jelly that burned with an intense heat on anything it touched, even water. The result was the development of napalm, dropped from fighter-bombers on German positions in the Normandy campaign in 1944.[6]

Arnold spent a great deal of his time as chief of the Air Services promoting the vanguard technologies that were transforming aviation, among them jet propulsion, rockets, and radar. He formed a close connection with the Hungarian scientist Theodore von Kármán. The meeting at La Guardia airport, when Arnold passed to Kármán the torch of air-force scientific development, features in Daso's account as a crucial turning point in the development of what became by the 1960s an independent air command that used jets, rockets, and advanced electronic communications, and was armed with nuclear bombs and warheads. No doubt much of this development would have taken place with or without Arnold, but the establishment of scientific priorities built around a close connection between the civilian science community and the air force bore Arnold's stamp.

The concern with science marked Arnold as a very modern commander. He did not share the fantastic or science-fiction view of airpower that was widespread in the interwar years, even among airmen themselves. His feet were firmly on the ground. Airpower for Arnold was a function of the ability of states to mobilize the key elements of the modern age—science, technology, mass production, corporate organization—in pursuit of a technically proficient and efficiently structured air force. Arnold symbolized the ability and readiness of the United States to forge ahead in the development of all these elements, both stimulated by and stimulating the modernization of the American military establishment and the industries and laboratories on which its evolution hinged.

This achievement was all the more remarkable for a man whose career began only shortly after the Wright Brothers first flew, and whose early experiences of aviation were formed by a very limited technical base and a confused and ill-defined sense of what aircraft could do in war. By the time Arnold died in 1950, both the technical possibilities and the doctrine had altered out of recognition. It is to Arnold's credit that this transformation did not leave him behind. He emerges in the pages of Dik Daso's shrewd and sympathetic biography as a man of real vision and commitment, who made it his job to marry the development of the air force he cared about so passionately to the rational scientific forces that were rapidly changing the material world around him.

Richard Overy

Notes

1. Gen. Hastings L. Ismay, *The Memoirs of Lord Ismay* (London: Heinemann, 1960), 253–54.
2. This is true also for the diary for Lord Alanbrooke, who sat alongside Arnold on the Com-

bined Chiefs of Staff for three years and yet had nothing of substance to say about him. See Arthur Bryant, *Triumph in the West: The War Diaries of Field Marshall Lord Alanbrooke* (London: Collins, 1959).
3. Library of Congress, Washington, D.C., Arnold Papers, Box 245, "Air Warfare," by Gen. Giulio Douhet.
4. National Archives, Washington, D.C., RG 94, 452-1, Arnold to adjutant-general, 9 June 1937. Arnold argued that the United States must provide "bombardment aviation at least the equal in numbers, range and speed performances, and striking power, to that of any other nation or possible coalition."
5. Jeffrey S. Underwood, *The Wings of Democracy: The Influence of Air Power on the Roosevelt Administration, 1933–1942* (College Station: Texas A & M University Press, 1991), 134–35.
6. Henry H. Arnold, *Global Mission* (New York: Harper & Row, 1949), 243. Use of napalm in Wesley Frank Craven and James Lea Cate, *The Army Air Force in World War II,* vol. 3 (Chicago, 1951), 233, 262.

PREFACE

When I graduated from the United States Air Force Academy in 1981, Brig. Gen. William "Billy" Mitchell was considered the Father of the Air Force. His legendary court-martial, it was believed by most cadets, was a tremendous example of self-sacrifice and personal courage—one to be emulated by any young officer. Today, as a lieutenant colonel, I wonder why that was true.

Mitchell was an insubordinate, often pompous, outspoken Army officer who was nonetheless revered by his subordinates. He set the early standard for the "swaggering" fighter pilot image so coveted by twenty-one-year-old pilots headed for the cockpits of the hottest planes in the world. His theories of strategic bombing and the 1921 bombardment tests struck fear into the fiscal heart of the Navy—another plus for an Air Force Academy graduate. Mitchell was our hero.

The reader may already perceive the inherent problems with such an ethos in today's military. Sexual harassment in all branches of service, breaches in superior-subordinate relationships, and the advent of the "political correctness" movement in both civilian and military culture—an effort to soften the realities of humanity—have politely but assuredly de-emphasized the legend of Billy Mitchell. During the last fifteen years, our society, and thus our military—both driven by a media sound bite–oriented age perpetuated by high-speed electronic computer technology—have evolved into something far different than they were in 1981, and vastly different than at the turn of the twentieth century.

After my first twelve years in the Air Force, all in flying assignments in supersonic jet trainers and fighters, I reluctantly began an academic sabbatical that culminated with the award of a doctorate in military history from the University of South Carolina in 1996. My undergraduate major had also been military history, although I received a bachelor of science degree along with the rest of my classmates at the USAF Academy. I initially had misgivings about taking a break from flight duty, but soon enough I became one of only a handful of Air Force fighter pilots with a Ph.D. in history. Many of my colleagues find this as amusing as I do—we often joke that the term *smart fighter pilot* seems oxymoronic. Spending significant periods of time away from the Air Force in civilian, primarily university, environments only served to emphasize the reasons for the relative decline in Mitchell's influence.

Upon my return to the "real" Air Force as a member of the USAF General Staff, serving in the Doctrine Division at the Pentagon, I was surprised to find that a "new-old" name had been resurrected and heralded as the historical focus for the fiftieth anniversary of the Air Force, 18 September 1997. The name that continually surfaced in the speeches of the secretary of the Air Force, Sheila Widnall, and the chief of staff, Gen. Ronald R. Fogleman, was General of the Air Force Henry Harley "Hap" Arnold.

My doctoral work had concentrated upon the technological origins and underpinnings of the Air Force and the individuals who were most directly involved in such affairs. General Arnold was one of these, so I was not totally unfamiliar with his career. But why such a dramatic shift from Mitchell to Arnold as an icon for the Air Force? Why this particular evolution? Arnold's private flaws of personality certainly rival Mitchell's public ones. My conclusion, after living and working in Washington for three years, is that Arnold—particularly from the perspective of a civilian—was far more politically correct than Mitchell.

Thus, I suggest, it is because Air Force leadership has, for the most part, learned its lesson about bucking the political system at too high a level that Arnold has become a vastly superior public role model upon which to link the history of the service. He entered West Point the same year that the Wright brothers successfully achieved powered flight, a convenient coincidence. His life was synchronized with the evolution of the airplane—and thus airpower—from bailing wire through the supersonic jet age. More important, Arnold's life symbolized the evolution of aviation from a single technological object to a complex megasystem that today spans continents and encircles the globe in air and space.

Although Arnold sometimes pressed the limits of discipline and made several near–career-ending errors during his lifetime, he learned to work effectively within military and political systems. He unwillingly became a very capable international bureaucrat, a servant and a staunch supporter of civil political leadership. In my view it is Arnold's journey through history, not his final destination in history, that offers the most critical insight into the mind and times of the commander of the most powerful Air Force ever assembled—even until this day. Any individual, not just military personnel, may gain significant insight from the story of Arnold's trials, victories, and defeats on the way to inheriting such staggering responsibility as being the United States's air commander during World War II. It seems appropriate, therefore, to update the scant Arnold historical literature by offering a fresh look at the life of the Air Force's only five-star general. Several colleagues, both military and civilian, agree with this assessment.

Arnold's life spanned three American wars—the Spanish-American War, World War I, and World War II. There is enough primary-source material buried in libraries and archives across the country to easily fill two, maybe even three detailed volumes about this man's wide-ranging experience. Because such a lengthy work was not practical (from my publisher's point of view, anyway), I decided to focus on the critical elements of science and technology that so influenced Arnold's personal and professional life, both inside and outside the military environment.

This approach seemed a logical choice, since the airplane, the technological achievement that most influenced warfare in the twentieth century, was the focal point of Arnold's military life for so many years. The people, the institutions, and the tough decisions that were associated with technological change of the nation's air forces, as we are today familiar with them, remain similar to those faced by top executives across this country every day.

It is a tremendous irony that this man, actively serving in the Army during two world wars, never personally fired a shot or dropped a bomb in combat. Those readers who enjoy combat history may be disappointed in the quantity of such narrative included herein, although there is some. Histories of the operational Army Air Forces line today's bookshelves, but biographies of air leaders—in fact, historical biography in general—have suffered of late, despite the belief of many academic historians that biography makes history come alive. In that, I wholeheartedly agree.

As an academy graduate, I found researching Arnold's West Point years both informative and familiar. Chapter 2 may seem long to the layman, but the information it contains is important. The influence of the academy years is crucial to understanding the career of any graduate officer, but, more important, it is crucial to understanding the nature of the military at that time. Coincidentally, Air Force Academy cadets and alumni may find answers to many of their nagging questions concerning academy life. Military Academy cadets will learn even more about their own school's history.

The name of the evolving Army air arm changed continually between 1907 and 1930. Throughout this book, I have done my best to refer to the service by the term that was correct at the time in question.

I have endeavored to tell Arnold's story at the most intimate and personal level possible. This is, after all, a book about a man—one whose spirit, dedication, insecurity, imagination, endurance, volatility, and compassion have been misinterpreted, and consequently misunderstood, over the past five decades. To write at this level, access to his personal papers was essential. Fortunately, Arnold's grandson Robert granted me access not only to the private letters between Arnold and his wife, Bee, but also to the Arnold ranch, El Rancho Feliz, in Sonoma, California.

Together we unburied boxes of dusty, rubber band–bound letters from Arnold to his wife, Beadle, dug through cobweb-covered artifacts and portraits, and drank a little California wine. Unfortunately Arnold was not the packrat that Bee was, and most of her letters to him no longer exist. However, many from Bee to her mother do survive. There were more than 1,500 letters from Arnold to Bee; we did not count them exactly. Some had been made available to researchers in the 1970s; many others were, at that time, stored away and unavailable.

All that are known to exist are now in Robert's possession, and he freely opened his personal archive for me on several occasions. The insight and the raw reality often revealed in these letters serve to liven the narrative a tremendous amount. Wherever possible, I have allowed the general to speak for himself, offering context and analysis of his words, balanced by additional official documents and appropriate secondary works. The candor of the letters frequently surprised the hell out of me, as I suspect they will the reader. I have made only rare and minor changes of punctuation and spelling in the letter excerpts, and only when it seemed necessary to ensure clarity.

This book is the result of many others' kindness and consideration. To Robert Arnold I owe my greatest debt and my most heartfelt thanks for warmly welcoming me into his home. I give Robert tremendous credit for encouraging me—in fact, insisting that I find the facts and write the truth; there are some warts in this story. It would have been easy for him to prefer hero worship, but he has never done so. Without that concern perched over my head, writing this book has been much easier, and I have no doubt that the final product is better because of it.

An early draft of this project was completed while I was serving as the Verville Fellow at the Smithsonian Institution, National Air and Space Museum in Washington, D.C., during 1997–98. As an Air Force pilot and historian, there is little that can compare with coming to work each day and standing beneath the Wright Flyer, the *Spirit of St. Louis,* the Bell *XP-59A* and *X-1,* in awe of the evolution of aviation technology that has occurred in less than a century. I admit it: I love airplanes and I love to fly. I hope that my experience as an Air Force pilot contributes both to the reader's technical understanding of aeronautics and to a better comprehension of those inner emotions that frequently accompany the thrills of military flying. These, I believe (except for the vast increase in pilots' confidence in their planes), have remained pretty much unchanged since 17 December 1903.

Initially an outsider, and entering the fellowship on the heels of the *Enola Gay* debacle that made national headlines and headaches for the entire museum staff, I was quickly made to feel a part of the NASM aeronautics family—an important part. To name all the fine members on the third floor would certainly slight someone. From the museum director to Louise, our diligent custodian, they all contributed to a tremendous year.

There were two, however, who assisted me above and well beyond the call of their assigned duties. My fellowship adviser, Michael J. Neufeld, carefully exposed flaws in early drafts, from poor logic to poor style. His gifted insight and delicate brutality significantly improved this work. Phil Edwards of the NASM library granted me access to the single greatest aeronautics-history fact finder ever known: himself. Phil is indeed a national treasure, and a sincerely humble one.

I owe special thanks as well to several friends and colleagues who took time to read sections of this manuscript. Dr. Stephen Grove, the West Point historian, offered critical comments to the chapter dealing with that institution. Maj. Bob White, USAF, and Dr. Jeff Underwood provided reality checks for the interwar chapters. Col. Phil Meilinger, Ph.D., USAF, read the entire work and provided insight that might only be available from another military biographer. I am deeply indebted to I. B. Holley, professor emeritus, Duke University. His half century of experience in researching and writing airpower-related history was offered and gratefully accepted; his contribution to this book can never be adequately repaid.

Several institutions also made vital contributions to the completion of this work. Many years ago, the USAF Historical Research Agency offered me a research grant so that I could begin my study of airpower and technology. Since that time I have made frequent visits to the HRA as well as to the Library of Congress, the USAF Academy Special Collections Division (under the care of Duane Reed), the National Archives, and other repositories that have never failed me in their kind efforts, even if material was scarce or nonexistent. I am grateful as well to research assistant John Tyree of Arlington National Cemetery, for helping me verify personal records and dates.

I would be remiss if I neglected to thank former Air Force chief of staff Gen. Ronald R. Fogleman, USAF (Ret.). Had he not authorized revisions in USAF personnel rules concerning mandatory changes of assignments when he did, I would have served out my days in the Pentagon as an action officer without any possibility of ever accepting any fellowship or researching this book. In this case, dumb luck and timing were the harbingers of opportunity. Ron Fogleman represents the finest of a dying breed, the true soldier/scholar. The epilogue of this book is dedicated specifically to him.

Finally, a book cannot be completed without a tolerant family. I am fortunate to have one of these. For that I am grateful.

INTRODUCTION

My Darling Beadle,

You can never imagine or conceive the number of ships en route between England and N. France and the tremendous concentration of ships at the beaches and yet not a single German plane has hit a ship. The German A.F. seems to have been bombed and fought out of existence. They have no punch left. They had a wonderful opportunity to sink some 4,000 ships and stop the invasion—an opportunity seldom presented to any air force. . . .

All my love,

Your

Hap[1]

B efore Arnold had arrived on the beaches of France the morning of 12 June 1944, Gen. Dwight David Eisenhower's son John recently graduated from West Point and on summer furlough, was invited on a short tour with the supreme commander to the beachhead. The closed-ranks parade of truck, tanks, and equipment would have astounded and appalled any West Pointer—to concentrate forces in the open, on a beachhead, was a clear violation of Army doctrine. Ike reassured his son, "If I didn't have air supremacy, I wouldn't be here."[2]

Even though German ground resistance was stiff in places, Allied surface forces possessed a distinct advantage at Normandy, particularly with the onset of fair weather. Air supremacy achieved, Allied ground troops were unconstrained by enemy aerial attacks. Meanwhile, Allied air forces remained free to assail enemy positions at will. Nevertheless, breakout from the beachhead would take until August.

Arnold's journey to Normandy started in London early on the morning of the twelfth. He, Gen. George C. Marshall, and Adm. Ernest J. King boarded prime minister Winston Churchill's private train to Portsmouth, where they transferred to the destroyer USS *Thompson*. Together with Adm. William D. Leahy, these four men made up the Joint Chiefs of Staff. After plowing through the concentrated mass of ships that spanned the English Channel, the group of "brass hats" were ushered aboard suitable landing craft. Through calm seas, several of the highest-ranking Allied officers in Europe then disembarked onto the beachhead.

There was no visible sign of the Luftwaffe.

After a situation briefing at First Army headquarters, Gen. Omar Bradley's outfit, the commanders went separate ways inspecting troops, extolling their courage and assuring further success. Bradley's after-action reports revealed that there had been no enemy air action the night before or throughout the day on 6 June, D day. It was not until nightfall that between 115 and 150 German aircraft dropped bombs, torpedoes, and mines against offshore shipping. During the following three weeks, 244 daytime enemy missions and 438 night attacks were flown. These raids were more an annoyance than anything else, as the Twelfth Army had prepared for 1,800 enemy sorties against the beachhead, when in fact there were far fewer. Bradley's report noted that "from D plus 15 forward, the German Air Force failed to count as a serious threat to Allied military operations. . . . During the rest of the campaign, our air superiority was so conclusive that it was an accepted factor in all planning."[3]

Perhaps this was the impetus behind Bradley's memo to Arnold, complimenting the Army Air Forces on a job well done. Admiral King, however, attributed much of the difficulty experienced by the invasion surface forces at "Omaha" beach to the Army Air Forces' curtailment of bombing operations due to foul weather that morning.[4] Nonetheless, Arnold was so impressed by the airmen he visited that he found nothing to "correct," an unusual occurrence for the demanding general.[5] For Gen. Hap Arnold, this visit to the Normandy beaches was one of the most satisfying of his military career—a career that spanned four decades.

Well satisfied by the D-day air situation, a jovial Arnold, his aide, and his theater commander, Gen. Carl "Tooey" Spaatz, boarded a fully armored B-17 that had landed on a 2,500-foot-long strip near the beach. Before an uneventful return to Bovingdon, England, their home base, Spaatz's pilot successfully cleared a hazardous gully at the end of the short runway and dodged several barrage balloons still tethered nearby.[6] Relieved and exhausted, Arnold, after a long, cool bath, retired to a deep sleep. He was not even disturbed by falling pulse-jet powered, V-1 buzz bombs.

The immensity of the war effort precluded any one individual from orchestrating the minute details of global air operations, massive aircraft-production efforts, personnel recruitment and training, or aviation research and development for the Army Air Forces. Arnold's responsibility was to place personnel in positions of authority from which these functions could be efficiently accomplished. Those individuals, military and civilian, men and women, senior and junior in rank, were selected to achieve particular results. Each relationship was unique; some were much more familiar than others. Each commander's abilities were distinct, and everyone, at all levels, reacted differently to the tremendous pressure of war. For Hap Arnold, winning the war transcended personal feelings. Most of his commanders understood that his reactions to unachieved goals and shattered expectations were nothing personal.

The ultimate achievements of the Army Air Forces in World War II did not come easily, quickly, or without cost in both dollars and lives. Yet the struggle to build American airpower had begun even before the First World War—and Arnold had been one of the first to realize the complexities involved in developing the airplane's full military potential.

Where Arnold differed from most other air commanders was in the breadth of his military experience and command responsibilities. After the spring of 1939, he had assumed responsibility both for American air operations around the globe and for the production and training programs required to create a fighting air force from a meager one. Of critical importance to Arnold were his commanders—those responsible for building planes, training pilots and mechanics, accomplishing necessary research and then applying the results to combat weapons and aircraft, building air bases and supplying them with the required personnel, and a host of other important behind-the-scenes jobs. Any one of these not accomplished quickly or efficiently might have adversely affected the establishment of massive and powerful American air force.

Another facet of Arnold's influence upon the creation of air force for the United States was a fascination with science and technology. Having been associated from the beginning with military aircraft, he came to understand the vital nature of technological change and its crucial relationship to aeronautical development. Over the span of his career, Arnold was informally educated by some of the greatest science and technology experts in the world.

In the early years of aviation, he studied at the Wright Brothers' ground school, worked with engineering wizard Charles Kettering, and forged relationships with Henry Ford, Donald Douglas, and other industrialists. By World War II, he was close associates with Dr. Theodore von Kármán, Dr. Edward Bowles, Dr. Vannevar Bush, and many others in the scientific and engineering community—experts in a wide range of developing aviation-related fields of study. All willingly spent time with Arnold, educating him, informing him, and convincing him that scientific inquiry and technological change were inherently, critically, and dynamically related to airpower.

To say that Gen. Hap Arnold was gregarious would be to understate the breadth and depth of his associations and relationships across a wide spectrum of professions and occupations. By the time the United States entered World War II, at the decision-making level Arnold was personally acquainted with nearly everyone who had anything to do with the development of American airpower—officers, industrialists, research scientists, and teachers. His associations often extended beyond aviation. He had many friends in Hollywood whom he used to bolster popular support for airpower; he made acquaintances in the broadcasting industry that allowed him to carry his message to still larger audiences.

Arnold was more than a commanding general, he was an airpower advocate, a vocal yet polite one. His skillful discourse was not always appreciated by his seafaring brethren, nor by some politicians. Arnold lived through many broadsides from the Navy during his Army career, and he masterfully learned how to deal with the Army-Navy rivalry that he had known since his West Point days.

From these experiences, and with the career-long help of scientists such as Dr. Robert Millikan, president of Caltech and 1923 Nobel laureate, Arnold came to understand that research, development, and production were related by factors of time. Research was often painstakingly slow; applying new ideas to aircraft took even more time; and mass production of the best possible aircraft, ones technologically and numerically superior, raised an immense challenge.

By the Second World War, Arnold had crystallized his philosophy of research and development. During peace, basic research into the theoretical aspects of aeronautics was needed if long-term improvements were to be made in aircraft technology. As war approached, however, this basic research came into conflict with continuous technological change. The practical aspects of mass production limited the application of technical changes that scientists and engineers had worked to incorporate into combat aircraft. Arnold had to decide the appropriate balance between the two. It was his experience and his convictions that directed the buildup and the balance of American air forces before and during World War II.

The term *air force* has, since World War I, been misapplied, misunderstood, and improperly used, even by airmen. It is crucial that the differences between *air force, airpower, air corps,* and *air service* be clearly understood, the way Arnold defined them in a 1945 report to the secretary of war.

> Air Power includes a nation's ability to deliver cargo, people, destructive missiles and war-making potential through the air to a desired destination to accomplish a desired purpose.
>
> Air Power is not composed alone of the war-making components of aviation. It is the total aviation activity—civilian and military, commercial and private, potential as well as existing.

> Military Air Power—or Air Force—is dependent upon the air potential provided by industry which, in turn, thrives best in an atmosphere of individual initiative and private enterprise. . . . Further, our concept of the implements of Air Power should not be confined to manned vehicles. Controlled or directed robots will be of increasing importance. . . .
>
> Our Air Force must be flexible in its basic structure and capable of successfully adapting itself to the vast changes which are bound to come in future. Whatever its numerical size may be, it must be second to none in range and striking power.[7]

Originally, *air service* was the term used to describe those airplanes attached directly to surface forces. Their functions were limited—reconnaissance and artillery spotting—they provided a service to the ground troops. The term *air corps* was similar, but reflected a larger organization with some limited offensive striking power, much like the Marine Corps and its relationship to its parent service, the Navy.

Airpower, as Arnold defined it, was used broadly and referred to the totality of a nation's air capability. It differed from *air force* in that the latter referred to attacking, from the air, targets independent from the engaged surface forces. In essence, air force meant strategic attacks upon targets well out of the range of naval or ground forces. To Hap Arnold, *air force,* or *military airpower,* terms that he used interchangeably, were composed of three fundamental pillars: aircraft and equipment, trained personnel, and air bases.[8] Arnold envisioned a symmetry of people, machines, and logistics as the foundation of a balanced air program. He had officially advocated this program since 1936.[9]

✪ ✪ ✪ ✪ ✪

In many ways, this book takes a traditional biographical approach to one man's life. In other ways, it is an examination of the evolution and struggle for the development and acceptance of air force as an element of military power. Arnold's participation in military aviation at the Wright flying school in 1911 was only the beginning of more than thirty-five years of military aviation service, both as a flier and as a staff officer. By the dawn of World War II, Arnold's experience spanned all facets of military aviation and a sizable portion of civil aviation as well. His knowledge of military aviation and his breadth of experience in that field were unsurpassed by his colleagues.

The essence of Arnold's story, then, lies not primarily in his command during World War II, though his performance during that crisis was significant. Rather, the key to understanding Arnold lies in careful examination of the years leading up to World War II. In those years of scarcity, exile, disappointment, disbelief, and danger in the air are hidden the foundations upon which was built Arnold's performance as the commander of the U.S. Army Air

Forces. It is there that we find the origins of his imagination, his compassion, his sternness, and his stubborn determination. Arnold's World War II effectiveness was the manifestation of experience that had been gained despite the fact that both political and military institutions remained overtly uninterested in military aviation until the late 1930s.

The simple soldier's stone, identical and in line with hundreds of others, stands near the top of a shady, rolling Arlington National Cemetery hill. Although an officer in the United States Army for more than forty years, and officially retired before the separation of the Air Force from the Army in September 1947, Henry H. Arnold died in January 1950, never having served a single day in the newly independent service, as General of the Air Force. President Truman had ordered the establishment of such a rank and awarded it to Hap Arnold in May 1949, and so his tombstone reads.[10]

Hap Arnold was the first and only General of the Air Force, the only American airman to ever wear the constellation of five stars. He once humbly explained to his son Bruce that his advancement to high rank was largely a matter of good luck: "I have been very fortunate—fortunate in many ways—one of which was that I was able to go into the Air just when it was young and stick with it up to the present time. So when you congratulate me, you are not congratulating me as a person but as a symbol—a symbol that gives to the Air Forces the rank which is consistent with the size of the organization."[11]

This is a story of the influential events in Hap Arnold's life. It is an intimate examination of his strengths and foibles, of how these traits contributed to his advance to the top spot in the World War II Army Air Forces, and of what he accomplished while he was there.

1

HENRY HARLEY ARNOLD
(1886–1903)

Young Philadelphian Henry Harley Arnold, born at 5:00 A.M. on 25 June 1886, was always called Harley at home. His namesake and great-great-grandfather on his mother's side, Henry Harley (b. 1754), fought during the War for Independence as a young man. Peter Arnold, the paternal side of the family tree, was in the first Arnold generation born in America and also served in the Revolutionary War, as a private in the 5th Battalion of the Philadelphia County Militia. Family members often recounted the tale of a British foraging party that raided the Arnold homestead, blasting a musket ball through the side of the house. The damage caused by the lead ball was never repaired so as to quell the guffaws of disbelievers.[1]

One of Peter's sons, Samuel, born in 1790, died of smallpox in May 1800, after receiving one of the first widely administered inoculations for the disease, a refined version of that used by George Washington's army at Valley Forge. Thomas Griffith Arnold, one of Peter's many grandchildren, was Harley's grandfather, a nail maker by trade. He fought in the Federal Army at the Battle of Gettysburg during the American Civil War.

Herbert Alonzo Arnold, Harley's father, born 4 August 1857, was his neighborhood's general practitioner and had served in Puerto Rico as a medic during the Spanish-American War in 1898.[2] Dr. Arnold remained active in the Pennsylvania National Guard during Harley's youth. Harley even accompanied his father to muster on occasion, a deliberate exposure to the military environment that Herbert had decided was appropriate for untamed young boys.

Herbert Arnold, a sturdy, serious man who wore a bushy mustache most of

7

his life, had begun his medical career in 1878, after graduating from Jefferson Medical College. He was a member of several professional medical organizations and delivered papers concerning "scientific subjects" at both state and national forums.[3] Because of the nature of his profession, he became intimately familiar with the explosion of scientific and technological advances flooding the medical profession as the new century approached. Advances in disease control pioneered and developed by Louis Pasteur, for example, seemed particularly promising at the time. (Yet even today the significance of Pasteur's work cannot be overstated.) Many advances were in some way related to cleanliness and sterilization. Rubber surgical gloves became common physician's raiment. Steam heat–treated surgical instruments ensured that bacteria were destroyed before surgery was performed.

Many of these developments occurred less than twenty years after the end of the Civil War, the last American war fought in which more individuals died of disease than died in actual combat—twice as many.[4] For many of the survivors, the horrors of the medical conditions had been inexorably etched into memory. The advances under way were lifesaving ones, at the leading edge of scientific and technological developments in the medical profession.

Herbert married Ann Louise Harley (b. 1857), six months his senior, on 22 April 1880. She was the only daughter of Henry Cassel Harley of Worchester Township, Pennsylvania. Whereas the Arnold side of the line had originated in Holland, Harley blood was German. "Lou," thick through the body in her later years, had been raised in the traditions of the Dunker sect of the Mennonite religion but, after her marriage to Herbert, she accepted the Baptist Church as her own. Her entire married life was spent with a stern, all-work-no-play husband, who generally had no time for anyone with a sense of humor. This was not uncommon in a nineteenth-century Pennsylvania Dutch family.

Family members remembered "Gangy" (mother Arnold) as very influential in Harley's formative life. He got his looks from her—thin lips and an infectious grin. He also inherited much of his broad-picture outlook from his mother, who was described as a "serene, radiant woman with a broad mind— in a family of narrow minds. She was modern in her ideas but she was not allowed to express them often," except to her children.[5]

Herbert's professional status as a physician and a National Guard officer ranked the family in the Philadelphia upper-middle class, above skilled laborers yet a mark below affluent bankers. The Arnolds lived in spacious accommodations but had no house servants to assist in the daily chores.

Dr. Arnold's dedication to medicine, coupled with a strict upbringing, appears by most accounts to have driven an impersonal wedge between himself and his family. Yet, as he contributed to the understanding and dissemination of modern medical ideas, Herbert's growing children must have sensed that his work was somehow different from most other occupations in their home just outside Philadelphia. Despite any overt affection for his children, his influence and dedication were strong enough to convince his fourth child, Clifford Hood, to join the medical profession and his third, Henry Harley, to join the military.

Of course, the children were not the only ones who felt the impact of Herbert's expectations. Lou was expected to wait on him, and she did so willingly, hand and foot. In quieter moments, he could be heard telling Lou that he yearned for the day when just the two of them could "sit in front of the fire together and talk." That day never came: Lou Arnold died of a massive, sudden heart attack in January 1931, leaving Herbert alone and suffering from emotional trauma. He loved his wife and had come to depend upon her careful administration of their household. He treated her as he—and she, for that matter—had been raised. "No one," it was said, "ever opened a door for a woman in those days."[6] Harley was, most certainly, aware of his father's treatment of his mother. He did not resent it, despite his strong affection for her. In his somewhat sheltered life as a child, Harley likely believed, just as his father had demonstrated all his life, that women were to be deferential to men around the home. This upbringing may also explain much of the relationship between himself and his own family in later years.

Relationships in many Pennsylvania Dutch families were very clearly delineated and were patriarchal in the extreme. The wife's specific functions enabled the husband to concentrate on earning the primary income that supported the family. To accomplish this, women tended to all home chores, raised the children to the father's specifications, and tried to make the father's life as comfortable as possible. Mrs. Arnold never benefited from labor- or time-saving devices, because Herbert did not allow these items in his home. He set the example of behavior for his children by his own job performance of long, hard hours and a total dedication to his medical practice. Hard physical labor acted as a form of penance; in fact, the doctor never owned a car for that very reason.

Dr. Arnold taught his brood the importance of diligence and dedication, even to the exclusion of a personal family life. Mother was more involved with the children but sought to teach them as the father would expect them to behave. This meant obedience, diligence, and honesty. It was a social structure that was accepted as the norm by those raised under its guidance, and the concept of gender equality would have to wait another generation or two. In large measure, this lifestyle molded Harley Arnold and his siblings during their youth.

Harley ended up as the middle of five children. Sophia Elizabeth (b. 1882), called Betty, was four years his senior. Thomas "Tommy" Herbert (b. 1884) was eighteen months older, while Clifford "Cliff" Hood (b. 1888) was two years younger. By all accounts, the three boys were a handful, particularly Harley, called Sunny by his mother, and Clifford. They "were a pretty tough pair for [Betty] because they were full of the dickens. . . . The doctor [Harley's father] used to tell wild stories about those boys."[7]

When Harley was five, another son, Isaac Johnson (b. 1891), was born into the sweltering August heat in Philadelphia. The family record notes that young Isaac died on 2 September 1891, just one week old.[8] Harley had lost a little brother, perhaps one of his earliest childhood memories. The event may also have contributed to the Arnolds move from Gladwyne to Ardmore, only a few miles up the road, in 1892. A new brother, Joseph Price, was born on 7 July 1894. Being six years the youngest, he was somewhat distanced from the other boys' lives.

The first three children had been born in an enormous house located at the corner of Conshohocken State and Youngsford Road that boasted three full levels, multiple fireplaces, and a workload for a mother of three that was too much to handle. It was shortly after Harley's birth that the family moved one block east, to the newly constructed, more modest, and more easily managed dwelling in Gladwyne. The 1892 move to Ardmore remedied the transportation difficulties of a lively but horse-drawn medical practice, and here Harley was enrolled in the Lower Merion Township school.[9]

Lower Merion High School suffered a calamitous fire during Harley's early years. The entire student body was forced to nearby Bryn Mawr School while the burned-out Ardmore school was repaired. Nevertheless, Harley, lanky and boyish, recalled his school years as a happy time. He played right end on the football team and threw the hammer on the track squad. Arnold regretted that Lower Merion "seldom beat Radnor," the cross-town rival, and his fondest memories were of team trips to neighboring towns—anything to get out of Ardmore for a while, as he joked at later talks given in his hometown area.[10]

But in fact, Harley was never fond of life in Ardmore. Before he married Eleanor Alexander Pool (usually called Bee or Beadle), also a resident of Ardmore and one of Dr. Arnold's patients, Harley explained that "I always was sure that Ardmore was no place to live in while one was young and I am more convinced of the fact every day."[11] Perhaps Harley, whose letter was written while he was just a second lieutenant, was merely trying to ease his bride-to-be away from her lifelong home. Perhaps, anticipating less than comfortable conditions for her as an Army wife, he was trying to prepare her.

This is unlikely, however. Harley was extremely aware that Bee was well traveled and well educated for a woman in the early 1900s, much more so than himself. It is far more probable that the letter simply expressed his belief that there was limited opportunity for excitement and adventure for young people in lazy Lower Merion Township.

Besides adding to Harley's longing to leave home after high school, his father's "formal and cold" demeanor "only made the boys . . . do things behind his back." Harley's pent-up teenage energy finally erupted in his junior year of high school. On 3 February 1902, Harley, along with eleven other boys (almost the entire male population of his class), was suspended from school for one week. The charge, "gross violation of discipline," must have been particularly irksome and embarrassing to the doctor, who lessened his son's school punishment to only two days by visiting the schoolmaster in person.[12] Harley's punishment at home was likely far more physical and far less tolerant than today's standards of discipline would allow.

But despite his apparent need for excitement, Harley was shy, even introverted, around girls. He far preferred playing a game of pickup football than doing anything involving a young lady, a characteristic that persisted until after he graduated from West Point Military Academy. To understand the depth of his shyness, consider the following major difference in recollections:

The Arnold family and the Pool family were friends. Dr. Arnold was the Pool family physician, and Lou Arnold and Annie Alexander Pool were well acquainted, although their children were not playmates. Harley claimed that he had met Bee during a social event in Ardmore, yet Bee has absolutely no recollection of Harley until 1907 at West Point.[13] It seems that Harley was the type to notice the girls in his town, but not the type to strike up a conversation or relationship with them. Even if he did attempt to make an acquaintance, he was soon forgotten by the young women in question. Harley lived for sports; aside from high school athletics, he also loved hunting and horseback riding.

The other family members were diverse in their interests and chosen careers. Thomas, the oldest, was supposed to attend West Point and continue the Arnold family tradition of American military service. Despite an impressive military legacy, Thomas rejected his father's persistent urging, which must have sorely disappointed the doctor. He had been seeking an appointment to the Military Academy for his son since 1901. In October of that year he had written his congressman, Irving P. Wanger, to inquire about the availability of appointments in the coming academic year. The congressman's reply had been encouraging: "I shall very gladly give due consideration to the claims of your son in the event that it falls to me to make a nomination of [a] cadet to either the U.S. Naval or U.S. Military Academy. It may not be amiss to suggest that when the nomination is to be made to the U.S. Military Academy next spring, that your older son will still be eligible in age and might in the event of the matter being subject to competition, be able to make a better fight than the younger. In the event of a competitive examination I can see no impropriety in both boys entering if that should be desired. . . ."[14]

The fact that Herbert had earlier inquired whether two sons at once could attend West Point suggests that Harley would have had an opportunity to attend the following year anyway, whether or not Thomas had accepted his father's wishes in 1902. Nonetheless, Thomas had already enrolled at Penn State the year prior to the West Point admission tests and discovered the freedom of being away from his boyhood home, away from harsh house rules and the mundane, small-town atmosphere. West Point, he likely determined, would be too much like returning home, particularly since his father had encouraged him to attend the Military Academy. So it was Harley who inherited the opportunity to carry on the family's military heritage, an opportunity created by his father's diligence.

Harley's situation was quite different from his older brother's. He had never been away from home; he had been trapped under the wing of his protective, older sister while living under the assumption that he would soon be off to nearby Bucknell College to study divinity and become a preacher, at the behest of his mother.[15] It was not Harley's father who wished him to become a "man of the cloth," it was his mother, and because of his tremendous respect for her, he might have actually followed through with her wishes. Dr. Arnold was still hoping for one West Point appointment. As for Bucknell, there is little doubt that Harley would have enjoyed this small Baptist college no more than he enjoyed living in Ardmore.

But evidence shows that he had applied and been accepted at Penn State by 18 June 1903, rather than Bucknell.[16] Favorable reports from his brother and a desire to escape Ardmore were certain influences upon his decision to apply. Besides, he needed a backup plan in case he was turned away by the Military Academy. Harley saw West Point, not the ministry, as his salvation. He would see the world by joining the Army; his teenage wanderlust could be satisfied at any one of many exotic Army outposts. West Point was a tremendous challenge for any young man. It was a challenge he would accept gladly, given the opportunity. This was his chance to escape sleepy Ardmore and the same dreary routine that had driven Thomas away the year before.

While Harley waited for news from West Point officials, he passed the summertime working part time at the Merion Title and Trust Company, where he served as a substitute clerk while the rest of the staff took summer vacations.[17] As the 15 June Academy start date came and went, Harley's spirits fell. Not for long.

2

CADET "PEWT" ARNOLD, WEST POINT CLASS OF '07 (1903–7)

The United States Military Academy, West Point, New York, an isolated fortress nestled up against a unique, narrow hook in the Hudson River, was established 16 March 1802 and opened on 4 July 1802 during Thomas Jefferson's presidency. Civil fears of the military establishment, bolstered by events like the Newburgh Conspiracy,[1] had subsided enough that the necessity had gradually become apparent for building an operational army from the unprepared, untrained national military force. At the heart of that force would be a corps of officers, efficiently trained in the "practical [technical] and theoretical" aspects vital for the military service of the United States.[2]

Originally built in 1775 to command the river, a somber, weathered complex of fortifications symbolized the both heroic and tragic elements of the American struggle, first for independence and then, in the 1860s, over union. Its eighteenth-century defenses consisted of several small "forts," a protective line of redoubts and shore batteries, a line of entrenched outposts, and a massive chain (each link nearly 3 feet across) that spanned the river during more temperate weather. Each of these supported the effort to foil any British attempt to traverse the crooked bend in the Hudson. By 1780, West Point was the strongest fortress in the newly independent United States of America.[3]

West Point was the first engineering college in the nation. During its first century, West Point easily matched reputations with the growing "ivy league" of colleges as one of the finest schools for engineers—military engineers. To ensure this continued excellence, only an Army engineer was authorized overall command of the school. It was not until 1866 that a superintendent from other than the Engineering Corps was authorized to serve in that post.[4]

In 1903, the year Harley entered the Military Academy, the narrow, dirt roads that led to the isolated, imposing locale made travel difficult. The countryside remained sparsely populated, and there were no routes leading north. Only a narrow, unimproved pass headed west out of West Point. The West Shore Railroad was the principal means of transportation in and out of West Point. For the most part, except for special occasions such as graduation, the only people at the Military Academy were cadets, faculty, and the faculty's families. A local tram, described as a "funny little train," was the most comfortable way to get from the local, main-line train station to the hotel near the post and was the chosen method of transport by out-of-town visitors, particularly lady friends. The ride up the hill, the final leg of the journey to "Flirtation Point," was provided by an early version of a taxi, a hack.[5]

Cadet training was as rugged and as difficult as the terrain. To step forward as member of the Corps of Cadets, young men had first to accomplish a series of examinations. Entrance examinations were difficult, and only a fraction of those taking them passed. Even passing the exams was no guarantee that a young man—women were not permitted to attend West Point, Annapolis, or the Air Force Academy until 1976—would actually enter with the new class, numbering initially around 160.

Harley Arnold was one of those who passed competitive exams, which he had taken with five other young men from the eighth district. But he was not immediately accepted into the class of 1907. Most new cadets arrived at West Point and began their ordeal at precisely 11:45 A.M. on 15 June 1903. But another candidate from Arnold's district had scored higher on the May entrance exams and was first in line.[6]

Finishing second turned out to be a remarkable stroke of luck, and, coupled with a strong case of teenage hormones, intervened to Harley's benefit. On 18 July, Arnold was notified that the candidate who had aced him out of the first slot had, inexplicably, married the day before "beast barracks" began. He was immediately disqualified and sent home. Harley was to take his place. At the age of seventeen years, one month, and two days, barely meeting the minimum age requirement, Arnold entered West Point on Monday morning, 27 July, as a member of the class of 1907. He, along with several others, were to arrive before 8:00 A.M. for the entry physical examination.[7]

This was more than luck: it was fate. If Harley had been first in line to attend West Point, he would have reported on 15 June 1903. And Army regulations were explicit in that "No candidate shall be admitted who is under seventeen." Harley did not turn seventeen until the 25 June; on 15 June, he was still sixteen. He would have been turned away. But in July, along with four other classmates with similar birth dates, he was seventeen and thus met the entry requirement for age.[8]

The challenge before him was formidable. Many cadets had prior experience at civilian colleges, and most were older than Harley. More than one-third of the class was over twenty years old. The "real life" experience gained in the intervening years between high school and West Point often enabled older, more mature cadets to handle more deftly the rigors of the freshman year—plebe life. Harley, almost before he realized it, had gone from high-school senior to plebe in less than one month without such a benefit.

Nearly one-third of those who entered West Point did not graduate. Arnold fell into the successful two-thirds, a feat he accomplished with seemingly shallow effort and, accordingly, minimal formal distinction. Nonetheless, he was destined to become part of the ever-extending long, gray line.[9]

Entering late, although a blessing for Arnold, did not come without penalty. The majority of the cadets had already moved out of the dormitory area and established the summer encampment, where basic field procedures were taught. The tents were erected past the cavalry plain near the tactical training ranges, less than a mile from the dorms. The twenty-eight who began training in July received special, almost individual, training attention. They were dubbed, according to tradition, Juliets, a bastardized addition to West Point lexicon originating in the combination of *July* and *-ette*.[10] The feminine allusion to Shakespeare's character was a derogatory bonus.

Beast barracks was not anything these young men had ever experienced before. It was sardonically defined in the 1906 version of the cadet yearbook the *Howitzer* as "Cadet barracks during the period when beasts use it for a summer resort." Gen. Carl "Tooey" Spaatz, West Point class of 1914, first chief of staff of the independent Air Force and a Pennsylvanian himself, described summer camp as "primarily not a hazing but a disciplinary period, a different kind of discipline than what you're used to when you're pretty much on your own around a small country town."[11]

To the relief of the entering class, hazing had been abolished at West Point a few classes earlier because of the unfortunate death of a freshman cadet. Any upper-class cadet who was found touching a new cadet or ordering one to do meaningless manual labor was expelled, no questions asked.[12] It is an interesting commentary on changing American culture that hazing, continually redefined by shifting cultural values, has been "eliminated" at military colleges many times since the early 1900s.

Different is perhaps a mild understatement to describe the plebe experience. Incoming candidates were first labeled beasts (from the French *bêtes*, meaning "animals" or "stupid"), then plebes (from the Latin *plebs*, meaning "mob" or "common herd") or Juliets, if applicable. From the moment the Juliets were ushered to the cadet area, the endless barking of commands and corrections began—plebes called it ragging and bracing. For those first three weeks they were beasts; they did not qualify as plebes until they moved from the barracks out to the tent city. Upperclassmen were constantly shouting commands. "Get your chin in. . . . Shoulders back and down. . . . Tack a 'sir' on to that statement, mister. . . . Drag in that chin!" The act of "dragging in one's chin" was immortalized in many cadet annuals in cartoon form. One of Arnold's class-mates was particularly impressed that Harley could, on demand, produce up to seven wrinkles under his chin.[13]

After a first day of following orders, the Juliets were ordered to sing a run-ning song as they double-timed to the cadet store, sporting crisp, maroon-colored banners that represented their class. At the store, the fledgling forma-tion was issued bedding, uniforms, a mattress, and a dipper for water. Then it was on to the dorms. Rooms were spartan. There was a plain iron bunk for each man and two alcoves (closets) in which to hang uniforms in a specified or-der. All other worldly belongings went in a footlocker.[14] "Everything was pre-scribed," as Hayden Wagner, West Point 1907, recalled. "The top drawer of your clothes press [closet organizer] was the only place you got to take any lib-erties whatsoever to arrange personal things. Most of them [cadets] had pho-tographs of girls up there." One of Harley's personal items was a photograph of his father and mother. Herbert had given it to Harley upon his departure from Ardmore in July 1903. He had scribed a candid message on the back re-minding his son to do what was expected and to act with "promptness and fi-delity" while living in sight of God and mother. "Self-control is essential to success," the note continued, admonishing the youth to be guided by the "Per-fect One as your example; you cannot fail and we shall not fear for you."[15] It was a message Harley struggled to follow for the rest of his life.

Each cadet had a washbasin and washstand. But, in what seemed like added harassment, the water had to be dragged from the quadrangle—the area in the center of the dormitories—back to the rooms. Despite the technological eu-phoria gripping the country at the time, running water and interior plumbing were nonexistent in West Point dormitories in 1903. Renovations in 1906 would remedy the situation, but that did not mitigate the problem for the plebe class of 1907. Cadet latrine facilities were inconveniently located on the second floor in a separate building on the quad. Toilets were divided by class rank: the first-class "sink," the second-class sink, and so on. Toilets lined one wall and tubs another, straight and tidy as a cadet parade formation.[16] After a quick latrine break, it was double-time back to the rooms, where the ragging increased in intensity again until the next scheduled duty.

Next came a trip to the ordnance department for rifles, bayonets, and en-trenching tools, a holdover from the successful siege campaigns of the Civil War. Then back to the rooms again. Drill formations began next. A soldier was not one until he could march in lockstep with a company of other soldiers while carrying a highly polished, bolt-action Springfield .30 rifle. Incredibly, by dinner on Arnold's very first day, the Juliets were keeping in step and looked like a sharp, gray-clad company of soldiers sans rifles; marching with rifles came a few days later.[17]

Day two established the model for the rest of beast barracks and was much more challenging than the partial first day. The newest members of the Corps of Cadets were rousted for the breakfast formation by the unnerving discharge of the reveille cannon at 0530, or 5:30 A.M. Immediately following the meal, the Juliets met the notorious 1st Lt. Herman J. Koehler, instructor of military gymnastics and physical culture. His job was to get the new candidates on an even physical par with the on-time plebes who had entered 15 June.[18] One might only imagine the colorful, malodorous splotches of sausage and flapjack vomit that littered the exercise field after the first half hour of nonstop calisthenics and running-in-place had passed. Several plebes fainted; others, unable to breathe, had "taken a knee" in an effort to catch their breath by collapsing to the ground, head down, one knee on the ground.[19] Harley handled the physical activity with more ease than many; his high-school track and football experience had left him in excellent physical condition.

Harley was gangly—some thought him too thin—but he had the build and the experience of a long-distance runner that had prepared him for these exercise periods. His dark brown hair was already receding high on his forehead. He had penetrating hazel eyes that turned a green-gray hue when he wore his gray flannel "plebe skins." He seemed always to wear a sly, tight-lipped grin. These days it might be described as Grinch-like.[20] Younger but taller than most of his classmates, Harley stood at about five feet ten inches and weighed 170 pounds by his senior year. During beast barracks he was a member of F Company, one of those on the end of the cadet formation, a "flank" company, so taller cadets usually ended up there.[21]

After a quick but necessary morning shower, drill recommenced. During drill periods, as one cadet wrote, "the sun was hotter, the guns heavier, the drills longer and the rests rarer than in any vocation in any other country on the planet."[22] Break periods were hardly worthy of the name. Plebes rushed back to their rooms to polish their brass buckles or buttons, clean rifles, or memorize upper-class cadet names and ranks. Then drill, drill, and more drill.

Meanwhile, most of the upper-class cadets practice-fired artillery. Many rode horses, and some worked on engineering projects. The first-classmen, seniors, worked and trained hard all morning but played polo, tennis, or went swimming all afternoon. For them summer camp was fun, even relaxing. There were even upper-class hops, sometimes three times a week during the summer. Sometimes local girls—faculty daughters or from nearby towns—made the journey, sometimes not. Hops were a privilege reserved exclusively for upperclassmen and were attended whether or not there were dance cards to fill. The plebes just drilled.[23]

Finally, at the end of the day, stomachs filled with "sammy" (molasses) and "slum" (mysterious stew meat), the new cadets found physical and mental relief. As Ben Castle, Harley's class athletic representative, recalled, "When tattoo [the bedtime bugle call] came at nine o'clock—that was the earliest we could go to bed—we just dropped into bed and went to sleep, a dreamless sleep. You were so damned tired, physically tired. Then, the next morning, up at quarter to six, breakfast at six, and the routine would be repeated. . . . It was amazing how quick they whipped us into shape."[24]

At some point during the first few days (likely Saturday, 1 August, the date on Arnold's admissions papers), the Juliets were ushered into a large lecture hall and quickly sworn in as "cadets of the United States Military Academy." Taking this oath obligated the young men to eight years of military service— four served as cadets and four upon graduation. There was no elaborate ceremony, no formality, just raised right hands, a quick "so help me God," and the deed was done.[25]

By the end of the third repetitive week, now indoctrinated to West Point's strict military regimen, the Juliets joined the rest of the cadets at summer encampment. Understandably, the new additions felt second-rate compared with those plebes who had been subjected to an additional five weeks of summer camp. The scornful but still vigilant eyes of the upperclassmen in charge of training did little to diminish this self-inflicted guilt. But the initial disparity vanished as the first official dress parade brought all the cadets together for the first time. It was the beginning of a four-year experience that transformed the individuals who entered the academy in 1903 into the united class of '07.

The first parade formation was not, however, an opportunity to relax. Upper-class cadets, now surrounding the newly tailored, stiffly starched, parade-dressed plebes on all sides, took the liberty of making verbal corrections even while the formation was passing in review directly in front of the West Point superintendent, Brig. Gen. Albert L. Mills. The constant din of corrections rumbled like distant thunder over the visitor stands, causing the uninitiated to wonder what the commotion was all about. None of the plebes enjoyed the constant disciplinary reminders, but they knew they were getting similar treatment as all previous graduates had received.[26] They were becoming part of the history, part of the legacy, part of the place where Ulysses S. Grant, Robert E. Lee, and Philip H. Sheridan had once suffered through the same initiation.

Evidence indicates that Harley did not stand out during beast barracks. Another Juliet in his class of twenty-eight latecomers, Hayden Wagner, did not even remember Arnold as one of his Juliet classmates, even though West Point records clearly show that he was.[27] Harley was riding the tide, falling into line with the rest of his classmates. That was, after all, the purpose of beast barracks.

❂   ❂   ❂   ❂   ❂

Just before Orville and Wilbur Wright began moving their most recent invention from Dayton, Ohio, to Kitty Hawk, North Carolina, the cadets were marching back to the cadet area anticipating the academic year. In those days, cadets did not leave West Point until two years after their initial arrival. No regular leave was permitted—none. Only extreme family emergencies warranted an excuse.

The Corps of Cadets returned from the plain to the dormitories on 31 August 1903. A large stack of textbooks awaited them, having been delivered to their rooms while they were yet in the field. The next day classes began. "There wasn't any fooling around. You had a lesson assigned the day before and you started in the first day to recite and be marked."[28] In addition to textbooks, cadets were issued a guard duty and drill manual called the Black Book. Failure to follow precisely the book's rules resulted in demerits and punishments.

Beyond the drill manual, cadets actually had a daily life characterized by a defined, rigid, routine. Aside from studies and sports, the young men also served periodic guard duty in twenty-four-hour shifts. Sunday church attendance was mandatory, as were all meals. All activities were preceded by a formation originating in the quad and ending up at the appointed destination. Weekends afforded the only opportunity for cadets to entertain visitors. On Saturdays and Sundays, even plebes had limited privileges.

For some, like Harley, West Point was their very first adventure away from home, but despite the potential to grow melancholy, Harley seldom wrote home. At this age he was not one who showed his feelings, particularly to his family. His father's stoic demeanor had been Harley's primary adult male influence. Although he may have missed his family, his longing for excitement was much stronger than any desire to return to Ardmore may have been. The strict military routine was deemed essential to internalizing the discipline that might one day ensure survival under austere field conditions or in combat, and there was little time to pine for home. But it was precisely the military environment, rather than the academic one, that interested Harley. Emotions— not normally associated with cold, calculating military officers—would have to wait.

The rigors of cadet life kept all classes so busy that time passed quickly, even for the plebes. There was so much to be accomplished that "weeks were stretched quite out of shape and could scarcely be made to fit into the little thirty-day month."[29] For most, academic studies took up a majority of free time. All plebes studied the same subjects during their first year at West Point: mathematics, French, English, and more drill. In fact, there were no electives in the entire cadet academic curriculum, and a "regular diploma" was awarded by the Academy staff as a requisite to commissioning. Mathematics was generally considered the most important subject, as far as studying went, and deficiency usually resulted in dismissal without appeal.

Harley's plebe year was an academic struggle, one that he never really conquered while at West Point. Out of 136 cadets that survived the entire plebe year, Harley finished 74th in his math class (see appendix 1). This ranking was high enough to avoid the deficiency-review process but was nothing he would write home to tell his parents. Of the twelve members of the class who were found to be academically lacking, eight were deficient in mathematics and four in French. The Corps of Cadets considered math the most difficult academic stumbling block, and it was a hurdle that did not go away until April of the third-class (sophomore) year.[30]

Fortunately, math was Harley's best plebe subject. Had it not been, Cadet Arnold might not have made it past his first semester. His French teacher, 2d Lt. Frank P. Lahm, who would win the first Bennett International Balloon Race in France in 1906, remembered only that the boyish Arnold was average—nothing outstanding. Perhaps his less-than-stellar performance in French, 98th out of 136, was the reason for Lahm's lackluster assessment.

Arnold finished even lower in English, 103d out of 136, but no one was expelled for low marks in English. Remarkably, fifty years of handwritten letters to his wife contain only a handful of misspellings, along with continual apologies for sloppy writing or breaches in style. Many of Arnold's letters were eloquent, demonstrating a gifted economy of language. In the English classroom, however, it appears that Harley did not put in much effort.[31]

Cadets in the middle of the bell curve got along without many worries. "Those who were at the head of the class were worrying about missing attendance," recalled Wagner, "and those at the tail of the class were worrying about getting flunked out."[32] Harley worried enough about his low plebe grades to raise his class standing from 82d to 63d as a "yearling"; his class size dropped to 119 during his second year. This effort earned him his highest marks in any subject while at the academy. It also gave him the margin of safety from academic disqualification that he needed to pursue his main interests, horsemanship and mischief.

Despite marginal academic achievement, Harley's military conduct marks were consistently high. Conduct grades were directly related to total demerits accumulated during the academic year. For his first three years, Harley's conduct marks approached the top 20 percent of his class. It was these marks that actually saved him from a lower final-class standing than his mediocre academic scores alone would have reflected.

Cadet life was not totally bleak: football season helped build esprit de corps, and victories over regional powerhouses, like Navy, often earned the Corps of Cadets special privileges such as postponed inspections or a canceled parade. Football in those days was a particularly brutal endeavor. There was no forward passing allowed until 1906, when that rule changed to accommodate a new—and certainly more exciting—game. Until then every play was a running play of some kind. Helmets were little more than leather caps, if worn at all. Games were played in thirty-minute halves rather than the familiar four quarters of today, and the rules were more like those of English rugby than modern-day football. Touchdowns were worth only five points, and field goals were worth four. This explains many of the odd scores that decided the winners at the turn of the century. A hard-fought, often low-scoring victory was appreciated in ways modern football fans might not understand.

The football season was a vital tonic for cadets. As testimony to that fact, twenty-three pages were devoted exclusively to the football squad and the games in the 1907 *Howitzer*. The three lower classes, in contrast, were only allotted a skimpy five pages each.[33] Army football was more than just a game: it was a reason to wear the gray proudly and one day recount the year's greatest struggle over their greatest rival, the Naval Academy.

During evening hours plebes were encouraged to visit the gymnasium, likely by the ever-present Lieutenant Koehler. Participation in fencing, swimming, or tumbling activities helped maintain their hard-earned summer physical condition. They had to take personal responsibility for their fitness level during winters, especially after parades ceased in November at the first snow, beginning again only after the spring thaw. Upperclassmen could sign for a horse and ride the cavalry plain until dark. Sometimes the cavalry plain was intentionally flooded to create a huge ice-skating area. Those who remained at West Point during the holidays were treated to a variety of entertainments, in an effort to raise fading cadet spirits. Guest speakers and other diversions were arranged, particularly on the weekends.[34]

One event, viewed as a tremendous privilege by the Corps of Cadets, occurred on 4 September 1903, at 6:19 P.M. The corps adjutant issued an order permitting all cadets to smoke pipes and cigars in their rooms during the evening academic period, as well as after studies and drill during the weekend. Cigarettes, commonly referred to as skags, were hand-rolled in those days with "Bull," Bull Durham tobacco. That night it appeared to some that the dormitory was oozing smoke from every possible crack and crevice—everybody, even nonsmokers, was smoking. This event was so memorable that it was immortalized in the *Howitzer* that year: on one page appeared a poem, on another a drawing of a cadet lighting up his skag.[35]

It may have been the award of this privilege that started Harley's modest smoking habit. He smoked more or less frequently until the mid-1920s, puffing primarily cigarettes, until a stomach ulcer and its subsequent treatment forced him to quit. The deleterious effects of smoking were not much of a concern in those days, although questions about a condition known as "tobacco heart" were clearly part of the entrance examinations in 1903. And many officers who smoked (there were indeed many of them) often paid a dear penalty later in life.[36]

But these were invincible young men. They had just completed the most grueling two months of their lives. "You have the confidence that you can do any damn thing," recalled Tooey Spaatz.[37] Tobacco was part of military culture; its use has only recently been actively discouraged by the Defense Department and the nation in general.[38] Cavalrymen particularly enjoyed it, chewing a big wad of leaf tobacco—"brown"—and seldom keeping the subsequent juicy, dark spittle from dribbling out the corner of their mouths. The chewing of tobacco was in fact expected of a true cavalry officer, at least in the minds of many still impressionable young cadets, including Harley Arnold.[39]

Approaching graduation for the class of 1904, and having weathered both physical and mental stress unlike any before in their lives, the plebes received a needed break in the rigorous routine of the preceding year. The entire Corps of Cadets traveled by train to the St. Louis World's Fair, and the plebes were even released from "bracing" to enjoy the trip. It lasted a full ten days and, not surprisingly, was well remembered by all cadets at the Military Academy.[40] For many plebes, this was the first time they had ever seen a city.

In 1904 the St. Louis World's Fair was more commonly known as the Louisiana Purchase Exposition, honoring the century since that vast expanse of land had been acquired from Napoleon's France. Featured at the exposition were such figures as band leader John Philip Sousa, president "Rough Rider" Teddy Roosevelt, and skilled orator and champion of isolationism William Jennings Bryan. Balloon races were held, Olympic-style track and field events took place, the Liberty Bell made an appearance, parades were frequent, and a variety of exhibits showcased the bursting technological optimism of the new century.

One of the focal points of the exposition, the Observation Wheel, gave visitors a bird's-eye view of the expansive grounds from an ultimate height of 250 feet. The wheel itself, a Ferris wheel, was an engineering feat. In the shape of a spoked bicycle wheel, the structure contained 4,200 tons of metal. The axle alone, weighing 70 tons, was suspended 125 feet in the air. The thirty-six cars had a capacity of 2,000 people and made lazy revolutions once every quarter hour. It was immense.[41]

Among the many exhibits was a massive turntable, on which sat a 164-ton locomotive and tender, capable of 60 miles an hour while hauling ten cars. The turntable motor was completely electric, and it continually rotated the engine around its 75-foot circular path.[42]

In the Pennsylvania State Building, Arnold missed seeing the Liberty Bell, on display from 8 June to 16 November; the Corps returned to West Point a week before it arrived. An emotional, well-orchestrated drive resulting from a petition signed by 75,000 school children convinced the keepers of the bell that the cause was worthy. Before leaving the fair, the cadets marched a dress parade in honor of the Liberty Bell in a driving rainstorm. Torrential showers soaked them, and their perfectly starched pants and woolen parade coats took on an odor of wet sheep.

One of the fair's largest exhibits displayed advancements in aeronautics. Aside from a collection of aeronautical artifacts in the Transportation Building, fourteen acres were set aside as an Aeronautic Concourse to accommodate the ongoing contests and aerial exhibitors. This concourse was directly adjacent to the track and field facilities and directly across from the parade grounds. Every cadet saw the variety of aerial contraptions on display, as well as "samples of everything applicable to the science; truly an exposition in itself and one of unexampled interest."[43] Most displays were related to ballooning, but many of the craft were gliders, the step before powered flight. It is inconceivable that some discussion of the Wright Brothers' achievement, although little attention had been drawn to the event by the news media, did not occur around the concourse.

One likely location for talk about the first powered flight was at the exhibit of Gustav Whitehead, a German aeronautical pioneer. He was responsible for a display that featured an "aeroplane flying machine." Besides being too heavy to be effective, its wings flapped like those of a bird. Yet Whitehead claimed that his craft had flown more than 1½ miles in 1901, and those who saw his craft or his display, including the cadets, were informed that powered flight had been achieved. His claim centered around the entry rules for the aeronautical prize money that required a prequalifying flight of more than 1 mile just to enter the World's Fair contests.[44] Despite the ongoing controversy of Whitehead's claims, the aeronautic exhibit in its entirety drew attention to the infancy of aeronautical engineering, a field destined to evolve alongside Harley's career in the Army.

Now back at West Point after the delightful ten-day junket, plebes' chins were dragged back in (for a few days, anyway) while final exams were taken. "Thirteen days of ninety-two hours each," explained a member of the class of 1905 awaiting his first furlough, "and then—oblivion."[45] The most significant event yet to occur was "recognition," meaning that the freshman class was accepted as an integral part of the Corps of Cadets. No more squared corners, no more drawn-in chins. Recognition was a monumental step back into a more human, less pressure-packed world.

Recognition took place after "hell week," the yearlings' last occasion to correct the plebes' posture and military bearing. After the graduation ceremony, it was official. For one day, there were no plebes at West Point. The graduates were essentially second lieutenants in the U. S. Army, while everyone else moved up one class in rank.

The transition from plebe to yearling was both instantaneous and miraculous. "What a glorious day it was," the *Howitzer* trumpeted; it marked a "complete metamorphosis of the class."[46] Wagner remembered the event with equal enthusiasm: "The day we became yearlings, oh yes, that was something!"[47] As for Harley, from the moment he became a yearling, he began searching for his niche at West Point. He knew it was not in the classroom.

✪ ✪ ✪ ✪ ✪

As Cadet Arnold roamed free across the cadet area, the Wright Brothers were fracturing the limitations that had bound flight to simple, straight lines. On 20 September 1904, Wilbur Wright accomplished the first airborne turns in the skies over Huffman Prairie, Ohio. Full control of the Wright machine was now clearly achievable. Uncertain at first in his newfound freedom, Arnold circled the cadet area tentatively, in much the same way as Wilbur made those first few turns over Huffman Prairie.[48]

The next day the yearling class of '07 moved lock, stock, and barrel to summer encampment, where the new beasts arrived the following day. Some of Harley's classmates stayed in the area to "greet" the new arrivals, and the rest of the class hiked out to yearling camp at nearby Camp Forse.

Artillery drill and riding skills were practiced each day, while afternoons were reserved for walks up Flirtation or for "deadbeating" under a shade tree. But summer encampment was not a total breeze. There was a noticeable, and welcome, lack of mental pressure as yearlings. Cadets began the process of learning about leadership at the basic level, while refining followership skills at an elevated level. For Harley, the most pleasurable hours of yearling camp were likely those he spent riding. The yearlings rode at least once each day, every day, in any weather. It was like being in the cavalry—sort of. Many yearlings did not appreciate their hours in the riding hall. Some, still cocky from their recent recognition, never understood why West Point cavalry horses seemed unmanageable: "Nothing can exceed him as an instrument of torture, with his rugged back, his stiff-legged trot, and his gentle bites and loving kicks distributed impartially. Endowed with super-equine intelligence, he seems to scent a yearling from afar and proceeds to run away with him and otherwise maltreat him, or else calmly stops, lies down, and rolls in the tanbark with the most exasperating sang-froid imaginable. See this same animal under a First Classman and he becomes a model of decorum and soldierly conduct."[49]

Experience, it turned out, counted for much on the cavalry plain at West Point. By the time they were seniors, the cadets were riding these same uppity horses around the indoor ring. They road bareback over perilous jumps with their arms crossed upon their chests, balanced only by will and skill and their strong, trained legs, a task unthinkable as yearlings only two years before.

Some cadets blossomed as young leaders during these cavalry drills, others during the instruction of plebes in the ways of West Point. Still others had to wait for the beginning of the school year, when they excelled in the classroom, leading by academic example. Harley was never one of these. Of all the courses he took, his highest ranking was in third-class mathematics—49th out of 119. He received his fewest demerits during his second-class year, only thirty-six, ranking him 21st in his class of 113 in conduct. Although Harley had entered the academy with a skewed reputation as a highly intellectual student (probably based upon his entry at such a young age), by the time he was in his final semester, yearbook writers noted that "he has overcome any hankering for work that he may have once had and now doesn't do any more than anyone else."[50]

Harley's doodling in his *Practical Astronomy* textbook may be an honest reflection of his academic attitude. The book's subtitle, written in by Harley on the title page, reads: "Or, Words Without a Meaning Used by the Unfortunate Cadets of the Second Class, USMA." He went even further, designing a new title page facing the real one. It reads: "An Impractical Astronomy" and is illustrated with a drawing of a cemetery-like iron gate, the entrance to a "torture chamber."[51] Apparently Harley didn't much care for astronomy class.

Outside of the classroom, only a chosen few demonstrated true leadership on the athletic fields, as teams were small and substitutes were rare. Despite Harley's slender appearance he was tough and strong, but he never met varsity participation requirements that entitled athletes to wear the coveted Army A upon their black pullover sweaters. He continued to run track during all four years at West Point, and he placed top three in the 16-pound shot-put event his junior and senior years with a best distance just shy of 36 feet. He played polo every summer and was a skilled equestrian, good enough to earn a spot on the graduation-ceremony drill team.[52]

In March 1905, the Corps of Cadets participated in the presidential inaugural parade for Theodore Roosevelt. Every cadet marched in one inaugural during their stay at the Military Academy; it was merely a question of which class year. Before departing the area for Washington, cadets were reminded of their obligation to behave. There was to be no unbuttoning of their tunics, no unauthorized visits to schools for women, and no language stronger than "Oh, Spludge." The 1905 train trip to Washington Barracks was brutally long and painfully slow, occurring in the midst of a damp drizzle that ensured the streets would be a mudbath the next morning—if they had not frozen first. After the oath was administered at noon on 5 March, the parade began. Officers in colorful sashes were a stark contrast to the gray-line incarnate. "Of course the President couldn't have safely been inaugurated without us," wrote one of Harley's classmates, "and the moral responsibility we felt was exceeded only by our appearance."[53] Cadets somehow maintained a sarcastic sense of humor.

By his second-class (junior) year, Arnold was on both the indoor and outdoor track teams and played football. Athletic programs in any college environment frequently inhibited academic excellence, particularly for football players. Time devoted to practice was extreme and usually lasted until the evening meal. After that, following the three-hour field workout, the mental effort necessary for study in light of physical fatigue created much more of a challenge than for those who spent most of their after-school time memorizing—"specking"—their assignments. For the football squad, the entire academic year served only one purpose: to support preparations to beat Navy in the annual winter grudge match.

During his second-class year, Harley "scrubbed" for the first-stringers who were learning a new game that included, for the first time, a play called the forward pass.[54] The task of the scrubs—pretending to be the upcoming rival team—was vital but thankless. Harley described a day at practice in a letter home to his mother in 1905, undated except for the indication "263 days till June."

> My Dear Mother,
> . . . I went out for foot-ball last week and today I played on the scrub against the varsity. I tell you the life of a man on the scrub is no cinch. He is

used for a dummy. If the varsity wants to try a new play they use the scrub to see if it is a success . . . the scrub gets battered and bumped and cussed out and everything else coming just because they are not as good as the varsity. I don't want you to think I am knocking or have the blues for I am not knocking and haven't the blues but I just feel like writing for the top of my head is full of bumps the size of hens eggs.[55]

By his senior year he had crawled up the football roster from junior scrub team to second-string halfback on the varsity squad. He never started a game, but he played against Tufts, Trinity, and Williams Colleges as many Army starters were injured during games in his senior year. While at West Point, Arnold saw two victories and one tie against Navy. It was unfortunate that the class of 1907 suffered a 10-0 defeat against the midshipmen in their senior year.[56]

During his junior and senior years, Harley built his physical toughness to new levels while balancing academics and other activities that challenged his mental facilities. Younger than almost everyone in his class, Harley was cultivating a style all his own. He was mentally tough, physically strong, and he knew how to work the system to accomplish tasks. But he was a bit less mature than his older classmates, and perhaps a bit insecure in this realization. He frequently could not control his tongue—he was well known for his profanity. Arnold was singled out for his perfection of the use of "sulphurous cusswords." Additionally, he had a propensity for tardiness, a shortcoming for which he earned several demerits.[57] In both positive and negative ways, he, like all the other cadets, was laying the bedrock for the rest of his career.

Although he participated in many officially sanctioned cadet activities, Harley demonstrated leadership and ingenuity in a less conventional, yet highly effective way. This brash, profane Pennsylvanian found his calling at the head of a small group of twenty cadets from E and F Company known as the Black Hand. The young men were tough and enjoyed spirited, rough games like pickup tackle football. When in action, they wore bandannas around their heads or necks as part of their getup. They did not go to hops and did not "drag girls" very often. They were too busy raising holy hell along the Hudson, and they enjoyed it. Harley was a prime mover in the Hand until he graduated. The Hand was not a secret organization—their pictures were in the yearbook, adorning a huge outline of an outstretched, dark-colored hand. Their outrageous activities were how they earned their reputation as bold pranksters.[58]

The story of the Black Hand has been told before, although melodramatically. Accounts of the excitement and daring of midnight rowdiness and cunning in the face of strict rules forbidding such activity are well documented. The Hand's adventures including rolling cannonballs down rickety, cavernous stairwells in the dark of night, hiding the reveille cannon, and—the most famous—a fireworks display from atop the dormitory honoring the class of

1907. All of their operations were carefully planned and well executed.[59] To accomplish the pranks required a certain amount of guile but also, more important, a unique form of trusting teamwork. These young men risked severe punishment, not only in the form of demerits, but also periods of confinement and disciplinary tour marching around the cadet area.

They knew the West Point system inside and out. They knew the guard and officer-of-the-day schedules; likely the guards and cadet officers as well. They developed a form of covert communications and night disguises, and after three years of this type of activity, a close comradeship forged under the fire and pressure of the academy foundry. They learned how to get around the system and accomplish their missions, and they became the rabble-rousers of the academy. Harley, their leader, was expert at these secret missions.

There was the Army way, and there was the way of the Hand. There is no doubt that the twenty-year-old Arnold, though he understood both methods, favored one over the other.[60] It was in this organization that he found his niche at West Point.

Harley gave way to the nickname Pewt during his third-class year. Pewt had its origins in a newspaper serial of the time (also a best-selling book in 1902), "The Real Diary of a Real Boy," by Henry A. Shute. This real-life diary, written by the main character "Plupy" Shute, chronicled the youthful adventures of a group of boys growing up in a small New England town in the 1860s. Among the sidekick characters was Pewter "Pewt" Purinton, a hayseed cigar-smoking, girl-hating mischief maker who frequently had to chop wood or had "the time licked out of him" to atone for his devilish behavior. The popularity of both the serial and the 1903 book made it an obvious source for secret names. Other cadets also purloined tags from the popular series. "Beany," the third major sidekick character, was adopted by cadet George R. Harrison (1907), a bawdy, song-writing member of the Hand. The stories were usually about some form of mischief—smoking behind the barn, shooting peas in school, exploding "snapcrackers" in each other's faces, or rough-housing instead of doing chores. So the nicknames were appropriately reserved for members of West Point's most mischievous organization.[61]

But Pewt was not Harley's only West Point name. His first-class yearbook photo and description noted that he was also called Benny, a shortened version of the obvious "Benedict Arnold." It is likely that he enhanced this nickname by illegally frequenting the only local pub, a known cadet hangout that was close enough to visit by foot and return without too much difficulty. The name of the pub was Benny Havens, immortal in the history of West Point. It was a ribald place, where cadets could smoke freely and drink a few tankards of beer, if they chose. Arnold likely joined in the drinking and the smoking, as did other impressionable, "pretend" cavalry officers.[62]

Harley saw the cavalry as his sole purpose in attending West Point. "It was what we lived for—our whole future. The Horse Cavalry!" Arnold once wrote, "It was the last romantic thing left on earth."[63] The cavalry had a culture all its own, and to be a cavalryman meant one must act the part. It was a culture of hard-playing, hard-working officers who lived with flash and a devil-may-care attitude. It was a culture that transferred, largely intact, to the follow-on maneuver force of the U.S. Army—the Air Service. In the cavalry, which most recognized as a separate culture within the Army, there was an atmosphere of adventure, the deafening sound of the charge, the dash of the wide yellow stripe on one's uniform trousers, and an undefinable attraction that most women could not resist—not that Pewt cared much about that.[64]

Considering Cadet Arnold's high regard for the cavalry, it is not surprising that even the launch of a hot-air balloon did not impress him, though he did write home to tell his parents about it. He described the launch of the 25-foot-diameter balloon with matter-of-factness. Having been filled with "illuminating gas" and piloted by Charles Levée, the sphere climbed upward, floated due north, and just kept on going. Harley never understood why the event was accomplished at West Point: it was near zero degrees, and fresh snow had covered the area two days earlier. Nor did he comprehend why the crowd that gathered was so large, particularly in light of the freezing-cold temperatures.[65]

The event was arranged by a delegation of the newly formed Aero Club of America. Courtland Field Bishop, Augustus M. Post, and A. Leo Stevens traveled from New York City to West Point, where they called upon Lieutenant Lahm, a balloonist himself and Harley's former French instructor, to arrange the balloon flight.[66] It was, for most, only a novelty.

For cadets at West Point, however, balloon launches were becoming almost routine. An unmanned balloon had been launched the week prior to Levée's flight, and a much larger balloon was launched on 31 March from the same Siege Battery as the others. Arnold was impressed enough to add a few photos of the 11 February flight to his scrapbook, but not impressed enough to write home about the other two flights.[67] The nearly silent balloons were a far cry from the deadly thunder of a cavalry charge.

Harley, youthful and handsome, exhibited as much interest in the "fairer sex" as he did in ballooning. His experiences with women at West Point is not a story worthy of a Harlequin romance. Courting at the Military Academy in the early 1900s might best be described as traditionally romantic; as with everything else at West Point, there were very strict rules governing behavior for both the cadets and their female guests. Woman arrived via the railroad, most of the time. They and their escort, be it mother, sister, or family friend, would eventually make their way to the quaint little hotel located at the base of the hill outside the campus. Legend held that it had been the former headquarters of George Washington's Continental Army during the Revolution—but it had not. The girls who were visiting "all jammed in together. . . . They had a great time," while the hotel's housemother ensured that protocol was strictly enforced.[68] A statue of Gen. George Washington upon his horse stood out front of the building, his arm outstretched as if delivering a benediction. Cadet lore held that Washington was actually saying, "Keep away from the hotel, boys. . . ."[69]

After evading the general's ominous apparition, cadets would present their calling card at the door and announce who it was that they were to meet. The card made its way up the long staircase to the anxious, primping visitors. The girls would peer out over the railing and flirt with their cadet until the bugle call announcing the parade formation. Only after Saturday classes and the noon meal were cadets free to walk Flirtation with their girls. The walk could not have been totally pleasant for the young ladies, sporting slipper-like shoes and long dresses over hilly, unpaved terrain. Saturday and Sunday afternoons were the only time that cadets were "alone" with their dates, although Flirtation was filled with cadets, all of whom knew each other. So there were frequent stops and conversations about cadet happenings and life in general, and in reality, cadets and their girlfriends were never alone.[70]

Following the evening meal on Saturday, cadets dressed for the hop while the women changed into their own hop attire. The dances highlighted everyone's weekend visit except the plebes', who were not yet permitted to attend hops. The upperclassmen escorted the plebes' ladies to the dance if they wanted to go. The hop ended promptly at the sounding of "Army Blue," the last dance at midnight. Escorts and guests headed back to the hotel on a bus, and then the cadets ran for the barracks. On Sundays everyone went to church, followed by a dress parade. Shortly after that and perhaps after one quick trip to Flirtation, the ladies took the tram back to the mainline for their journey home. They were gone by 4:00 P.M.[71]

At least, that was how it worked for most cadets. Not Harley. Harley was painfully reserved around women. His youthful entrance into West Point had everything to do with this particular disposition. Having been reared in an extremely restrictive environment, he never had time and was never instructed as to the ways of the world, particularly those involving women. This inexperience resulted in undue shyness; Harley was so bashful that he did not attend a hop voluntarily until his first-class year. It appears that women did not much interest him until after he left West Point.

Pewt was much more interested in horsing around with his classmates than in "dragging" girls around Flirtation, although he did so on several occasions. His West Point photo album holds pictures of many women within its pages, neatly arranged in military fashion. This would seem to verify that he did not have one particular love interest, but enjoyed the pleasant company of many young women. It may also be that Harley was an unwilling participant in gathering dates for his less "appetizing" classmates. Some of his Black Hand brethren complained that they were not having any luck finding a girl suitable for marriage. Pewt's revealing response was, "Well, my trouble is in keeping away from the girls that like me."[72]

Perhaps this is why Pewt was so stricken by Eleanor "Bee" Pool: she paid him no attention whatsoever until he was near graduation in 1907. Bee's first recollection of Harley was of a visit to West Point one weekend during his first-class year. They never even got close enough to talk. Harley was serving punishments for hanging "100 Days" banners, reflecting the number of days remaining until graduation, from the cadet academic building in the quiet hours of 23 February 1907. He spent the ensuing two months confined and marching the area.[73] Being the cadet leader of the Hand, Pewt often bore the brunt of the punishment issued by academy authorities.

Bee had come with Harley's older sister, Betty, to escape a nagging illness that weekend. Daddy Doc—Dr. Arnold—had prescribed a trip to the Military Academy as a cure for her symptoms; perhaps he felt that Miss Pool would make an appropriate wife for his son, the soon-to-be-graduating Army officer. Perhaps he was, in reality, setting them up, an act he would have categorically denied.[74]

But Harley was an immature rogue. His behavior at that time fell far below the Pool standard for its gentlemen. Bee had no misgivings about attending the hop with one of Harley's classmates instead; she saw no use in wasting a trip all the way from Ardmore. Although she revisited West Point twice more that year, she and Harley never really became acquainted, at least from her point of view—there was certainly no talk of love.[75]

Apparently for Harley, on the other hand, his two subsequent, yet innocent, meetings with Bee on Flirtation resulted in a severe case of love at first sight. For the next seven years, with varying degrees of intensity, Pewt thought about Bee. Much like his transformation from plebe into yearling, Harley began to understand the pervasive and complex feelings and emotions—from infatuation to head over heels—of true and lasting love between a man and a woman. It was the last phase of his four-year West Point education, the last lesson that molded a boy into a man, a lesson not taught by any academy instructor. As with his entry into West Point in 1903, Harley's first step toward an intimate relationship happened late in the game. But before he could pursue any relationship with Beadle, he had other goals: first graduation, then an assignment to his professional love, the horse cavalry.

Pewt's first-class year had been different than his first three years. He had figured out the academic system well enough to graduate without failure, including lackluster performances in military law and history. The West Point history curriculum was divided into ancient, regional, and world studies. Military history as a separate course was not included; American history centered around the creation of an independent United States, and some discussion on the War for Independence. The American Civil War was not formally addressed in any significant measure, except for a short summer field trip to Gettysburg's battlefield. The rest of the Army's advanced schools, particularly those located at Fort Leavenworth, Kansas, were making major efforts to include Civil War history in their curricula. The 1903 Root Reforms, an effort to increase efficiency and performance within the Army, had yet to reach West Point's academic departments in any great measure by 1907.[76]

Perhaps the lessons of the Civil War seemed too near in time to be considered history. After all, it had not yet been a half century since the last Confederate shots had been fired. There were instructors at West Point who had served as lieutenants during the war, and at least one civilian chemistry professor who frequently told of his combat experiences. Some military history writers believed that history was wasted on the young, while others sought great revelations and formulas for victory in Sherman's generalship or in Antoine-Henri Jomini's writings. In essence, military studies at West Point consisted of fortress engineering and small-unit tactics for each branch of service: cavalry, infantry, artillery, and engineering.[77]

But his involvement with the Black Hand, and the leadership role he played in it, eroded Harley's conduct marks from 21st to 52d out of 111 cadets. His attitude became cocky in the extreme, even to the point of making an impertinent remark to the senior cavalry instructor after being ordered to spit out a large chunk of "brown" he had crammed into his mouth. "Sir," Arnold quipped, "I thought all good cavalrymen chewed tobacco?" This almost-childish rejoinder, one sure to bring a stiff penalty, was indicative of Harley's lack of maturity and his inability to hold his fiery tongue at critical moments. As expected, the name Arnold topped the "skin list," and punishment was harsh for a soon-to-be-graduating senior. He was to be an AB (area bird) and march the area until graduation. When he wasn't marching the area, he was confined to quarters, again.[78] He did not mind the confinement too much; it was only for three or four days. He *really* did not mind missing the senior hop either, because he knew Bee was unavailable for graduation weekend anyway. But the consequences of his outburst may have been more severe and longer lasting than he anticipated.

Pewt graduated 66th out of 111 in his class, which normally would have qualified him for cavalry duty, but not for the engineering corps. In those days graduation order was treated with much more import than today; graduates who held faculty positions at West Point were listed in the *Howitzer* by name, rank, class year, class standing, and job title.[79] Surprisingly, the realization that he was not engineer-qualified disappointed his mother more than his father. Bee remembered Louise Arnold's hopes for her son: "I always wanted him to be an engineer, but he wasn't an engineer."[80] Herbert, however, now had the best of both worlds. His eldest son, Thomas, had become an engineer, while Harley was on the brink of a commission. It was, until that time, perhaps Daddy Doc's proudest moment as a father.

3
SECOND LIEUTENANT
HENRY H. ARNOLD, INFANTRY
(1907–11)

Graduation day, Friday, 14 June 1907, was as much a relief as a triumph. As in 1903 when he had left Ardmore for West Point, Harley was once again free of strict rules and seemingly ridiculous punishments. Leaving West Point brought no teary goodbyes. The departure defined the essence of the unofficial class cheer, "1907, never again!"[1] This cheer had been adopted by the class of '07 on the final day of summer encampment in 1906, and it was dutifully repeated upon the completion of any number of significant "last time" events during their first class year. Arnold went home on furlough anxiously awaiting news of which cavalry unit would be gaining one of the Army's finest new horsemen lieutenants. Commissioning paperwork and assignments were expected in the mail by the end of June.

Dr. Herbert Arnold always left the house before sunrise to begin his local rounds. The clip-clop of his horse and buggy signaled the beginning of his twelve- to fifteen-hour workday. Harley and his mother were enjoying breakfast one morning during summer furlough when the postman arrived with a letter from the War Department. Believing it to be a mere formality, he tossed it to his mother unopened. She carefully opened the commission and read it to herself while Harley explained how tremendous a rider he had become over the past four years. Familiar with the details of her husband's military career as a medic in a cavalry unit, Mrs. Arnold was well aware of the differences between cavalry and infantry.[2]

Lou's eyes signaled impending disaster to her young horseman, and sympathetically she could only watch as Harley read, then reread the orders she had just handed him: "Henry H. Arnold, 2nd Lieutenant of Infantry."[3] He did not

32

believe his own eyes. Shock, a queasy, stunned, perplexed look, fell over him for a moment—then anger. Harley had invested four years of his life in the Army with only one purpose: to become a cavalry officer. Now that dream was gone. Hundreds of hours perfecting equitation at the Military Academy now appeared useless. Fortunately it was his mother who sat with him that morning, not his father. Mrs. Arnold had significant influence on Harley, a much different influence than his father. She was a voice of reason concerning emotional matters such as this one.[4] Mother and son shared the disappointment together, allowing rising blood pressures to fall back into more normal ranges by the time the doctor returned from his rounds that evening.

Harley knew all too well what this infantry assignment meant. In those days each branch of the Army had separate lists, each consisting of a well-defined number of personnel. Once assigned to a particular branch, it was nearly impossible to switch, particularly to the cavalry. The cavalry was the most prestigious branch of the Army—the branch with the widest gold stripe. Promotions, however, lagged behind the infantry by two years. To transfer to the cavalry from the infantry, a volunteer from within the cavalry had to be willing to move. But "nobody would do it," recalled Tommy Milling (West Point, 1909), whose own first assignment was in the cavalry.[5]

Everyone in the Army was familiar with how the branches worked. Arnold realized that his best, and maybe his only chance to join the cavalry was upon graduation from West Point. His assignment to the infantry was one that, for better or worse, would determine the rest of his Army career, and he knew it.

So did his father, who immediately cabled Congressman Irving P. Wanger, the same gentleman who had offered Arnold his appointment to West Point in 1903. Before too long, the congressman and Boies Penrose, senior senator from Pennsylvania and a Philadelphian, accompanied by Harley and his father, boarded a train for Washington. If this mainline team could not rectify the commission situation, it could not be changed. In that case, Harley would have two choices: to refuse or to accept his commission into the infantry. His personal account of the fiery meeting that took place between this posse and the adjutant general of the Army is perhaps a bit exaggerated, colored by the recollection of youthful disappointment and an overzealous editor. In fact, a meeting took place during which Arnold threatened to decline his commission. Finally he accepted his fate, his commission, and an infantry assignment to the Philippine Islands. Even Dr. Arnold's political clout, considerable because of his service in the Pennsylvania National Guard, was limp against the administrative necessity for a proper balance of numbers in each Army branch, as determined by the adjutant general.[6]

In 1907 the Philippines was home to the only fully manned, combat-ready infantry force in the U.S. Army. Additionally, the islands were the only location where soldiers received foreign-service credit on their records. The secretary of war, William Howard Taft, the only man in the Army who could change Arnold's assignment, was himself in the islands overseeing the establishment of new Army posts. Although Arnold may have considered tracking him down and pleading his case in person, he must have realized that the secretary of war would not long remain overseas.[7] It is much more likely that Arnold chose the Philippine Island assignment for the first two reasons. It was an opportunity for actual combat, and at the same time it filled the foreign-service block contained in his military records.

✪ ✪ ✪ ✪ ✪

While Arnold was making these futile attempts to change his infantry assignment, the chief Signal officer, Brig. Gen. James Allen, had taken the first steps toward recognizing that aviation activities were growing in importance. Allen brought Maj. George O. Squier directly to Washington in July 1907, following Squier's completion of Command and General Staff School at Fort Leavenworth, Kansas. While at Staff School, Squier, who held a doctorate in electronics and magnetism, had concentrated his efforts on command and the field of aeronautics.

On 1 August 1907, perhaps influenced by Squier's work, Allen created the Aeronautical Division within the Signal Corps. This division was charged with responsibility for all military aeronautical matters, including operation of balloons and air machines. Rectifying earlier short-sightedness, the War Department, via the Signal Corps, finally announced its intention to buy a military, heavier-than-air flying machine. The Army required that the craft must carry two men aloft for one hour at 40 mph velocity.[8]

By the time the trials of the Wright Brothers' "heavier than air flying machine" began at Fort Myer, Virginia, in mid-September, Arnold and his classmate Ben Castle had reported for duty in San Francisco, awaiting transportation to the Philippine Islands. On 7 November 1907, they boarded the transport ship *Buford,* a converted rough-sailing cattle carrier, in San Francisco Bay and steamed toward the wondrous Philippines by way of Honolulu and Guam.[9] The new lieutenants were unaware of the newest developments in organized aeronautics within the Signal Corps.

After arriving in Manila, Lieutenants Arnold, Castle, and Wiley Evans "Wobbly" Dawson, another classmate, were all assigned to the Twenty-ninth Infantry that was newly established in the islands. The three officers moved directly to the bachelors' quarters on Fort McKinley, a cavernous building for only three men. Soon the place was up to Army standards, and Castle, the only married officer (his wife had accompanied him on the journey), was placed in charge of the mess. He and his wife occupied a far corner of the building, away from Arnold and Dawson. Castle hired a local youth to clean the quarters and a local Chinese cook, who was made responsible for ensuring that meals were adequate and on schedule.[10]

Typically the workday began at 5:00 A.M., and drill practice began one hour later. Drill was normally close-order sessions but also included target practice, wall scaling, and swimming in full combat uniform. After the four-hour drill period, the officers completed administrative duties until noon. These duties varied from checking morning reports to organizing guard duties for subordinates. Because of the extreme midday heat, a long siesta was observed from noon until 5:00 P.M. Evenings were social events, unless an officer had guard duty. Nearing the dinner hour, officers donned their dress-white uniforms and called on fellow officers at their homes across the post.[11]

This ritual, one that Arnold loathed, ranked equally with his limited experience at cadet hops and walks on Flirtation for enjoyment—a convention he thought he had just escaped.[12] The tradition supported the observation that Fort McKinley was purported to be "one of the greatest marrying grounds in the world." Generals sent their daughters, officers sent their sisters, any girl who just wanted to get married came to Manila. Lonely men immediately latched on to the visiting females and became enamored. Only those who were "very, very unattractive" were not immediately besieged.[13] Yet Lieutenant Arnold refrained. This environment was hardly the exotic one he had envisioned.

In actuality, Fort McKinley seemed like an adult version of West Point. The only real boon was a recent policy directed by the brigade commander, Brig. Gen. John J. Pershing, requiring that all officers maintain proficiency in horsemanship. The opportunity for an infantryman to mount up was rare, and Arnold took full advantage. His overall disappointment with his situation, however, was still apparent to his buddies as well as his superior, known only as Colonel Mason. Mason was a solid infantry commander and, believing in the importance of knowing his subordinate officers, had personally familiarized himself with his young troops. When an opening on mapping detail became available, Mason offered it to Arnold. The adventure-starved lieutenant accepted without hesitation.[14]

Mapping required that a team made up of two engineer soldiers, six Philippine scouts, two packers, and eight mules abandon the comforts of Fort McKinley and venture out "in the *bosque*" (pronounced "bosky" by the soldiers). Using machetes, the team hacked its way through the jungle, detailing the topography of the islands of Luzon and Corregidor. Conditions were harsh. The pests were frequently unbearable; the weather varied from torrential rains to abhorrent heat. Camp equipment was moved by cart until the trail became too narrow, then by *cargadores* (porters) until the trails became too steep, and then by pack train. Canvas tents were home. Arnold loved it.[15] This was real adventure.

Arnold, sporting a ragged beard, carried a shotgun in his personal equipment and hunted at every opportunity while in the bosque. He hunted wild chicken, pigeon, duck, and doves until he ran out of shotgun shells. Although deer were also plentiful, the animals only foraged at night, demanding too much time awake for him and his men. In the field Arnold's men worked a demanding schedule, one much different than that at the fort. Work began at 6:30 A.M. and continued straight through until 4:00 P.M., when a combined lunch-dinner was prepared. Aside from the game birds Arnold and the others gathered, they ate bacon and hardtack as well as local fare, such as eggs, from the *barrio* when they happened upon one. On 31 January 1909, Harley wrote a letter from the field describing these events: "I sure like the work," he wrote, "and am quite content to do my own washing, cook my own meals when necessary. . . ."[16] The apparent purpose of this closing line was to emphasize his self-reliance, a development his father would have encouraged.

Dr. Arnold, despite Harley's developing independence, had already revived the issue of his son's assignment to the cavalry. In January 1908, the doctor had written a friendly letter to Col. H. L. Scott, West Point's superintendent since 1906, in which he described his son's exceptional equestrian skills. One year later he sent another message, to newly promoted Lt. Col. Charles M. Gandy, surgeon on the superintendent's staff and head of the Department of Hygiene at West Point, again questioning the circumstances surrounding Harley's assignment to the infantry.[17] A polite response dutifully explained that Secretary of War Taft had listened to complaints about assignments for several cadets in the class of '07, not just Harley's. Although Taft expressed interest, it was a bureaucratic dodge and nothing ever came of the issue.

Locked away in the West Point archives was the real reason for the rebuke. In a 14 October 1907 internal response to a staff request for Arnold's transfer to the cavalry, Maj. Gen. Fred C. Ainsworth, the U.S. Army's adjutant general (commissioned in the Medical Corps) wrote, "Henry H. Arnold is not S.Q. and regretfully, transfer is not possible."[18] Ainsworth's letter revealed the existence of a cavalry qualification that was unknown to all but the Military Academy's highest authorities. There is no evidence that Arnold, his father, his congressional representatives, or even Lt. Col. Charles Gandy, a department head at West Point, were ever made aware of "S.Q.," special-qualification, status.[19]

Harley and others who were not assigned to the cavalry had not received (or had lost) special-qualification status for the cavalry. S.Q. was a mysterious label that, if not attached to a graduate's personal folder, disqualified him from cavalry service, apparently for life. Arnold did not hold S.Q. status and was therefore not eligible for the cavalry.[20]

How this rating was awarded remains a mystery. It is possible that Arnold's impertinent remark to the chief cavalry officer concerning chewing tobacco only days prior to his West Point graduation had cost him S.Q. status. S.Q. required a certain amount of objective evaluation by academy faculty, and none had more influence in selecting cavalry officers than the chief cavalry officer himself. It is likely that after Arnold's brash outburst, his S.Q. status—if he had earned it before—was summarily revoked.

While on mapping detail, Arnold escaped the mundane routine of drill and officer calls and found the exotic adventure he had signed up for. He plodded through every variety of landscape found throughout the islands. In one expedition alone, he and his team traversed rice paddies, cane fields, tropical swamp, *cogon* grass over fourteen feet high, mountains, and rolling hills. He encountered "monkeys, crocodiles, and the short wolley [*sic*] haired negritoes [*sic*; natives] galore."[21]

As they trudged around the jungle, Arnold's team also ran across Japanese men. "We seemed to be accompanied or met by Japanese photographers," Arnold recalled, "itinerant Japanese 'peddlers' or Jap [*sic*] botanists . . . whose best specimens always happened to be growing just where we had set up our instruments."[22] Some of these were what they claimed to be, but others were Japanese map makers. Arnold's classmate Ben Castle recalled, "We were picking up Japanese spies all the time."[23] Encountering these teams only reinforced the belief that war with Japan could occur "at any minute."[24]

Surprisingly, Arnold found fieldwork exhilarating, but it was the hard work and personal contacts he made during his tour that he considered "a tremendous professional advantage." His mapping details had familiarized him with many foreign nationals, but, more important, these details allowed younger officers to "become far better acquainted with [their] own seniors and with naval officers than would have been possible at home."[25] This unique aspect of his remote service, which broke down barriers of rank, allowed Arnold to relax around superior officers. He never lost the ability to be at ease around those who outranked him.

One of these contacts was Capt. Arthur S. Cowan. Cowan and Arnold had crossed paths while doing the business of mapping. They knew each other well enough that Cowan was aware of Arnold's distaste for infantry life, and in a later assignment, he remembered it. Cowan's next duty placed him in charge of finding officers willing to participate in a new Signal Corps program, flight training. One of his first inquiries went to Arnold. Realizing a chance to bail out of the infantry, Arnold responded favorably and had his name added to Cowan's list. Yet three more years would pass before there would be a place in the Signal Corps's fledgling aviation program, permitting Arnold to leave the infantry—and the ground—for the first time.[26]

✪　✪　✪　✪　✪

Flight trials began on 3 September 1908 at Fort Myer. Orville Wright flew the tests that were to prove that the air machine met the Army's stated specifications.[27] Initial flights were tremendously successful. Orville's solo and passenger-carrying flights left large crowds awestruck, as they did the members of the Aeronautical Board evaluation committee. This elation did not last.

The first in a long line of aerial tragedies occurred on 17 September 1908, when the Wright Flyer's propeller blade fractured. It warped out of shape and then snagged one of the fragile support wires that had come loose during the ensuing vibrations caused by the now-unbalanced propeller rotations. The plane went out of control and crashed to earth from its perch slightly higher than 100 feet above the ground.[28] Orville had taken an unfortunate passenger, 1st Lt. Thomas Selfridge (West Point, 1903), along for the flight. Selfridge, one of the Army's most experienced in the field of aeronautics and a member of the Aeronautical Board, was entitled to a personal evaluation flight.[29]

The Wright Military Flyer impacted the ground at a steep angle, nose first. Seat restraints had not yet been introduced, thus the occupants were hurled headlong into the parade field. Selfridge's skull fracture rendered him unconscious and produced an injury from which he could not recover. He died following emergency surgery. Lt. Thomas Selfridge was the first military man killed in an aircraft accident. Orville was critically injured; most serious was a broken left thigh and an injured back that hobbled him for the rest of his life. He spent seven weeks recuperating in the Fort Myer hospital, under the care of a nurse and his sister, Katherine, before he was well enough to return to Dayton. Not until June 1909 did the tests resume. They were completed successfully, with Orville at the controls, on 29 July.[30]

That same month, the Twenty-ninth Infantry was transferred to Fort Jay on Governors Island, New York. They had done their time in a remote location and were on normal rotation back to the States. Having saved some of his pay, Lieutenant Arnold decided to avail himself the opportunity to explore the world a bit on his way home, particularly since the journey itself would cost him nothing.[31] Every three months, a transport ship traveled the long way around the globe from Manila Bay. En route to New York, Arnold visited Hong Kong, Singapore, Egypt (including the pyramids), Genoa, and then traveled overland to Lucerne, Switzerland, his true destination. Arnold's intentions remain unknown, but it seems likely he may have had two ideas in mind for his journey. First, Switzerland was near the region of his ancestral home, and he had never visited there. Second, and far more important, Bee Pool was in Lucerne.[32]

Harley had been informed from home, likely by his father, that Bee Pool was in Switzerland at Lake Lucerne, enjoying a vacation with her mother.[33] After arriving in Lucerne, he arranged with Mrs. Pool to surprise Beadle, a childhood nickname given her because of her unusually tiny build, and went to meet her down at the Lake Lucerne boat dock. Her diary entry for 31 July 1909 described this meeting. "As we got off the boat and walked up the river to the bridge who should we see but Harley Arnold. I was so surprised because I had never received any answer from the letters I had written him in Naples and Genoa and thought he had decided not to travel in Europe after all!" The implication, clearly, was that both parties had attempted to arrange a meeting. Bee, her sister Lois, and Harley had lunch, during which he entertained them with stories of his adventures in the bosque. Then they visited the Museum of Peace and War, examining relics and battle displays. Bee noticed that Harley "looked terribly thin but very brown so does not look ill." More important, she recalled having a "very jolly time."[34]

Harley and Bee spent nearly the entire next day together. That morning they took the twelve-year-old Pool twins, Joe and Jack, to a nearby grotto to escape the stifling heat. In the afternoon, Bee and Harley sat and talked on the hotel balcony. Harley was expecting a visitor that day, someone who had traveled on the ship with him, and because of some undetermined glitch in their plans, he grudgingly had to return to Lucerne from Bee's chalet for two days.

On 4 August Harley returned to the Pools' villa via the eleven o'clock boat. For the rest of the day, he and Bee hiked around the countryside, exploring the terrain and each other's frame of mind. In typical Arnold fashion, the two hikers "trespassed on a dozen or more 'verboten' signs," as Bee recorded in her diary, "but finally reached a little terrace where the view was excellent. . . . Such a rough journey I have never taken."[35] No one would have guessed from this innocent flirtation that their challenging journeys together were just beginning.

For the next four days, long walks, flower gathering, long talks, and very happy times were the routine. On Harley's second Saturday in town, he and Bee were scolded by the madame of the hotel for "staying up until 10:30 on the balcony [apparently unsupervised]." Bee and Harley made definite efforts to create time alone. On one day trip to nearby Altdorf, the couple decided to take the train back to Lake Lucerne while the rest of the family walked. Suddenly, on Monday, 9 August, Harley received word that his father was very ill and his condition was not improving as expected. Betty, Harley's older sister, likely concocted the message that begged his return. Harley reluctantly set out for home via Paris.[36] He would not see Bee again for any appreciable length of time, and certainly not in such a romantic setting, until 1912.

It was during his hectic return to Philadelphia that Arnold became aware of the air machine as more than just a curiosity. He briefly viewed the Blériot airplane while waiting in Paris for his transport. Louis Blériot had successfully flown across the English Channel just recently, on the morning of 25 July 1909.[37] The single-engine, fabric-covered monoplane hung triumphantly near the Place de l'Opéra. In his memoirs, Arnold recalled his thoughts at that moment. "If one man could do it once, what if a lot of men did it together at the same time? What happens then to England's splendid isolation?"[38]

But sometime before World War I, he wrote about the Blériot craft in an article that was never published, titled, "Pioneers of the Aerial Trails." In that article Arnold wrote that he was "not very greatly inspired by its appearance for it seemed to be too fragile-looking to have any real value as a means of transportation."[39] At that point in the young lieutenant's career, the latter was likely the more accurate assessment of his true feelings about airplanes.

Arnold's 1909 journey from Hong Kong to Genoa on the *Grosse Kurfuerst* transport ship had been packed with German, British, and American officers on their way to and from military duty locations. The Royal Navy, undeniably the strongest naval force in the world in 1909, seemed a popular topic of conversation among the Europeans on board.[40] These conversations were still fresh and clear in Arnold's mind as he looked at the frail air machine hanging above the curious Parisian crowd. But he was bound for an assignment that he thought was "probably the dullest garrison job in the Army."[41] Certainly it would be, after two years in the bosque.

Upon Arnold's arrival in Ardmore, he found his father well on the road to recovery. Relieved, he set out for New York City and Fort Jay in September 1909. In stark contrast to the bosque-loving lieutenant of Fort McKinley, Arnold had shown a definite softer side. His timid, ineffective attempts at courtship had not even been perceived as such by Miss Pool. In fact, Bee became engaged to a newspaperman from Rochester, New York, later that year.[42]

Arnold arrived at Fort Jay, Governors Island, in September, and officially reported for duty on 1 October 1909. Governors Island was flat, so flat that even riding a spirited horse was not enjoyable.[43] But Fort Jay, an ammunition-storage facility and harbor-defense post, was only a few miles from New York City and all the diversions available there. Why, then, was Arnold so dreading duty on the island? Here was a young, handsome, Army officer—a worthy prize for any young woman—only a short ferry ride away from one of the most exciting cities in America. Certainly this was too good to be true for a young, adventure-seeking Army lieutenant.

Additionally, social life on the fort itself was tedious for single officers. "There is not much doing in the social line," Arnold wrote to his mother. "Every Tuesday night there is the regular concert at the club and every Friday the hop. Evening calling seems to have gone out of style."[44] In reality, there was plenty of social activity available for the young officers. Yet Arnold complained that there was "not much doing." Why did he perceive this to be so?

The above letter was written 16 March 1910, long after Arnold's first Christmas in Ardmore following his Philippine tour. During the holidays he visited home, where his family held a traditional Christmas party. In attendance was Miss Beadle Pool. During the party, though the details remain somewhat sketchy, Arnold expressed to Beadle his innermost feelings for her. It was only then that Bee realized for the first time that Harley was interested in her as more than a family friend.[45]

Bee had many suitors. In fact, at the time of this meeting, Bee was engaged. In the next few years, while attending school in Berlin, affluent foreigners—German, Italian, Swiss—continually pursued her hand in marriage. One German youth named Billy kept in touch with her even after her marriage to Harley.[46] Italians begged her hand while she was on vacations. It was no wonder that Harley's attempts at courtship were brushed aside as innocent. Even after the Arnolds' 1909 Christmas party, Bee recalled that there was virtually no courtship with Harley.[47] During 1910 and 1911, however, it was Bee, not Harley, who was out of touch while schooling in Germany. There is no record of correspondence between the couple until nearly a year after Bee had returned from Europe, and Arnold had been assigned to flight training at College Park Field, Maryland.

Arnold had fallen in love with Bee Pool, and, in his own clumsy way, he was trying to let her know how he felt. This explains why a striking, single Army officer had nothing to do in New York City. He saw no purpose to enjoyment without his true love at his side. Her engagement to another man did not seem to dissuade his desire or lessen his feelings for her, implying that some sort of mutual pre-engagement arrangement may have been made during the family party. Yet it would be over three years until their own official engagement.

Arnold passed the time at Fort Jay by riding and accomplishing his routine garrison duties. The flat, open ground on the island did serve one significant purpose—it provided a landing field for two of America's aviation pioneers—Wilbur Wright and Glenn Curtiss. The Wright Military Flyer arrived at Governors Island on 20 September 1909, fresh from successful flight evaluation at Fort Myer. Glenn Curtiss arrived the next day, following his accomplishments at Rheims, France. Both were contractual participants in the Hudson-Fulton Centennial and were preparing to make record-breaking flights from Governors Island up the Hudson River, around Grant's Tomb, and back, a route just a bit over 20 miles.[48]

These pioneers were not just demonstrating the capabilities of their machines, they were after prize money. The New York *World* newspaper had announced a purse of $10,000 for the pilot who flew the route from New York to Albany during the celebration honoring the centennial of the first voyage of Robert Fulton's North River steamboat and the 300th anniversary of Capt. Henry Hudson's entry into New York Harbor. The celebration's organizing committee had searched for aviators willing to accept contracts that paid handsome sums for aerial demonstrations and broken aviation records. The Wrights had just filed suit against Curtiss for patent infringements related to the design of his aircraft-control system, and in an awkward turn of events, both Wilbur Wright and Glenn Curtiss accepted the record-breaking challenge.[49]

Curtiss could not stay in New York for the entire duration of the affair, and therefore he contracted with the committee for $5,000. He was to fly from New York to the tomb and back, or make several short flights from the tomb across the river to astound the crowds.[50] The Wrights had contracted for $15,000, promising a flight of 10 or more miles, or one hour-long flight plus shorter local hops to please the crowds during the rest of the two-week event.[51]

Unfortunately for Curtiss, poor weather, strong winds in particular, severely limited the amount of flying that could safely be accomplished during the first week. Determined to collect some of the contract money, Curtiss made one short official flight on Governors Island and called it quits, then departed to meet a commitment in St. Louis. By Monday morning, 4 October 1909, the weather had calmed, and Wilbur announced that he would attempt to satisfy the terms not only of his contract, but of Curtiss's as well. The round-trip flight to Grant's Tomb took just over half an hour. The prize money was secure.[52]

Arnold certainly witnessed at least one of these flights while stationed on Governors Island during the tricentennial event. His autobiography, however, inaccurately describes a Curtiss-made flight, even implying that he flew as far away as West Point during the celebrations. This did not occur. Curtiss did make the flight from Albany to New York City seven months later, on 29 May 1910, passing by West Point.[53]

It is probable that Arnold, along with nearly a million other New Yorkers, witnessed the takeoff and landing of Wilbur's prize-winning flight up the Hudson River. The Wright Flyer sported a unique modification for the over-water competition: Wilbur had obtained a fire-engine red canoe, sealed the top closed with canvas and "dope," a lacquer-like sealant used on airplane wings of the day, and affixed it between the airplane's skids. This makeshift raft was intended to keep the craft afloat long enough to pull it from the river in case of a dire emergency.[54] Even if Arnold did not witness the event personally, the aviators were in the media headlines during the entire celebration. Certainly he read of their accomplishments.

The dull routine of garrison life and the absence of his lady friend was broken only by an occasional air show nearby or some other special event in New York City. Still trying to escape the infantry, Arnold took every possible opportunity to better his chances for a transfer. He had earlier reapplied for a transfer to the cavalry and been denied. He took the entrance tests for the Ordnance Department, which held the greatest promise for early promotion; the lowest rank allowed in this division was first lieutenant. He even submitted a short note to the adjutant general requesting duty with the Aeronautical Division of the Signal Corps that was operating at College Park, Maryland.

While awaiting the results of the mathematics and physics exams (which he failed), Arnold received a letter from the War Department offering him a rare opportunity and his chance to escape the infantry—an assignment to flying school.[55] Captain Cowan had apparently come through. Arnold's two-year-old response to Cowan's initial inquiry, coupled with his note to the adjutant, had finally reached the top of the pile. His association and friendship with Cowan, along with his persistence, finally proved to be his ticket out of the infantry.[56]

The catalyst for Arnold's assignment occurred on 3 March 1911, when Congress approved War Department appropriations specifically for aeronautical pursuits. Although the bill was for fiscal year 1912 (FY 1912 began 1 July 1911), $25,000 were made immediately available to procure the airplanes.[57] Three Wright Flyers and two Curtiss craft were purchased. With the Wright contract came the provision for training one pilot per airplane at the school in Dayton.

The War Department already had files on those who had volunteered for aviation duty, such as Arnold, and when the funds were allocated in March, the candidates were notified of their new duties as quickly as administrative procedures permitted. Arnold and Thomas DeWitt "Tommy" Milling were on the top of that list. By 21 April, the orders had been cut and the deal was official.[58]

Against the advice of his commander, but realizing an opportunity to free himself from infantry ties, Arnold accepted these new orders. He recalled his commanding officer's warning, "Young man, I know of no better way for a person to commit suicide!"[59] The young second lieutenant considered those words a challenge and probably did not think much about the dangers involved in piloting early flying machines. By the end of April 1911, Arnold and Milling—another handsome youngster, later nicknamed Dashing—were in Dayton, Ohio, to begin flying lessons at Simms Station, the home of the Wright Brothers' flying school. It was the ultimate adventure for any young man.

4

"THEY ARE HERE TO LEARN TO FLY" (1911–12)

The above words, written on 7 May 1911 by Bishop Milton Wright, Orville and Wilbur's father, summed up Arnold's reason for moving to Dayton, Ohio. Packing his few belongings, he bid farewell to Governors Island and the infantry, for how long he did not know. During the last week in April he arrived in Dayton, where he met up with the dashing "Tommy" Milling. After finding a place to live in town, the young lieutenants reported to the Wright flying school at Simms Station. This was nothing more than a hundred acres of pasture and one wooden hangar. Exact dates for the completion of initial ground school do not exist, but we can ascertain that they lasted no more than one week from the fact that Arnold's first training flight occurred on Wednesday, 3 May.[1]

Early ground lessons were basically an introduction to the flying machine and its mechanical workings. The Wrights themselves frequently taught elementary flying techniques during these ground lessons and were assisted with the maintenance portion of the instruction by their mechanics.[2] Mechanical lessons took place in the factory that was located in Dayton. The small brick building was the factory and housed Orville's office, one large room in which the planes were built, and one smaller room in which the engines were assembled and tested. All flying was done at Simms Station, an 8-mile electric-streetcar ride east of town.[3]

The Wright Model B engine was a four-cylinder gasoline-powered motor weighing 178 pounds, capable of developing up to 40 horsepower. The original 1903 engine weighed 160 pounds not including oil, water, or the magneto, and produced only 12 horsepower.[4] In these early days, 1 horsepower was approximately equivalent to five propeller revolutions per minute at peak engine-operating efficiency. The less horsepower the fewer screw rotations, and thus less thrust for flying.[5] As the narrow margin between flying speed and stall speed—the speed at which sufficient lift for flight is no longer generated—was often less than 10 miles per hour, every bit of power was absolutely essential.

The engine powered two wooden propellers that were driven by chains affixed to a cogwheel on the engine drive shaft. The chains resembled bicycle chains, only larger, and they were geared down so that the maximum revolutions of the engine drive shaft could be turned into slower, more powerful propeller rotations. The extreme pitch of the propellers (the higher the pitch, the more propeller surface strikes the air) required power, not speed, to bite into the still air and accelerate it rearward, creating the necessary thrust for flight. This gearing solution was how the Wrights solved the early problem of finding an engine light enough to propel a man and an airplane on its own power. It was only one of several major obstacles that the Wrights eventually overcame.[6]

To picture the basic workings of the engine and the propellers, imagine riding a ten-speed bicycle up a very steep hill. Using the low gears allows the rider to pedal quickly but comfortably, while the wheels rotate slowly, pushing the bicycle up the hill. In the case of the Wright Flyer, the engine acted in the same way as the bicycle rider, expending energy by pedaling quickly. The propellors did the job of the bicycle wheels, turning the engine's work into power (thrust) through the use of gears.

Together, Arnold and Milling spent hours learning how the delicate machine was assembled, disassembled, greased, tightened, and repaired. Sharing the experience of becoming new aviators, the two young lieutenants developed a unique friendship that endured nearly forty years. Both were grateful for the time spent in the factory because, although the Army had decided to train pilots, it had not begun training mechanics or crew chiefs. In 1911, every pilot was also a mechanic of sorts.[7] All early aviators became intimately familiar with the workings and assembly of their planes.[8]

The second and more challenging problem concerned stability and control in flight, a problem largely conquered in the 1902 Wright Glider.[9] Until the Wrights began working on a flyable craft, previous failures by other inventors had been result of an inability to maintain balance in the air. Otto Lilienthal had met his end that way.[10] What Orville really meant by *balance* was that for an airplane to actually fly, it would have to be under complete control at the hands of the pilot at all times, in all three axes of motion, to maintain equilibrium.

The process that finally led the Wrights to the development of the 1903 Flyer was a methodical study using both empirical and theoretical research.[11] First, all available sources were consulted to establish a baseline of knowledge from which to begin experimentation. Then hundreds of tests over a period of years, using both gliders and a homemade wind tunnel, resulted in the accumulation of data in sufficient quantity to ensure final success. Data on lift, drift, and center of pressure were recorded and eventually utilized to maximize performance of wing shapes and flight controls for the first airplane.[12]

The Wrights were not purely empirical in their methods, although they did a large amount of trial-and-error testing. They invented tools to help them measure forces and compare designs. They built a wind tunnel to refine wing design. They incorporated the lessons they had learned in their laboratory to practical application in refining the wing construction of gliders, and, in the end, the powered airplane. Insight came at different times in almost random, chaotic fashion. Unexpected results that often forced modifications in design were seen not as roadblocks but as detours. By the fall of 1902 the Wright brothers knew they could fly, they just did not know exactly when they would.[13]

The Wrights' practical experience was put to use in their flying school every day. Before their first flight, all students were instructed in the workings of the Flyer's flight controls. To control the machine required full-time use of both hands and at least one foot. Additionally, the 1910–11 Wright Model B did not have dual controls. This meant that once a student learned to fly from one seat—Arnold and Milling both learned to fly in the left seat—they flew only from that seat. In turn, new students were taught to fly from the other seat, a rather confusing arrangement to say the least. The problem was rectified by adding dual controls to the airplanes that were delivered to College Park in late 1911 and early 1912.[14]

Thrust, which produced velocity, was controlled by a foot pedal that engaged a magneto. The magneto was two-cylinder attached to a flywheel that produced the spark to ignite the fuel inside the engine. It was, practically speaking, a large spark plug. The engine ran full power at all times while the foot pedal was not depressed. Depressing the foot pedal lengthened the spark, slowing down combustion. Airspeed was controlled by alternately pushing the pedal in and letting it spring back out. The magneto control acted something like a gas pedal in an automobile, but instead of providing more fuel, it provided less spark that reduced engine speed. This on-off operation resulted in a characteristic pulsating-engine sound while the machine was flying. In 1912 the procedure was reversed to operate more like a true gas pedal. There was also an emergency engine-shutoff string that hung over the pilot's head, and pulling the string killed the clanky, putt-putting motor by opening the engine valves. The motor could be restarted by resetting the valves.[15]

Altitude was regulated by the elevator and was therefore an important control for takeoff and landing. The elevator control was located on the outside of each seat—for the left seat it was on the left side. The natural motion of pushing or pulling the control stick in flight moved the elevator: pushing caused the airplane to descend, while pulling initiated a climb. Arnold flew with the elevator control in his left hand.[16]

Direction was changed by a combination of lifting a wing and pulling back on the elevator control. The Wright machine used "wing warping" to change the shape of the wing and either create or decrease lift generated by each side of it. In so doing, one wingtip began to rise or bank to the right or left. This movement shifted the direction of lift from straight up to some angular direction. By pulling the elevator up slightly after initiating a bank, the vector of lift actually pivoted the nose of the machine to a new direction. This combination of moves generated turns. During advanced piloting lessons, Orville often demonstrated steep turn techniques (executing banks greater than 45 degrees) and emphasized "the paramount importance at all times of maintaining ample forward velocity in order to prevent loss of control that results from lessened speed, commonly called 'stalling.'"[17]

Instead of a natural left-right movement for the warping lever control, however, it moved forward and back, just like the elevator control.[18] Pushing forward increased the wing camber, and thus increased lift created by the right wing, initiating a left bank. Pulling had the opposite effect. The rudder handle, which rotated atop the wing-warping lever, also operated independently, if needed.[19] Students had to consciously learn to use the warping lever properly to avoid disaster. This required the formation of a totally unnatural, new habit pattern—push to turn left, pull to turn right, while twisting the rudder handle at the same time.

The complexity of these motions, at least to the uninitiated airmen, required some form of ground training, and a simulator had been erected in the Wrights' factory for this purpose. An old machine, stripped of landing struts and tail, hung balanced on a sawhorse. The warping lever was connected to a series of pulleys and cables, and when the lever was actuated, the machine tilted in the corresponding direction.[20] In this way young pilots established flying-habit patterns essential for survival in the air. It was with this nascent technology, along with that provided by Glenn Curtiss and his flying school, that American military airpower first found its wings.[21]

No flight was routine in 1911: there were no ground or flight checklists. There was only common sense, good judgment based upon experience, and, often, natural skill that prevented accidents. There was little specialized equipment. Civilian attire was worn at the Wright school, and hats were simply donned backward to keep them from blowing off the pilots' heads. Until Arnold took a bug square in the eye during one particular flight, goggles had not been worn. After successful removal of the bug's wings from Arnold's eye, goggles became a standard piece of flying gear.[22]

Before flying, the condition of the craft was checked. "When the plane was tuned up," recalled Milling, the airplane was "like a drum—if you touched it with your fingers, you'd see the cloth and everything had to be tight, and the wires had to be a certain tension, and you could test it by the sound."[23] A plucked support wire resonated like a long, thick wire inside an open grand piano. Ever since Orville's crash at Fort Myer in 1908, after a propeller had fractured and severed some of the airplane support wires, fliers checked for appropriate tension, particularly around the propeller section of the craft. Checklists carried by pilots today, both civilian and military, contain procedures and cross-checks that serve as a constant reminder of the fate of many fliers, crew, and passengers killed or injured in aircraft accidents over the years.[24]

Orville and Wilbur Wright, when available, taught the ground lessons personally, but they could not instruct every student pilot in the air. Lieutenant Arnold's flight instructor was Wright employee Art L. "Al," or "Owl," Welsh. Orville had taught Welsh to fly in May 1910; he was one of the many Washingtonians who had witnessed the Wright flight trials at Fort Myer.[25] Arnold himself never flew with either Orville or Wilbur Wright. Between 3 May and 13 May, he flew every one of his twenty-eight lessons with Welsh—the average flight lasted only eight minutes.

A typical flight started with a short discussion setting goals for the flight. After the ground inspection of the machine, Arnold and Welsh climbed aboard, and formal instruction began. Progress was incremental over Arnold's first twenty-eight flights. He rode as a passenger during the first two, then progressed in ten work days to having a "hand on elevator," then to "handled levers nearly all the time," and finally to "landed without assistance."[26]

The Wrights never flew on Sundays. Flights were normally in the afternoon, as the winds were generally most calm late in the day. "Wright would not allow you to go and do any training unless we had completely still air," Milling recalled, because "you couldn't tell whether you were controlling the plane or the wind was knocking it about."[27] It was critical to fly these early flights in ideal weather to establish a personal baseline, as far as control and confidence were concerned. Arnold soloed after a total of three hours and forty-eight minutes in the air with Al Welsh. In practical terms, he became a pilot on the day of his first solo, 13 May 1911, a Saturday. His civilian airplane-pilot certificate (FAI, Fédération Aéronautique Internationale) was awarded on 6 July 1911. The first official military-aviator ratings were not awarded until 22 July 1912, as reflected in War Department General Order No. 40.

It took Arnold a few days longer than Milling to complete the program of instruction. This supported Orville's belief that anyone having good coordination, the proper size (not too heavy), and enough "smarts" could learn how to fly a plane, given enough time. To many young pilots, there was nothing natural about controlling a Wright Flyer, but to a few, such as Milling, flying came more easily. It is because of Milling's early completion of his instruction that he has been described as a natural flier, whereas Arnold has never held that distinction. Arnold took a bit longer to learn, but after mastering the basic skills, it was like riding a bicycle.[28] The rest of his flights in Dayton were "made alone for experience."[29]

By 10 June Arnold had amassed thirty-three solo flights, totaling six hours and twenty-six minutes of flying time. During idle hours or bad weather, he studied how the machines were built and helped to make minor repairs caused by the inevitable crackups that were, then, common occurrences.[30]

Following initial checkout and much solo practice time, Arnold and Milling crated up the Army's newest Wright machine and sent it by train to College Park, Maryland, about to become the home of the first Signal Corps flight school. A second Wright Model B had been reassigned from Fort Sam Houston, Texas, and arrived at College Park about the same time Arnold and Milling did. The boxcars arrived at the airfield via the Baltimore and Ohio Railroad near the end of June.[31]

The hours spent on the Wright factory floor now paid off. Arnold and Milling assembled the craft themselves in preparation for the opening of the flight school. The only job to be done was to assemble the machines and get them flying. "We have been up every day since the arrival of the machine," Arnold wrote his father. "Yesterday we had our first cross country trip when I took Milling for a ride to the outskirts of Washington and back to College Park."[32]

The only two active Army pilots were now its only flight instructors as well. Topping their new tasks was teaching two other officers, who had been assigned to College Park on setup detail, to fly. The unit commander, Capt. Charles deForest Chandler, arrived at College Park on 20 June direct from Fort Leavenworth's Staff School. He and the young lieutenant who had established the airfield while Arnold and Milling had been in Dayton, Lt. Roy Kirtland, began flying lessons immediately.[33] Most flying took place in the afternoon, and all of these young officers had other functions for which they were responsible. Chandler, aside being the commander, was also responsible for aviation at Signal Corps headquarters in Washington, D.C. The officers shared one large room at the War Department building at 17th Street and Pennsylvania Avenue. Arnold and Milling, aside from instructor duties, were wrapped up in trying to invent missions for these new contraptions.[34] For these pioneer aviators, uncertainty and innovation were daily watchwords.

Arnold, as Chandler's instructor, easily overcame the problem of teaching his student to fly right-handed.[35] Chandler visited the Wright flying school in person after he had been checked out at College Park: as the commander, he needed to be familiar with all aspects of flying, including some fine-tuning in the air under Orville's personal guidance. Following Chandler's mid-summer visit, Arnold's innovative instruction prompted Orville to write him a note, complimenting his flying as well as his instructor skills. "I was pleased to hear the newspaper men who infested our camp at Kill Devil Hill speak so well of your flying; but I knew that you must be flying well, or you could not have given Captain Chandler such good training. He flew in excellent style when he was here."[36]

Arnold had become not only a skilled pilot, but a skilled airplane mechanic as well. He and Milling created the first *Dash-1*, the airplane technical manual, including pictures of the craft and the motor, with each of the parts meticulously labeled by hand. This early manual was invaluable to each pilot who daily tinkered with his air machine.[37]

When headquarters obligations had been met and instruction had ended for the day, Arnold, Milling, Kirtland, and also Capt. Paul Beck pressed the limits of known aerial achievements. Beck had trained with Curtiss in California and was now assigned to College Park, along with the arrival of the first Curtiss airplane.

Arnold excelled at breaking altitude records:

> NEAR DEATH IN AERO
> Lieut. Arnold Benumbed by Cold at High Altitude
>
> MAKES NEW ARMY RECORD
> Nearly Loses Control of Machine
> When 4,167 Feet in Air[38]

Arnold was embarrassed by the sensational 19 July 1912 headlines. He wrote his mother, "I was up over 4100 feet the other day and found it quite cold but not as cold as the newspapers printed it."[39]

This followed by one week an earlier innocent flight-turned-red-faced for Arnold. He and Lt. Kirtland had taken a short hop around Washington, enjoying the sights and practicing air navigation. Unfortunately, a visit from famed aviator Harry Atwood was anticipated the same day by many in the capital city, but Atwood had been delayed in Baltimore. Arnold's plane was thought to be Atwood's by some over-anxious observer, who notified the Congress of the awaited arrival. Both houses hastily adjourned and hurried to see the plane land out front of the capital. Among the bustling bureaucrats was none other than Arnold's own senior senator Boies Penrose, whose ineffective effort to change the lieutenant's infantry assignment had been indirectly responsible for Arnold's reassignment to the Signal Corps.

Arnold's plane simply circled at an altitude of 2,400 feet, turned northeast, and headed back to College Park, unaware of the hubbub. Arnold recounted the incident matter-of-factly. "I do not know whether I wrote about my flight over Washington or not," he described to his mother. "In any case it caused Congress to adjourn."[40] For the rest of the summer and most of that fall, Arnold personally turned his eye toward improving the Army's few aircraft.

In September he continued to turn heads, while participating in an aviation meet at Nassau Boulevard, New York. On 24 September he made the first "aero mail-carrying" run from Nassau to Garden City, New York—about five miles. That run made headlines in *Aero: America's Aviation Weekly*. By the end of the meet, aerial scouting demonstrations had been flown, as well as a demonstration by pioneer aviatrix Miss Harriet Quimby. There had been airplane rides, too, for those willing to pay the fee.[41]

Israel Ludlow, one of the air meet's promoters, sought out Arnold to act as a stunt pilot in two motion pictures that featured flying scenes in their dramatic climaxes. In *The Military Airscout,* Arnold's character succeeded in delivering a message to his commanding general through a barrage of gunfire. The airplane was used to sweep the aviator's love interest off her feet in a second film, *The Elopement.* The nature of aviation garb—a long leather coat, knickerbockers, helmet, and goggles—tricked the audience into believing the screen actor was also the daring pilot. It was in ways such as this, and by winning prizes at air meets and races, that early aviators supplemented their Army pay.[42]

Now with a full six months' flight experience to draw from, Arnold realized that the Army's planes were adequate for basic flight instruction and little else. The Army had a total of six planes in its inventory—one hung silently in the Smithsonian's National Museum, one was on its way to the Philippine Islands, and four were at College Park.[43] By 6 November, Arnold had informed Orville that soon "machines that will carry more weight and climb faster" would be needed to meet anticipated aviation-school requirements. As an interim measure, he queried Orville about the maximum performance of both the propellers and the drive chain.[44] This suggested that Arnold was ready to modify the engines to produce more power.

Early experiments in bomb dropping, "wireless" operations, and gunnery made it clear that the greater the weight placed on the aircraft, the worse the performance became. Riley E. Scott's bomb-dropping trials at College Park demonstrated the narrowness of the margins involved. Scott's bombsight weighed about 60 pounds, and he carried two 18-pound bombs. Along with his own burly six-foot frame, the device, the bombs, and the pilot, only the bantam-weight Milling, a spry 140 pounds, could fly for the tests. Even Arnold, a tall, slim 175 pounds, pushed load limits too far.[45] Milling was also selected to test Isaac N. Lewis's powerful machine gun while Chandler fired it from the air. Although the tests were a success, the Army did not purchase the Lewis gun for aerial use.

It was an unfortunate fact that the Army did not purchase any aeronautical combat equipment to speak of, and there was no money for development projects of any kind. The Lewis gun was unfunded because the Army had purchased the Benet-Mercier machine gun, which Arnold described as "a very satisfactory weapon—on the ground. As an aircraft weapon it was impossible. With the Benet-Mercier mounted aboard, the controls of the Wright airplane could not be operated and the movement of the Curtiss wheel yoke was interfered with."[46] Money allotted to the aviation section was only enough to purchase the plane, and none of the supporting infrastructure necessary for operations, such as airfields and repair tools. "This short-sightedness," recalled Milling, "was one of the major reasons we had neither combat aircraft nor combat crews in our military structure at the beginning of World War I."[47]

The ongoing experiments demonstrated obvious deficiencies in the 1911 airplanes. To resolve the weaknesses, the inquisitive Arnold began seeking advice on improvements for the machines. Wilbur answered his letter with detailed specifications for propeller rotation, motor performance, and testing procedures. Warnings were issued reminding the young aviators that the motors should "never be run without plenty of water in the radiator, and oil in the tank." Overheating eventually caused warping in the cylinders that decreased engine performance. As to the issue of chain strength, "The propellers and chains have a large factor of safety and if sudden jerks are avoided," Wilbur wrote, "will easily carry 25% more power than our present motors give."[48] This large safety margin immediately suggested that a more powerful motor might be used as a substitute for the older, four-cylinder models.

In fact, Arnold spelled out exactly what he had in mind after reading Wilbur's incomplete response. "Could we put a 60 or 70 H.P. engine in the standard machine and put 2 or 3 more teeth in the engine sprocket. This would give us much more power when it was needed." Under normal conditions, however, normal power would remain adequate.[49] In modern terms, Arnold wanted afterburners on his Wright Flyer. He wanted a margin of extra power not only to improve performance, particularly during takeoff and climb, but also to salvage unexpected flight conditions, whether natural or self-induced.[50]

Orville was about to provide Arnold an ill-fated approximation of what he wanted: the Wright Model C, a six-cylinder, 55-horsepower, improved version of the Model B.[51] Dated one day before Arnold's request for bigger engines (mail return took about one week), Orville promised "one and possibly two new motors for next season, of six or eight cylinders." Orville anticipated an enormous surplus of power adequate to quickly lift heavy loads. Perceptively, Orville also pointed out that increased power meant better control in gusty wind conditions, still one of the greatest dangers to fliers.[52] Arnold and Wright were in sync.

Flight at that time was still a fair-weather game. On 28 November 1911, as winter settled over the Washington area, the aviators boxed up their planes and moved to Barnes farm near Augusta, Georgia, hoping for more temperate flying weather. In the first-ever aerial-unit deployment, all personnel (thirty-nine Signal Corps specialists plus the officers), equipment (motor vehicles, horses, mules, aircraft), and spare parts were loaded upon several train cars and transported to the deployed operating location.[53]

Unlike the planes of today, these could not be left out in the open. They were cloth and wood, and, even though they were finished with good protection for weather and flying, they could not stand bad weather for any length of time. They would deteriorate: "The way we shipped the Wright plane at that time was to take off the tail, remove the skids, undo them and put them over the wings, leave the wings as they were, and just shove it into a boxcar, endwise. Then the tail assembly could be shoved in with it and also the landing assembly, so that the plane could be assembled very quickly after you arrived at your destination."[54]

By 7 December flying had begun. Arnold remained so busy that a trip to Ardmore for the holidays was impossible. "So please all have a good time for me," he wrote. "I only wish that I could help you partake of the Christmas dinner."[55]

The weather did not cooperate as expected during the deployment. In January a blizzard, the first to hit Augusta in fifteen years, grounded the airplanes. The tents in which they were hangared collapsed due to the strain of the heavy, moist snow. A less-powerful yet persistent snow halted operations again in February. Predictably, spring thaws swelled the Savannah River past its flood limits and covered the flying field in several feet of water. Although the planes and the horses were kept high and dry, nature's interference prevented a full season of aviation activities.[56]

Beginning in January 1912, improvements were also being made to the existing military aircraft. New parts were mailed directly to the deployed unit from the Wright Company in Dayton. The installation of the new equipment was, however, not always easily understood or well explained, as this exchange of letters between Arnold and Wright illuminates.

> 24 February 1912, Augusta, GA
> Dear Sir:
> Amongst the new set of fittings which were sent to us from Dayton was a new type of magneto spring. I request that you furnish me a sketch showing method of fastening on engine. I believe it is a new type to be used in connection with the new foot pedal which you have furnished us.
> There is also a set of four nickel plates with upturned edge each with two holes in center portion. These plates exactly fit on the main skids but I cannot see for what purpose they are to be used. Kindly send me some information concerning these also.
> Sincerely,
> Henry H. Arnold,
> 2nd. Lieut. 29th. U.S. Infantry.[57]

> 2 March 1912, Dayton, OH
> My Dear Lieutenant Arnold:
> The magneto set was of the new type intended to be used with the new foot pedal. We have no sketches at present, showing the method of attachment, but we will have one made and sent to you within a few days.
> The nickel plated plates are, no doubt, the plates that go on the skids at the point where the starting wheel brackets are fastened to the skid. They are intended to keep the bolts, which hold the bracket, from tearing out. . . .
> The new foot pedal is intended to operate so as to advance the spark

when it is pushed forward against the spring. The old spring and pedal worked in just the reverse way, but of course, the new pedal may be used with the old spring, in the method with which you are already familiar. Sincerely yours,
The Wright Company[58]

Parts were sent without installation instructions or explanation of their proposed function. It fell to the airmen to figure it out and then, when stumped, to ask for detailed help from the factory. This process of improvement was the forerunner of modern-day production research and development (R and D) for existing aircraft. Problems manifest during everyday flying operations, such as the wear imparted upon the strut bracket, were studied; then, as a result of the study, modifications or improvements were made to the aircraft, such as the installation of reinforcing nickel plates.[59]

In conjunction with the aircraft improvements and despite less than perfect weather conditions, important flying training and experimentation were attempted. Arnold trained Captain Beck in the operation of the Wright aircraft; this made Beck the first pilot in the unit qualified in both types of aircraft. Milling soon taught himself to fly the single-seat Curtiss machine, assisted by Beck's ground instruction. The tendency for early aviators to be trained in several different types of airplane began in this very first flying unit. A small, battery-powered "wireless radio sending set" arrived at Barnes farm in January 1912. The set was affixed to one of the planes and tested successfully on several occasions. Continued experiments with aerial photography, spotting and reconnaissance, bomb dropping, and aerial gunnery also occupied the aviators before they returned to College Park in April 1912.[60]

From these early experiments that explored the potential uses of Army aircraft came the realization that to accomplish particular missions, aircraft with particular capabilities were required. To drop bombs, for example, an aircraft designed and built to carry heavy loads was the primary requirement, while reconnaissance flights required speed and the ability to climb rapidly. Captain Chandler recalled, "It was agreed that the weight-carrying feature and high speed could not be combined satisfactorily in the same airplane with the power plants then available; therefore the military requirements as announced that winter [1911–12] provided for two classes of airplanes. One of these was designated as a reconnaissance or 'Scout' type . . . and was designed especially for carrying radio and photographic equipment. The second type was called a 'Speed Scout' machine . . . the objective was to secure greater speed, carrying only the pilot."[61]

The Scout was to be the weight-carrying machine, designed to carry two pilots and 450 pounds of equipment for four hours. Climb rate for this craft was only 2,000 feet per ten minutes, at a minimum speed of 45 miles per hour. The Speed Scout was to carry one pilot for one hour, achieving a climb to 1,800 feet in three minutes while sustaining a speed of 65 miles per hour. An additional requirement for the "largest possible field of vision" reflected requirements for an airplane with a reconnaissance mission.[62] Thus, nascent airpower doctrinal applications determined which airplanes and which technological capabilities were requested and purchased by the Army Signal Corps in 1912. It was Arnold who wrote the requests based upon conversations with other fliers and upon his understanding of air doctrine as it existed at the time.[63]

For the rest of that year, tragedy seemed to stalk the flying community. Wilbur Wright contracted typhoid fever and died on 30 May 1912. His individual influence upon the young Arnold cannot be accurately measured; Arnold always looked upon the Wrights as miracle workers. "Without any formal scientific training whatever," Arnold wrote, "two 'ordinary' young Americans from an ordinary town in the state of Ohio had not only grasped and advanced the whole known science of aerodynamics—they had become its admitted masters."[64]

Despite Wilbur's mastery of the air, Arnold never forgot the older brother's hesitancy to give answers to technical questions "without first consulting the little black notebook of aeronautical data he always carried with him."[65] When Wilbur spoke, he spoke with confidence gained through experience, both technical and practical.

Less than one week after that tragedy, Arnold had dinner with Miss Katherine and Orville Wright, who "both seem to be just getting themselves together after Wilbur's death." Arnold was a close friend during a difficult time.[66]

Another disaster struck when Al Welsh and his unfortunate passenger, Lt. Leighton "Ty" W. Hazlehurst Jr., died while speed-testing the new Wright C in trials at College Park, on 11 June. Milling, who was watching the test, described the incident as a stall followed by a violent nose-first crash.[67] His influence upon Arnold had been one of a mentor and teacher: "He taught me all he knew," Arnold wrote. "Or, rather, he taught me all he could *teach*. He knew much more."[68] He had given Arnold the basic skills required to survive early flying and all the unexplained hazards that went along with it. His student, though, deeply saddened by the teacher's passing, realized that accidental death was often part of military flying.

Then in July, Arnold and Kirtland crashed just off the coast of Plymouth, Massachusetts, in a new Burgess-Wright "tractor" seaplane. Tractors had the motor and propellers in the front of the airplane, like those that are more familiar to us today. Initial impressions were excellent: "The new Burgess military machine was a peach and we were tickled to death with it. It handled fine in the air and on a fairly calm day was as steady as an automobile on a good smooth road."[69] Perhaps expecting more performance that day than the machine could deliver, Arnold had attempted to take off carrying too much baggage, plus Kirtland, during variable wind conditions.

Although he was able to raise the craft out of the water by taking off facing into the wind, as soon as he turned the craft he lost the advantage of the head-wind. "Then I did not have anything to support me and down I dropped." One pontoon was wrecked, the propeller was destroyed, and one wingtip was crumpled. "The damage done," Arnold wrote, "was very slight."[70] It was in that crash that Arnold received the distinctive scar below his lower lip on his chin that he wore for the rest of his life. A passing boat eventually gave them a lift ashore.

Others were less fortunate. Two more aviators were killed on 28 September, Lt. Lewis C. Rockwell and Corp. Frank Scott, the first enlisted man to perish in an aircraft accident. Additionally, there were troubles with the newly delivered Wright C airplane engines.[71]

Arnold had already experienced an engine failure while at 50 feet above the ground during a landing approach. Upon inspection after landing, he found that "a small bolt (?) [sic] had come loose in the magneto and gotten in between the cogs of the brass wheels in the magneto and torn them all to pieces." The tremendous noise caused by the catastrophic failure had forced Arnold to shut down the engine.[72]

Of greater concern were the problems he found while repairing that original shattered magneto. He wrote that "in repairing my motor by taking of the magneto from one of the spare motors to put on mine I found that the parts did not fit and had to make a new steel piece to fasten the control rod to. Then the forks that move the magneto control cylinder back and forth would not fit. They were not interchangeable."[73] The lack of perfect fit among replacement parts had further serious ramifications.

"Also today the motor caught fire again. This time on the ground while I was watching it. The valves were released and two men were turning the propellers to get the gasoline flowing. I saw the gasoline start to drop down, a blue spark across the magneto spark gap, a small blue flame at the same place and then a general combustion. After turning off the gas and using pyrene we put it out without much damage. But the idea is not pleasant. . . . I know that a magneto cover properly made will stop the fire but there ought to be some other method of obtaining the same result."[74]

To Arnold, the importance of finely machined, interchangeable replacement parts for aircraft engines was glaringly apparent as early as 1912.

In September, the officers from College Park traveled to Chicago to act as judges for the aviation meet scheduled for 13 September 1912. It was in this way that Arnold became familiar with the superior capabilities of civilian aircraft of the day. He enviously witnessed one of his West Point classmates, Roy "Mick" Staver, who had resigned from service to pursue business interests, "fly at the rate of 105 miles an hour over a circular course for one hundred and twenty-eight miles. The engine never missed a stroke and there was not a single hitch in the whole performance."[75] Civilian aviation technology, like several of those demonstrated at Chicago, had a great advantage over most military aircraft in those days, and the military aviators knew it—including those naval aviators, such as John Towers, with whom Arnold had become acquainted.

On the brighter side, in October Arnold earned the first Mackay Trophy for the most outstanding military flight of the year. Arnold and Milling had been challenged to fly a triangular route between Fort Myer, College Park, and Washington, D.C., and pinpoint a troop concentration. In winning the award, Arnold completed the reconnaissance course and reported the simulated enemy-troop concentrations to the event judges. In one respect, it was really not a contest at all: Milling, the only other participant, had aircraft problems that kept him on the ground. Nevertheless, it was a significant accomplishment, and one that would positively affect his career for years to come.

The day prior to the award ceremony, Arnold was a bit concerned about speaking in front of an extremely distinguished crowd of officials. "You can imagine my making an address, especially when there are a few Secretaries of War on hand, Chiefs of Staff present. . . . I only hope that I do not make too many blunders in my little talk or act too awkward in my movements. It would be such a shame if I tripped over my own feet."[76]

After the big event, he related, "General Allen [retired] introduced Mr. Hawley president of the Aero Club of America. He turned the cup over to the Assistant Secretary of War. That gentleman, after a long harangue told me how brave and how wonderful I was to win it. Knowing he was mistaken I simply said thank you and let it go at that. If he had not been so loud in his praises for me I would have made my little speech but I couldn't have made mine under any circumstances after his."[77]

The flight demonstrated one of the doctrinal missions for army aviation, something the Army air arm was still struggling to define (as demonstrated by the variety of missions practiced while they were bivouacked in Georgia). Perhaps because of these circumstances, Arnold did not take himself or his accomplishment too seriously. The young lieutenant wrote, "It [the trophy] certainly is handsome. I figure that it will hold about four gallons so I cannot see how you can fill it with anything but beer."[78] But the well-deserved celebration would soon give way to another Wright C accident.

At the end of October, Arnold, Milling, and the rest of the College Park airmen traveled to Fort Riley, Kansas, to participate in Army ground-force exercises. "Our machines arrived here last Saturday [26 October 1912] and after working all day we had put them together in time to make a flight late Saturday afternoon. . . . Since that time the wind has been blowing a gale both night and day and we have done nothing but enjoy ourselves and view the scenery. . . . This morning [Thursday, 31 October] it started snowing and has been keeping it up all day." The weather, particularly the wind, was worrisome to Arnold, as he was now in command of the detachment. Captain Hennessy, the ranking flier, had been recalled to Washington to care for his ailing wife. The poor flying weather did permit Arnold several days' worth of horse-back riding, a pastime he missed.[79]

Whereas Arnold had rekindled his love of riding, his considerable enthusiasm for flying was temporarily doused by a near-fatal airplane flight on 5 November 1912. After completing a live-fire artillery spotting mission, Lieutenant Arnold and his observer, Lt. Alfred L. P. Sands, were inexplicably thrown uncontrolled toward the ground. Arnold miraculously righted the craft and missed a violent crash by only a few seconds and tens of feet. It was not by skill or calculation that this crash was avoided—it was dumb luck. "I am unable to account for it," he freely admitted to Captain Chandler, his commanding officer at what was now officially called the Signal Corps Aviation School.[80]

The onboard altitude-measuring device, a barograph, clearly recorded a drop of 300 feet in ten seconds, ending up just above the ground-zero line. It was too close a call for Arnold. He was so rattled that not only did he walk back to the airfield from the site of his near-crash, he also immediately requested three weeks' leave and temporarily removed himself from flying status. Sands, only a passenger, had been oblivious to the danger and would have died fearlessly.

"From the way I feel now," Arnold explained, "I do not see how I can get in a machine with safety for the next month or two."[81] His relief was so great that he and several of his bachelor friends were later found "gathered around a table imbibing champagne rather freely under the justification of his narrow escape."[82] But Arnold had also achieved several aviation firsts: winning the first Mackay Trophy, carrying the first air mail, setting several altitude records, flying as a movie stunt pilot, and—somewhat more dubiously—accomplishing, mostly by luck, the first successful recovery in an uncontrolled airplane.

Arnold's experience has most often been described as a spin, a condition that develops after a near-complete stalled condition of the aircraft wing has occurred. Closer examination of the available evidence suggests a different, more plausible explanation. The incident occurred near the end of the mission, so the possibility that excessive weight due to fuel might have caused the problem is easily eliminated. Photographic evidence clearly shows that cloud cover was prevalent during the mission.[83] Although not significant by itself, Lieutenant Milling's recollection of that day—he landed from his mission a short time after Arnold—supports the conclusion that winds were gusty and played some part in the near accident. "When I got over the field, one of the miniature whirlwinds that occur on sunshiney [*sic*] days in that country struck my plane and turned it more than 90 degrees. The plane stalled, but by diving it a short distance I regained speed and pulled it out for a safe landing."[84] The fact that Milling landed in sunshine, while Arnold's flight took place under cloud cover, indicates that low, rapid-moving clouds associated with blustery frontal boundaries were the likely conditions of the day. Milling's stalled condition was immediately due to the loss of forward velocity over the wing surface, a condition remedied by turning the plane back into the relative wind and diving slightly.

Arnold's situation began in similar fashion to Milling's—a gust of wind upset the forward velocity of the airplane. In Arnold's case, however, he had already begun to spiral toward the landing site, as was the common practice at the end of a flight. This was similar to Orville's steep-turn maneuver, using 45 degrees of bank with elevator controlling the turn. Having plenty of speed initially, Arnold's natural tendency was to pull back on the elevator control in an effort to stop the uncommanded dive that resulted from the induced stalled condition. In this case, the stall was the result of control inputs that exceeded the physical-performance capability of the airplane, rather than the result of inadequate speed. Instead of releasing the backward pressure on the controls and allowing the machine to accelerate in the downward direction for a short while, the constant back pressure caused what is commonly known today as an accelerated stall, and not a spin.[85] The circular motion described by Arnold was a result of having already begun the spiral pattern for landing.[86]

As to the final recovery of the situation, there are two possibilities. Eyewitnesses described a near-vertical dive in extremely close proximity to the ground, exactly the action required to save the situation. Arnold must have released pressure on the controls just enough to decrease the wing's angle of attack, the angle between the wing cord line and the relative wind. Thus the plane's forward velocity was sufficient to regain control. Fortunately this occurred a few feet above the ground, allowing him to pull up level and control the landing, although all evidence indicates that he did not do this intentionally.

It is also possible that the dive actually allowed the Wright C to gain enough speed to right itself before impacting the ground. "When a machine of this type acquires excessive speed due to gravity," Orville once explained to Mr. Israel Ludlow, a prominent movie producer, "the center of gravity and the center of momentum being below the center of resistance causes the machine to right itself instead of pointing downward."[87] Perhaps a fortunate combination of the two saved Arnold and Sands from certain death, but the experience staggered Arnold's confidence in his plane and his flying. And, according to the Wright brothers, these were the elements essential to survival as a pilot.[88]

"At the present time my nervous system is in such a condition that I will not get in any machine. That being the case it appears that my work here must simply be in a matter of supply officer . . . I personally do not care to get in any machine either as passenger or pilot for some time to come. I therefore request instructions concerning the shipment of that machine [No. 10]."[89]

Those few weeks of grounding grew into a few months and then a year, as desk-bound Arnold effectively served as the assistant to the officer in charge of aviation in the office of the chief Signal officer, Brig. Gen. James Allen (until 5 March 1913) and then Brig. Gen. George P. Scriven. When the young lieutenant married Eleanor Pool in September 1913, he was effectively removed from the active flying roster. At that time, Army fliers were not encouraged to marry and remain on flying status.[90] Although this requirement would soften by World War I, Arnold, at his own request, was relegated to ground duties until November 1916.[91]

5

"A CUSHION-CHAIR OFFICER"
(1912–16)

Lieutenant Arnold's near-tragedy may have had more fortunate consequences than he imagined at the time. "I suppose," he explained, "that I must have had a guardian angel guiding my hand, but whatever it was I am duly thankful."[1] That angel kept him on the ground just when airplane crashes were becoming much more frequent and fatal.

During 1913 and 1914, the Wright Model C established a notorious reputation as a pilot killer. Al Welsh and Lt. Ty Hazlehurst were the first to die. Second Lt. Henry B. Post "rode one in" to the San Diego Bay just after setting a new altitude record of 12,140 feet. Eyewitness reports suggest a nearly identical scenario to the one that had almost killed Arnold at Fort Riley—a banked, accelerated stall. By mid-1914, all six Army Wright Model C aircraft had been destroyed in accidents. A total of six men had died while trying to tame the unruly C.[2]

The extra power generated by the 60-horsepower engine created more thrust than the C's aerodynamic design was capable of supporting under most flight conditions. But the C was so durable that, even considering the more powerful power plant, there was little chance of structural failure in flight.[3] Orville explained to Arnold, "Our Model C will stand a test far in excess of the load that is required of it in flight. . . . In the test just mentioned the outer uprights carried a load over ten times the normal strain in flight, and showed no indication of buckling. . . . The wing spars of the last section were subjected to a strain over five times the normal strain in flight, and showed no indication of buckling. . . . When it flies at speed of 38 to 40 miles an hour with its full load as required in the government tests, its center of pressure is just one third back from the front edge of the surfaces; but when flying at 55 miles an hour as in the speed tests, its center of pressure would be 44% back."[4]

The 40-horsepower engine on the Wright B had not provided the pilot enough excess thrust to allow him to pull the airplane into a stalled condition with any ease—in level flight, there simply was inadequate speed for such a maneuver. The added power in the C allowed the pilot, while flying in the upper controllable speed range (near 55 miles an hour), to displace the plane's elevator enough so that the aircraft angle of attack rapidly increased from normal flight conditions directly into stalled conditions. Additionally, the shift of the center of pressure to 44 percent aft at high speeds made this maneuver all the easier and all the more deadly.

Although recovery from this condition was immediate if the angle of attack was decreased by releasing back pressure on the control stick, the pilot was still required to patiently wait for the stabilization of the ensuing dive, which accelerated the craft and allowed the pilot to pull up to level, controlled flight. An impatient recovery attempt or excessive pull on the stick resulted in an immediate return to the stalled condition. As airspeed decreased, due to the increased drag of consecutive stalls, aircraft control was often lost, and unpredictable gyrations frequently resulted. This phenomenon—the accelerated stall—remained unknown in these early years, and the death toll mounted because of it. Arnold was the only Army pilot lucky enough to survive his brush with this unexplained phenomenon.[5]

By Christmas 1912, Arnold was enjoying the convalescent leave he had requested after his near-catastrophic flight. He joined his family in Ardmore for a traditional Christmas party. In attendance was his heartthrob, Bee Pool, now finished with her studies in Berlin. The two spent the evening sharing stories and becoming reacquainted. Harley had only written her twice in the past two years, and she had not replied—if she even received the letters.[6]

That she did not reply was no surprise. Bee's Berlin diary for January 1912 described close relationships with no less than three different men, none of them Harley. On 3 January she wrote, "Rodo" spent the afternoon with her: "He brought a lovely bunch of violets and some drawings he [had] made."[7] On 6 and 8 January Bee lamented the distance between herself and "Dawd," who was 3,000 miles away in Rochester. At the time, Bee and Dawd, the newspaper man, were secretly engaged. "No one will ever imagine that 'Dawd' is the unlucky man until I return home in the summer," Bee humorously wrote. On the same day she received a letter from "Billy Boy," inviting her to two different social affairs—one she declined and one she was "delighted to accept," as the local "Ball" was a "rare thing to witness."[8] Yet, after the 1912 Ardmore Christmas party, everything changed.

For the first month of 1913 Arnold returned to Dayton, where he spent many hours at the Wright factory and many evenings at the Wrights' home for dinner. He lamented that most people he had known in Dayton were gone and worried that "the Wrights are more than nice and invite me up there so often that I will never wear out my welcome. They are certainly wonderful people."[9]

Soon Arnold returned to Washington, D.C. The carefree, rough but determined young Army officer and the worldly, refined, socialite found the one thing that had been missing in their lives: love. Their courtship consisted of a series of weekend visits between Philadelphia and Washington, usually only when Arnold's hectic War Department schedule allowed. During May, Bee's annual hay fever resulted in a prescription for another journey—this time to Washington, D.C. The suggested journey, once again the work of Dr. Arnold, seemed odd, since the wilting cherry blossoms signaled the beginning of pollen season all over Washington. Once again, Arnold's sister, Betty, accompanied Bee during her therapeutic vacation.[10] Betty and Bee did some sightseeing, but mainly they relaxed, often spending time with Harley throughout the day.

At the War Department, Arnold now worked directly for chief Signal officer Brig. Gen. George P. Scriven (West Point, 1878), a portly, handlebar-moustached representative of the "old Army." As the War Department's expert on airpower, Arnold was called in the summer of 1913 before the Hay Committee, where he testified against the establishment of a separate, independent Air Corps within the Army.[11] At the time, he was the most famous Army pilot around; it was just a few months ago that he had been presented with the Mackay Trophy. His opinions about U.S. military air capabilities would be seriously considered. He commented upon House Resolution 28728, the first bill that proposed the separation of aviation from the Signal Corps. Like most others who testified, he objected to the separation on several terms—they were too small and unprepared to stand alone. HR 28728 was shelved by the Military Affairs Committee, never making it to the floor of the Senate for a vote.[12]

It was too soon. The Army was still in what Arnold called the "instructional phase" of aviation development. In preparation for these hearings, Scriven had ordered Arnold to prepare a 150-page report covering all aspects of aeronautics. Arnold described the difficulty he was facing in compiling such a report in such a short time. "Ever since I have been a cushion-chair officer I have regretted very much that I did not take a literary course at some institution as part of my education. This grasping and groping for words while trying to write an article is not what it is cracked up to be. As an editor on the Chief's staff my value may be assessed at—well somewhere between zero and minus infinity. However, about two more days will find all of the material together."[13]

The final report described the deplorable disparity in appropriated funding between several foreign air forces and his own Signal Corps aviation branch—Germany, $45 million; Russia, $22.5 million; Austria, $3 million; Great Britain, $1.1 million; Italy, $.8 million. The United States had appropriated only $250,000 for aviation, placing them fourteenth out of the twenty-six countries surveyed. This testimony shamed the isolationist Congress into increasing Aviation Division funding to $300,000 in March 1915.[14] The increase was comparably insignificant.

Even with the increase in air appropriations in 1915, in terms of technology, production, research, and experience, American military aviation was falling steadily behind that of the warring nations. Overwhelming disparities in appropriations would affect Arnold and the development of Army aviation throughout most of his career. Dealing with strict budgetary restrictions—particularly in the middle of the efficiency movements such as those initiated by Frederick Winslow Taylor's "scientific management"—enabled the Army to maximize the usefulness of its comparably meager aviation budget.

Arnold was also responsible for Army aircraft production and specifications compliance for both airframes and engines. His many and varied duties took him frequently to College Park, right up until the day it closed in June 1913. On a few occasions he took Bee and the meddlesome Betty to the airfield with him, and after flying trials concluded, they attended a baseball game or other social event. His love interest won, he entertained her as best he could, showing her everything about the world he hoped she would soon be joining.

Among his responsibilites was to observe qualification tests for new Army aircraft. Some passed, some failed—Arnold watched them all.[15] But the weather at College Park did not allow year-round flying, and the tight aviation budget was forcing the Army to make administrative changes anyway, specifically in its basing for airplanes. Training bases needed as much good weather as possible; thus the migration of flying bases to the fair-weather south and southwest.[16] Although he remained in D.C., Arnold closed the Army's College Park flying school with mixed emotions: "I have had some of the worst experiences of my life there," he wrote Bee, "and I have had some of the best, so that the average should make me feel indifferent on the subject."[17]

Functioning frequently as the Army's airplane-engine inspector, Arnold traveled between Washington and the Navy Engineering Experiment Station Plant, across the Severn River from the Naval Academy in Annapolis, Maryland. This plant, adjacent to the naval-aviation camp at Greenbury Point, provided many of the engines for the Army's Curtiss airplanes and flying boats.[18] Arnold personally supervised the engine tests, ensuring that safety margins were adequate and performance was nominal.

It was during these duties that he and an earlier acquaintance, Navy lieutenant John H. "Jack" Towers, whom Arnold had met while flying at College Park, solidified a lifelong friendship and unique professional relationship. Both officers experienced the frustration involved with testing new aircraft and engines for their service. Both had nearly died in similar accidents involving Wright aircraft. Both still suffered from that experience: Towers physically, and Arnold, to a lesser degree, mentally.

Towers's June 1913 crash had far more gruesome results than Arnold's mishap. During the initial stall-recovery pitchover and dive, his pilot, William D. Billingsley, was thrown completely clear of the plane while still 1,500 feet above the Chesapeake Bay, falling to his death. Towers was tossed out of his seat and into the support wires of the Wright B (designated B-2 by the Navy), where he clung tenuously to the aircraft structure. The plane went down, totally out of control. After several wild gyrations, the Wright B hit the water engine first, upside down and backward. This stroke of luck was the primary reason Towers, hanging on so tightly that he separated one of his ribs from his sternum, survived.

Some good did come of the event, however: seat restraints became mandatory on all Army and Navy aircraft beginning the next day.[19] Having cheated death, in both cases by unbelievable luck, the youthful Arnold and Towers shared a lasting bond. Tommy "Dashing" Milling recalled that in the early years all fliers were close, "like a fraternity."[20] Arnold and Towers, bound by the common experiences of flying Wright airplanes, would butt heads during World War II as high-level commanders, but their professionalism and long-time friendship usually resulted in productive arguments that achieved decisions beneficial to the nation.[21]

After reviewing Towers's accident report, Arnold explained the similarity of the two mishaps to Bee, emphasizing how "really lucky" he himself had been to survive. "Sometimes it looks as if there is an unseen hand that reaches out and turns these machines over in the air," Arnold wrote, certainly not bolstering Bee's confidence, "for there have been so many accidents which have never been explained."[22]

In Washington, Arnold frequently visited the Army's engine-test facility at the National Bureau of Standards.[23] During May 1913, he even took Bee along and introduced her to a few of his acquaintances there. This visit made quite an impression on the well-educated Bee Pool, who later recalled that Arnold "worked there all the time with the scientists. He was always interested in that phase. Even before we were married, I met some of his friends at the Bureau of Standards in Washington. That was always one part of his life. Very few people know that . . . [Harley] was in his element with those people . . . and he never neglected to talk to scientists and get their views on what could be done, in the air. Very few people realize the fact that this was always in the back of [his] mind, that science and the air should work together. The air needed scientists and scientists could get a great deal from the air."[24]

Another of his daily responsibilities was listening to proposals by inventors and then reporting his recommendations to Chief Scriven. Arnold was the only Army officer who regularly dealt with scientists and engineers during these early years of Army aviation. Consequently, by mid-1913 Arnold was internalizing the critical connection between science, technology, and airpower. His understanding of the relationship between these issues heralded the beginning of a revolutionary change in military culture. In Arnold's eyes, aeronautical science and technological development were inherently and necessarily tied to the creation of effective, powerful air forces. Evolutionary advances in weapons occurred regularly in both the Army and the Navy, but the basic doctrine concerning the application of forces remained fundamentally unchanged over time. Arnold began to envision the potential of airpower as a way to change the very nature of surface warfare—he envisioned a new form of three-dimensional maneuver warfare from the air.[25]

Perhaps understanding that his enthusiasm for technology could be quite useful, aircraft manufacturers began requesting that Arnold personally make inspection trips to their factories. Although Scriven was willing to send him, the Signal Corps budget precluded any reimbursement for travel expenses. So the inspection tours were put on hold.[26] The freeze on travel funds did have one happy effect: it allowed the courting to continue, interrupted only by Arnold's older sister, Betty.

On a sunny Sunday, 1 June 1913, the twenty-six-year-old Arnold and Bee, having just celebrated her own twenty-sixth birthday the previous day, escaped Betty's ever-watchful eye to privately enjoy the sights of Washington. It was Bee's final vacation day in Washington. After strolling around the White House grounds, the couple ambled across Pennsylvania Avenue to Lafayette Park. There the nervous lieutenant and Bee sat upon a bench facing the White House, and it was there that he asked her to be his wife. She accepted, but only after a lengthy, perhaps dramatic, pause.[27] He dutifully handed over his hard-won West Point ring, the traditional symbol of engagement for graduates, and the deed was done. The couple then headed for the train station, meeting up with Betty for the return trip to Philadelphia.

The proposal, like the courtship, was far from romantic. Arnold realized it even before Bee had arrived back in Ardmore that evening, once again an engaged woman. He wrote: "Please Bee, when you think over what has happened today do not think that I am such a cold blooded, matter of fact individual for I am not entirely lacking in sentiment. I will admit that my actions and words today did resemble more or less those of a transaction but considering the short time we had together alone and the nature of the surrounding country I believe that I did fairly well. Please pardon the conceit."[28]

Bee's acceptance had an immediate and permanent effect upon Harley. The only true love of his life was now to be his wife. Now that they were again separated, years of pent-up emotions came gushing out in a flood of love letters. Harley Arnold began his first letter to his new fiancée with what turned out to be an ironic disclaimer. "Just because I am writing this letter," he wrote, "there is no reason to believe that I am going to bore you with a letter every day for such is not my intention."[29] But from that day until their wedding, on 10 September 1913, Harley wrote Bee Pool one letter every day (sometimes two or three), unless they were together. By the time Arnold died in 1950, he had written hundreds of personal letters.[30] After their marriage, the majority of those letters began with the same three words: My Darling Beadle.[31]

Arnold's daily correspondence with Bee illustrates many aspects of both his personality and his realization of his own shortcomings. Arnold immediately felt that Bee had a "wonderful influence," a calming effect, over his bachelor-like "method of living."

"Now let me tell you something about your future husband," he wrote. "First, he stopped drinking—not that he ever did much—but he quit entirely. Second he quit smoking. Third he seems to be perfectly content to hang around the club and has quit all the running around he used to do. . . . People tell me that I am subdued and quiet. I suppose I am, for I spend most of my time thinking about you. There has been a big change in me but I am glad that there has and I am more than glad that you are responsible for it."[32]

These were the promises of a man still trying to convince his betrothed that he was a worthy prize. Harley's shyness reflected low self-confidence concerning his perceived appeal to women, particularly Bee. "Sometimes I wish that the engagement was announced for I feel as if I would like to have every one know about it."[33] The public announcement would solidify things, he felt. He would have to wait until August for the official announcement, but Betty told the families the day she and Bee returned to Ardmore. Harley's promises to stop drinking and smoking were not immediately fulfilled; to give up drink was unnecessary. He continued smoking and took drinks in moderation, until serious gastric ulcers forced a change of lifestyle in 1922. Even then he found it difficult to quit cigarettes, until the mid-1920s. Bee didn't really care if Harley had a drink or two—she had been known to imbibe on occasion herself, a reflection of her social education in Berlin and the influence of her father, who enjoyed a scotch now and then.[34]

Harley went to extremes to ensure that Bee's wishes were heard and, if possible, acted upon. The one area over which Arnold had no control was the Army's assignment system. From June to August, the wedding date changed three times on account of Army orders. Arnold was frustrated, even angry, while Bee seemed to take the changes in stride. Yet Harley was able to see some humor in the upheaval. "There is one consolation," he wrote, "there can only be about six more changes of station for us—3 to Ft. Thomas and 3 back to Ft. Roots, by that time I will have been in about every company in the Regiment."[35]

Both Bee and Harley learned early in their relationship about the unpredictability of military life. Later in their lives, periods of separation during many long-distance travels, some Harley's and others Bee's, were accepted as routine. Bee understood the Army way—most of the time—and Harley would continue writing letters throughout the years. He frequently explained to Bee before the wedding that the many uncertainties were "more or less training for Army life for then we must act on very short notice but, dear, I believe that we are the combination that can do it."[36] Arnold never lost his can-do attitude in anything he did.

Somewhat surprisingly, Arnold's letters to Bee reflected a refined, yet almost totally neglected sense of humor. In his first letter after their engagement, he asked for her ring size so that he could order wedding bands. "If you cannot [send me the size of your ring finger] I suppose that you will have to wait until I can get you and your finger and myself together."[37] By mid-month, Bee was handling all the wedding plans—and Arnold had listed the following measures to ensure her happiness:

1. It seems to me that I am forgetting that this is your wedding and making too many suggestions.
2. I will quit making suggestions and wait until I am asked before making known my ideas on any subject.
3. Kindly disregard any and all of my suggestions that have been forced upon you.
4. I will be good.[38]

Arnold rarely subordinated his take-charge attitude, except with Bee.

He used humor to ease the pressures of the approaching event: "The invitation to our wedding reached me today and I was sort of glad to get it as I was afraid that I might not get invited."[39] Arnold's subtle sense of humor was genuine, but reserved for his intimate friends and family, his inner circle. And it remained that way throughout his life. For this reason, many perceived him as overly serious or humorless. Significantly, those who never witnessed the lighthearted humor that Arnold kept well guarded were not generally considered close friends or confidants by Arnold or his family.

He often described everyday events in comical ways; during a 100-degree-plus heatwave in Washington, for example, the sweat-soaked Arnold summarized his discomfort by writing simply, "I am going to change my residence to the inside of a refrigeration plant." Later that summer he noted, "The thermometer has been so high that it was necessary to get a ladder to read it."[40] Arnold took a certain amount of pride in his penmanship, and when an error was made, such as ink spilled into an unusual blotch, he sometimes shrugged it off with a humorous side note. Next to one airship-shaped blob, he added an arrow and the note, "That's a dirigible."[41]

On 4 August 1913, his letter to Bee ended with a self-portrait drawn to resemble a popular Chicago-area cartoon character of the day, Billikens. A curly lock of hair, all that remained between the high forehead of a rapidly receding hairline, was accentuated for effect.[42] Arnold was not afraid to poke fun at himself, even while seeking Bee's approval during their engagement.

But the outward explosion of emotions surrounding the engagement illustrated a most profound internal change in Arnold. His youthful tendency to ignore anything emotionally serious began to crumble after he gave away his West Point ring.

> Before I fell in love with you I could take everything as more or less of a joke—I could always see the funny side of everything. Things were always taken as they came—an accident in an aeroplane amounted to nothing and was even funny in spite of the accompanying bruises and cuts. . . . I can not understand why I can take everything so indifferently and in such a matter of fact way but this. . . . But without exaggeration I would rather fall 420 feet in an aeroplane than go two days without a letter from you. . . . I am sorry, dearest, that I have no self control and sense about this business but . . . I never before in my life took anything really serious and I wouldn't take things so serious if I could help it.[43]

Harley was uncomfortable with these newfound emotions and how they affected him, so he developed a simple solution: "I will practice the theory of effect of emotion I used to have—no matter how much I feel anything internally never show it externally. That only applies to the unpleasant feelings. Pleasures continue as formerly."[44] He carried through with this plan, which had unfavorable results: keeping feelings bottled up, except while alone with Bee, created internal stress that affected his health over the next thirty years.

Sometimes his disgust could not be subdued. After the Army changed his orders from Washington for the sixth time, he "cussed enough for six men not because we are to go to Ft. Thomas but because they will not leave us alone when we begin to get acclimated . . . I am about ready to hold up both my hands and say, 'Go ahead do your worst. Send me to Siberia for station and then I would welcome a change.'"[45] Arnold never totally understood why, once the Army had made up its mind, it had never really made up its mind.

These early experiences only reinforced within the young lieutenant the deleterious impact of indiscriminate decision changing. Arnold realized that the troops in the field bore the greatest strain of such changes, not the decision makers in Washington. This indicated to him that quick, accurate decisions were best for the troops. Such influences shaped his decision making later in his career, and many who were accustomed to bureaucratic Army staff procedures perceived Arnold as impatient.

This impatience was a characteristic of which he was well aware and that he never earnestly attempted to change. The day he proposed to Bee, she told him point-blank that he had acted impatiently while awaiting her reply to his marriage proposal. "Well, my characteristics have not changed any in that line," he wrote.[46] He had earlier promised to quit smoking and drinking, activities he apparently considered vices; he made no such promise concerning his tendency toward impatience. In fact, he commented, "my impatience, my unreasonableness, etc. do you [Bee] not think that you have a hard proposition ahead, to control those undesirable qualities. However one thing is sure— when you are with me the cause is removed so they are nonexistent."[47] Arnold's belief in the quick and accurate decision was a result of confidence in his own knowledge and of his trust in the knowledge of others. For the most part, however, when Bee was around he kept his impatience in check.

On the weekend of 7 June 1913, Arnold went to Ardmore, where he accepted warm congratulations from his family. He spent most of his time at the Pool house, beaming in Bee's company. "I enjoyed yesterday more than any day in my life and I hope that you enjoyed it as much as I did. The whole setting was complete—the time, the place and the girl."[48] These were powerful feelings for Arnold, and he knew it.

"Bee I am so much in love with you that it is beginning to hurt. It looks as if my indifference in the past is not helping me any in the present and will not in the future. . . ."[49] Later he passionately wrote, "I love you more all the time. I thought I knew what the word meant a couple of weeks ago but I didn't. I am learning all the time to love you more and by so doing be more happy."[50]

Arnold's upbringing had not prepared him for these most powerful of human emotions, and he realized his shortcomings as far as expressions of love were concerned. His time away from Bee became more difficult with each passing week. He was so consumed by her that at times he even lost focus on his War Department duties. By the end of July, after many frustrating attempts to successfully test an aircraft engine at the Annapolis plant, he simply "had the motor packed up for shipment without even giving it a complete test."[51] The usually thorough Arnold had been smitten by the dainty Miss Pool and her elegant charms to the point of distraction from duty.

That summer, Arnold's stoic approach to work-related incidents was brutally tested. On 8 July he received word from Texas City that an old friend had crashed while riding a motorcycle, and that he lay near death (Lt. Harry Graham later recovered and served in the Air Service until his retirement in 1929). Later that same day, Arnold was presented with an accident report describing the death of another close friend, 1st Lt. Loren H. Call, in a Wright Model B plane. He served as a pallbearer at Call's funeral the following week, and later he described the rainy event that soaked everyone in attendance: "I hope that I do not have to go on any more such missions. Call is buried right along side of Rockwell."[52]

Arnold's distaste for Washington, which he kept no secret during the rest of his life, began during that summer of his 1913 War Department tour. "I certainly wish that I could leave this city at once and for all. I am sick and tired of getting such reports. Being here as I am, I am forced to receive such reports [as that of Call's death] without any show of feelings and it hurts. . . . I will certainly be glad when I say good bye to Washington D.C. and find a complete change of surroundings."[53]

Arnold endured the frustration of testing poorly built engines and planes; testified before Congress in front of many who had no comprehension of airpower, yet would make funding decisions precluding any serious advances in the field; and lost close friends to accidents, all while carrying on a long-distance romance with Bee. It is little wonder that he wanted to marry and bail out of Washington, a place he often sarcastically referred to as a "sleepy town" or "that quiet little burg."

For Arnold, as for his father, withholding emotional displays was inborn. We know today that stress can have long-term physical effects on the human body, particularly the cardiac muscle. Although it is impossible to prove, Arnold's inability or unwillingness to vent his inner feelings, both in his personal life and in his military positions, likely contributed to his deteriorating cardiac health later in life.[54]

Additionally, during his time in Washington he rarely exercised. He openly complained to Bee about his inactivity while working at the War Department, and only exerted himself while away from D.C. On one occasion when he was stuck at Annapolis during engine testing, he played three sets of tennis, prompting him to write, "That is the first real exercise I have taken in . . . I do not remember when."[55] While visiting the Burgess factory during the last week in August, he enjoyed a relaxing respite from the rigors of Washington. "I am afraid that you would not know me if I stayed here a month," he wrote to Bee. "Lots of exercise—sun burn and sleep. However 3 days is not enough to make much change."[56] The benefits of regular cardiac exercise and fitness were only basically understood in 1913, and even less was known about the critical importance of diet and weight management.

At Bee's insistence Arnold began a "milk diet," in an effort to gain a little weight. Ever since he had visited Lucerne, Bee had felt that he was excessively thin. Dutifully, he drank more milk than ever before—and there was no low-fat milk in 1913—but, thanks to the sweltering heat of the Washington summer, he actually began losing more weight. "I went rapidly up to 174, stopped to admire the scenery for two days and slowly went in the opposite direction until I arrived at 164, where I have been stopping ever since." He had earlier tried comforting Bee by writing, "Do not be alarmed for I am not going to get as thin as a lamp post or look like a needle if I shut one eye."[57]

Although Arnold had also promised Bee that he would stay away from flying, he hedged away from that pledge in a 5 August 1913 letter: "I believe that I will take you up myself, at Marblehead or Dayton. There are so few aviators that I would be willing to trust you with that it is going to be some problem for you to get that ride."[58] Arnold's comment reflects his awareness of the growing fatality rate among aviators, rather than any personal mistrust of his fellow Army pilots. The Washington job required constant review of all military-aircraft accident and aviation-personnel casualty reports.

On 24 August Arnold demonstrated that he had, in large measure, overcome his fear of flying. "This is certainly a glorious day and I wish that you might be here to enjoy it with me," he wrote to Bee from the Burgess Company at Marblehead. "This morning I went out in a flying boat—no I did not leave the water except for short jumps but it was certainly fine. I did not take a flight so did not go back on my word."[59] If the Wrights' first flight, totaling 120 feet, was flying, then Arnold's "short jumps" excuse was a mere technicality. In fact, Lt. Harley Arnold had been flying again. Bee's response was likely delivered in person and is lost to the record. We do know that Arnold did not press the limits of his promise again, until he was officially called back to flight duty in 1916. Despite his claims to the contrary, there was still a streak of adventure within Arnold's character that surfaced periodically during the next four decades.

While serving as a "cushion-chair officer," Arnold never wavered in his belief in the overall importance of airpower. He later recalled that in 1913, fliers fought a constant uphill battle for acceptance within the Army, as well as for procurement of modern equipment. "At that time," Arnold explained, "we in the Air Service looked to foreign countries for engines that might give us better performance."[60] Throughout his career, he never hesitated to look beyond American shores for aviation advances. Arnold realized that progress and funding were usually positively related; nearly every other major nation was spending many times the amount on aviation as was the United States.

For example, on 11 August 1913, Arnold and Milling witnessed the trial flight of a French-built copy of the latest Blériot monoplane. After the test they were invited to dine with the builder, the pilot, and the trip manager. After Milling made an early departure, Arnold was "forced to listen to the builder's tale of woe—suffer a cross-examination on why the [U.S.] government was not buying any of those machines, answer all their questions without telling them anything . . . and convince them that I was not responsible for the kind of machines purchased by the government."[61] Meanwhile, even as a lieutenant in Washington, Arnold sought the best technology available. He was always pushing to improve what budgets would allow, while keeping in mind for his future reference that which remained out of reach.

Arnold's earliest personal aeronautical influence was, of course, the Wright Brothers. But he also became friends with other aircraft designers and manufacturers, such as Glenn Curtiss and entrepreneur W. Starling Burgess.[62] He dined with the Curtiss family on 23 August, and the following evening he spent with Burgess and his wife. Arnold became close enough to Burgess that he and Bee were invited to spend their honeymoon with the wealthy couple on a cruise to Europe. Arnold, his plans already made for a more intimate trip to Panama, politely declined.[63] The potential conflict of interest that such a trip might today stir did not raise an eyebrow back then. On the contrary, Arnold's close ties to industrialists would serve throughout his military career to expedite production, hasten development, and minimize bottlenecks.

Concurrent with his other duties, Arnold continued his written inquiries to Orville Wright. "If machines are inverted and given the sand test what factor of safety should be required?" And "What other tests could be given for determining the factor of safeties of any important parts?"[64] His quest for safer aircraft accelerated after the Fort Riley accident and never slowed.

Before long, Arnold returned to making more detailed inquiries about performance and design. "As it is desired by this office to incorporate a stress test of some kind in our specifications for machines," he wrote, "we would greatly appreciate it if you would send to us . . . the chart showing the travel of the center of pressure for various speeds and weights." In another request, he asked, "Will you kindly tell me what, if any, are the objections to having the propellers turn in the opposite direction to what they turn now in your machines." New aircraft designs were under continual review: "The light scout machines have caused more or less controversy but I think the Signal Corps is at last persuaded as to the necessity of having them even though there is no one capable of flying them but Milling."[65] The Wrights always answered his letters in detail, but it seemed each response generated more questions.

Arnold's inquisitive attitude about design and performance had resulted from his early piloting and maintenance experiences. He was not an expert in aerodynamics; he did not always understand the particulars of the science behind or the difficulty of the engineering problems associated with his queries. For example changing propeller direction, according to the Wrights, would have required the reversal of nearly everything internal to the machine.[66] Yet Arnold was never fully satisfied with an air machine as it stood. As a demanding pilot, he insisted upon safer aircraft capable of ever-increasing performance—higher altitude, better load-carrying capability, greater range, and faster speed. As a mechanic, of sorts, he saw the need for interchangeable parts, peak engine performance, and substantial margins of safety in construction. He well understood both the operational requirements for and the production limitations of Army aircraft.

Important as his job was as the War Department's expert in technical air matters, Arnold's later involvement with the administration of the Aeronautical Division would become just as critical. During that summer of 1913, the myriad responsibilities that helped shape the future administrator and negotiator included that of go-between. Arnold was directly involved in quelling unrest among aviators who were forced to fly substandard airplanes on the Mexican border while revolution swept the southern country. Arnold's impossible job was to remedy their complaints, most of which concerned the safety of the airplanes and requested changes in the aviation command structure to include more aviators. Arnold acted as the mediator between General Scriven and the pilots. He was well aware of the shortcomings of their planes, but unsympathetic to their demanding—almost threatening—methods. Scriven and the Signal Corps made compromises that satisfied the aviators, and a final resolution was reached. The Texas unit was disbanded shortly thereafter and moved to North Island, California.[67]

As the aviators moved west to California, Arnold's time ended in Washington; Gen. Leonard Wood, the chief of staff, was not certain that a lieutenant belonged there. Aside from the rank difference between Arnold and most of the other officers at the War Department, living in Washington was a very expensive proposition for a soon-to-be newly married Army lieutenant. In a fatherly way, Wood moved Arnold out for his own financial good.

After another Army-assignment fiasco concerning the determination of his new unit, Arnold and Bee were finally notified that they would depart Washington at the end of September for a brief two-month reintroduction to infantry life at Fort Thomas, Kentucky. But before the new assignment, one pleasurable task remained.

Harley had been hard at work trying to provide six groomsmen to meet the wedding requirements that Bee had issued him. The list changed as often as the weather, but he kept good humor through most of the Army's indecision. At one point, he decided that the traditional poem describing a variety of "necessaries" for superstitious brides (something old, new, borrowed, and blue) had been designed specifically and exclusively for women. Harley devised his own verse to correct the lack of one for men. His poem was: "Something red, something bright, something stolen, something tight." To fulfill these requirements, he had promised to wear a red-bandanna handkerchief (reminiscent of his Black Hand getup), flaunt a monocle, purloin one of the ushers' watches, and wear tight shoes—certainly a sight to behold.[68] But he changed back into his military dress uniform before the wedding ceremony began.

Harley Arnold and Bee Pool were married 10 September 1913, in Ardmore. Tommy Milling was the best man, and Bee's sister, Lois, was maid of honor. The wedding was huge: six bridesmaids, six groomsmen, and an invitation list approaching 500. It was held at the First Unitarian Church in Philadelphia, 9 miles from Ardmore, and did not come off without a hitch.[69]

Harley's sister, the fickle Betty, refused to stand as one of the wedding party just one hour before the ceremony began. Although she eventually agreed to participate, making quite a scene to gain attention, the incident apparently embarrassed Harley so much that he did not even mention his own wedding in his memoirs. Bee would only politely say many years later, "We had a little difficulty at the wedding. . . ."[70]

After the service, the newlyweds darted for the bride's limousine. Tommy and Lois beat them to it, however, and convinced the driver that they were the bride and groom. Harley and Bee ended up in the second-best car. "Oh, that Tommy was a monkey, you know!" the new Mrs. Arnold recalled.[71] Both Bee and Harley thought the world of their mischievous friend Tommy Milling.

The reception at the Pool house was no picnic either. Despite the promise that Bee's father had made to the dry Dr. Arnold to remove champagne from the menu, a loaded cellarette was tucked away upstairs. As the evening progressed, lieutenants from the wedding party mysteriously vanished and then reappeared in remarkably fine spirits. The gradual inebriation of the groomsmen might have gone unnoticed, but for the fact that Tommy Milling, lacking requisite self-control, shattered a glass window in the bathroom door near the stash. It was unfortunate that his cuts were serious enough that medical attention was required. Dr. Arnold was notified of the accident and was ushered upstairs. The gig was up.[72]

Harley and Bee spent the night at the Bellevue-Stratford Hotel, thus escaping the family friction that resulted from Betty's childish behavior and the discovery of the liquor cabinet. The real honeymoon featured a two-week round trip on a transport ship to Panama. "We loved the sea," Bee recalled, "and we were going to be in Kentucky." Harley was so anxious to get on with his new life that he failed to notify the Army of his travel plans abroad, a mistake forgiven upon his return to New York.[73]

After what he recalled as "two very pleasant months with the 9th Infantry," Arnold and his bride were off to foreign service in the Philippine Islands. He left the nation's capital much matured as a man, and vastly more experienced as a lieutenant. He disliked the nature of staff work in Washington, yet he understood the many benefits of working directly for the chief of the Signal Corps. "It has taken me over two years to make the friends I have now, to obtain the position I occupy in the office, and I am a little sad because I have to leave it all. Here all that was required to make good was a little common sense. Here the reputation was easily made. So every thing will not run so smoothly after we join at Ft. Thomas as it has here."[74]

Arnold realized that he was acknowledged by many senior-ranking officers as the most erudite airman in Washington. In the civilian-aviation world, he was personally acquainted with many of the East Coast aircraft and engine makers that were propelling the infant industry forward as fast as they could. No other Army officer, including those who outranked him, had gained the unique experience that Lieutenant Arnold possessed in 1913: a flying and staff background coupled with ties to the aviation-industrial base.

In his new assignment Arnold was, practically speaking, starting from scratch. He and his new wife would be unknowns at a new post while Arnold relearned his infantry job. The changes for both him and Bee were stressful. Following a two-month stay in Kentucky, the newlyweds were to move halfway around the globe to the exotic and sometimes dangerous Philippine Islands. Moreover, Bee had just discovered that she was pregnant.

✪ ✪ ✪ ✪ ✪

They sailed for the Philippines from San Francisco during December. The morning the ship was to leave, Harley surprised Bee with a large bunch of violets. This had special significance, as she later recalled: "If your beau liked you well enough, he would send you a big bunch of violets to wear."[75] But it was a treat Harley did not believe he would not be able to afford often: the newly-weds were on a strict budget. The Army did not pay travel expenses for wives, so traveling overseas became a costly affair. After Harley had paid all their lodging bills, he found he still had one five dollar gold piece left. Wanting to use the money to surprise Bee, he slipped down to a flower shop near their hotel, on Powell Street. Back East, violets were expensive—four or five dollars a bunch. Here, he picked out a big bunch of violets and turned over his gold coin.

The shop owner gave him $4.75 change. Harley was dumbfounded: "All this time we've been going without violets because I thought they were $5.00 a bunch!" Bee later spoke of how memorable that event was to her. "That showed the gentler side of [Harley]—which is hard for people to realize . . . who know him only as a soldier."[76] The private Arnold was a compassionate, caring man. It was a good thing, too: before they reached Manila Bay, he and Bee would endure an entire month afloat on the ship (except for one day on Guam), including the Christmas holiday.

Although Benjamin Foulois had just established an aviation section on Fort William McKinley in Manila, Arnold would have nothing to do with it. Lieu-tenant Arnold was assigned to the Thirteenth Infantry—he was a doughboy, pure and simple. The Arnolds' first real military assignment together did not begin very happily. Apparently the trip and the surroundings were just too much for the petite Bee Arnold to handle physically, and she miscarried in mid-January. This event was traumatic for both Harley and Bee.[77]

The situation worsened as Lieutenant Arnold was immediately ordered away to participate in a combat exercise near Batangas for more than one month. Bee was still in the Manila hospital recovering when Harley left. He was distraught much of the time he was away, constantly worried and deeply concerned when no letters were received out in the field. "I hope dearest that we never have to go through those troubles again. It caused me more serious thought than anything that has happened in the last 28 years of my life."[78] It took nearly a month before Arnold's worries subsided enough for him to begin suggesting that he and Bee would soon be making love again, each and every day. Her response to this idea is not recorded, but Bee was pregnant again by May 1914.[79]

The Arnolds did not immediately tell their families of the miscarriage. "Female problems" were generally off limits, except in the most extreme cases. Neither Bee nor Harley ever dared write the word *miscarriage*, even in their personal letters. The event was most frequently referred to as "those troubles." February 1914 letters from home asked for news of Bee's health, offered suggestions on child rearing, and mentioned that those at home were praying for the new family.[80] The second try to enlarge the Arnold family met with greater success.

During the rest of 1914 and again in 1915, Lieutenant Arnold participated in a variety of practice attacks on different Philippine Islands. He was reluctantly back "on the bosque." Professionally, though, this would be a most useful tour of duty. During the troublesome Batangas exercises immediately after Bee's miscarriage, Arnold watched his next-door neighbor plan and order the execution of a flawless attack. He commented to Bee that the young lieutenant "still holds the 'job as main guy' for this detachment and tells the colonels where to take their regiments and what to do with them." Clarifying the field situation, he explained: "However, everyone agrees that he has the ability to handle the situation so that there is no hard feelings any where."[81] Arnold was so impressed that he told Bee upon his return that he had served with a future Army chief of staff. The young man, George Catlett Marshall, would become his close personal friend, military commander, and staunch supporter nearly a quarter of a century later. The Arnolds developed a fond relationship with Marshall and his first wife, Lily, who suffered from thyroid troubles.[82] The Marshalls were also sympathetic and helpful during Bee's frequent physical problems during that tour, and the relationship that germinated would mature into a crucial element in the evolution of American airpower during World War II.

Arnold was no longer directly involved in Army aviation, but he still kept up with developments in military flying around the world. Friends made at College Park reported the state of air affairs periodically; Tommy Milling, for example, sent "Pewt" a lengthy report from France, describing the state of French aviation in significant and revealing detail. "Ease your mind on the supremacy of the French; they are great little advertisers and have a few specialists in the flying line but the percentage of real flyers is very small. This holds true in both the military and civil end of the work—in fact there are very few in the Army that can really fly. . . . The Army has an immense number of machines of all types—easily over a thousand, but they are not all suited to military purposes. They continue to buy them, single and two seaters, large and small, and as far as I have been able to determine, they are simply stuck in hangars at the different centers and left there."[83]

Milling continued to detail the shortcomings in French flight instruction, biplane design, and high accident rates. His experience at the Blériot school had also left him disgusted. He had flown an underpowered 50 Gnome aircraft many times, but when he asked to try the 80 Gnome, the fee was suddenly raised. "Blériot is nothing but a tight-wad of the first order, and as he wanted to rob me in the process, I didn't do so."[84] Dashing finally inquired whether Pewt had seen the new Hay Bill just introduced in Congress. He promised to report further upon his return to the States.

For Arnold's future professional development, having an aviation unit on the post at Manila did not hurt either. Lt. Bert Dargue, assigned to Foulois's flying unit, became close friends with the Arnolds. Captain Chandler, Arnold's

first flight student, was also assigned to that unit. They frequently met on social occasions, and certainly they exchanged all the current "dope" on flying
Additionally, Arnold was an avid reader of the *Army-Navy Journal,* which he
took with him into the field. He was as well informed as his assignment allowed him to be, but it was a far cry from his direct involvement in air matters
back in Washington.[85]

Without question, the most important family event of the tour occurred on
16 January 1915, when Lois Elizabeth Arnold was born in Manila. Named after both Bee's and Harley's older sisters, Lois, affectionately called Snooks,
brought relief and joy into the Arnold house—at least while she was still
young. Bee took all precautions after the birth to relax and build her strength
as quickly as possible. She informed her mother-in-law that "Harley is running the house and it works like a charm—his three weeks of bachelor training," while Bee was in the hospital after giving birth, "was fine preparation
and I haven't a thing in the world to think about."[86]

This news certainly would have relieved Bee's mother, who had cautioned
her to remain in bed a full two months prior to the birth. But her trepidation
over the pregnancy was lessened by Harley's presence: "I am sure that there is
no man like Harley, indeed I could never have allowed you so far away, with
anyone else."[87] By April Harley was ordered back in the field, where he stayed
until May. And in the middle of it all, the Arnolds moved to Batangas from
Fort McKinley. Shortly thereafter Bee was taken ill by some unknown afflic-
tion, so serious that she was at one point thought to be near death.[88] Harley
was beside himself, but she did eventually recover. With Bee nearly back to
normal, it was finally time to return stateside. Fortunately, the hectic two-year
tour was over.

In early February 1916, the Arnolds boarded a San Francisco–bound transport. The ship was packed full. Bee remained somewhat ill, and caring for
baby Lois was a major draw on her energy. Harley had his hands full watching
over them both. Thankfully, one of Harley's bachelor friends, Hubert "Miff"
Harmon, was also on the transport. Miff acted as the babysitter when the
Arnolds needed a few hours to relax. "He was a precious person," Bee later recalled.[89]

Somewhere in the middle of the Pacific Ocean, a cable reached Lieutenant
Arnold. The message was an invitation to return to flying, with a promotion to
captain. The Arnolds suspected that Billy Mitchell, now acting director of the
Aviation Section of the Signal Corps and one of Harley's old acquaintances,
was behind the query.

Mitchell had testified before the Hay Committee in 1913 and had a hand in
drafting follow-on legislation sponsored by Hay. In early 1916, Mitchell began a crusade to enlarge flight training among active-duty Army fliers, and
Arnold's experience fit these plans ideally.[90] Additionally, Bert Dargue may
have played a role in bringing Arnold back into aviation. From flying at Fort

McKinley, Dargue had gone to North Island, California, as a flight instructor.[91] But from either location he might have suggested to Mitchell that Arnold, who likely spoke with his friends of returning to flying, might be convinced to return to the cockpit. If so, Mitchell, now running the Washington office, capitalized on the suggestion.[92]

Army wheels were difficult to stop in mid-rotation, so the Arnolds ended up back on the East Coast by mid-March. Arnold was stationed at Madison Barracks, New York, home of the Third Infantry; Bee moved into an apartment near Ardmore. She eventually joined Harley, but by June they were on their collective way back to the West Coast, to join the Signal Corps Aviation School located at North Island, near San Diego. Arnold was not initially assigned as a pilot; he was the post supply officer. But Bee knew that he "wouldn't be a supply officer very long."[93] She was right.

6

CAPTAIN TO COLONEL:
THE GREAT WAR
(1916–18)

The Arnolds' journey west began under clouds of uncertainty, as Europe was firmly entrenched in the stalemate of World War I. President Woodrow Wilson had stuck to the policy of isolationism and, despite incidents as flagrant as the sinking of the British liner *Lusitania,* had successfully kept the United States out of the war. "The paper told today of the sinking of the Lousitania [*sic*]," Arnold wrote. "I have been expecting that all the time. People will stop taking those trips to England now I guess."[1]

Harley and Bee had only occasionally written of the developments in Europe, as passing topics in their letters of 1914 and 1915. On 25 August 1915, while still in the Philippines, Arnold had commented to Bee, "What do you think of the Japs joining the Russians to lick the Germans? It looks as if England is determined to beat the Germans."[2] Much serious discussion about the war also occurred between Harley, his father, and his mother. In the Arnold family, critical discussion of war and politics took place equally between the men and the women, this in a time when such subjects were largely the domain of men.[3]

War remained a remote possibility for the United States in the spring of 1916, as the Arnolds prepared for their move to North Island, California. Longtime Arnold acquaintance Henry S. Molineau, a civilian mechanic who had worked on early Wright and Curtiss aircraft engines in Dayton, was also now employed at North Island. He was the most experienced mechanic-engineer on the post. On 30 March 1916, Molineau wrote Arnold a letter warning of a tragically shabby state of flying operations. Although not delineated, the implication was clearly that leadership was lacking and morale was

80

low. The root of the problem was a growing rift between those who were pilots and those who were not.

Pilots felt that "ground-pounders" had no understanding of the potential of the air, yet they were under the bureaucratic control of such men.[4] By April 1916, the situation had become so inflamed that the secretary of war, Newton D. Baker, called for an independent investigation of the Aviation Section of the Signal Corps.[5] Lt. Bert Dargue, one of the most vocal of the airmen, testified before the committee. He explained that there were no officers in the Signal Corps capable of commanding the Aviation Section with any credibility. By June the inquiry was complete, and the General Staff recommendation was clear: aviation should be separated from the Signal Corps.[6]

Arnold was aware of, but unprepared for, the true gravity of the situation when he arrived at North Island in late May 1916.[7] Despite Molineau's warning, Arnold could do little to reverse the dismal situation: there was no budget money, and even less enthusiasm for aviation among the commanders than he had imagined. By the time Arnold was ready to leave North Island, in January 1917, he was convinced that the only method for change was to complain directly to the Inspector General of the Army.[8] And Arnold would feel the sting of North Island's leadership after leaving the post.

While the Arnolds made their way out west, the country's scientific and technological gold rush was well under way. Alexander Graham Bell made the first transcontinental phone call, from New York to San Francisco; and the Panama Canal was completing its first full year in operation. In 1915 the National Advisory Committee for Aeronautics (NACA) had been established, the first government organization chartered specifically to pursue aeronautical research. This marked the beginning of the second major phase of American aeronautical development, that of turning infant theory and experimentation into a tangible, organized program of inquiry.

Although joint Army-Navy aeronautical committees had existed before the NACA, they had no statutory status and even less authority over the progress of aeronautical science. The need for a committee with legitimate power to direct research and offer advice became apparent after Brig. Gen. John J. Pershing's punitive expedition into Mexico demonstrated the incapacity of Army aviation to perform operationally. Unfortunately, the NACA could not immediately solve that problem; it had no direct authority to direct Army research.[9]

In what turned out to be an aeronautical calamity, eight planes of the 1st Aero Squadron from San Antonio, Texas, were deployed to support Pershing's expedition in mid-March 1916. By the end of April, none were flyable. One plane was lost before the operation even began, while another crashed a few days later, leaving only six of the original eight for operations. The aircraft, the modified Curtiss JN-2 (later called the JN-3), had insufficient power to climb over the mountains and insufficient strength to withstand unpredictable southwestern winds and storms. Replacements were unavailable.[10]

Although many successful reconnaissance missions were flown over Mexico through August 1916, the early operational disasters that marked the Mexican expedition, coupled with the juxtaposition of the increasing utility of airplanes in the European war, influenced the substance of the June 1916 National Defense Act. The act increased the size of the Aviation Section, removed age and married-status limitations earlier placed upon fliers, and paved the way for an unheard-of $13 million appropriation for aviation that August. But the appropriation, the largest ever for American military aviation (by many multiples of previous funds), would be too late to ensure any sizable contribution by a meager, ill-prepared aviation industry.[11]

As the 3 June act was passed, Arnold was adjusting to his assignment as supply officer at the Aviation School at Rockwell Field, North Island. He held the new "junior military aviator" rating, because of his previous flying experience, and he wore a fresh set of captain's bars—as promised by Billy Mitchell. Now, however, he was officially eligible to return to flying, despite the fact that he was married. Arnold arrived in May as a support officer and became eligible to fly again in June. But his requalification training did not begin until 18 November 1916. In the meantime, Arnold spent many hours studying to pass his promotion exams: an aviation captain was a step down from a line officer.[12]

One bright, sunny Saturday afternoon, Harley and his close friend Bert Dargue, recently returned from the Mexican expeditionary debacle, entered the Arnold house, each sporting fresh goggle imprints on their now-sun-burned faces, Arnold's accentuated by an ever-receding hairline. Both men went about their business as if nothing had happened at the field. Finally Bee was forced to shatter their illusion that they might have actually gotten away with something. "Well, did you have a good trip today?" the five-month-pregnant Bee inquired. Harley's grin revealed the truth: this time his prenuptial promise to remain landlocked had been broken for good and all.

Bee knew that because she was expecting their second child, Harley was a bit unwilling to shock her system with the news. She had not handled her earlier pregnancies very well. Nevertheless, she had come to the realization that Harley belonged in the air. "It's perfectly alright," she said. "If you want to, go ahead and [fly]. That's your life."[13] Six days later Capt. Harley Arnold was a qualified Army pilot once again, but he was never officially assigned to a flying position at North Island.

Almost as soon as he was requalified, he and a few of the other young pilots met with trouble. On 10 January 1917, two fliers, Lt. William A. Robertson and his observer, Lt. Col. Harry Bishop, got lost on a cross-country flight. A malfunctioning compass helped steer them well off their planned course, deep into the California desert. After a few days of idle discussion by Army leadership on whether or not a search should be mounted, tempers among the aviators' friends began to flare: Arnold, Dargue, and B. Q. Jones, among others, had endured enough. With tacit approval from their commander, Col. William A. Glassford, the young airmen mounted the search themselves. The effort was futile, and the lost duo was never located by air; they were rescued after nine days by a rancher. Glassford was censured by his superiors for his inaction, and several of the insolent airmen suffered Glassford's military wrath, in the form of scathing performance reports, when he was forced to retire.[14]

Arnold was lucky: he had already been assigned command of the 7th Aero Squadron in the Panama Canal Zone. There were, however, other concerns at the Arnold house. Bee gave birth to their first son, Henry Harley Arnold Jr., on 29 January 1917, a full two months' premature. Mother and son both appeared to be in good shape, but Harley senior, unfortunately, could not remain in Coronado with his family. His new squadron of fifty men (sans airplanes) needed a home and, only a few days after the birth of his son, he was off to Panama via Washington, D.C., and New York.[15]

Bee really was in better shape than Arnold realized. A few weeks after he left for Panama, she demonstrated her own adventurous side. On short notice, she was gathered up by one of her husband's closest friends and ushered to the airfield. She donned a greasy pair of too-big coveralls and a mechanic's hat and hopped aboard one of the nearby "Jennies." Her flight was a thrill, but moreover, the sortie helped her to realize why her husband loved the air as much as he did. In light of the hot water Arnold was almost in, her excursion was truly risky. Whether he ever knew of this hop remains unknown.[16]

During the first week in February, Arnold was called to Washington for a personal briefing that described his new responsibilities, this before any official inquiry into the North Island affair had even begun. It was not until 13 February that Brigadier General Squier, now head of the Aviation Section, asked for all of Arnold's papers concerning the controversial Robertson-Bishop flight. Arnold added some small print to his 13 February letter to Beadle explaining what was going on, as if to whisper, "Apparently an investigation."[17]

Some believed the Canal Zone assignment was a punishment for his actions at North Island—an "exile" for Arnold. This is not reflected in the record. In fact, he was given the added responsibility for locating and establishing the base for the yet-to-be-formed and only partially equipped unit, one of only seven aero squadrons in the U.S. Army. Additionally, he was to be on the commanding general's staff for the entire Canal Zone, and his aviation command was expected to grow from one to three squadrons during his tour of duty.[18] This type of command assignment would not have been given to an untrusted or negligent officer in the Army of 1917.

In 1917 Arnold did not perceive anything negative from his new duty assignment, even though his later autobiography implied otherwise. Upon notification of his duties he wrote to Bee, "The Panama job is a big thing from the way it is outlined here [Washington]. Balloons—aero squadrons and hydro squadrons. I hope that I am big enough to handle it. It will grow slowly so that maybe I can grow with it." [19]

Only after the assignment had been explained to Arnold and orders had been issued did he find out about certain individuals who objected to the move. "I stand in well with some," he wrote, "and not so well with others. Before I leave I hope to stand in well with all. I am trying to be very conservative." [20] This last comment revealed another lesson that Arnold was well on his way to learning and understanding: advancement in the Army bureaucracy often required some form of tacit higher-up committee approval. In the face of the developing North Island investigation, he took the opportunity to smooth the waters at the Army staff; it might be called schmoozing. By February 1917, Arnold was cutting his bureaucratic and political teeth, to ensure that he kept what he perceived to be a challenging and important job.

Arnold had two weeks to prepare for his 28 February port call aboard the *Kilpatrick*. He used much of his free time to inspect training facilities and interview designers and engineers. The day prior to his departure, he visited the Sperry factory, two hours outside of New York. Elmer Sperry and his son Lawrence became well known for their work on gyroscopes that were used in the first automatic flight controls for airplanes, as well as in other secret Army projects. The following day, Arnold visited the pilot-training facilities at Mineola, New York, to "see the bunch out there and have dinner." [21] He seemed never to waste a moment, particularly when he was away from home and Beadle.

Although his North Island performance report was terrible, his new commander in Panama, Maj. Gen. Clarence Edwards, did not appear to hold it against Arnold. He lived in the general's house and had free use of his car during the first month of his tour of duty. It may have been the general's tolerance that prompted Arnold to write, "He is a real man, the first real General I have ever met." [22]

Arnold shrugged off Glassford's report with minimal dismay in his letter to Beadle: "Don't say anything about it but Col. G_____ gave me an awful efficiency report. The general told me and I am going to ask to see it tomorrow. After all I did at the school and after his asking me to fly over to Calexico and not putting me on flying status I think he might at least have been noncommittal. However, that is neither here nor there—the deed is done—I am glad I have one or two good reports to my credit. I wonder what kind he will give Jones and Dargue?" [23]

Only once did Arnold let his dander up, when on 20 March 1917 he candidly wrote Bee: "You can not make me mad if you never see Mrs. L_____ or Mrs. G_____ again. I tried to get the general to let me see my efficiency report but he wouldn't. He told me that it was so rotten that it made me stink. Hence Col. G_____ must like me very much. I hope he gets tried by a G.C.M. [general court-martial] before he gets out." [24]

This letter, incidentally, describes the origins of a lifelong animosity between Arnold and Frank P. Lahm, his former French instructor at West Point and an aviation pioneer. Colonel Glassford, the commander, and Captain Lahm, the executive officer, were responsible for the delayed desert search as well as the stinging efficiency reports. It was not until much later in life that Arnold and Lahm ever publicly reconciled their differences resulting from the incident. Privately, on both sides the animosity remained.[25]

Bee too saw the Panama job as a major challenge. "It must be wonderful to be starting such a big affair as the first squadron in the zone," she innocently wrote from California, "I can imagine it is going to be just as interesting as anything you will ever get to do."[26]

Arnold's first priority was to find an acceptable location for an air base on which to land his planes. The task of canal defense could only be accomplished after the base had been established. "I have been all over the Isthmus from Gatun to the Flamingo Islands with the general. Today Cowan," who had influenced Arnold's first flying assignment, "and I will go across to Colon and look around there."[27]

After several weeks of searching, no consensus could be reached on a location. When one was acceptable to the Americans, it was unacceptable to the Panamanians. When another was acceptable to the Army, it was unacceptable to the Navy. Frustration and dead ends forced Arnold back to Washington to take up the matter directly with Gen. Leonard Wood. "Things are not going smooth enough in the organization," Arnold announced in his letter telling Bee he was coming. "As usual it looks as if the War Department has forgotten all about us." He concluded, "Hence it is up to me to wake them up."[28]

It was aboard ship while on his way to Washington to issue the wake-up call that Arnold heard news of the United States's entry into the Great War. On 6 April 1917, his transport ship began blackouts and zigzag patterns in the sea, and a new seriousness of attitude spread throughout the ship. Arnold knew he would not be back to Panama anytime soon.[29] He hoped to obtain a command of a flying squadron bound for Europe, but he was destined to remain in Washington, a noncombat staff officer.

At port, Arnold received his new orders to the War Department. By telephoning his in-laws, he learned that Bee had already packed up the household in San Diego and was one day's travel from Ardmore. She and Harley had suffered from a poor mail system in the Canal Zone, and, although many letters were exchanged, Bee had never been able to inform Harley of her plans to move back East. All turned out well, though, as the family—Bee, Lois, and "Bunkie," now nearly four months old—were reunited with Harley at the old homestead in Ardmore.

While Bee recovered from her cross-country journey, still weak from the premature birth but motivated by her flight, Arnold proceeded to Washington. By June he had been promoted to major in the Aviation Section of the Sig-

nal Corps. Wartime brought rapid military expansion, and those few who
were already in the Aviation Section represented the corporate knowledge for
air matters. They were quickly elevated in rank. As testimony to this fact, on 5
August 1917 Henry Arnold was "jumped" to full colonel (temporary) as executive officer of the Air Division. However, he was not officially notified of
the new rank until early September. His rank was backdated to the fifteenth
and then again to the fifth of August. At that moment, Arnold was the
youngest full colonel in the Army. But as the war progressed, others several
years his junior also were promoted temporarily to that rank.[30]

Immediately, from his desk at the Mills Building on Pennsylvania Avenue,
Arnold began to attack his wartime tasks. These included expansion of training facilities, planes, and trainees.[31] Fortunately, appropriations for the
wartime air arm finally became available. At least he didn't have to worry
much about procurement money.

At the heart of the massive expansion of the Aviation Section were the con-
tents of a 24 May 1917 cable from the French premier Alexandre Ribot to
President Wilson: the Ribot Cable. The message requested that an American
force of 4,500 planes, 5,000 pilots, and 50,000 mechanics be shipped to
France by spring 1918. Evidence suggests that the essence of the cable had
been transposed from correspondence between Billy Mitchell and Premier Ribot, but not all the detail. What remained unclear was the requested mix of aircraft types. Mitchell had suggested that bombers and fighters should make up
the majority of the 4,500 planes. His advice, if heard at all in America, came
too late. The Signal Corps, assisted by Pershing himself, opted to place high
priority on reconnaissance and observation aircraft—those missions already
proven plausible by the air arm.

Nonetheless, the Ribot Cable became the rough basis for American wartime
aircraft production.[32] In an effort to clarify the ambiguity in the Ribot Cable,
the chief Signal officer sent a small committee to France under the leadership
of Maj. Raynal Cawthorne Bolling. Bolling, a graduate of the Harvard Law
School and a lawyer for the U.S. Steel Corporation, National Guardsman, and
pilot, would be killed in hand-to-hand combat in the trenches on 26 March
1918.[33]

This group was to investigate which type planes were actually needed and
write a report. By July 1917, the report finished, Bolling recommended that
four planes be produced by the United States en masse: the British de Havilland DH-4 for observation and bombing, the French SPAD and British Bristol
as fighters, the Italian Caproni for night bombing, and the Curtiss JN-4
"Jenny" as the backbone of the training force. The realities of war, however,
resulted in the mass production of only the DH-4.

General Pershing and his staff decided that the time differential between Europe and America was too great to keep up with the near-daily technological
advances in fighter-type airplanes.[34] Thus the United States's single aircraft

contribution to the war effort, the DH-4, was made possible by the already-established European aviation industry. It was by this method—borrowing from others already well advanced in aeronautics—that American aviation technology "caught up" with the rest of the world after a decade of under-funded neglect.[35]

This experience only reinforced previous efforts to improve American technology, efforts that Arnold had already seen during his 1913 Washington tour of duty. It was a lesson he internalized and would use effectively during the next war as well. Arnold's War Department assignment involved direct experience in the administration, training, and massive expansion of American airpower in the face of a national military crisis. He would deal with remarkably similar circumstances again in 1938.

As he had done in 1913, Arnold became indispensable to his superiors, who, although supportive, had little knowledge of air matters. While in this War Department assignment, he saw firsthand the immense problems facing the Air Division: lack of trained mechanics, lack of pilots, and lack of an aircraft-production system. These problems were Arnold's biggest headache of the war. The young colonel spent a huge chunk of his time traveling around the United States checking on the progress of training expansion programs for pilots and mechanics, as well as on aircraft production and development and on keeping his superiors informed of the plodding progress made in these areas.[36]

Many production problems could be attributed to the United States's policy of neutrality that, until February 1917, was publicly supported by President Wilson. To build the American military in any form—despite some pressures to do just that—was, in the perception of that time, to abandon neutrality as a policy. Not until unrestricted U-boat warfare threatened American overseas trade with Continental Europe did public opinion shift dramatically toward active intervention. The interception of the Zimmermann Telegram, a memo from Berlin to Mexico City seeking a military alliance against the United States, added insult to injury, but interventionist politics had already ensured funding for the military. Still, this funding, totaling slightly over $58 million by 1 June 1917, came too late to build a fully functional air arm.[37] There was no head start for industry during this war; many manufacturers who had never built a plane were truly starting from scratch.

By July 1917, Army aviation had money and production goals. Colonel Arnold, assistant director of military aeronautics since the 21 May internal reorganization of the division, inherited much of the responsibility for training the requisite pilots and mechanics to meet the Bolling Commission's numerical goals while also pushing the production of the planes.[38] The combination of these duties with other more secret projects, such as unmanned flying bombs, occupied Arnold's life until November 1918.

During May and June, he set out to develop a system for training pilots that would meet the ever-increasing numbers of available cockpits during the war.

Arnold opened ground schools across the country, most of them located at civilian universities such as Ohio State, Massachusetts Institute of Technology (MIT), and Cornell University. By the end of June, 21,000 young men had passed the physical and completed ground school, qualifying them for flight school.[39] The problem of establishing sufficient flight schools for these ready candidates fell next on Arnold's to-do list.

From 2 to 19 August 1917, he and several other junior officers visited twenty-three cities from Washington as far west as San Antonio, and from New Orleans as far north as Ontario, Canada. His team was searching for new airfields from which to begin training pilots. When one was found satisfactory, it was leased on the spot and plowed flat immediately. More than thirty fields were built in this way by the fall of 1918. Additionally, research facilities were inspected, ensuring that production and development was on schedule. On 15 August, for example, Arnold visited Detroit, home of the Liberty engine.[40]

The Liberty engine program picked up speed after a meeting between Col. Edward Deeds of the Air Service and Lt. Cols. E. J. Hall and J. G. Vincent, two engineers-turned-officers for the war. They met to finalize plans to build the American version of the DH-4 combat airplane. Bee later remembered heated discussions in her living room between Harley, Colonel Deeds, and other members of industry during these months. Colonel Arnold tried accelerating engine and production timetables, but industry, for any number of legitimate reasons, could not comply with his requests.[41]

In Deeds's Washington, D.C., hotel room that May, the designers solved the problems associated with six- and eight-cylinder engines that were designed for the British de Havilland DH-4. By August, the 400-plus-horsepower Liberty engine was approaching the production phase. The first twelve-cylinder model of the engine was tested on 25 August, and mass production began shortly thereafter.[42] The Liberty engine was the United States's singular independent technological contribution to the war effort.

American engine production overall was a remarkable success story. By the time of the armistice, more than 15,500 Liberty engines had been produced. Additionally, the auto industry continued production of other engines that had been licensed for production in America. Le Rhône, Hispano-Suiza, Gnome, Hall-Scott, and XO engines were also built in significant numbers. In eighteen months, more than 32,000 aircraft engines had been built by American industry. "It was unfortunate," Arnold lamented, "that our industry was not able to produce combat planes with the same ease and in the same numbers."[43]

During his August 1917 trip, Arnold's typical day had no beginning and no end. In daylight the team was either inspecting a potential field or traveling between two sites. Sleep was only possible on the Pullman cars between major stops; the rest of the time they were so busy inspecting and searching for adequate fields that days blended together. In Rantoul, Illinois, Arnold was impressed by the flight school: "They start the students at 4:30 A.M. and keep them going until 7:00 P.M. Then they are so tired that they are perfectly willing to go to bed. . . . The machines are in the air all the time. The students are the finest looking bunch of youngsters that I have seen yet and are being turned out as R.M.A.'s [reserve military aviators] rapidly."[44] This school had the right idea, he thought: long hours, hard work, mission accomplishment. A can-do attitude.

Even while Arnold was busy traveling, he still took time to find presents for his family. He was distressed in New Orleans that he could not find an "appropriate" doll for his daughter Lois, now called Lolie, only a black-colored one. Interestingly, despite the slur, he understood that buying a black doll might be insulting to his black housekeepers back home in D.C. "But it certainly was cute."[45]

Arnold had been raised and lived in a day where racial separation and disparaging terms were the social norm. Even the socially adept and well-educated Bee referred to blacks as "darkies." Throughout his career Arnold actually showed great compassion and care for his housekeepers, most of whom were black, and one of whom, Maggie, was with them for a decade and received money from Bee until the early 1970s.

Yet Arnold had no compunction about ruthlessly generalizing the appearance of all English women. He showed little compassion when describing them upon his arrival in England later in the war. "They look like H_____ [hell]. They don't know how to wear their clothes and they have no clothes which look like anything. They have ankles like fence posts. Taking them all in all they are messes."[46] Today he would be termed a racist. Of course, so would every general, journalist, radio host, and mother of a soldier during wartime, when Japanese were "Japs" or "Nips," and Germans were "Huns," "Bosche," or "Krauts." Arnold simply expressed himself using the common jargon of the times.

During the fall of 1917, Arnold visited production facilities in Detroit, Buffalo, Toledo, and Dayton. Afterward, he returned to Washington and reported his observations first to the chief Signal officer, Maj. Gen. George Squier, and then to the new director of the Aeronautics Division, Brig. Gen. William L. Kenly. But Arnold was not idle while in Washington. During September he wrote to Jerome C. Hunsaker, a naval construction contractor at the time, requesting advice on the classification of certain types of "float construction" for military planes. Hunsaker would go on to join the MIT faculty and become actively involved in the American radar program during the next war.[47]

Arnold's jobs during World War I included, primarily, solving the problems associated with massive aircrew expansion and training. Additionally, the young colonel dealt with administrative headaches, coordinating and directing the expansion in aircraft production then just beginning, and coping with modifications in design that resulted in bottlenecks. He accomplished these duties diligently, often in person, and frequently with little rest or relaxation time for himself or his staff. He was seldom home during daylight. It was the way he accomplished these important support functions that made him indispensable to Generals Squier and Kenly.

After 20 May 1918, Arnold's responsibilities for monitoring aircraft production and development diminished. President Wilson separated aviation from the Signal Corps when he signed the Overman Bill. The aviation branch then was divided into the Bureau of Aircraft Production, under John D. Ryan; and the Division of Military Aeronautics, commanded by Maj. Gen. William L. Kenly. Kenly's division held responsibility for operations and training. Arnold's specialty was training and all that went with expansion in that area.[48]

On the operations side, Arnold also became involved with top-secret military weapons projects. The impact of these projects on the young colonel is illustrated by his War Department involvement in the creation of the Army's first guided missile, code-named Liberty Eagle, also called the Flying Bomb or Kettering Bug. Colonel Arnold was more directly involved in the development of the Liberty engine than with the Liberty Eagle project, but both fell under his jurisdiction.

Officially known as the Liberty Eagle, the Ammunition Carrier, and in secret correspondence simply "FB" (Flying Bomb), this unmanned biplane's fuselage housed a four-cylinder, two-cycle engine and carried 180 pounds of explosives. The Bug had no wheels and was launched from a wagon-like contraption that ran on a long section of portable track. The missile's engine was cranked at one end of the track that was pointed directly at the intended target. Project members became convinced that thousands of these easily mass-produced weapons could be launched toward the enemy simultaneously, annihilating a wide area of a city or an industrial complex in a matter of moments. Most of the Army's high command remained unaware of the weapon's development.[49]

When the engine was fully revved, the mechanical counter was engaged and the Bug was released. When it reached flying speed, it lifted off and flew straight ahead toward the target, climbing to a preset altitude that was controlled by a supersensitive aneroid barometer. When it reached its altitude, the Bug's barometer sent signals to small flight controls that were moved by a system of cranks and a bellows (from a player piano) for altitude control. A gyro helped maintain the stability of the craft and the barometer helped maintain altitude, but only the design of the wings assured directional stability.[50]

The Bug flew until a mechanical counter sensed the calculated number of engine rotations required to carry the weapon the intended distance. When the preset number of revolutions was attained, a cam fell into place and cut fuel to the engine. Then the Bug silently glided to the target like a diving falcon. Kettering's Bug was rarely as deadly as a falcon, and certainly not as fast. Eventually, lateral controls were added that rectified the instability problem caused by overdependence upon the dihedral—the slightly upward angle of the wings for lateral stability.[51]

During the first official test of the weapon in the first week of October 1918, the miniature craft lifted into the air precisely on cue. The development team began to smile, and the visiting "brass hats" wondered how this new missile could be used in Europe. But then the slowly climbing bird pivoted off its course, swooped and dove like a kite flying without enough wind, and headed straight for the reviewing stands. The distinguished crowd now seemed less so as they dove haphazardly under the bleachers to avoid potential disaster. Fortunately, the unarmed craft crash-landed a few hundred feet from the invited guests, much to the embarrassment of the once-confident development team.[52] Arnold recalled, "At about six to eight hundred feet, as if possessed by the devil, it turned over, made Immelmann turns, and seeming to spot the group of brass hats below dived on them, scattering them in all directions."[53]

A subsequent test the following week, though more successful than the one described above, resulted in a high-speed chase through the farmlands around Dayton. The Bug initially flew straight and level, but then began a lazy encirclement of the town, drawing unwanted attention to the experiment from the local population. After the limited fuel supply was exhausted, the miniplane crash-landed near Xenia, 20 miles east of Dayton, in a farmer's field. A crowd gathered around the device before Arnold's team arrived on the scene. The locals were frantically searching for the pilot of the plane, who, they believed, had somehow escaped the wreck. A bit of quick thinking and a little white lie calmed the crowd and preserved the secret of the pilotless airplane. The Bug project officer from Dayton, Lt. Col. Bion J. Arnold (no relation to our protagonist), pulled an unsuspecting passenger, a flight-suit-clad visitor, out of the chase car. The officer carefully explained, as he gestured toward the man, who was obviously a pilot, that he had bailed out of the plane before it crashed. The excited farmers breathed a sigh of relief, oblivious to the fact that the Air Service used no parachutes in 1918. The breach of security surrounding the project forced an immediate change in the testing location, from Dayton to Arcadia, what is today Eglin Air Force Base near Fort Walton Beach, Florida.[54]

On the Bug team were Orville Wright, C. H. Wills, Elmer Sperry, Robert Millikan, and Charles Kettering, an amazing collection of scientists and engineers. Orville Wright remained quietly active in aviation technology his entire life and was frequently consulted by Arnold when he faced any difficult problem. Henry Ford's chief engine engineer, C. H. Wills, designed and built the engine specifically for the Bug. Dr. Elmer Sperry had just finished working on a Navy project, the "aerial torpedo," which transformed old airplanes into unmanned air weapons. His working knowledge of gyroscopes was essential to the Bug's flight stability. Dr. Robert Millikan had been commissioned into the Army and was serving as the chief of aeronautical research during the war. He became the president of the newly renamed California Institute of Technology (Caltech) in 1921, and received the 1923 Nobel Prize for Physics for his earlier charged-particles research. Charles K. Kettering, of the Dayton Engineering Laboratories Company (Delco), was the primary project engineer. "Ket" Kettering had solved the problem of pings and knocks in sparkplug-powered gasoline engines and also invented the self-starter for automobiles. His ingenuity was well respected by Arnold, who admired his ability to accomplish impossible things.

More important than the gadget itself were these team members, particularly Millikan, who would play a vital scientific and technical role for the air arm in the 1930s and again during the Second World War.[55] Arnold never forgot the Bug, nor did he forget the men who had helped create the missile. The top-secret project became dormant shortly after the end of the war.[56] Though neither Arnold nor the Bug ever flew in combat, valuable lessons were learned during the process of readiness for war.

Arnold had already been aware of the importance of each individual on the team, but he now also became familiar with new concepts and processes. While working Bug-related issues from Washington, Arnold learned the importance of secrecy in certain military projects. Too many with knowledge of the project often resulted in everyone having knowledge of the project. He learned the value of trusting the team members, not only in construction but also in the conceptualization phases of a project. Trust yielded a confidence that allowed him to work on other important issues while the Bug project moved forward. From a purely military perspective, Arnold was establishing his own doctrinal base for unmanned and guided aerial weapons. He realized that the early versions of the Bug, although grossly inaccurate, might one day evolve into a weapon more precise than any other in the force.[57]

Somehow, in the middle of the wartime madhouse in Washington, the Arnolds were practicing their own methods of mass production. Bee gave birth to William Bruce on 17 July 1918. Colonel Arnold again was not home long before pressing duties and inspection schedules forced him back on the road.

Colonel Arnold and his boss, Brigadier General Kenly, having realized the Bug's potential contribution to combat operations, convinced the Army staff to send Arnold to Europe in an effort to persuade Gen. John J. Pershing to use it against the Germans before World War I ended. Arnold saw this as his opportunity to make it to the combat zone, and probably pushed the issue himself. His actual involvement in the development of the Bug had only been tangential, but he had attended the initial test of the machine and had drafted the letter assigning Bion Arnold as project officer. Kenly had signed that order and also insisted on sending someone over to brief General Pershing. Arnold was that man.[58]

Additionally, Arnold, who self-admittedly feared a limited Army future without any combat experience on his record, probably used the opportunity to make the trip to Europe. Squier, his former boss, had refused any attempts he had previously made to join the fighting. Arnold's experience was unique on Squier's staff: he had dealt with wartime industry, and he had a flying background. Realistically, Squier could not send Arnold and all his experience to Europe: a void in Squier's Signal Corps would then exist. Arnold, a young wartime colonel, at this point seemed more interested in his own career progression than in supporting the needs of his commander. Kenly, however, was friendly with Arnold and even wrote him and Bee personal letters. He may have believed that there was some truth in Arnold's complaints about combat and promotion and, in that light and suspecting war's end, finally selected Arnold to brief Pershing.[59]

Despite several setbacks, Arnold did, after two previously aborted attempts, make it to Europe. Officially his orders were to sail by mid-October and become familiar with training-organization methods in France and combat operations at the front. His trip was, however, unsuccessful. After a quick family visit in Ardmore, he arrived in New York, the debarkation point, but soon fell victim to the Spanish Flu that was then rampant on the East Coast. Perhaps not coincidentally, Arnold's daughter had become desperately ill with the same type of flu the day after he had departed for his port call.[60]

After transferring tickets to a faster ship in an effort to reach the combat zone more quickly, Arnold had a few days of idle time in the New York area. In typical fashion he arranged to visit the torpedo station at New London, Connecticut; inspect the flying school on Long Island; and meet with General Kenly to "talk things over."[61] Censorship of military mail prevented any detailed discussion with Bee of what the conversation was about; it likely covered a variety of topics including, certainly, the Bug.

But all was not work. The day before his departure, Arnold met up with several of his friends who were just returning from combat tours in France, among others Tooey Spaatz. The two had met in 1917, while Arnold was inspecting training bases in Texas. Upon his return to Washington, D.C., Arnold had commented to Bee that Spaatz was a "fine young man and would go far." Shortly thereafter, his newfound friend departed for France.[62] Now back home, Spaatz met Arnold in New York, where they saw a show, ate a grand dinner, and toasted the aviator's safe return with expensive champagne. It was war.[63]

Perhaps feeling a bit guilty for having such a wonderful time while Bee was in Ardmore with three young children, Harley wrote an apologetic letter of appreciation to the woman he loved so much.

> I think that you deserve more credit for this war business than I do. I have been so busy for over a year that I have only had time in a cursory way to see what was going on any where but in the office. In the meantime you were

running the whole show at the house and keeping me going besides. I have
relaxed a bit now and have had a chance to think again so I want you to
know dearest that I appreciate your work then and most of all now when
Lolie is so sick.

    After the war is over I hope that we can go somewhere and get acquainted
again. I'd like to have nothing to do for an hour—a half day or all day but sit
down and talk to you or let you talk or just sit. I miss you terribly darling.[64]

On 17 October 1918, Arnold sailed on the fast transport ship *Olympic*. He
was hoping for a relaxing journey, one that might soothe his own "nervous
strain," a result of his many travels and long working hours. But just before he
stepped aboard, he fell dreadfully ill, still with the flu. For the next seven days
he never left his stateroom; Arnold had been afforded one of the largest set of
quarters because of his rank. His accommodations were "as large as our front
room—a private bath attached," he wrote Bee.[65] The flu forced him to remain
bedridden, with a 102-degree temperature and mild bronchitis. Friends on
board saw to his needs, in particular one young Maj. Reuben "Rube" Fleet,
whom Arnold had tasked to establish air-mail service between Washington
and New York earlier that year. It was probably Fleet who told Arnold all
about the six Navy destroyers that escorted the transport for the last three
days of her journey.[66]

    Upon arrival in England, Arnold was carried off the ship on a stretcher after
a useless protest against such a measure. He later retold the story of his
stretcher trip as more harrowing than the entire boat journey. "They carried
me off—down—many flight of stairs—sometimes I was standing on my head
and sometimes on my feet."[67] With him on board the *Olympic* had been a
number of military chaplains, notorious for their unmilitary appearance and
marching abilities. Arnold, the ranking officer on board, had charged Rube
Fleet with marching these chaplains to their barracks the night of their arrival.
The last thing Arnold heard as he was placed into the awaiting ambulance was
Fleet shouting marching orders to the undisciplined padres. "Left, two, three,
four. . . . Keep in step you G_____ D_____ chaplains, keep in step!" Trying to hide his laughter, Arnold was immediately carried off to an American-
run hospital, where he was placed on a strict regimen of rest and fluid intake.[68]

    Arnold was discharged from the hospital on 1 November 1918, his recovery
impaired by the week-long transatlantic voyage and a minor relapse the day he
debarked the ship. By 4 November he was in France. Along the way, he met an
unnamed French captain, who related the dreadful experiences of life as a pris-
oner of war in Germany. He also heard that Billy Mitchell held a reputation as
the best-dressed American officer in the war—not a surprise to Arnold, who
knew of Mitchell's wealthy family background.[69]

    On 6 November, Arnold had a meeting with Gen. Mason Patrick during
which, presumably, he told him about the Liberty Eagle project. His next task

was to inspect the airplanes of the First and Second Army. He described to Beadle his journey from Paris to Chaumont: "I came here by way of Meaux-Chateau Thierry-Dormans-Epernay-Chalons—by automobile. It was a wonderful trip—the ruins of Chateau Thierry and the Dormans were very bad. Shell holes every where—Also graves. Houses down and partly down—Bridges wrecked and rebuilt. Barbed wire almost from one town to another—Trenches without number. Villages completely deserted."[70]

Arnold was astounded by the plentiful food available in "starving France," more than in America. It was rumored that the war would last only three weeks to three months longer; no one thought it would be only three days. On 9 November, Arnold wrote about the kaiser's abdication, the signing of the informal armistice, and the cease-fire that was to begin the tenth, one day before the historic eleventh hour of the eleventh day of the eleventh month. Arnold held mixed emotions about such an unexpected end to the war. Although relieved, he felt an element of disappointment: "I did not get my ride over the lines so I am not much of a battle-scarred veteran."[71] But he continued trying.

The next day, he and Monk Hunter, who years later would bring Eighth Fighter Command to England, got in a car and drove as far as they could toward the front lines, passing miles of trenches and scores of artillery batteries. By the time they reached the farthest-forward deployed American troops, the fog had grown so thick that they "could just see the Bosche in his line on the crest of a hill beyond."[72]

The formal armistice went into effect while they were there. Upon returning to Souilly, Arnold and Hunter drove through what remained of the Saint-Mihiel salient. "We saw so much that I can not record it," he wrote in awe.[73] He had seen the results of the first-ever mass aerial attack, and it had marked his memory.

The weather finally broke, allowing the commencement of flying operations once again. Arnold was given a ride over Verdun and the former front lines. It was 14 November 1918. On the way back to the field to land, the aircraft crankshaft shattered, and he and his pilot made a forced landing in the middle of a field of artillery craters. They hiked more than 3 miles just to reach a balloon company from which they could arrange transportation back to the airfield. Arnold's experiences made a dynamic impression upon him at the time: "Darling," he admitted to Beadle, "I see so much and so many terrible and wonderful things that I can not sleep at night. I would not have missed this trip for anything."[74]

Arnold never saw General Pershing, and activating the Bug did not occur before the guns fell silent. Arnold never saw any action, though he desperately tried to get as close to the front lines as he could. He actually made it to the most forward-deployed American Expeditionary Force unit, but the real shooting had already been called to a halt, and only a few distant shots were heard. Arnold saw German prisoners of war being escorted behind the Allied lines. He even managed to obtain a German army helmet, which he sent home to Bee.[75] Despite the fact that he saw no action, Colonel Arnold had made it to the theater before the armistice had been signed and was, by regulation, entitled to the decorations accorded combat soldiers.[76] It would have been foolish not to accept these honors, as they had been his purpose in making the excursion, and Arnold was very interested in his future in the Army.

The trip to France included a surprisingly bright moment when, in the middle of a road near Verdun, partly by accident and partly by design, Harley met up with his brother Clifford, now a physician in the Pennsylvania National Guard.[77] Clifford had suffered through two gassings, and was recovering with his unit when Harley found him near Audincourt. His other brother, Price, was also serving in France but never came in touch with Harley: he was in the hospital with the flu while Harley was in the theater. Clearly the Arnold family tradition of military service during wartime was never in doubt.

Arnold later recalled the importance of many advances that occurred in aviation during the war years. Some of the most significant were oxygen masks combined with communications devices, air-to-ground radio sets, automatic cameras, armored pilot seats, increased firepower for strafing, and improved aeromedical research equipment. Additionally, the establishment of the NACA held promise for the future of aeronautical research and development.[78]

Aircraft production, however, never reached acceptable levels. Even though Liberty engines were produced in great quantity, the United States never figured out how to build enough aircraft for the engines. By the end of the war, 1,213 American DH-4 aircraft had made it overseas, but only about 600 of them had been sent to the front.[79] Arnold had witnessed the production bottlenecks firsthand, and would remember the consequences of a failed production arrangement throughout his career.

He detailed these production failures in his report, "Airplanes, Less Engines, Including Propellers and Airplane Parachutes, January 1922."[80] An examination of this study reveals the lessons Arnold learned from his World War I experiences. He gathered data from the industries involved in aircraft production during the war, most of which he had dealt with personally in his Aeronautics Division duties. He took issue with some of findings of the famous postwar study by Col. Edgar S. Gorrell, particularly concerning production bottlenecks versus personnel shortfalls, since these had fallen under Arnold's responsibility during the war.[81]

In his own report, Arnold's most significant observations centered around existing differences between automobiles and aircraft. In automobile production, supplies such as rods, bolts, nuts, and steel conformed to certain specified standards. But in the case of airplane production, standards for exactness of part size and material quality were much more stringent. The smallest deviation could mean the ultimate failure of the plane. Additionally, the auto industry's need for spare parts did not even approach that of the aircraft-production industry. Lack of spare parts resulted in the cannibalization of hundreds of training airplanes so that others could remain in the air.[82]

Although Arnold realized the need for spare aircraft and engine parts—based upon previous deployment experiences—he did not grasp the gravity or the magnitude of the wartime situation until near its end. Despite his efforts during the first year of the war, he could not solve the industrial problems faced by the Air Service. It was one of the lessons he internalized and would remember as World War II approached.

Industry remained uninformed of aircraft requirements and unwilling to alter production lines permanently, despite Arnold's efforts. Initially, executives allowed foreign-industry representatives to sway them away from choices made by disparaging competitors, who were trying to sell their own products. Industrial inspectors, largely hired from commercial firms, were found serving in positions for which they had no preliminary training whatsoever. To Arnold, these represented the "big picture" mistakes made that prevented U.S. aircraft production from "getting on its feet as soon as it should have."[83]

More specific problems resulted from inexperience and a competitive desire to provide the finest, most advanced craft in the world. When the Army assigned more than one model to a manufacturer, the problem was further complicated by diluting already inadequate engineering staffs, machine-tool specifications, and manufacture. The industry simply lacked the experience to deal with such demands. After the production line had been established, changes were incorporated haphazardly, in an effort to incorporate the most advanced equipment available.

This shortfall was exemplified by the DH-4 production line, which introduced more than 6,700 separate modifications after the initial designs and specifications had been delivered to the factory. The ensuing production logjam was exactly what Arnold had referred to as the "neck of the bottle." He wrote in his report: "Undoubtedly some of the changes were necessary; but the majority of them could have been eliminated by proper tests and designs that should have been made by the experimental machine before the articles were submitted to the factories for quantity production."[84] The method by which modifications occurred—not the modifications themselves—remained a tremendous challenge.

This problem evolved into a philosophy that resulted in production research and development in later years. But during World War I, a system of manufacture capable of dealing with such rapid and continuous modifications did not exist.[85]

Of major importance was the lack of coordination between component-part manufacturers and production lines across the country. In some cases, one factory would have an abundance of gas-line connectors while another had none, forcing the production line to close until the parts were obtained.

Tires ran out at one of the DH-4 factories, so, to keep the line in operation, tires were rotated from the planes awaiting delivery back to the end of the assembly line. There they were affixed to newly completed DH-4s. The process continued until new tires arrived.[86]

Arnold's report concluded that the most important factor in successful mass production concerned the stability of the aircraft design itself. "A change in design during production," Arnold's report stated, "always causes more trouble than any other one factor."[87] Of all the lessons he learned during the Great War, this was the most important. But it was only part of the problem of developing a system that could handle the many complexities of aircraft production. Arnold visualized the solution in too-simple terms, and from too great a distance during the last year of the war.

At the top of the list of sixteen recommendations to ensure "airplane production in large quantities in time of necessity" was the acknowledgment that once production had begun, the line must be allowed to run undisturbed. Any new improvements should wait until a specified point. American industry was already capable of producing 30,000 airplanes each year in an emergency, Arnold concluded, and advanced aviation technologies and production methods would significantly improve upon that number. Mass production required certain sacrifices in technological advancement, he reported; the trick was to be aware of what was needed before production began, "and then to stick to it for a certain period even though it can be improved, until such time as the improvement can be incorporated without materially affecting production."[88]

Few believed in the ultimate capability of American aircraft production as Arnold did. His report suggested that the United States must lead the way in cooperation in aeronautical science, aviation technology, and military needs if an adequate buffer for mass production was ever to work as he envisioned. "There should be closer cooperation between the designer of the airplanes and accessories and those who will be required to operate the airplanes in time of emergency," Arnold reported, "for, in the last analysis, the man who operates the machine is the one who knows what he wants, and knows what should be required of a given plane and its accessories."[89] The United States had a long way to go to achieve such a goal.

Arnold finished his study with a forecast. Considering what he had gathered from his data, he said of the potential future of aircraft production: "The total estimated output of all existing and probable sources of supply, based upon extreme emergency conditions, would, at the time of maximum production, amount to 2,500 airplanes per month, unless some new type of airplane is developed which makes it possible to stamp out in metal the component parts, and thus do away with the long, tedious hand work necessary at present."[90]

✪   ✪   ✪   ✪   ✪

Arnold celebrated the armistice in France in the company of old friends such as Tommy Milling. One in particular, Billy Mitchell, who had impressively organized and led the massive air offensives at Saint-Mihiel and Meuse-Argonne, asked for Arnold's help when they returned to Washington. It was assumed that back in D.C., Mitchell would take up the reins of the Aeronautics Division.[91] Arnold obliged the man who had recalled him to flying in 1916—he did as Mitchell asked.

But Mitchell was not appointed chief of the Air Service. He was appointed director of Military Aeronautics, and Maj. Gen. Charles T. Menoher was made director of the Air Service. However, many airmen—including Arnold—who supported air-force operations as separate from supporting ground troops resented Menoher. His World War I experience had convinced him that in fact, air forces should support ground troops and little else. This opposed Mitchell's theories. Arnold wrote: "Our chief, General Menoher, was not only unable and wholly unwilling to cope with Mitchell's ideas, he could not handle Billy Mitchell. Also, to make matters worse, he did not fly much."[92] It was within the bounds of his new job that Mitchell launched his campaign to energize the Army's air arm. His insubordinate tactics led, eventually, to his court-martial.[93]

After returning from Europe, and just before Christmas 1918, Arnold, no longer needed in the rapidly shrinking War Department, received orders to return to Rockwell Field, California. There he was to assume the post of district supervisor, Western District of the Air Service. On 26 December Arnold was relieved of duty in Washington, and by early January the Arnold clan had packed up the house and were once again headed across the country to California.

From January to June 1919, Arnold supervised a portion of the United States's traditional postwar demobilization from Rockwell Field.[94] Soon, however, he found himself in charge of all Army aviation in the western United States under the command of Gen. Hunter Liggett, former commander of the First Army in France. Yet even while dealing with drastic reductions in the size of the Army air arm, Arnold tried promoting Army aviation any way he could.

Until the end of World War I, Arnold had been gaining experience and forging his tools, both as a military officer and as a man. His first thirty-two years had molded and shaped him, as he learned and sorted out those ideas he agreed with and those he only tolerated.

Arnold learned that industrial capacity in the United States had few boundaries, but those that existed needed much work. He continued making acquaintances within industry, scientific fields, political circles, and Hollywood that he utilized to the Air Corps's benefit in later years. Arnold had visited—in fact he had established—most air bases and ground training facilities during these past few years. During World War II, this background would allow him a greater ability to visualize the necessary process and to administratively lead training and expansion efforts. Arnold built a foundation of knowledge, albeit incomplete in some areas, in training, administration, production, supply, logistics, and communications. It was a foundation upon which his future assignments would build clearer understanding and necessary experience for the challenges that awaited him. He also developed his own theory of airpower employment—similar to Mitchell's, yet broader in its application—from logistics to precision bombing.

During the coming two decades, Arnold matured. He learned difficult lessons and faced adverse situations. His tools became tempered and finely honed during the years of cutbacks, demobilization and depression, enthusiastic technological advancement, and aeronautical discovery. At the same time, he continually expanded his network of individual and institutional contacts in industry, science, academia, and politics.

7

INTERWAR YEARS,
A DIFFICULT EDUCATION
(1918–29)

While dealing with massive reductions in the size of the Army, Colonel Arnold showcased aviation as best he could. It was not easy. Appropriations for air dropped from $460 million during fiscal year 1919 to $25 million the next. Wartime strength of the Air Service shrank from 190,000 officers and enlisted personnel in November 1918 to 81,000 only two months later. By the end of June 1919, the Air Service consisted of 5,500 officers and 21,500 enlisted. Equipment production was halted, contracts were terminated and training programs ceased; mountains of wartime machines were sold. In all, nearly 95 percent of the officers commissioned for the war and all of the wartime enlistees were discharged. Airfields and depot locations were abandoned in droves, making post–Cold War base-closure debates seem ludicrous in their small scope.[1] The American tradition of postwar demobilization continued, and American air forces were being gutted along with the rest of the Army and Navy.

Even as the demobilization continued, air shows or flying circuses remained popular events at Army airfields. At Rockwell Field, a flyover of more than 200 planes honoring World War I veterans awed huge crowds. The Rockwell Low Flying Team also thrilled onlookers with daring formation flying and stunts. At one of these events, Arnold "decorated" movie star Mary Pickford with a banner proclaiming her an Honorary Ace. At another, more seriously, Arnold decorated one of his most recent acquaintances, Maj. Carl Tooey Spaatz, with the French Croix de Guerre for downing three enemy aircraft in three weeks during the war.[2] The positive publicity generated by events such as these was desperately needed during the immediate postwar years.[3] Arnold realized public opinion's power as a tool for maintaining support for the ailing Air Service, but immediate results in the form of appropriations did not occur.[4]

As publicity stunts went, the amazing "Jimmy" Doolittle caught Arnold's attention after pulling off a dangerous flying trick for a gathered crowd at Rockwell Field. It is held that Cecil B. DeMille, famous filmmaker, had a motion-picture camera trained on an airplane that was coming in for a landing. Under the fuselage, between the wheels, sat a bold young aviator, Doolittle, his audacity caught on film. But the developed footage did not impress unit commander Col. Harvey S. Burwell, who immediately had his executive officer, likely Colonel Arnold, ground the young second lieutenant for one month. Later, despite such insane bravery—or perhaps because of it—Arnold would call on Jimmy Doolittle to orchestrate and lead the famous World War II raid on Tokyo.[5]

When Rockwell Field closed temporarily in May 1919, Arnold assumed duty at the Presidio, San Francisco, as air liaison officer for the Ninth Corps Area. Here Arnold met a young first lieutenant, Ira C. Eaker, assistant adjutant. Lieutenant Eaker (Infantry) was not yet twenty-three—ten years younger than Arnold. In their short time together, from January to July 1919, Arnold impressed Eaker as a "tremendous personality. He won your complete admiration and support just by being there."[6] Eaker, likewise, impressed Arnold with efficiency and loyalty, traits that were important to Arnold.[7] During subsequent tours together, Arnold used Eaker's writing skills—he had been trained in journalism—to complete three books. These were intended to educate airmen on the nature of their profession, the nature of flying, and the potential of airpower.[8] They attempted to delineate a common culture of the air: what made airmen different from soldiers and sailors.

Tooey Spaatz, a true war veteran and newfound friend, soon joined Arnold at the Presidio. Upon his return to the States in the fall of 1918, Spaatz had taken charge of the western flying circus based out of San Antonio, Texas, but he moved to the Presidio after the drawdown of such stunt units. In October 1919, he participated in the first transcontinental air race, the Transcontinental Reliability Test, devised by Billy Mitchell to publicize the potential of airplanes. Spaatz flew a modified DH-4 from the Presidio across the northern United States to Mineola, Long Island. Although he arrived first on the East Coast, he erroneously landed at the wrong airfield, allowing a slower but more accurate airman to claim the first prize. It was one of the few mistakes he ever made. Spaatz was extremely skilled at solving difficult problems. He got results; that was all Arnold needed to know.[9]

As if he had nothing else to do, Colonel Arnold also took command of the 818th Depot Squadron, San Francisco.[10] There, West Coast Air Service planes underwent modifications and improvements. At least the depot's nearness to the Presidio minimized inspection time away from home.

Having witnessed the deleterious effects of the rapid Air Service drawdown, Arnold was determined to do what he could to bolster support for airpower. Acting on orders from Maj. Gen. Charles T. Menoher, director of Air Service, Arnold established "forest patrols" over the western region. Although this concept had been suggested by the Forest Service as early as 1909, it was not until a decade later that an official request for forest patrols was made to secretary of war Newton D. Baker. Arnold, now Air Service Officer, Western Department, organized the patrols, consolidated his aircraft assets, deployed planes to locations near fire-prone areas, and delegated his airplanes according to range and endurance requirements until older Jennies could be replaced by longer-range, war-surplus DH-4s. By August Arnold's forest-patrol teams were serving from Oregon to Southern California as the eyes of the Forest Service. Besides fire spotting, the airmen mapped bug-infested areas and helped ground crews complete road surveys.[11]

By 30 June 1920, the worst of Army demobilization was over. The Army revoked its emergency wartime commissions, and officers reverted to their peacetime ranks. Thus, Arnold's orders reduced him to his permanent grade of captain. However, on 1 July he was promoted to the permanent rank of major. Technically, he never wore the rank of captain, but administrative paperwork required that a rank be shown on the discharge papers, and since he had never been a permanent major (or lieutenant colonel, for that matter), his last official rank, captain, was written in.[12]

Legend holds that Arnold walked into Spaatz's office after his rank had reverted and offered him the command, because their dates of rank had been reversed. This myth exaggerates what started as a simple practical joke between the spirited Arnold and the "straight man," Spaatz. Whereas Arnold was the resident expert in the administration of Western Department operations, Spaatz had changed duty locations every other month since the end of the war. He seemed always in-between jobs. Arnold's command was never in jeopardy, and both men knew it. Spaatz realized, however, that his opportunity for command in the same place as Arnold was less than if he were stationed elsewhere, and he requested a transfer in search of that opportunity.[13]

Rank notwithstanding, there was no doubt as to the effectiveness of Arnold's forest patrols. In August 1920, for example, the detachment stationed in Eugene, Oregon, reported more than 170 new fires. Near Red Bluff, California, fliers detected more than 100 fires in just one week. One eagle-eyed crew flying out of March Field spotted five fires within thirty minutes.[14] These early fire notifications saved thousands of acres of timber, and millions of dollars as well. Arnold's activities caught the public's and his commander's attention. A peacetime use for military airplanes kept the shrinking service in the air, at least for a while. By 1925, however, the Forest Service had obtained its own DH-4s and begun flying forest patrols without Air Service help. Two years later, the Forest Service contracted the task to civilian flying companies.[15]

More hazardous than searching for fires were border-patrol missions. Since Pershing's 1916 punitive expedition into Mexico in pursuit of Pancho Villa, Army airplanes had occasionally flown above the Mexican border. Searching for potential trouble, these missions covered the vast, open areas of the desert Southwest, an unforgiving territory. Air navigation was imprecise, and airplanes were not 100-percent reliable. Compass errors or engine malfunctions often resulted in life-or-death struggles for survival against the desert or the Mexicans. To make matters worse, in 1919 the Air Service tried to fly border patrols and forest-fire patrols with only limited resources.

Like his men and planes, Arnold became overtasked as he administered both programs. In June 1919 he met Brig. Gen. Billy Mitchell in El Paso, Texas, to discuss border-patrol issues. In May 1920 he traveled between Sacramento, Red Bluff, and Fresno, California; and Salem and Eugene, Oregon, in connection with forest-patrol station inspections. In between these appointments, Arnold traveled to Washington, D.C., in December 1919, to testify before the House Committee on Military Affairs.[16] He took care of the Western Department's administrative matters, and his subordinates ran the day-to-day flying operations.

On one mission, Arnold became personally involved with operations. When a DH-4 disappeared while on an inspection flight from Rockwell to Fort Huachuca, Arizona, Arnold remembered Colonel Glassford's delayed decision to search for a missing crew in late 1916. He quickly mounted the most extensive ground and aerial search possible. He launched every aircraft from Rockwell, called in fliers and planes from other bases, and even commandeered three visiting airplanes from cross-country visitors. He asked nearby infantry and cavalry units to canvass the proposed flight path on foot and on horseback. He sought and received help from Navy fliers stationed at the naval air station in San Diego.

In times of crisis, Arnold did not hesitate to utilize all airpower assets available—Army, Navy, and civilian. The effort proved futile. The plane had crashed near the top of nearby Cuyamaca Peak in fog, thirty minutes after takeoff, and was totally destroyed, killing the crew. It was only by chance, nearly five months after the crew had been given up for dead, that a farmer discovered the wreck.[17] Arnold's actions in the matter had clearly been driven by his earlier experiences at Rockwell, when he had been so outraged by command inaction that repeating such a mistake was unthinkable. Yet the ability to find missing planes had not much improved in five years.

Arnold did not participate in the search as a pilot. At that time, he was suffering from acute gastric ulcers and was medically grounded—little wonder, considering his travel schedule and extensive responsibilities. Arnold suggested that his internal injuries had resulted from the crash landing he had made in a LePere at Rockwell Field in 1919. However, there is no medical evidence supporting this claim. On 22 July 1922, he wrote his father: "I have been

X-rayed and flouriscoped until there should be nothing within me they haven't seen. I have swallowed 75 feet of garden hose and with great effort kept one end in my stomach for 3½ hours. To make matters worse they further aggravated me by taking samples out every 15 min. Then when they have taken all their pictures—charted their specimens they tell me exactly what they did two years ago—They think my symptoms are indicative of a gastric ulcer but they are not sure."[18]

Medical orders grounded Arnold from 1 July to 3 October 1922.[19] His grounding was welcomed at home: the previous August, in 1921, Bee had given birth to their fourth child and third son, John Linton, nicknamed Jackie.[20] Jackie, the Arnold jewel, earned the reputation of a perfect child, one with whom Arnold spent many peaceful hours during those months while his ulcer healed.

The episode with the flight doctors also served to curtail Arnold's already moderate drinking habits. Early in his career he had sometimes drunk alcohol while entertaining friends, but from 1922 on, Arnold rarely drank at all. When he did, he never drank to drunkenness.[21] He often acted as bartender at family gatherings, but did not drink. Nevertheless, he remained the life of any party.[22] It was not until the manifestation of heart disease in the mid-1930s that orders from his physician prescribed one or two servings of alcohol each day to thin the blood.[23]

During these years on the West Coast, Arnold's close working relationship with Doolittle, Eaker, and Spaatz took shape. All became critically important associates and remained so for the rest of Arnold's career. But Billy Mitchell contributed the most to Arnold's personal development and understanding of the politics of national military airpower. His association with Mitchell became as important as any he had during his life, and their deference was mutual. "But do not ever forget," Mitchell wrote Arnold, "that I have very high respect for your ability and some day may be able to show it."[24]

Mitchell's zealous, insubordinate approach to creating an independent air force taught Arnold how not to tackle political problems. He later recalled that Mitchell himself had warned him away from outspoken methods that he had been using to draw attention to airpower. Mitchell, son of a U.S. senator from Wisconsin and well-off monetarily, was aware of his financial ability to survive expulsion from the Army, while most of his followers had no such means.[25]

While Arnold successfully stirred publicity out West, Mitchell held most of the aviation headlines everywhere else. On 21 and 22 July 1921, Mitchell's bombers sank the German battleship *Ostfriesland,* considered unsinkable by most naval officers (the United States did not sign an official peace treaty with Germany until August 1921, during Warren Harding's administration). The wild publicity—favorable to the Air Service—marked the event as the first major victory over the Navy in terms of service roles and missions. Mitchell's success led to the immediate development of an aircraft designed specifically to fulfill the dream of true strategic bombardment, the NBL-1, at that time the largest airplane in the world.

The NBL-1 (or XNBL-1), more commonly referred to by the name of its designer, Walter H. Barling, was built by the Wittemann Aircraft Corporation, Hasbrouck Heights, New Jersey, during 1923. The Barling Bomber featured three wings; two contained flight-control surfaces, while the mid-wing provided a lifting surface only. The first American airplane built with a wingspan as long as the distance of the Wright Brothers' first flight, 120 feet, the Barling stood three stories tall and 65 feet long. Six Liberty engines (four tractors and two pushers) provided thrust enough to allow a cruising speed of 100 miles an hour, and the 2,000-gallon fuel capacity allowed the plane to remain airborne for a full twelve hours without bombs. It was capable of carrying one 10,000-pound bomb (still under development) for two hours. The immense Barling carried seven self-protection guns at five locations, and it required a crew of four.[26]

Additionally, this behemoth contained a unique landing-gear system consisting of two "trucks," one of them toward the forward area of the plane for landing, the other aft for taxiing. When the pilot lowered the front truck during landing, the initial shock was absorbed. Then, as the plane settled to the ground, the pilot transferred the load to the rear truck and the tail skid.[27] The Barling flew for the first time at McCook Field on 22 August 1923, but it performed poorly.[28] It could not fly directly between Dayton and Washington while fully fueled, because the Appalachian Mountains exceeded its service ceiling. When fueled and loaded with simulated bombs, it was so heavy that only two runways in the country could tolerate its weight.[29]

Still, the Barling was not a total loss. Valuable wind-tunnel data, parts design, and other aeronautical-engineering problems were addressed and solved during its development. In that way, the Barling influenced the design of the B-17, B-24, and B-29 bombers that became the backbone of the United States's strategic-bombing campaign during World War II. Additionally, a huge portable hangar designed and built specifically for the Barling employed construction techniques that were used as aircraft size and airborne mobility increased. Furthermore, fuel hoses were created to decrease fueling time. No plane had ever held so much gas, and normal hoses would have required excessively long ground delays for refueling.

At this time, however, Air Service planners perceived the 40,000-pound Barling as only a stepping stone to massive 200,000-pound bombers. As described in *U.S. Air Service* magazine, "the Barling Bomber is to be looked upon as a small big airplane rather than a big small one."[30] Although Arnold later found the Barling to be operationally worthless, he also realized that sometimes "the full-scale article must be built to get the pattern for the future."[31]

Strategic bombers needed to be able to fly tremendous distances. To increase aircraft range for pursuit planes and bombers, Arnold approved the trials of a new, dangerous, potentially revolutionary advance in aviation operations—midair refueling. Nothing more than hoses, ropes, and gas cans provided such capability. Audacity and fearlessness played a larger role in the success of the trials than did the machinery involved. On 27 June 1923, 1st Lts. Frank Seifert and Virgil Hine achieved two successful contacts in a modified DH-4 aircraft. A second, even more successful test occurred in August.[32]

Arnold had no doubt of the potential import of this event, still considered a stunt by most of the general public, and even by many aviators as well. Arnold's Rockwell Field "Holiday Greetings" letter revealed his pride:

> In performing the two aforementioned flights Rockwell Field presented to the world a new mode of replenishing gasoline and oil supply of an airplane while in flight. While the great benefits to be derived from refueling in the air are probably unappreciated at this time by many people in aviation circles, it can only be a matter of a few years until the pioneer refueling work done at this station will be the basis for operating airplanes on long cross-country flights whenever it is needed to carry great loads or carry materiel or personnel to greater distances than the capacity of gas and oil tanks will permit. . . . These things were done in spite of the handicaps under which we labored . . . such as decrease in personnel, limited appropriations and inadequate supplies during the year that has passed . . . and were only possible by every one working at the Depot cooperating to the fullest extent and giving their utmost support to all projects underway, loyalty to their superiors and strict compliance with instructions received regardless of whether or not the individual believed such instructions to be the best possible under the circumstances. Our successes during the past year are such that we should all be proud of them.[33]

This memo not only sent out heartfelt congratulations on a job well done, it also delineated those qualities that Arnold demanded of and admired in his subordinates: humility, loyalty, diligence, and strict compliance with orders.

In the midst of the remarkable accomplishments of the refueling trials, tragedy struck the Arnold family as young Bill Bruce contracted a nearly fatal case of scarlet fever. Then, suddenly and inexplicably, two-year-old John Linton became ill and died, on 30 July 1923. It was later determined that he had suffered a ruptured appendix. The loss of their son hit both Bee and Harley with tremendous force. Arnold's hair turned totally gray by the end of that summer. But he had his work to occupy his time and his mind. Bee had the children, and they were her life.[34] Eventually, the loss was too much for her to handle on her own. By May 1924, she had retreated to Ardmore to recover from not only the loss of her child, but also from past childbirth- and obstetrics-related surgery. Bee needed to regain her health.[35]

It took almost a full year before Harley could even write of his own feeling of loss. On 2 June 1924, he wrote one simple sentence: "We all miss you very much [Beadle] and in addition I, somehow now more than for some time, miss the presence of John Linton's sunny smile."[36] With the expert help of Eula the nursemaid, Harley kept the children out in California. This allowed Bee to recuperate in peace, both mentally and physically.

Now the commanding officer at the newly reopened Rockwell Field, Arnold continued to operate forest patrols on a diminished scale. He wrote to Bee, "I took Red," Paul G. Redington, chief forester in California District 5, "up for a ride over the mountains back of Quiamaca and we picked up three fires. One was a very big one over about fifteen miles East of Quiamaca. . . . The fire had started down in the bottom of that canyon and had burned up to the top."[37] This flight was one of his last forest-patrol missions in California.

On 10 June 1924, Arnold received a personal letter directly from Maj. Gen. Mason Patrick, director of Air Service. It said:

> I recollect very clearly that when at Rockwell Field last year I told you that you would remain there for another year. The time has now come when I think you can render better service somewhere else. I am asking for an order which will bring you here to Washington where you must report about the first of September, and you will for the first six months thereafter take a course in the Army Industrial College. I am satisfied that your previous experience will fit you for this duty and that the completion of the course will make you a more valuable officer. After the course is concluded, you will be on duty in my office.[38]

Patrick, a classmate of "Black Jack" Pershing, had been so impressed with Arnold's performance on the West Coast that he had added a personal commendation to his military record.[39]

The move was not a surprise to Arnold, who matter-of-factly sent Bee a copy of Patrick's letter. In this instance, considering Bee's overall condition, Arnold probably welcomed the move back to Washington, only a few hours from Ardmore and both sets of eager grandparents. Bee, who had just undergone additional surgery in mid-June, was likely relieved by the move as well. She was well enough by the end of August to return to Coronado, help pack the household, and move back East once again.[40]

Before her arrival, to celebrate the Fourth of July, Arnold openly demonstrated his affection for children by hosting an ice-cream social for the entire population of Rockwell Field's youth. Aside from his own, twelve attended. "They all had two ice cream cones and after they had finished them I gave them the freezer," in which the cream was iced, "to clean up. They went at it with spoons, hands and anything else that they could find. They all had a beautifully, smearry [*sic*], creamy time. Sticky but happy."[41] The vision of a goo-covered, giddy Major Arnold surrounded by eager ice-cream-loving children is one not normally associated with H. H. Arnold.

Other social affairs in the area generated a somewhat more stern reaction. At an officers' call at Crissy Field, the Presidio, Arnold was disgusted by the behavior of "so-called ladies" who, after imbibing too heavily of the mild punch, "forgot that certain things are not done by refined people. . . . Late in the evening one might have thought that he was at a soldier's dance rather than at an officer's dance."[42] The clear distinction between officers and enlisted men in Arnold's mind is apparent in these harsh remarks, as is a certain disdain for public drunkenness among officers and their wives.

Competitions between Rockwell and Crissy in skeet shooting and track and field events took place regularly. Arnold strongly believed in the positive effects of friendly competition among the troops. But in one instance, the "friendliness" Arnold intended was discarded by the Crissy participants. Arnold wrote that he had told the teams "that this series of athletic events was gotten up for the purpose of everyone getting out of doors and having a good time but if they were going into it for the purpose of winning everything and for the sole purpose of getting the cup, I would give them the cup now with the compliments of Rockwell Field."[43]

Arnold felt that some on the Crissy Field teams, who picked the events and had twice as many officers to choose from on the post, were first-class whiners. He punctuated his feelings by writing, "I hope that we take every point that remains."[44] Arnold had trouble with anyone he felt simply "crabbed" all the time. He wanted to prove to them that complaining did not solve problems. In any activity, a team spirit and hard work were essential to success. Arnold thought so much of the overall team effort at Rockwell that he later referred to it as the "West Point of military aviation."[45]

The summer of 1924 tested the Arnolds' relationship. Aside from the personal tragedy they endured with Jackie's death, Harley commanded at Rockwell, Bee had several more or less severe medical problems, and they struggled financially, though they could afford a nursemaid. Communications from coast to coast were most often accomplished by letter or telegram, since phone service was extremely expensive. Harley had little understanding of Bee's female troubles and might have seemed callous in his letters suggesting that she simply get over her mental problems and return to him as her old self. Bee did not help much either, as she rarely wrote, and much of the information Harley received was relayed from family and friends back East. This arrangement would have pressed the limits of any marriage, but the Arnolds survived the difficulties and were soon reunited in Washington, D.C.

Before returning to Washington, Major Arnold, now looking older than his years, took leave for the entire month of August. He and Bee packed up the house and immediately headed to Ardmore. The children had missed their mother, and he had missed his wife. By 2 September 1924, Arnold returned to

Washington as a member of the Army Industrial College class to graduate in January 1925. He was not totally happy about being back in Washington.[46] Further, Bee had suggested that she and the children would remain in Ardmore. Arnold voiced his protest against such a decision: "Nothing to that stuff—If I could get the house now, I would take, beg or steal time off and go up to Phila[delphia] and bring you down here tonight. Washington at best is a nightmare and without you it is H_____l."[47]

Coincidentally, this same letter recounted the arrival in Washington of the Air Service "Flight Around the World." The first successful circumnavigation of the globe was a massive cooperative logistical effort. Besides the Fairfield Air Depot's prepositioning of supplies and parts, the U.S. Navy, Coast Guard, State Department, Signal Corps, and other agencies held responsibility for many important parts of the mission, from passports to weather reports. The flight had begun in Seattle on 6 April 1924, initially consisting of four Douglas World Cruisers (DWC), and it took a total of 175 days to complete.[48] Before the Arnolds departed Rockwell, Bee had even taken a ride in Lowell Smith's Douglas Cruiser on the way to Seattle for the "hop off" of the flight. Smith piloted the *Chicago,* one of two planes to make the entire trip. "After feeling the steadiness and strength of the plane," she explained to her mother with a certain clairvoyance, "I am not one bit skeptical about the trip."[49]

Upon the Around the World Flyers' arrival in Washington, D.C., they were greeted by the president and the entire upper echelon of the War Department. After the political activities and photographs, Arnold met with a few of the crew, 1st Lts. Lowell Smith and Erik Nelson, and they discussed the successes and failures of the airplanes on the journey. "They were all very outspoken in their praise for the Rockwell engines and also outspoken in their condemnation of the McCook jobs."[50] Reports of this nature did not build any strong feelings of confidence within Arnold as far as the capabilities of McCook Field. His personal experience with this West Coast depot seemed much reinforced. Nonetheless, the flight marked a new milestone in aviation history, and the Air Service had been responsible for its success.

Arnold was one of two Air Service officers in his Industrial College class of thirteen. The course, only the second time it had been taught, was administered as a series of case studies examining a cross section of industrial and military problems that had been encountered in previous experiences. During the six-month course, students worked in small groups on several cases. When sufficient study and examination yielded a solution, they briefed the rest of the class and the faculty, and a critical discussion and evaluation followed the briefing. A mix of service-branch representatives was intentionally sought, in hopes that the "free and frank interchange of ideas would tend toward interservice understanding and the harmonizing of procurement practices in all branches."[51] At the Army Industrial College, Arnold was exposed to many of the intricacies of the procurement and logistics system operating in the Army.

More important, he became familiar with both the nature and the potential of the national military complex, with its civilian production and its brutal fiscal realities.

World War I experiences with aircraft production had disappointed Arnold, and now he knew why: Army planners still insisted upon the American auto industry as the primary contractor to manufacture airplanes in times of crisis. Arnold lobbied for a different approach, arguing that the aircraft industry should remain the primary contractor, while the auto industry should be utilized for small-parts production and other subcontracting jobs. This short college assignment was one of the most valuable of Arnold's career, one that he said "was to stand me in good stead in later years."[52]

Not only did Major Arnold formulate a plan for future expansion, but he realized that his civilian industry contacts from earlier tours would be essential if a sizable production scheme had any hope of success. Glenn Curtiss, Elmer Sperry and Henry Ford were only a few of those contacts. Additionally, Arnold's friend Donald Douglas, California aircraft manufacturing mogul, was vital to explaining many of these links between industrial capacity, fiscal capability, and military necessity.[53]

Beginning in February 1925, Arnold served as Patrick's chief of information. In this function he remained vigilant to new developments in foreign and domestic aviation, in both the civilian and the military arenas. He also found time to write for *U.S. Air Service* magazine. "The Performance of Future Airplanes" was published in the July 1925 issue.

In this article, Arnold explained that long-term predictions of aircraft performance were difficult, but in the near term—four or five years—there existed a "fair enough basis on which to estimate something about how fast, how far, and how high airplanes of various types may be expected to go."[54] He used a basic linear interpretation of available data, such as aircraft speed records, to forecast future performance. Although Arnold's approach is simplistic today, in 1925 he forged new ground by making moderate predictions concerning airplane improvements. Forecasting the performance of aircraft always interested Arnold.

Moreover, he demonstrated a remarkable understanding of the potential of aeronautics when he wrote: "Somewhere, we know, there should be a 'terminal velocity' governed by the head resistance of the airplane and the power available to drive it. When this point is reached, however, it is probable that the wings of the airplane will have mostly disappeared, it being presumed that sufficient lift to support the craft in the air will be provided at such great speeds with an extremely small amount of surface."[55]

The sleek Lockheed F-104 Starfighter immediately comes to mind as a modern manifestation of Arnold's vision. Despite the fact that propellers were seen as the only practical method of propulsion in 1925, Arnold suggested that an engine might one day be designed that "weighs only a fraction of our present power plants for the same horse power and which requires only a fraction of the fuel on which to operate."[56] Additionally, Arnold discussed range, altitude, and endurance limits during that period. He mentioned the necessity for "provisions for the pilot," such as oxygen masks, sealed cockpits, and electric flight suits, as ways to improve the parameters of flight.[57] To fully realize the potential of the machine, the performance of the pilot required maximization. Even in 1925, Arnold eclipsed most aviation authorities in understanding the capability and potential of airplanes.

Meanwhile, he failed to get his close friend and mentor, Billy Mitchell, to temper his language and writings while campaigning for an independent air force. Mitchell, still rocking the Navy's boat, had been "exiled" to Fort Sam Houston in San Antonio, Texas, in February 1925, the same month Arnold graduated from the Army Industrial College.

There was some irony in Mitchell's treatment of airpower in sister services. Although he has been characterized as an advocate of independent air forces, Mitchell held no prejudice against Navy or Marine Corps pilots. Just before he left for Texas, Mitchell wrote a letter to John K. Montgomery, who had worked for him in Washington, clarifying his views on airpower. "Actual flying officers of the Naval forces are one of us [Air Corps airmen] in every way; they are as capable, efficient and as daring as this fine class of Americans are. . . . Every measure that I have advocated, been consulted about or projected, handles them exactly in the same way as Army aviators, Marine aviators and other flying officers. This will always continue to be my policy."[58]

To Mitchell, real airpower had no service affiliation. For if it did, its greatest potential was lost. He realized that those who understood airpower the best applied it the best. To Mitchell, that was clearly not the high command of the U.S. Navy. His belief formed the foundation of Arnold's later concept for a unified air force—all airplanes under one command. Arnold, as one of Mitchell's "boys," felt as he did, but Arnold tried to unify airpower in the combat environment with teamwork and competition, as he had done at Fort Riley and Rockwell Field. He wrote that Mitchell in uniform "had made military dumbness a national crime, and maybe in the long run he was right."[59]

Soon, Mitchell returned to face a military court-martial for conduct prejudicial to good order and military discipline, and for conduct bringing discredit upon the military service. The charges against him had originated in the office of the president of the United States, Calvin Coolidge. This fact played directly into Mitchell's ultimate purpose: to sway public opinion toward an independent air force. Arnold, as chief of Patrick's Information Department, became actively involved in the court-martial and acted as Mitchell's Washington liaison officer. He, along with Spaatz and many others, testified before the court on Mitchell's behalf, even though Patrick had admonished the younger officers not to become too closely associated with Mitchell at a personal level. Career progression might be jeopardized by such an association.[60]

Just before the trial, the Morrow Board, an investigation into the use of aircraft for national defense that had been ordered by President Coolidge in September 1925, determined that five-year planning and a slight increase in personnel would rectify the shortcomings of the Air Service. The board also recommended changing the name of the service to the Air Corps.[61] To Arnold's chagrin, Mitchell chose simply to read massive segments of his writings on independent air employment into the record. Watching the testimony, Arnold felt like urging Mitchell to put his book away and tell story to the board, as he had told it to him and others so many times before, with fire and conviction. It was not to be.[62]

The court-martial began immediately after the Morrow Board completed its investigations. For the most part, Arnold could only watch silently as his friend and mentor went down in flames. But he now perceived himself a target for Patrick. Arnold had lobbied several politicians for support of the most recent appropriations bill for air. In so doing, he had produced a fact sheet using Army supplies and equipment; it had once been suggested to Arnold that such practice was acceptable. Bee recalled that he had even been encouraged to contact congressmen in search of local support. But that had been out West in California, while he had been a commander far from the hub of national politics. In Washington, military officers did not lobby congressional representatives.

It has been suggested that this administrative violation, not Arnold's testimony in the Mitchell trial, spurred General Patrick, possibly insecure in his command authority over a group of upstart airmen, to bring charges against Major Arnold. Just one year short of retirement eligibility, Patrick gave Arnold the choice between a court-martial and resignation from the Army.[63]

Arnold's choice was impossible, and he had only twenty-four hours in which to make it. Bee recalled that he came home "completely deflated."[64] But not for long: she reminded him about previous encouragements made by high-level staff in Washington while he had been stationed in California. Arnold also remembered that an old West Point buddy of his, now fairly high up in the Judge Advocate General's office, might provide him sound legal advice. However, it remains unknown whether he actually consulted that officer. Arnold believed he had done nothing drastically wrong. He admitted acting against Army administrative regulations, but nothing deserving of a court.

The next day he approached Patrick, who until this time had been supportive of Arnold, and demanded the court-martial. Although their conversation remained undocumented, Arnold certainly reminded the general that it was Patrick himself who had advocated such lobbying of congressional officials in the past. These facts would have emerged in a court, and Patrick would have realized that.[65]

Arnold was backed into a very tight corner. He did not want to leave the Army, despite a prosperous national economy and plentiful civilian job opportunities for pilots. To salvage what remained of his career, he reacted as any desperate man might; he used any tool he could think of to survive. In this case, he threatened to expose (some might call it blackmail) his superior officer. He threatened to reveal facts that would undoubtedly, he believed, damage Patrick's reputation and position.

Arnold had nothing to lose. If his plan failed he was out; if he did nothing he was out; but if it worked, he might later get another chance. He had survived disastrous performance reports before. When the situation required it, Arnold could be as ruthless as any officer in the Army. Whether or not it was because Patrick chose not to face potentially damaging testimony in a court, he sent Arnold to the "worst post in the army," Fort Riley, Kansas. There he was to command the 16th Observation Squadron, "whatever that was," Arnold later quipped.[66] At least he would be flying airplanes.

On the heels of Mitchell's court-martial and Arnold's exile came an inkling of the realization that airpower had greater potential than had yet been realized. The Air Corps Act of 1926, signed into law by President Coolidge on 2 July 1926, provided for modest expansion of the air arm over a five-year period. Chiefs of industry perceived the Morrow Board and the Air Corps Act as the catalyst that would change things for Army aviation. Appropriations for aircraft began to rise, as did negotiated contracts authorizing experimental aircraft. These appropriations and the system of negotiated contracts allowed the aircraft industry to avoid many of the deleterious effects of the Great Depression that began in 1929.[67]

In 1926 the Air Service became the Air Corps, an assistant secretary of war (for air) was created, and additional general officers were authorized to act as assistants to the chief of the Air Corps, Maj. Gen. Mason Patrick. F. Trubee Davidson, an aviation enthusiast and the administrator of the Guggenheim Fund for the Promotion of Aeronautics, was named as the man who would act as the civilian link to secretary of war Dwight F. Davis. Arnold once described Davidson as a man who listened well and "knew his onions."[68]

Davidson's ties to the Guggenheim Fund were crucial. Daniel Guggenheim, wealthy entrepreneur, saw great potential in the technological advancement of aviation across the vast expanses of the United States. He, as well as his son, Harry, saw aviation as a method to increase commerce. Aviation, particularly education in aeronautical engineering, was a worthy investment. Trubee Davidson held the same philosophy.[69]

In 1926 the Guggenheim Fund began selecting schools to receive significant aeronautical-department stipends. The Guggenheims "wanted to make aviation practical, safe, and of great value to the commercial development of this country."[70] Although the intent of the fund was to improve American civil aviation, ultimately the same aeronautical engineers trained at Guggenheim universities became involved in the design and production of military planes. The Guggenheims poured millions of dollars into the national education system for the betterment of American aviation. Monies allowed building of facilities and hiring of gifted young aeronautical engineers.

Initially these schools were concentrated on the East Coast. After Robert Millikan made a well-argued case, however, Caltech also appeared on the list of seven universities that launched American aeronautics into competition with the Europeans.[71] The key to Millikan's argument centered around acquiring the talented Hungarian aeronautical engineer Theodore von Kármán and his scientific methodology. Although Harry Guggenheim favored Ludwig Prandtl, Europe's leading aeronautical scientist, Millikan finally agreed that Kármán's youth, vibrance, and practicality better fit the hip Pasadena scene.[72]

Robert Millikan's goals were to thrust Caltech science programs to national preeminence and to bring aviation interest—and industry—to Southern California.[73] Millikan believed that science, "knowledge of the facts, the laws, and the process of nature," was vital to American destiny, as long as it was applied properly to practical uses such as aviation. Others held similar beliefs, but Millikan, supported by Guggenheim money, accelerated the building-up process at Caltech.[74] Daniel Guggenheim himself took an interest in Caltech, Millikan, and the possibility of luring a notable European away from that continent. Thus, the foundations of American aeronautical engineering germinated just as Arnold arrived at Fort Riley.

Coincidentally, Arnold's first major book was published just after the Air Corps was named. It was a technical summary, *Airmen and Aircraft: An Introduction to Aeronautics*. The purpose of the book, as Arnold described it in his son Bruce's copy at Fort Riley in September 1926, was as follows: "This book should in future years be a means whereby you can compare the aircraft of that day with the aircraft as you now see it. The development in the next 20 years will be most marked."[75]

By Christmas 1926, with Mitchell martyred and Arnold exiled to the Army's largest cavalry post, the Arnolds entered their new assignment with tremendous trepidation. Brig. Gen. Ewing E. "Barnie" Booth, the commander at Fort Riley, had been a judge on Mitchell's court. The Arnolds did not know whether Booth would throw them "out into the street" or allow them to move in. Fortunately, with open arms and an open mind, Booth welcomed the Arnold family—it was a great relief to Beadle.[76]

Not only did Arnold command the 16th Observation Squadron, he also inherited the responsibility for supplying air assets to the entire Seventh Corps area, essentially the entire midwestern United States. Arnold also put his flight experience to use as the senior air instructor at Riley, where he was able to spread the word about airpower to many of the most promising young cavalrymen in the Army. He ensured that as many of the students as possible actually flew as observers in one of the antiquated DH-4s or JN-3s that provided the air training on the post.

By the end of the year, Arnold had received Booth's highest recommendation and support for his request to attend the Command and General Staff School at Fort Leavenworth. "I consider that the progress in training between the Air Corps and the other combat units of this post has been of exceptional value and is improving all the time. His method of instruction and training of observers, 90 of whom are taking the course here, is exceptionally good. In fact, I can not conceive of a more desirable condition existing than does exist here between Major Arnold and his unit and the other units in this post. . . . I shall be very sorry to see Major Arnold leave the post but feel that his excellent services here entitle him to as favorable a recommendation as I can give him."[77]

In essence, Arnold had participated in the air arm's first joint training and education program. Airmen taught ground soldiers the strengths and weaknesses of their weapons, while cavalry and infantry officers reciprocated.[78]

But not everything succeeded at Riley. During one "concentration exercise," night reconnaissance flights were dismal failures. Crews dropped flares on ground troops, could not locate troop concentrations, or were so engrossed in flying the airplane that they neglected to observe at all. "Net result—zero," Arnold noted.[79] Night-flight capability was hampered by inadequate flight instrumentation in military airplanes. Flying at night under most conditions except full moonlight resembled flying in clouds; it required special instrumentation and training not yet developed and tested by the Army Air Corps.

Fort Riley, despite its reputation as a mediocre location, turned out to be one of the Arnold's most pleasant and personally satisfying assignments. Arnold himself continued to demonstrate a certain strength and vitality. The arrival of his newest son, David Lee, occurred in February 1927 and would be the last Arnold birth. Bee had recovered from her various surgeries and was enjoying life on the plains; she really loved her stay at Fort Riley.[80] Major Arnold, however, carried one heavy personal burden: he had been deeply scarred by his problems with Mason Patrick.

Arnold's autobiography remained lukewarm toward that officer, but a personal letter to his brother Clifford, on 15 March 1927 from Fort Riley, was written in the form of a fable and revealed Arnold's feelings. His description labeled Patrick the "King of the Egos," small of stature and of mind. Further, "he [Patrick] knew little of the arts and sciences of his tribe but was wont to put up a bold front always endeavoring to put his subjects in awe of him by drowning their advice and counsel in long sentences of nothingness and froth."[81] Arnold perceived that Patrick had used him as a "goat to sacrifice to re-establish himself in the eyes of the people."[82] As described above, Arnold began harboring these feelings after Patrick's objections to both his lobbying efforts and his testimony before the Morrow Board and the Mitchell court. In both cases, Arnold had made Patrick appear to be uninformed as a commander in front of many of his peers, particularly when Arnold, unknown to Patrick, arranged for thirty-five Air Corps airplanes to fly over the Capitol during his testimony. The airplanes, he exaggerated, represented "everything we could get together from all over the United States."[83] He ordered the majority of operational Air Corps aircraft to buzz the Capitol in order to illustrate the service's weakness.[84]

It is unlikely that Arnold intended to diminish Patrick's reputation. He had received strong performance reports from Patrick until after the "flyover" testimony, during which Patrick—rightfully so—felt "back-doored" by Arnold. The major would have done better to inform his boss of the nature of his planned testimony, including the multi-aircraft flyover of the Capitol, despite Patrick's annoying propensity to be inattentive to some of his staff officers, such as Arnold.

Bee verified that Arnold's relationship with Patrick deteriorated after these events. "Oh, no he [Arnold] didn't get along well personally with Patrick! Gen. Patrick threw a bottle of ink at him once. . . . I didn't like him. He was a superficial, insincere type . . . and he was egotistical."[85] After Mitchell's trial, Arnold had little personal fondness for Patrick. He successfully concealed these fiery, yet perhaps immature, feelings at the professional level, demonstrating remarkable restraint in the face of what he perceived as an illegitimate exile and a scathing proficiency report.

Patrick wrote: "This officer displays above average intelligence . . . in my opinion . . . in judgement and common sense, he fell below average . . . I think he is liable to lose his head. . . . I should now hesitate to entrust to him any important mission."[86] The collapse of the relationship was mutual.

Arnold's change of heart toward Patrick demonstrated both his strong feelings about anyone in authority whom he did not respect, and his own lack of emotional maturity. Arnold took Patrick's actions against him personally, with a certain amount of childlike anger. His extreme emotionalism concerning this issue may also reflect the angst that he felt about being removed from Washington, the center of Army Air Corps power.

In reality, reassigning Arnold to Fort Riley did him a tremendous service. Here he interacted with cavalrymen and taught them about airpower from an airman's perspective. He went as far as to write a basic airpower textbook to use at the Command and General Staff School while he was a student there.[87] In a real way, Patrick helped Arnold's career by forcing his interaction with the ground Army.

Arnold must have enjoyed his tour too, for it was at Fort Riley that he made his choice to remain a military officer despite the feeling that he had suffered numerous career disappointments. He had never been assigned to the cavalry, even after repeated requests. Ironically, he worked with the cavalry as an airman. He had been denied the opportunity to participate in combat during the Great War, primarily because Army leaders thought that his experience with Air Service supply and logistics was irreplaceable. He had testified on Mitchell's behalf despite warnings from his superiors.

Additionally, the national economic picture was very good. The New York Stock Exchange was higher than it had been on the same date for the previous five years. Cotton and coffee hit all-time highs in the market, and General Motors reported record profits during the week of 23–30 July 1927. Even in 1928, according to Donald Douglas, Wall Street was booming. "Anything was a cinch for financing . . . we had a good well established business, a good record over a number of years, we were making money."[88]

By June 1927, Arnold had reached his twentieth year of military service. Twenty years' service entitled him half pay and full benefits in retirement. He even went out of his way to attend his West Point twentieth class reunion—"1907, Never Again!"[89] Perhaps the old class motto crossed his mind as he labored over his decision to remain in the Army or give up his career. That summer, John K. Montgomery, a captain in the Air Reserve and president of American International Airways (a branch of Pan Am), offered Arnold a lucrative position as the first president of Pan Am Airlines, including significant stock options and an impressive salary.[90]

Civilian airline companies were just beginning to swell with orders as designs and positive publicity began to reach new peaks. Donald Douglas, Larry Bell, Jack Northrop, and others were feeling the early impact of aviation production in the military and commercial markets. "From mid-1927, when Lindbergh mania was at its peak, to the end of 1929, when the stock market fell apart, the rising level of investment in aviation reached tidal wave proportions." Arnold had an offer to get in on the ground floor.[91]

On 24 July 1927, Arnold replied: "As much as I would like to tell you that I will resign and take up work with the company, I hesitate doing it on account of the obligations which I have with my family." He suggested that he might take four months' leave to work for Pan Am, and then make his final decision.[92] This leave was apparently never taken, even though Montgomery called Maj. Jack Jouett, an Army personnel officer in Washington and friend of both Arnold and Montgomery, to expedite the request for it.[93] Family concerns appeared to be foremost on Arnold's mind at the time his final decision was made. Remarkably, despite the overwhelming advantages available in the commercial sector, Major Arnold and his family remained in the Army.

But in his memoirs, Arnold never mentioned his family as a motive. He wrote, "I couldn't very well quit the service under fire."[94] One writer has suggested that the frustrated Major Arnold had many things to accomplish in the Air Corps, many ideas to test.[95] At that moment, however, there was no chance that Arnold would ever hold a position allowing him to test anything. He had been banished from Washington, his reputation tarnished, and sent to an undesirable post—for aviators, anyway—as punishment for his clear violation of official regulations. Henry Harley Arnold was lucky he was still an Army aviator at all.

It is difficult to determine precisely why Arnold decided to continue his career in the Army. If his family truly came first, a civil airline presidency plus his Army retirement check at half pay would have afforded him an extremely comfortable life. He could have settled in one location, spent more time with his family, and forever escaped the political and military bureaucracies he claimed he hated.

There are other considerations that might explain what otherwise appears an irrational decision. Perhaps he simply loved flying so much that he was unwilling to give up the opportunity to fly military airplanes—even for a high-paying executive desk job. Additionally, and perhaps as important, Arnold enjoyed military command and the many opportunities to travel the country and the world. The wanderlust of his youth may have contributed to his final decision to remain a military aviator.[96] The Arnold family tradition of patriotism and military service added pressure to remain on active duty. Arnold's father, and two of his brothers, remained very active in the Pennsylvania National Guard. Arnold's strict upbringing and his father's stern example had instilled the importance of weathering adversity as part of life. All of these factors doubtlessly played a part in his final decision to remain in the service of his country, despite dismal potential for advancement through the ranks.

Arnold made a variety of contributions during his time at Fort Riley. He indoctrinated cavalry officers in the uses of airpower. He wrote children's stories about pilots and flying and named the hero after his middle son, Bill Bruce. In all, he wrote six Bill Bruce books, from 1926 to 1928, earning about $200 for each one. He also wrote books for his other two living sons that were never published.[97] The Davey Lee series told the tale of a young West Point cadet who created an unpiloted atomic bomb in the basement of a hidden laboratory. However, the political climate forbade publication of such a children's story in 1947. Another story included adventures with the Kettering Flying Bug and the secrecy surrounding that weapon.[98]

His unit delivered President Coolidge's vacation mail for a time. On one occasion he met, flew, and dined with Will Rogers, the famous satirist.[99] He survived the tour and finally, upon the approval of newly promoted Brig. Gen. James E. Fechet, attended the Army Staff College at Fort Leavenworth, Kansas. Fechet, a former Air Service officer of the Southern Department and Arnold's contemporary, replaced Patrick in December 1927. Arnold's appointment to Staff College occurred despite the protests of the college's commandant, Brig. Gen. Edward L. King, who had also served as one of the many judges on Mitchell's court. Arnold started the course of instruction on 5 September 1928 and graduated in June 1929.[100]

Arnold's memoirs barely mention his Staff College tour. He had already experienced General Staff work during wartime, and it is unlikely that he learned much that he did not already understand. For the most part, he tried to keep a low profile. He did teach and write about airpower issues at the school, and in that way influenced the ground soldiers in his class, as well as several classes that followed. Arnold had always been an advocate of airpower and the potential of true air force.[101]

Arnold's difficult, and predominantly formal, military education had ended. He had learned political finesse from his experiences with Billy Mitchell. At the Army Industrial College, he had learned about the Army's logistics and procurement system—and how those systems did not work well with airplane production and development. While on duty as an instructor at Fort Riley and as a student at Fort Leavenworth, he had learned that many Army officers were open to understanding airpower's capabilities.

Throughout industry and the Army, he had established numerous contacts, civilian and military, that he would build upon during his next few tours of duty. Arnold had a feel for the advancement of aviation technology, but he had not enjoyed any of it in his assignments—he was still flying vintage DH-4s at Riley. From 1919 to 1929, much of the foundation had been laid that would support Arnold's later strength at administrative high command. Next, he would receive an introductory-level crash course in technology that expanded during the rest of his career. He and his family departed Leavenworth for Fairfield Air Depot near Dayton, the new home of Army Air Corps research and development.

Top: Henry Harley Arnold was born in this Gladwyne, Pennsylvania, home early on the morning of 25 June 1886. (Robert Arnold Collection, Sonoma, Calif.)

Bottom left: Dr. Herbert Alonzo Arnold with son Harley during a National Guard encampment in 1896. Dr. Arnold believed that military discipline was tonic for unruly young men. (Robert Arnold Collection, Sonoma)

Bottom right: Harley Arnold at twelve. A hint of his mischievous grin is clear in this 30 August 1898 photograph, taken in Ardmore, Pennsylvania. (Robert Arnold Collection, Sonoma)

Above: Harley Arnold, second from left, graduated from Lower Merion High School, class of 1903. (Robert Arnold Collection, Sonoma)

Left: Charles Levée thrilled West Point cadets in 1906, when he ascended skyward in a 25-foot balloon filled with "illuminating gas" and drifted out of sight to the north. (Robert Arnold Collection, Sonoma)

"Pewt" Arnold (in photo below that of building) became the leader of the Black Hand. The class of 1907 "Hundredth Night" fireworks display highlighted the membership poster. (West Point Archives, West Point, N.Y.)

Pewt (second row, third from left) ran track for his class and played varsity football in his junior and senior years. (West Point Archives, West Point, N.Y.)

In 1909, in an effort to win 10,000 dollars in prize money, Orville Wright successfully retraced by air the path of the early Hudson River explorers. This one-of-a-kind photo shows the Wright Flyer as a float plane. A bright red canoe is strapped to the plane's midsection. (Library of Congress, Washington, D.C.)

Above: On the *bosque*. Lieutenant Arnold
(far right) enjoyed his time mapping the
Philippine Islands with this tough troop of
soldiers and natives. (Robert Arnold Collection, Sonoma)

Left: Orville Wright's crash at Fort Myer in
1908. His passenger, Lt. Thomas Selfridge,
became the first military man to be killed in
an aircraft accident. Wright suffered lifelong
injuries. (Robert Arnold Collection,
Sonoma)

Top: In May 1911, Arnold, John Rogers (USN), and Thomas DeWitt Milling (left to right) arrived in Dayton, Ohio, for flight training at the Wright Brothers' school. (Library of Congress, Washington, D.C.)

Bottom: Al "Owl" Welsh (left) flew Arnold's first twenty-eight sorties. Welsh was killed when his Wright C aircraft crashed in 1912. (Library of Congress, Washington, D.C.)

Left: Orville Wright frequently visited Arnold and Milling at College Park, the home of the Army flight school, during 1911 and 1912. This photograph, taken at dusk, utilized early flash techniques to illuminate the subjects. (National Archives, College Park Annex, College Park, Md.)

Below: In 1911 Lieutenant Arnold (driver's seat) commuted the eight miles from Washington, D.C., to College Park each day with his mechanics. (National Air and Space Museum, Washington, D.C.)

Lieutenant Arnold (right) flew with Glenn Curtiss, but never once with Orville or Wilbur Wright. This image was taken in September 1911. (Library of Congress, Washington, D.C.)

In a Wright Military Flyer, a grinning Lt. "Pewt" Arnold soars above the College Park airfield, June 1912. (Robert Arnold Collection, Sonoma)

The Wright Military Flyer, when disassembled, fit neatly into one train car. During 1912, such mobility helped the deployment of the College Park school to Augusta, Georgia. The weather did not cooperate. (Robert Arnold Collection, Sonoma)

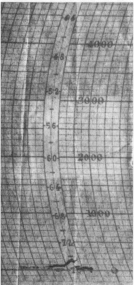

Top: The College Park fliers experimented with airborne wireless radio sets to assist in artillery spotting and reconnaissance. (Robert Arnold Collection, Sonoma)

Middle: During November 1912 at Fort Riley, Kansas, Arnold (kneeling, center) and Lt. J. O. Maubourgne of the Signal Corps tested the ground receiver. (National Air and Space Museum, Washington, D.C.)

Left: Arnold's 5 November 1912 barograph tape. This earliest of "black boxes" recorded his near-fatal accelerated stall and plunge to earth with his passenger, Lt. Alfred P. Sands. (Library of Congress, Washington, D.C.)

Pre-wedding photos of Eleanor Pool and Harley Arnold, circa September 1913. The wedding, a fiasco by all accounts, was seldom discussed in later years. (Robert Arnold Collection, Sonoma)

Top: Arnold's self-portrait resembled a popular cartoon character of the day, Billikens, a pet name Bee then used for several months in her letters. (Robert Arnold Collection, Sonoma)

Bottom: From left, Arnold's older brother, Tommy; Harley; and younger brother Cliff circa 1915. (Robert Arnold Collection, Sonoma)

Top left: Captain Arnold, North Island, California, 1916. Impending war loosened pilot restrictions. Married men became eligible, and "Billy" Mitchell convinced Arnold to requalify. (Official Army photo, courtesy National Archives, College Park Annex, College Park, Md.)

Top right: By August 1917, Henry H. Arnold was the youngest full colonel in the Army—for a few weeks, anyway. He still wore Signal Corps insignia in this picture. His job was to find, then build up stateside aircrew-training bases and help ease production logjams wherever possible. (Official Army photo, courtesy National Archives, College Park Annex, College Park, Md.)

Bottom: Arnold stands next to the first Ford company's Liberty engine, delivered to San Diego Air Depot in 1919. Many other companies built these engines during wartime. (National Air and Space Museum, Washington, D.C.)

Top: The production line for the "FB," also known as the Kettering Flying Bug, turned out about fifty of these unmanned missiles. The operation provided Arnold's ticket to Europe at the end of World War I. (Library of Congress, Washington, D.C.)

Bottom: Arnold flew a LePere to supervise his units up and down the West Coast. This photo was taken at Crissy Field, circa 1924. (Robert Arnold Collection, Sonoma)

Top left: Major Arnold holds the "Jewel" of the family, John Linton, who died suddenly in July 1923 of appendicitis. (Robert Arnold Collection, Sonoma)

Bottom: From left, Bruce, Hank, and Lois, holding John at the Presidio in 1922. All the children, including David (b. 1927), did not see as much of their father as they, like Arnold, desired. (Robert Arnold Collection, Sonoma)

Top right: Major H. H. Arnold's twenty-year West Point reunion portrait, 1927. Sophomore Cadet Arnold is pictured in the oval, 1905. (Official West Point photo, courtesy Robert Arnold Collection, Sonoma)

The Barling Bomber, the United States's first strategic bomber. Even in failure, the Barling contributed in minor ways to the success of the B-17, B-24, and B-29 bombers. Billy Mitchell (center, in uniform) and Walter Barling (third from left) appear dwarfed by the six-engine bomber. (Robert Arnold Collection, Sonoma)

Arnold (back to camera, hat in hand) exchanges greetings with the "Around the World Flyers" at Bolling Field, September 1924. (Robert Arnold Collection, Sonoma)

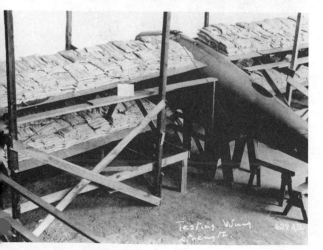

The sand test, an early Wright Brothers' method of testing wing strength, is still used in modified form to test modern airplanes. (Robert Arnold Collection, Sonoma)

In this 1924 photo, note the military-aviator badge (Arnold helped design it) and the prop and wings on the collar, rather than Signal Corps flags. Arnold's smoking habit diminished during the 1920s, but some evidence indicates that he never gave up the habit entirely. (National Air and Space Museum, Washington, D.C.)

Maj. Gen. Malin Craig and Lt. Col. Hap Arnold, early 1930s. Craig staunchly supported Arnold and was largely responsible for his return to Washington in 1925. (National Air and Space Museum, Washington, D.C.)

Left: While at March Field, California, Arnold entertained celebrities and other notables. Here, aviatrix Amelia Earhart and Nobel laureate Robert Millikan visit Arnold's First Wing, August 1932. (Robert Arnold Collection, Sonoma)

Above: From left, the flamboyant Air Corps chief Benny Foulois, Arnold, and Carl "Tooey" Spatz at March Field, early 1930s. (Robert Arnold Collection, Sonoma)

Top: Arnold welcomes GHQ Air Force commander Frank Andrews to March Field. Andrews (left) was a pure operator, while Arnold excelled in administration and training. (Robert Arnold Collection, Sonoma)

Bottom left: Lt. Col. H. H. Arnold commanded the Western Zone during the air-mail episode, spring 1934. Poor weather, inexperience, and aging planes contributed to casualties suffered by the Air Corps during the operation. (National Air and Space Museum, Washington, D.C.)

Bottom right: Lt. Col. Hap Arnold commands ten Martin B-10 bombers from his cockpit. The 9,000-mile flight was the first of such distance that maintained constant radio contact with ground stations while en route. (Robert Arnold Collection, Sonoma)

Arnold's B-10s circled the Washington Monument as they departed for Alaska. (Robert Arnold Collection, Sonoma)

Tail 145 spent a week in the repair shop after crash-landing in Cooks Bay. The durability of the B-10, in flight and after undergoing repairs, indicated that the potential offered by long-range bombers was improving. (Hewitt Photo Shop, courtesy Robert Arnold Collection, Sonoma)

Arnold presents Secretary of War Dern with a gift from the people of Fairbanks, Alaska. Hugh Knerr (behind totem wing, left) did much of the early planning for the mission. Benny Foulois (left, wearing boots) selected Arnold as his stand-in when duties in Washington precluded his departure for an extended time. (Robert Arnold Collection, Sonoma)

Top: In November 1938, President Roosevelt and newly appointed chief of the Air Corps Hap Arnold inspected the United States's airpower, including the underpowered B-15, at Bolling Field. FDR, while assistant secretary of the Navy, had seen little use for independent airpower. But as president he understood its necessity, and Air Corps bombers gave him the political and military options that he used in the early years of the war. (Robert Arnold Collection, Sonoma)

Bottom: The chief of the Air Corps automatically held a seat on the NACA Main Committee. In 1939, this committee consisted of several aviation all-stars, including Charles Lindbergh (fifth from left), Orville Wright (next), and Jerome Hunsaker (next). Vannevar Bush, seated at center head of table, was the chair. Arnold (third from right) sat on the committee for six years. (NACA photo, courtesy Robert Arnold Collection, Sonoma)

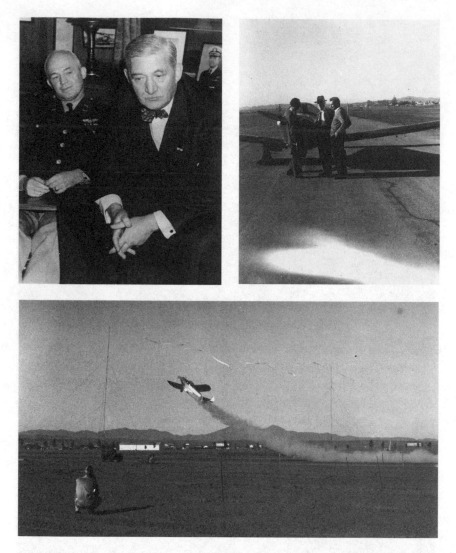

Top left: Maj. Gen. Hap Arnold counted on William Knudsen, later commissioned a three-star general, to lead the massive industrial expansion that was required to meet wartime Army Air Forces needs. (National Air and Space Museum, Washington, D.C.)

Top right: Drs. Frank Malina (left), William Durand, and Theodore von Kármán (right) discuss final details before test flights of the JATO system. (Jet Propulsion Laboratory, Pasadena, California)

Bottom: Capt. Homer Boushey ignites the JATO rockets and leaps skyward over the 50-foot-high test ribbon. (Jet Propulsion Laboratory, Pasadena, California)

Bee sees Hap off as he departs for England in April 1941. During this trip, he convinced air marshal Portal to share the plans for the Whittle jet engine. (Robert Arnold Collection, Sonoma)

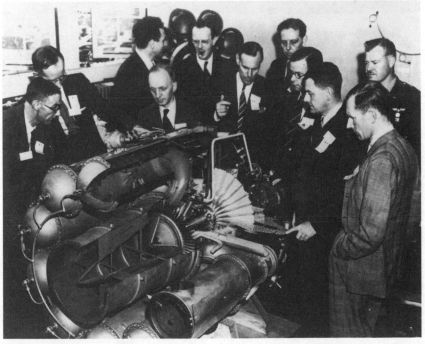

The first time British designers see the Whittle engine after American modifications. Team designer D. F. "Truly" Warner (top center, with cigar and glasses) shows off his team's work. (Air Force Materiel Command, Office of History, GE Collection)

Top: From left, test pilot Bob Stanley, Brig. Gen. Ben Chidlaw, Col. Don Keirn, Col. Ralph Swofford, and Larry Bell headed the team that built and tested one of the Army Air Forces' most secret aircraft, the XP-59A. This model is a YP-59. (Air Force Materiel Command, Office of History, GE Collection)

Bottom: Lieutenant General Arnold addresses a graduating class of new airmen at Randolph Field in 1943. As he had done in World War I, Arnold pressed for training—lots of it. (Official Army Air Forces photo, courtesy Gay Morris Collection, Alexandria, Virginia)

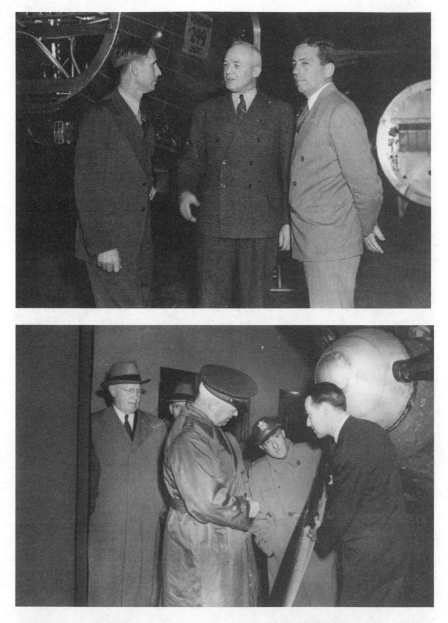

Top: From left, Douglas test pilot Carl Cover, Arnold, and Don Douglas tour the plant in California, 1943. The Douglas and Arnold families had been close for many years, so close that Arnold's son Bruce married Douglas's daughter Barbara the next year. (Robert Arnold Collection, Sonoma)

Bottom: Arnold also visited scientific and engineering locations during the war. Here, Dr. George Lewis (left) and Mr. Wilson Hunter (right) show Arnold the detrimental effects of ice on airplane propellers at the NACA facility located near Cleveland, Ohio. (NACA photo, courtesy Robert Arnold Collection, Sonoma)

Left: Arnold meets with longtime associate Henry Ford during one of his whirlwind World War II tours. (Robert Arnold Collection, Sonoma)

Below: Lieutenant General Arnold, en route to the Middle East, has just left the Casablanca Conference where the strategy of around-the-clock bombing was approved by Churchill and FDR. Americans would bomb precision targets at high altitude by day, and British forces would bomb industrial areas and cities by night. (National Air and Space Museum, Washington, D.C.)

Project Aphrodite, staunchly supported by Arnold, consisted of automated explosive-laden, war-weary bombers called Weary Willies: B-17, B-24, and naval aircraft. In addition, glide bombs such as the one pictured here were built to keep aircrews from overflying enemy targets directly. Some used radio and television guidance. (USAF Historical Research Agency, Maxwell AFB, Ala.)

After one of Arnold's many global trips during the war, Robert Lovett, assistant secretary of war for air, decorates him for conspicuous leadership. Lovett's calm balanced Arnold's fire. (Robert Arnold Collection, Sonoma)

Harry Hopkins (right), personal adviser to FDR, ensured that the president's door opened at the times when Arnold and Lovett most needed access. (Robert Arnold Collection, Sonoma)

Top: Curtis E. LeMay (left) replaced Haywood S. Hansell (right) when the Twenty-first Bomber Command's results fell below Arnold's expectations. Hansell understood Arnold's decision, while LeMay stumbled upon low-altitude fire bombing to avoid terrible weather. (USAF Historical Research Agency, Maxwell AFB, Ala.)

Bottom left: Sir John Dill (left), the Royal Air Force's liaison in Washington during the war, and Arnold spent significant time together. Dill is the only foreign officer buried in Arlington National Cemetery, a symbol of the importance of his service to the United States. (Robert Arnold Collection, Sonoma)

Bottom right: Sir Peter Portal (left), Arnold's direct counterpart in the RAF, was instrumental in aviation-technology transfers and Lend-Lease policy successes. (Library of Congress, Washington, D.C.)

Top: Gen. Hap Arnold took a naval transport from England to France in early June 1944; he hopped an AAF B-17 back the same night. (Robert Arnold Collection, Sonoma)

Bottom: On 12 June 1944 Arnold joined the rest of the Joint Chiefs of Staff and several of the combat commanders on a tour of the Normandy beachhead. From left: Arnold, Ike, Marshall, Bradley, and King on the beach. (Robert Arnold Collection, Sonoma)

Above left: Arnold (left) walks with Omar Bradley at the landing site in France. Bradley praised the AAF publicly, but his official report was less complimentary. (Robert Arnold Collection, Sonoma)

Above right: Arnold traveled to see Carl A. Spaatz at his headquarters immediately following the Normandy tour. (Robert Arnold Collection, Sonoma)

Left: Arnold visited Jackie Cochran's WASP school in Sweetwater, Texas, on 6 December 1944. He praised American women pilots for their many accomplishments during the war. This occasion marked the last WASP graduation. (National Air and Space Museum, Washington, D.C.)

MacArthur's airman, George Kenney (right), directed airpower operations for the fiery Army general in the Southern Pacific theater. (Robert Arnold Collection, Sonoma)

Operation Lusty (Luftwaffe Secret Technology) uncovered German technological advances only conceptualized in the States. A jet-powered helicopter (pictured) and swept-back wing designs were two of the most significant. (USAF Historical Research Agency, Maxwell AFB, Ala.)

This ship, the *H. H. Arnold,* was used to track missile test-firings during the mid-1960s off the Atlantic Coast of Florida. (Robert Arnold Collection, Sonoma)

Top: Five-star Arnold decorated Kármán at the end of the Scientific Advisory Group's first year. Kármán remained a vital part of the USAF's technological development until his death in 1963. (U.S. Air Force photo)

Bottom left: Those who knew Hap Arnold well expressed the opinion that this photo of him on his favorite horse, Duke, captures the Arnold they knew best. (Robert Arnold Collection, Sonoma)

Bottom right: Arnold never lost his ability to work a crowd. On Air Forces Day, 1 August 1945, 30,000 locals jammed Mitchel Field, Long Island. Here, a young man receives a friendly embrace from the five-star air general. (National Air and Space Museum, Washington, D.C.)

El Rancho Feliz, built on forty acres near Sonoma, California, became the Arnolds' retirement home. Arnold wrote about the wildlife in the Valley of the Moon, but he most enjoyed spending time with Bee and their dogs, and woodworking. (Robert Arnold Collection, Sonoma)

Above: Hap Arnold's body was transported from Sonoma to Washington in a simple pine box. His final resting place is somewhat more formal. He was buried in his Air Force blue uniform—General of the Air Force, 19 January 1950. (Robert Arnold Collection, Sonoma)
Left: General of the Army Hap Arnold, 1945. (Robert Arnold Collection, Sonoma)

8
INTERWAR YEARS, COMMAND EXPERIENCE (1929–38)

After his tour at the Staff College, on 25 June 1929, Arnold took command of the Fairfield Air Depot Reservation (FADR) near Dayton, Ohio. Earlier, in October 1927, Wright Field had been officially dedicated and replaced nearby McCook Field, along with most of the newly created Materiel Division functions still located there. The 1926 Air Corps Act had authorized the establishment of the Air Corps Materiel Division at Wright Field, and Fairfield Depot became a large section of that new division. In an expanded role, from August 1930 to February 1931, Arnold, now a few pounds heavier with a bit less gray hair, also served as executive officer to the chief of the Materiel Division, Brig. Gen. H. Conger Pratt. Only Maj. Augustine Warner Robins had ever held both of Arnold's positions, along with the responsibility that went with them, in the fall of 1927.[1]

As FADR commander, Arnold oversaw the distribution of supplies and the regularly scheduled refits and overhauls of all Air Corps airplanes over three-fourths of the continental United States. Arnold was more responsible, as FADR commander, for shipping nuts and bolts than for the oversight of aircraft R and D.

After the consolidation of the Materiel Division, funding became available for construction of hangar and testing facilities. Of course, Arnold could not resist holding an air show for the local populace to celebrate the conclusion of the new construction projects at Fairfield. The same month as the hangar refurbishing was complete, he opened the gates for a widely publicized Air Corps Carnival that featured military bands, one-dollar airplane rides, fireworks, and a dance. Arnold realized that winning the support of the local pop-

121

ulation could head off conflicts that sometimes resulted from airplane noise at all hours of the day and night. The friendly approach he had taken in Dayton preceded events like the massive May 1931 Air Corps maneuvers. More than 650 airplanes and their crews flocked to Wright Field; the planes were parked wingtip to wingtip as far as one could see across the flight line.[2] The local merchants, suffering from the Depression, benefited from such an influx of aircrew, the engine noise a small price to pay for such a fiscal windfall.

The purpose of the exercise involved consolidating air forces while staging from multiple locations, and then evaluating the successes and failures involved in launching attacks from bases dispersed across the eastern United States. The problem was a monumental logistical one, and Arnold, temporarily serving under Brig. Gen. Benjamin "Benny" Foulois, acting First Provisional Air Division commander, was instrumental in managing the prepositioning of essential supplies before the exercise began. During this event, Arnold witnessed the crucial nature of logistics and preplanning during major air force deployments. This reinforced his appreciation for the importance of logistics and the employment of airpower—without adequate logistics, there was no airpower.[3] The lesson shaped Arnold's views of airpower and its application for the remainder of his career. It was, tangentially, while serving in these different assignments in supply and logistics that he was for the first time exposed to the Air Corps's formal R and D system.[4]

Back in 1922, Gardner W. Carr, the assistant chief of production for the Engineering Division at McCook Field, had written a three-part article for *U.S. Air Service* magazine that broadly described two functions of the Engineering Division. First, the engineers designed, tested, and improved the Air Service's equipment. Second, McCook engineers collected, classified, and disseminated technical information of value to the Air Service. Many believed that solutions to aeronautical problems often involved diverse branches of "fundamental sciences."[5]

Air Service aeronautical engineering at McCook Field had begun only after the war. Carr explained that "our entry into the conflict found the United States not only without an organized Air Service, but without airplanes, flyers, or even engineers trained in either design or construction of military aircraft." The Engineering Division was created to prevent technological unpreparedness in the future. By July 1921, more than 1,500 civilians and 109 officers and enlisted personnel formed the backbone of McCook Field's manpower.[6] During the next decade, McCook developers contributed to advances such as the Supercharger (allowing airplanes to climb to higher altitudes by compressing outside air for combustion), leakproof gas tanks, parachutes, and new engine designs. Additionally, they categorized aircraft into fifteen types, in an effort to standardize both parts and functions.[7]

However, McCook engineers did not limit their work to airplanes. For several years, radio-controlled cars had been under development. The "Radio

Dog" received much publicity in the early 1920s, as it drove through the streets of Dayton obeying all traffic regulations.[8] During World War II General Arnold would revive the radio-controlled-car idea, incorporating it into planes and a series of radio-controlled bombs.

But experimentation of this nature during the early 1920s met with inadequate funding. A few projects were specifically applicable to "civilian interests"; aerial crop dusting gained the interest of local farmers, who frequently saw the airplanes as a noisy nuisance. At least one farmer became a hearty supporter of aviation when McCook test pilots dusted his grove, saving him a week's time and labor fees normally paid out to hired help.[9]

Yet, despite all the apparent good work going on at McCook Field, the foundations of conflict were forming. As Carr described, "much of the work done by the Engineering Division is purely research." More specifically, "the Engineering Division has the personnel and equipment for handling the problems of aviation and is striving to act as a clearing house and experimental laboratory on all technical questions arising in both the military air services and the general aviation industry."[10] Since 1915, the NACA had been operating under a similar charter.

The pressures toward efficiency driven by Progressivism and the European war had resulted in the establishment of the NACA on 3 March 1915. Modeled after the British Advisory Committee for Aeronautics, the NACA consisted of a cross section of representatives from government agencies and institutions, the military services, and up to five other representatives familiar with "the needs of aeronautical science . . . or skilled in aeronautical engineering or its applied science."[11] The NACA was supposed to represent a pool of knowledge that was enriched by each of the participants' special fields of expertise. Group discussion was expected to generate ideas beyond the capacity of an individual—"produce a new body of knowledge greater than the sum of its parts." This was the essence of the committee system as it was envisioned.[12] But with its meager $5,000-a year budget, the NACA could do little but advise during its first five years. Successfully mediating the Wright-Curtiss wing-warping lawsuit was an early achievement, but to remain a simple advisory committee was never the NACA's plan. Its founders argued long and hard for their own laboratory as the foundation of their organization.[13] The control of government research dollars was always in question, and the decisions prioritizing projects, despite the military representation on the committee, created rifts.

The struggle between the air arm and the NACA over who would control aeronautical research was the manifestation of a more universal issue: civil control of military functions. In this case, military necessity often dictated that projects remain confidential, making them "of little interest to the outside world." Fears that government functionaries might compromise or disregard military projects ran high. The U.S. air forces and the NACA would butt heads well after the NACA had been transformed into the National Aeronautics and Space Administration, NASA, in 1958.[14] Arnold lived with and worked around such struggles in later years.

Circumstances like those surrounding the disposition of the Barling Bomber soured Arnold's opinion of War Department logistic and supply staffs. The Barling cost the Air Service $375,000, and it cost the manufacturer their business, when the cost overrun of $150,000 surpassed the company's liquid assets. The now combined Wittemen-Lewis Company had won the bid for the bomber, but in those days there were few provisions that excused overruns of that magnitude. The lone Barling had not flown since May 1925.[15] An embellished tale, as told by Arnold's son Bruce, demonstrates Arnold's frustration with the Air Corps's logistics system during his tour in Dayton.

It was lunchtime that Saturday during the summer of 1930, and warm enough for a cool glass of lemonade hand-squeezed by Bee. Arnold had appeared home in the middle of a working day, a rare occurrence. His puzzled twelve-year-old son, Bruce, met him on the front porch.[16]

"Hey Pop, whatcha doin' home?"

"Just thought I'd take a little break, son, I've been on the phone with Washington all day trying to get rid of that damned Barling Bomber that Billy Mitchell built."

The Barling sat disassembled in one of the depot hangars just taking up space. It lay along side vintage WW I planes that had been stored in the dusty, wood-framed buildings since the end of the Great War. More importantly, the War Department books still carried the "Barling" as a flyable Air Corps airplane.

"Did they tell you no again?" Bee was sympathetic but still wondered why her husband was home in the middle of the day. He rarely came home during the duty day, even on the sixth day of the work week.

"Yup. No Soap."

The one and only Barling bomber was a throw-back to the early 1920s when Mitchell had it built as the answer to the early challenges of strategic bombing. Unfortunately, even the six surplus Liberty engines that powered the behemoth in flight were not enough to make the plane an operational success. Thousands of WW I surplus Liberty engines, many stored at Wright Field, continued to power everything from modified DH-4s to the six-engine Barling. Arnold realized that until the surplus was gone, the Army Air Corps would be stuck with outdated equipment lacking the capability of more modern aircraft engines under development elsewhere.

As Bee watched him eat lunch, her curiosity was too much to hold inside her petite frame. It was almost half past noon when Arnold looked carefully at his wrist watch.

"Harley, what is going on?" Bee, fully aware of the telltale signs of mischief which Arnold had perfected during his West Point days, half-expected a furtive response.

"Yeh, Pop, why do ya keep lookin at your watch?"

"Well son . . . there's gonna be a fire." This revelation resulted in a moment of puzzlement on both Bruce and Bee's faces which resolved into casual disbelief.

Just about then, the wail of the airfield fire brigade siren rose in the distance. The scream echoed off the angular walls of nearby military housing. The sound grew louder as the fire brigade raced from the service side of the depot to the flight line side. Soon it became apparent to Bruce and Bee that the fire was billowing from one of the old storage hangars. Major Arnold never looked up from his lunch.

Coyly, Bee asked, "What was in that old hangar?"

"Well Beadle," he lifted his head in the direction of the flight line without shifting his eyes, "it looks like the hangar where we kept that old Barling bomber. What a shame. I'll have to notify Washington." He finished his lunch, his Billikens-like grin stretched wide across his thin, boyish face. The reality of events was really not far from Bruce's boyhood recollections. It is most likely, though the documents authorizing the destruction of "one heavy bomber" have not survived, that Arnold had tacit permission from Washington to destroy an outdated bomber, not specifically the Barling. Nonetheless, the fire was ordered and the deed was done.[17] An eyewitness recalled that one of the storage hangars at Wright Field held burned airplane parts. The hangar itself remained intact. In fact, the Barling had been disassembled for some years and was simply added to the burn pile.

Had Arnold destroyed a perfectly useful hangar, he would have been questioned about its destruction. As it appears, the story—over many years—has suffered from exaggeration, perhaps to show Arnold as a fiery get-things-done officer. Nonetheless, this was not the only fire that Arnold set during the remainder of his forty-year military career.

Sickened by the lack of progress that he perceived at Wright Field, Arnold lamented the "advancement" represented by the Douglas O-38 two-seat observation biplane. It was capable of only 130 miles an hour. "What the hell have we gained in twenty years?" he rhetorically asked his oldest son, Hank, "Nothing!"[18] These perceptions of stagnation were etched deeply into his memory and stayed with him the rest of his career. It did not matter that Arnold's perceptions were largely misplaced and, in many ways, incorrect. He was too involved with supply problems to appreciate the real success in Army Air Corps R and D. Technological change was constant, if methodical, at Wright, and usually beneficial to aircraft design; many important contributions had been made to aeronautics by the engineering staff. There were other reasons why Arnold had such disdain for the Air Corps Materiel Division and the R and D system, none of them related to technological advancement or scientific progress.

Arnold's Fairfield assignment, although critical to his understanding of the Air Corps's procurement, logistic, and R and D system, was nothing less than a financial disaster for his family. Although the Great Depression's impact on the military and the aviation industry was not as serious as it was for American society in general, it seriously damaged the Arnolds' financial well-being.[19] Arnold had been sending money to his father for deposit in the family savings and loan bank, Lower Merion Trust, since he had graduated from West Point. His father had all his retirement savings in the same institution. When banks started to disintegrate, all of the Arnolds' money was lost. Bee's father, a banker himself, was swindled by his partner, and the pressures of losing his savings contributed to a series of crippling strokes that killed him one month before the stock market crashed in October 1929.[20]

By 18 January 1931, the pressures on Daddy Doc and Gangy Arnold had grown too overwhelming. That Sunday morning, at 7:00 A.M., Gangy awoke as usual, but soon experienced pain enough to inform her husband that something was wrong. By 7:20 she lay dead, stricken by a massive heart attack. Arnold, feeling guilty that he had missed his parents' golden wedding anniversary during the previous spring while stuck in California on duty, rushed to his father's side. After the funeral, Daddy Doc fell into a deep depression, and he never recovered after his wife's sudden death.[21]

Gangy's death also had a deep and lasting impact on Harley. In his youth, his mother had been loving and available for the children while Daddy Doc had been making his rounds. She had been with Harley at pivotal moments in his young life, the most memorable being his unexpected commissioning into the infantry in 1907. Gangy usually called Harley by a pet name, Sunny. The name had carried over into his marriage to Bee, who had affectionately called him Sunny since the days of their courtship until January 1931. This was not surprising, since Harley had taken Bee's family nickname, Beadle, as his pet name for her. Most of her private correspondence to him began with "Dear Sunny," and his return letters were signed, "Your Own, Sunny." After January 1931 the letters suddenly changed.

As with other traumatic events in Arnold's life, his tendency was to suppress the memory and never speak of it openly. After the shock of his mother's death, signing his letters with "Sunny" seemed a constant reminder. By May 1931, Arnold started to conceal the memory by changing his personal signature from Harley "Sunny" Arnold to "Hap." Whether Bee had anything to do with the name remains unknown, but in later years she would sometimes refer to Arnold as Happy instead of Hap. The origin of this famous nickname—a secret, personal reaction to the memory of his mother—has been the greatest mystery of his life, as well as, it turns out, the greatest irony.[22] The name derives from the single most horrible emotional blow he had ever received, even more devastating than the loss of John Linton.

There was no irony in the fact that the Arnolds, both elder and younger, were essentially bankrupt. Bee's family was little better off, and their lives had changed forever. Arnold would carry such painful memories of his family experiences at Fairfield and Wright Field that he devoted less than two pages in *Global Mission* to that near-three-year tour of duty, and he wrote nothing of a personal nature.[23] As he had omitted the description of his wedding, a debacle at best, he skipped over the ruinous years spent near Dayton. He preferred to keep his negative emotional experiences to himself. Coupled with his often immature reaction to emotionally charged events, these experiences may explain Arnold's aversion to the Wright Field complex of R and D, logistics, and procurement, despite much of the excellent work going on at those facilities.

While Arnold supplied aircraft with parts and materiel, the Army tried to supply the Air Corps with a mission. Early in January 1931, Gen. Douglas MacArthur and Adm. William V. Pratt, chiefs of their respective services, reached an agreement concerning the employment of air forces. Essentially, the Air Corps assumed the mission of coastal defense of the United States and other overseas possessions. Anticipating the requirements of this newly approved mission, bases were established from which to stage actual coast-defense operations. That meant at least one base on each coast, and one more centrally located as rapid reserve for either engaged coastal base.

The First Wing at March Field, near Los Angeles, became the West Coast base, and Arnold was placed in command. He left Wright Field in October 1931 and happily moved his clan back to California. By Thanksgiving, he was out of the support field and in charge of creating, from what was then only a small training outfit, the General Headquarters Air Force's largest operational combat unit.[24]

✪ ✪ ✪ ✪ ✪

While waiting for new planes and new personnel to arrive at March Field, Lt. Col. Hap Arnold rekindled old acquaintances. His World War I associate, Dr. Robert Millikan, forty miles away in Pasadena, was now Caltech's president. The 1923 physics Nobel Prize winner continued his cosmic-ray research in the face of a challenge to its validity by Karl Compton of MIT. Arnold had little understanding of the nature of these experiments, which involved moving a lead sphere to different altitudes and taking electronic measurements. Nonetheless, Millikan had no trouble convincing him to lend a specially modified Curtiss B-2 "Condor" bomber, backbone of the bombardment group, to complete his charged-particle experiments. Others might have balked at the suggestion that a civilian should be allowed to use a military plane for experimentation. Arnold, who had an inquiring mind and wide-ranging interests, encouraged the tests despite the absence of written authorization.[25]

Arnold had his March Field mechanics build a special "bomb" rack for the sphere that was affixed to the Condor. These experiments were carried out from Canada to Mexico over a period of months. As part of the project, measurements were also taken underground, in mines and at a variety of elevations on the earth. One time, Millikan transported the ball to Lake Arrowhead, California, on top of a high mountain peak. Unfortunately, the ball was so heavy that it crashed through the bottom of the rickety boat in which he was transporting the experiment. It sank to the bottom of the lake. Arnold recalled that the first time they met following the unfortunate mishap, he addressed the professor as Admiral Millikan.[26]

While reestablishing his contacts at Caltech, Arnold's command was in operational limbo. Coastal defense had opened some doors to procurement and appropriations, but the Air Corps was far from effective at the increasingly nebulous mission. While the debate continued in Washington, Arnold kept his First Wing busy. For example, during the winter of 1932–33, unusually devastating snowstorms swept through an enormous portion of the desert Southwest, isolating several Indian villages. Arnold's fliers were called to resupply the stranded villagers. After quickly solving the problems involved in dropping foodstuffs without aide of parachutes, the fliers braved the winter storms while navigating around treacherous mountain terrain and swirling-weather phenomenon in their B-2 Condors and B-4, B-5, and B-6 "Keystone" biplane bombers. The aircrews located the villages with the airborne assistance of Indian agents, and they "bombed them with food." In his draft memoirs, Arnold later referred to the operation as an "ancestor" of the great Berlin Airlift.[27]

As the weather improved for the Indian villagers, the national political climate also seemed to thaw. Franklin Delano Roosevelt was sworn in to the office of the presidency in March 1933, bringing the New Deal with him. FDR's election had immediate effects on the First Wing. Relief policies such as the Civilian Conservation Corps were assigned to military units for implementation. Although they were in the middle of maneuvers in May, when the first orders to establish CCC camps were issued, the First Wing's can-do spirit quickly provided shelter and food for 3,000 youngsters sent west from around the country.

These young people, who were among the more than 2.5 million Americans employed nationwide between 1933 and 1935, worked on conservation and reforestation projects around Los Angeles. One of the more challenging projects that Arnold supervised was the improvement of roads and the construction of public camps throughout Death Valley. Arnold's aircraft continually flew in large quantities of water, food, and necessary construction supplies for CCC Companies 529 and 530. A February 1934 Department of the Interior press release stated: "the men of the CCC camps have done their part in making the glories of Death Valley accessible."[28]

It was in the course of establishing these CCC camps that Arnold became known to Mr. Harry L. Hopkins, director of the Civil Works Administration, devoted social worker, and advisor to FDR. Hopkins's CWA, one of the largest government organizations in history, was challenged to provide jobs for more than four million men and women. The CWA and CCC were different in that the former attempted to employ out-of-work individuals in jobs that were similar to those in which they were already trained. The latter was for untrained youth whose families were really needy. These workers did mostly manual labor. Hopkins's philosophy, one of "getting relief to the miserable and getting it there quickly," was in line with Arnold's methods. The success of Arnold's thirty-plus CCC camps certainly had come to Hopkins's attention, even though there was no official link between the two organizations.[29] The impression that Arnold, or the First Wing, made on Hopkins at that time is undocumented, but Arnold's style certainly fit with Hopkins's social philosophy. Later, the relationship between these two men benefited Arnold at both the personal and professional levels.

While New Deal reforms, air shows, public-relations campaigns, and exercises, as well as support of scientific research, occupied the First Wing, Daddy Doc had come to stay with his son during 1933 and occupied much of Hap's limited spare time. The loss of his wife and his money left Daddy Doc bitter and beaten. The bitterness carried over into the Arnolds' home in the form of unwanted efforts at child discipline and lectures about the evils of drink. Despite his respect for his father, Hap was forced to ask him to return to Ardmore in August 1933. The doctor died two months later, a resentful man, and Hap never openly spoke of his death.

There are two possible reasons for Arnold's silence. Perhaps he felt guilty about asking his father to leave March Field, even though he was disrupting Hap's own family life. Or maybe he simply continued in his proven ways, suppressing his emotional loss deep inside himself.[30]

✪ ✪ ✪ ✪ ✪

Even though the American economy would be slow to recover, Arnold did not neglect the technical development of his airplanes. Procurement took precedence over many creature comforts on his base; palm trees for base beautification, for instance, were added only when donated by a local farmer who needed to rid his field of the California landmarks.[31] Military funding continued at forecast levels into 1934, but it faded somewhat with the advent of FDR's massive social programs. Air shows at March Field were major public events in Southern California, as they had been at Rockwell and Wright Fields during Arnold's tours there. Movie stars and celebrities of all sorts visited the field on show days. The inevitable result was favorable publicity in several Southern California newspapers.[32]

Arnold's wing was not just a showpiece for Hollywood. By 1934, it had developed into the "best military combat operation in the world."[33] At least that was the opinion of Arnold's operations officer, Tooey Spaatz. The command arrangement between Arnold and Spaatz at March Field actually reflected the structure for future air-base wings. Arnold, as wing commander, was in charge of all personnel, structures, and maintenance functions; Spaatz, as his executive officer, was in charge of flying operations. Under Spaatz were Monk

Hunter, pursuit commander, and Joe McNarney, bombardment commander.[34] In layman's terms, Arnold was in command of the entire base and all its
functions, from the hospital to the quartermaster. Spaatz was in command of
only the operational flying at the base. Eventually the First Wing included airplanes from March, Rockwell, and Hamilton Fields, but the command structure remained the same as it had at March Field. This structure, on a much
larger scale, would resemble the command relationship between Arnold and
Spaatz during World War II.[35] Arnold took care of the "base," while Spaatz
took care of operations.

While command relations within the Air Corps at March Field were fairly
clear, the relationships between the Army and Air Corps were a bit more confusing. The command problem came to a head during another First Wing operation, which originated after the devastating Long Beach earthquake of
March 1933. Arnold had been made aware that food kitchens were desperately needed by the local population. He provided the mobile kitchens and the
food required until cleanup efforts were well under way.[36] Unfortunately, he
ignored the Army's chain of command.

During actual operations, the First Wing fell under the Corps Area commander, Maj. Gen. Malin Craig, based in San Francisco. Orders were issued
by the War Department through the Area commander to the First Wing, and
requests to operate flowed in the opposite direction. Craig, who had not immediately been available after the quake in Los Angeles, had not been informed of Arnold's efforts at relief. Arnold had acted of his own volition, outside standard Army procedures.[37]

Moreover, now chief of the Air Corps, Major General Foulois, had no direct
operational authority over Arnold. He had only "technical control," an am-
biguous term at best, over Arnold. "It was a very mixed up, jumbled up way of
running a military organization," Spaatz recalled.[38] The Corps Area commander, a non-flier, controlled all Army operations within his area of responsibility. The Air Corps was still a part of the Army and was expected to support
ground operations, rather than to operate independently of troops. The chief
of the Air Corps held the responsibility for procurement of equipment and personnel issues (such as promotion), but held no authority over the operational
employment of forces.[39] Fortunately, Arnold and General Craig got along
very well. After Arnold recounted to his immediate boss the events of the
earthquake and the needs of the population, the chain-of-command issue was
dropped—no threat of a court-martial this time.

This confusing and difficult command relationship existed in February
1934, when postmaster general James A. Farley canceled all air-mail contracts
because they had been let without competitive bidding and at costs "wholly
unjustified by the services rendered."[40] Foulois pledged that the Air Corps
would carry the air mail until new contracts had been negotiated. During the
ensuing four months, a dozen airmen died. Only one fatal accident occurred
while a pilot was actually transporting the mail; the others were killed while

training to fly the routes or while transporting airplanes for operations. These deaths resulted in very negative press reporting and enormous political pressure upon both Farley and Foulois. In a way, their plights were similar. Jim Farley took much of the public pressure for President Roosevelt, while Benny Foulois became the whipping boy for the Air Corps. Many thought this a bold action; some called it foolish.[41]

○   ○   ○   ○   ○

Foulois had assigned Brig. Gen. Oscar Westover as overall commander of the air-mail operation. His job was to coordinate routes between the three zones of operation across the country. Arnold commanded the Western Zone, Maj. Byron Q. Jones commanded the Eastern Zone, and Lt. Col. Horace M. Hickam was given responsibility from Chicago to Cheyenne.[42] Arnold created a provisional headquarters on 18 February 1934, in Salt Lake City. It was centrally located and facilitated communications throughout his zone. By the twentieth, Arnold's command center was getting organized, and he described the situation to Bee: "We may and most certainly will not get the mail through uninterrupted but we will get it through when we can. I have preached and ordered that in case of doubt the planes will stay on the ground. I told them I didn't care if no mail moved in bad weather. I hope that everyone will follow that policy."[43]

Arnold had followed the orders issued by General Foulois on 17 February to ensure compliance with the "safety-first policy of the Air Corps."[44] But his best intentions, even when the orders were followed by his pilots, could not prevent mishaps caused by inexperience. On 2 March a young aviator, flying a B-7 twin-engine biplane bomber at night, met bad weather and attempted to turn back to avoid a storm. He was not experienced in night flying and may have been anxious to extricate himself from the clouds. He turned too tight, pulled too hard, and put his plane into a spin. Having no instruments to help him recover, he cleverly dropped a flare for illumination. He was able to see the ground and then, regaining his orientation, was able to recover the plane and crash-land in the middle of the Mojave Desert uninjured. Daylight revealed that the accident had occurred over the only dry-lake bed in the area. The depression it formed had provided enough altitude to save the situation. "Who says there is no such thing as luck—predestination—or fate?" Arnold wrote about the fortunate airman, remembering his own near-disaster at Fort Riley twenty-two years earlier.[45]

Hap correctly perceived the air-mail assignment as a "political football." Aware that Foulois was taking a beating in Washington, he wrote to Bee that "poor old Benny looks worse every day. So far he hasn't much to his credit but lots of mistakes and errors chalked up against him."[46] But he did not blame Foulois for taking on the job; he believed that anyone in command of the Air Corps would have done the same.[47]

Arnold's letters to Beadle describing the troubles during operations illustrate the complexity of the political situation, as well as the reality of the Air Corps's readiness to accomplish the mission.

> The Army Air Corps was asked to take over a system of air routes covering the entire U.S. We didn't have enough experienced pilots to carry on and had to use inexperienced flyers who lacked the mature judgement, who were afraid to turn back, who did not know when they were getting into trouble and who had too high an opinion of their own capabilities. Add to that the lack of intimate knowledge of the air routes, the lack of knowledge of the details of weather changes which occur so rapidly in winter and a desire of the air lines to see us fail—these things together with sensation hunting—supercritical newspapers and a congress which was looking for a political football—made our task a most impossible one. Did you note that no one has yet given us credit for the amount of mail which we have carried—the miles we have flown.[48]

Arnold's uncharacteristic description of the situation as "most impossible" signified how grave it had become: the word *impossible* was anathema to Arnold. In frustration, he looked for explanations for and solutions to the Air Corps dilemma. The negative publicity really irked him, particularly in light of the many successful air shows and public programs he had championed during his recent command. In that moment, Arnold could only wonder what was really going on in Washington. "Are all the officers of high rank afraid to assert themselves? . . . We haven't a single friend in court."[49]

His perception of Foulois's efforts is a telling revelation. Without naming names, Arnold was apparently questioning General Foulois's effectiveness as chief of the Air Corps. Although he treasured his operational command, the implication in his letters home was that he felt he might better serve the Air Corps in the political environment of Washington: he might be a better spokesman for airpower. Despite his continual complaints about Washington, Arnold was, perhaps, beginning to believe that he belonged there, that he could do the most good for the Air Corps by serving at the War Department.[50]

Returning to D.C. seemed a distant possibility, though, as he missed promotion to brigadier general during the air-mail operations. Jake Fickel and James E. Chaney were selected instead. Arnold's disappointment surfaced in a letter home on 20 March. "Foulois told me (truth or fiction) about the 2 B.G.s [brigadier generals]. I will tell you when I see you."[51] There is some evidence to show that Foulois had targeted Arnold for a star by the end of the air-mail mess, but promises irritated Arnold, whether or not he understood the complexities of the Army's promotion system.

To relieve some of the pressures, he returned to March Field a few times to see Bee, while delivering mail himself. But he felt constantly obliged to remain in Salt Lake during operations. He did not understand B. Q. Jones's operation and complained to Bee that "Hickam has an awful time coordinating his actions with Jones. I can't understand why they don't send Jones back to Langley."[52] The younger Jones had made a few decisions in his command, such as abolishing rank structure, that Arnold considered unacceptable and unmilitary.

Accidents in other commands caused Arnold constant worry over his fliers' safety. "I have given out instructions for safety in every way that I can think of and yet—the young pilots will not turn back. . . . I will need three vacations when I get over this job."[53]

Despite mounting negative publicity as a result of the accidents, some still stood by the Air Corps. Not surprisingly, Postmaster Farley was one of these. FDR, Army chief of staff Douglas MacArthur, and others washed their hands of the entire affair.[54] Before the Air Corps totally handed the mail back to civilian airlines, Arnold reminded the public that the service had demonstrated determination and audacity, even in the face of one of the worst winters on record. Nevertheless, the media continued to use Air Corps accidents to attack Roosevelt's administration. The Air Corps could not stop it.[55]

In retrospect, the Air Corps 1934 air-mail service remained a pivotal event for the development of American airpower. The media's politically driven attacks, initially waged foolishly against the popular Roosevelt administration and then transferred to Foulois, only served to emphasize the deplorable state of readiness and the outdated technology in the Air Corps. Foulois and Spaatz both figured, according to Hap, that the Air Corps would "get something out of the mess—new legislation."[56]

The budget for 1935 included no increase in Air Corps funds; New Deal programs were still in full swing. Beginning in 1936, however, FDR no longer impounded Air Corps monies, as he had in 1933 and 1934. Appropriations from 1936 onward increased incrementally.[57] Foulois had unknowingly accepted a mission doomed to failure in the short term, but it was also one that forced the American people to recognize the deplorable state of American military aviation. The fliers who died during that harsh winter of 1934 became silent heroes of airpower advancement in the years before World War II.

Moreover, the public began to realize that American airpower consisted of more than just military planes. Civil aviation, ahead of the Air Corps technologically in the areas of navigation and blind flying, was vital to the national infrastructure, and Postmaster Farley's cancellation of air-mail contracts showed that the United States's growing airpower base was built on an uncoordinated combination of civil airliners and military aircraft. It would not be long before civil aviation and the Air Corps were inexorably merged in "supporting the expansion of all facets of aviation," both for war and for peace.[58]

More personally, Arnold endured the air-mail months under constant pressure to succeed—or, perhaps more accurately, not to fail. General MacArthur had promised that once the Air Corps began delivering the mail, it would be delivered without delay, difficulty, or interruptions. Partly because Foulois had convinced MacArthur that these expectations were possible, Foulois's own troubles began to multiply.[59] Bold statements in front of investigators and military commanders only exacerbated his situation.

On Thursday, 12 April 1934, Arnold took a flight that signaled changes in the Air Corps. On that day, he flew the new Martin B-10 bomber for the first time. He mentioned the bomber's "wonderful performance" to Beadle and notified her that the rest of the allotment of new airplanes was to arrive the next day.[60] The B-10 only carried the mail for a few weeks, but in that short time the airplane demonstrated that it had capability surpassing even the most advanced civil airliner, including a near-record coast-to-coast flight.

How had the Air Corps procured the Martin B-10 in the face of the restricted budgets of 1933 and 1934? Under the provisions of Army Regulation 5-240, certain circumstances existed where competitive bidding seemed impractical due to the experimental nature of the end product. The Air Corps had delicately worked within these regulations and contracted with Glenn L. Martin's aircraft company for the production of ten YB-10 aircraft for service testing. After the testing had been satisfactorily completed and procurement officers had certified that no comparable product existed in industry, a production contract was authorized under the procurement-without-competition provisions of AR 5-240. Thus, the B-10 bomber was purchased and made available to the Air Corps by the spring of 1934.[61]

Although cleverly accomplished, the regular use of sole-source contracts had previously backfired on the Air Corps. During the congressional hearings in January 1934, financial improprieties throughout the War Department and aviation industry had come under close investigation. One of the investigations, led by senator Hugo L. Black, had resulted in the cancellation of air-mail contracts; another had implicated a few senators in stock-market insider trading. The Navy and certain engine manufacturers had suffered through similar scrutiny.[62] Many of these investigations continued throughout the year, and Arnold testified in at least one of them.[63]

As Arnold's air-mail assignment was winding down, Bee, acting in her position as the First Wing commander's wife, had an official occasion to host General and Mrs. Patrick, now retired, for a dinner at March Field. Upon hearing the news, Hap scribed a letter to Bee:

> My Darling Beadle,
>   So you are going to entertain Gen. And Mrs. Patrick. Be a good girl and pour tea and smile and pull the old mans "toup" off and push the old lady down the toilet and tell the old man what a poor double crossing fish he is and have a good time generally. I am sorry that I am not there to put glass and tacks on the road in front of the auto rut in the middle of the sand stretch near Inueville [*sic*] during a Santa Anna. So be it.[64]

He followed up the next day: "Give them both a dose of castor oil with my compliments."[65] In this case, Hap demonstrated that he was perfectly capable of holding an eight-year grudge. The Patricks never became aware of Arnold's true feelings; he successfully concealed them from the public.

On 8 May the last load of Army Air Corps mail left Salt Lake City. "It has been a very educational experience," Arnold wrote, "and one which we will probably never get again but I don't believe that anyone will ask for a repeat."[66] All told, more than 300,000 pounds had been delivered by the Air Corps during the entire operation. The B-10s that contributed near the end increased the average weight transported and the average speed of delivery between stops.[67] The B-10 proved a formidable aircraft, one that Arnold would push to new limits only two months after the final mail run. Had the B-10 been available to the Air Corps the previous February, the air-mail story might have ended differently.

○ ○ ○ ○ ○

Another of Arnold's significant achievements while he was commander at March Field did not occur there. Lt. Col. Hap Arnold won his second Mackay Trophy as commander of a flight of ten new Martin B-10 bombers that flew round-trip from Washington, D.C., to Fairbanks, Alaska, from July to September 1934. The first all-metal, low-wing, retractable-gear monoplane, the B-10 was the most technologically advanced airplane in the Air Corps inventory.

Planning was meticulous. A poor showing as a result of a poor plan would have been a catastrophic embarrassment, particularly since the Air Corps was still stinging from its performance while carrying the U.S. mail.[68] The trip had not been Arnold's idea. It was probably assistant chief of the Air Corps Oscar Westover's answer to the media's assault on Foulois and the Air Corps. Westover's intent was to justify the sole-source purchase of the Air Corps's newest bomber. Arnold was selected to lead the flight because, according to executive officer for the mission Hugh J. Knerr, he was substituting for Westover, who could not escape his responsibilities in Washington.[69] Testimony before a variety of ongoing investigative boards and committees was a regular affair in the halls of the Capitol Building, and "Tubby" Westover could not be spared.[70]

Arnold arrived at Wright Field the last week in June, to find planners hard at work on the mission. In assessing the progress, the possibilities for distribution of logistics, and the readiness of the planes, he determined that the earliest departure date might be 10 July.[71] Arnold informed Foulois and Westover that adjustments to the proposed date were required, and he was called to Washington to discuss the particular objectives for the mission. During the ensuing meetings over the next two days, Arnold was given complete authority for the flight. "I received about 4 sets of letters telling me that I was holding the sack with regards to safety, hazard, success, and risk! I in turn told them that I would not say when I would start on the flight until the planes were ready."[72] He immediately returned to Dayton to oversee the final preparations.

Unexpected problems arose with the supply lines to Fairbanks, the target destination: striking longshoremen prevented commercial ships from moving supplies. Rail routes through Canada were available but could not transport the total amount of supplies needed. The U.S. Navy did not care to assist, and a transport ship normally reserved for soldiers was even considered as a possible alternative. Finally the Army acquired a small barge, *El Aquario,* that carried half of the gasoline required for the Alaskan portion of the journey. The rest went by rail.

Additionally, the B-10s were not ready. Each was having a new radio set installed and was landlocked at the depot. By 6 July, six planes were ready for a shakedown flight. Arnold selected Maj. Hugh Knerr, the flight leader for the second flight of three Alaska-bound B-10s, to lead it. At dinner that night, he briefed Knerr on the requirements for the mission, a nonstop flight to Dallas and a nonstop return. Knerr was to test and record the gas and oil consumption of the planes, so that flight planning could be fine-tuned for the longer flight.[73] Arnold realized that a mission of this nature was dependent upon prepositioned supplies. This shakedown flight was specifically designed to refine the necessary logistics—critically restricted by striking longshoremen— so that only the absolute minimum tonnage would be shipped to Alaska. This type of operational planning was essential to smooth operations away from local facilities. The Dallas trip was an important part of the Alaska mission.[74]

The six aircraft were to fly to Dallas on Saturday, 7 July, and return the following day. Actually, the planes flew to Dallas and back the same day, demonstrating remarkable range and reliability. All went as planned, and Arnold called it a "magnificent flight."[75] He hoped that the other planes would be ready after refit. "Sometimes," he explained in a letter to Bee, "I think that we are just marking time here—Then I know that we are moving forward— slowly but surely. We have one grief after another but perhaps there are not so many of them now."[76] The success of the test flight reinforced Arnold's hopes. After the Dallas six-ship formation had returned, plans were finalized, and the departure date was set for 18 July 1934.

Foulois, initially disappointed in the date, realized that a perfect showing one week later was far more desirable than accidents caused by a rushed departure. For the next few days, Arnold had a few moments to relax. In his correspondence, he praised the enlisted men who worked all day and night to ready the aircraft: "They are a mighty fine bunch." He assigned each individual aircrew to one specific plane, believing that the crews would take a greater interest in their aircraft if they were flying it.[77]

Just two days before departing, logistics concerns befuddled Arnold once again. "Well our military establishment most certainly breaks down when an extra load is imposed. Sometimes it is personnel and sometimes it is materiel—who knows which it will be in advance. . . . We have been delayed day after day due to mechanical defects and adjustments which—in my humble opinion—should have been corrected before we ever arrived here."[78]

The logistician in Arnold was disappointed in certain aspects of B-10 production; the supply officer in him pulled out what little hair remained, trying to resolve fuel and consumables issues; and the pilot in him was raring to get going. His experiences served only to reinforce that which he already knew too well: without superior production and appropriate supply, there was no true airpower.

On Tuesday, 18 July, the ten Martin B-10s departed Wright Field at 7:00 A.M.. They arrived in Washington at 9:00 A.M., to a media circus. "I had my picture taken shaking hands with Secy. Woodring so many times that I thought they would never quit." Arnold took Woodring for a short B-10 flight around the Washington area, and then he went to the War Department.[79] There he received his final briefing. Arnold's mission had three specific purposes: first, to test the newest Air Corps bombers, including photo capability; second, to determine the practicability of moving a tactical squadron from the continental United States to Alaska; and third, to demonstrate U.S. goodwill to the people of Alaska, not yet a state.[80]

The team departed Washington the following morning—first stop, Wright Field. On the next leg, two aircraft developed engine trouble and returned to Dayton. After quick repairs, they caught up with the others at Minneapolis. The remainder of the journey to Fairbanks was marked by smooth airplane performance and warm welcomes at every landing place. On 22 July Arnold decided to lay over one day, so that the mechanics could accomplish required periodic checks and maintenance on the bombers. "This day of rest was extremely beneficial to the airplanes," he explained to Bee.[81]

The publicity portion of the mission tried Arnold's patience. "I am getting good willed to death," he complained. He could not wait to reach the wilderness areas of Fairbanks. "When we get out of the entertainment area we will all be much better off. The people are all wonderfully hospitable, too much so but I guess that is all in the game."[82]

Even while airborne, the travelers could not escape the goodwill mission. Halfway between Prince George (British Columbia) and Whitehorse (in the Yukon), Arnold received a radio message from the governor of Alaska offering an official welcome. The radios that had been installed at Wright Field worked tremendously. According to Arnold, they had a "wonderfully big range."[83] In fact, this flight to Alaska was the first Air Corps long-distance mission that maintained continual contact with ground stations along the entire route of flight, even deep into Canada. It was a tribute to the equipment and to the logistic planning.[84] Moreover, the B-10s made the journey from Whitehorse to Fairbanks in four and a half hours. The same journey took two weeks by boat; one month over land. The harsh terrain and lack of improved roads only emphasized the practical aspects of air travel in the Yukon.[85]

The expedition staged sporadic photo operations out of Fairbanks and Anchorage for the next two weeks, even finding an opportunity to stop off in Juneau to accept a totem pole from the mayor of the city. The weather, on the whole, was not very cooperative, but, despite many clouds and low ceilings, the aviators did successfully photograph a majority of the planned target area, including the archipelago.[86]

The only glitch in the mission occurred on a flight out of Anchorage. On the morning of 3 August, rain clouds broke and an opportunity presented itself to photograph some terrain. Arnold recounted the events to Beadle: "Everything went along well until Bobzien," a member of the photo team, not one of the regular crew, "took off. His engines both quit soon after takeoff and he landed in Cooks Inlet. No damage to the plane other than salt water or injury to personnel other than a good wetting." Arnold later found out, though, that Bobzien's mechanic, Sergeant Bush, broke his leg in the ditching. "We are salvaging the plane now. However, I doubt if the plane will ever be used again on account of the salt water bath."[87]

The pilot had mishandled the fuel-control switches and cut off the fuel to the engines.[88] The decision to allow a pilot from outside the mission team to fly the B-10 was one that Arnold certainly regretted and for which he took responsibility. Nowhere in Arnold's correspondence did he ever lay blame for the accident, not even upon the inexperienced pilot.

The working airplanes returned to Fairbanks to complete their photo mission, while Arnold left a mechanical crew in Anchorage to get the still damp Airplane No. 145 in working order if possible. Through superhuman diligence, the ditched B-10 rejoined the rest of the contingent at Fairbanks one week later.[89] The mechanics had not only saved Arnold's reputation after a bad decision, they had also saved the Air Corps considerable embarrassment. To Arnold, those young men were heroes.

The mission was not all work: poor weather afforded a few days of leisure time. Arnold went fishing. On the trip upriver, he saw a menagerie of game and wild flora and fauna. Hap Arnold loved being in the outdoors; he loved to hunt and fish, and he reveled in successes. The fishing trip was a resounding triumph. According to Arnold, he caught "a fish on every cast."[90]

A peculiar yet particularly influential event occurred during one of the "rotten weather" days. While relaxing in his Fairbanks hotel room, Arnold received a call from an unknown local resident asking for a meeting, and Arnold obliged. The gentleman, speaking with a stiff German accent, informed him that he was a spy, and warned him that the Germans were well on their way to rebuilding their air forces. He said that the Martin B-10 was already behind German advances in airpower and technology. Arnold, shocked, called the visitor "a damned liar!"[91]

Before the U.S. Army's intelligence network could investigate these claims, in the spring of 1935 Hermann Goering announced the rebuilding of the Luftwaffe. In the back of his mind Arnold became worried. His concerns preoccupied him, and he would anxiously receive most intelligence reports that came out of Germany before World War II.[92]

On 17 August 1934, the disturbing information about the Luftwaffe a fresh memory, the flight of B-10s left Alaska for the United States. Three days later they landed at Bolling Field, Washington, D.C. The "Alaska Flight" was over, but Arnold's mission was not. That evening he dined with General MacArthur and Secretary of War Dern and was charged to take the B-10s from coast to coast in a demonstration of their speed and reliability.

Arnold took the B-10s back to March Field and prepared for the flight. But when the word finally arrived to launch the mission, gasoline and weather problems prevented the B-10s from making the flight from March Field to Mitchel Field, New York.[93]

After one month's preparation, Arnold had taken his planes nearly 8,000 miles and remained in constant radio contact with the ground. There had been only one major foul-up, and no aircraft had been lost along the way. The round-trip distance to Alaska was 7,360 miles, but Arnold's planes flew aerial mapping missions while deployed there, increasing their total miles flown. A continuation of the flight was accomplished shortly after their return to Washington: westward to March Field and then back to New York. The total mileage flown on the mission, according to Arnold's trip diary, was 18,010 flight miles at an average speed of 168 miles an hour.[94] The success of the mission earned Arnold the Distinguished Flying Cross (DFC) and a second Mackay Trophy. It also proved that long-range bombers could threaten formerly impenetrable and isolated territorial boundaries—both those of potential enemies and those of the United States.

Unfortunately, Arnold's personal recognition also earned him the scorn of at least one of the other flight leaders, Maj. Hugh Knerr.[95] At the conclusion of the mission, Arnold recommended that all the flight crew should receive the DFC for their achievement, but War Department General Staff officials who approved such awards were not fliers; they failed to recognize the contribution made by each pilot. They determined that only the commander of the mission, Hap Arnold, should receive the medal. Arnold had nothing to do with the deliberations on the subject. But Knerr, who had been the primary mission planner until Arnold's arrival in Dayton at the end of June, felt that Arnold was being rewarded for work he had not accomplished—more accurately, that Arnold had received the DFC for work Knerr had accomplished. In the end, Knerr blamed Arnold for Knerr's not receiving a DFC.[96] Knerr was unaware that Arnold had questioned the decision of the War Department and had voiced his complaint directly to Gen. Hugh Drum on 14 November 1934. "Told him it was awfully hard to be loyal to Gen. Staff when they pulled things like that," he wrote to Beadle. "No one could understand why 3 men got it for jumping out of a balloon [*Explorer I*] and we were denied it after flying 18,000 miles. . . . He agreed to reopen case."[97] Arnold's men never got the medal, but he did.

❂ ❂ ❂ ❂ ❂

In November 1934, Arnold once again returned to Washington from March Field, this time to testify before the Howell Commission. FDR had selected the editor of the *Atlanta Constitution,* Clark Howell, a longtime Democratic National Committeeman, to head a Federal Aviation Commission to study American aviation.[98] Arnold traveled via Dayton and participated in a Pursuit Board conference that included many Air Corps operational commanders: Conger Pratt, Frank M. Andrews, B. Q. Jones, Ralph Royce, and others. The mood became somber at the news of Horace Hickam's death in an aircraft accident. Hap explained to Bee that the death was "an almost irreparable loss to the Air Corps. Looking over the crop of Field Officers I can see, right now, no one to fill his place—at this time when need strong men so badly."[99]

Once in Washington, Arnold discovered that none of the Air Corps leadership knew of the purpose behind his summons to testify. That he was permitted to testify was remarkable in itself. A barrage of War Department instructions had severely limited the openness of official testimony. Arnold had been in the office of the Army chief of staff, Malin Craig, just prior to his testimony and had received tacit permission to take the stand. He spent three hours on the witness stand, where he produced "extremely guarded and careful" answers to a host of questions. Perhaps views of the windswept, endless plains of Fort Riley, Kansas, the location of his former exile, were instrumental in Arnold's personal restraint. Only for the final question did he answer more directly.

"Colonel Arnold," one committee member posed, "I am going to ask you a question which you may find embarrassing—Could you straighten out the Air Corps if you were given the opportunity?"

After a brief hesitation, Arnold replied, "If I were given the authority I am sure that I could."[100] That was the end of his testimony. While the commission was packing up, Mr. Howell approached Arnold and asked him to lunch. Arnold accepted. This luncheon provided him an opportunity to assess how his testimony had been received. It turned out that Arnold had done remarkably well.[101] He wrote to Bee, "I believe that I kept my shirt on and made a good impression with the commission. . . . Mr. Howell is a peach—took a shine to me and wants me to visit him in Atlanta. Says I should head the Air Corps."[102] Arnold had just taken his first big step as a spokesman for the Air Corps in the political jungle of Washington.

He returned to testify again after spending the weekend with his brother in Philadelphia, where the siblings were still attempting to resolve estate issues resulting from his father's death. The afternoon he returned to Washington, President Roosevelt wanted to see him. Hap Arnold hurried to the White House, where, during a ten-minute meeting, FDR offered congratulations on the success of the Alaska mission and asked "a hundred questions" about the Yukon.[103] The meeting, Arnold's first alone with the president, was a pleasant success. On a cloud, and with brand-new B-10s under his command, Arnold returned to March Field.

✪   ✪   ✪   ✪   ✪

Arnold always pushed for improvement. One of his favorite places to search for improvements in aeronautics was Caltech, where "Admiral" Millikan had gone a long way in fulfilling his dreams for American aviation. Caltech had the best wind-tunnel facilities in the western United States, and it had one of the finest academic faculties in the nation. The Caltech atmospheric-sciences department, under Dr. Irving Krick, had made remarkable strides in weather forecasting. The civil-aviation industry was beginning to locate nearby in Southern California. Caltech definitely impressed the commanding officer at March Field.[104]

By March 1935, Millikan had introduced Brig. Gen. Hap Arnold to Dr. Theodore von Kármán, director of the Guggenheim Aeronautical Laboratory, California Institute of Technology wind tunnels. The two had become well acquainted.[105] Kármán recalled that he had first seen Arnold as a major, perhaps on one of Arnold's frequent inspection tours to the Los Angeles area while still assigned to Wright Field. "Major Arnold," Kármán remembered in his thick Hungarian accent, "came alvays in the vind toonel and asked me questions."[106] In late 1930, Kármán, in the field of aeronautics second only to his former professor Ludwig Prandtl, had come permanently to Caltech from Aachen, Germany, enticed by a Guggenheim Fund stipend.

Back in 1925, Daniel Guggenheim had donated $500,000 to New York University to speed along the realization of the possibilities of aerial navigation.[107] Through 1930, Guggenheim had funded a variety of aeronautical programs at ten other universities, some to establish schools of aeronautics and others to solve particular aeronautical problems such as blind flying. Guggenheim saw his contributions as a "step toward the up building of civil aviation in this country." He never intended to train pilots. Rather, his intention was to enhance the "training and education of boys . . . in the practical work of designing, building and scientific developing of aircraft and aircraft engines for the utilization of the airplane on a commercial basis."[108]

What Guggenheim failed to assess with any accuracy was the inevitable links that would develop between military aviation and civil aviation. A complex network of established relationships—such as Arnold's with Millikan, Kármán, and aircraft manufacturer Donald Douglas—grew into mutually beneficial working relationships between the Air Corps, university staff, and, most strongly, the aviation industry. The late 1920s, then, witnessed the fertilization of the American airpower megasystem even while, technologically, commercial aviation forged ahead of military air forces. Commercial advantages over the Air Corps were manifest when Postmaster Farley canceled the mail contracts in 1934.[109]

Guggenheim's largesse brought Kármán to America; Millikan's long-term plan for Caltech's eminence brought Arnold to Kármán. Arnold's association with the Jewish Hungarian professor provided him a lifelong, personal tutor in theoretical aeronautical science and its practical application to airpower. The nearness of Caltech to March Field cemented the Air Corps's connection with that school, both personally and institutionally. From 1931 to 1936, Arnold and Kármán developed similar visions for military aviation. Although they arrived at their conclusions from different angles, both men realized that the United States needed a cooperative aeronautics establishment to meld civilian scientific and industrial expertise with the real-world needs of the Army Air Corps.[110] To Arnold, such collaboration meant better combat airplanes—always his primary concern. To Millikan and Kármán, it meant greater influence and funding for Caltech within the West Coast aviation industry—always Millikan's primary concern.

Based on the reports of the Drum Board, the Baker Board, and the Howell Commission, as well as on the experiences gained from experiments with the Provisional General Headquarters formed in late 1934, the General Headquarters Air Force was finally created. GHQ Air Force was capable of organizing independent air operations, directly supporting ground forces, and maintaining responsibility for coastal air defense. The Drum Board had issued the requirement for 2,320 aircraft, a requirement that remained unchanged by the other two committees, largely because of the need for expediency and budget preservation throughout the committee process. The GHQ Air Force became a reality on 1 March 1935.[111]

The new organization's rank structure placed it more in line with that of contemporary ground units. Andrews finalized the restructuring with Drum in January 1935. A brigadier general was to be added on each coast, and the unanimous choice for the West Coast was Hap Arnold.[112] Andrews accomplished what Foulois had only promised. Arnold's promotion to brigadier general in March that year was symbolic of Andrews's respect for Arnold's ability and performance. It did not hurt that they were friends.[113]

The GHQ Air Force, the first manifestation of a truly independent air arm, included an independent mission within the Army. As Spaatz explained it: "The GHQ Air Force was not a compromise; it was quite a step forward at that time, because GHQ Air Force was responsible for strategic targets," which would affect future battles. The service was not, Spaatz emphasized, responsible for tactical targets that affected engaged tactical forces.[114]

In the following testimony, Brigadier General Arnold clearly described the new GHQ Air Force setup to a House Appropriations Committee at March Field:

> An understanding of the setup is necessary to a proper appreciation of the GHQ Air Force and its relationship with the Army as a whole. The components of the Army Air Corps may be considered as falling within three general classifications:
>
> Training Schools
>
> Supply agencies
>
> Tactical units
>
> All training schools and supply agencies are under the jurisdiction of The Chief of the Air Corps. His office is responsible for the procurement and training of personnel and for the development, procurement, and supply of all equipment.
>
> When personnel and equipment so produced are brought together and organized into tactical units, these units become part of the field forces of the Army and consequently pass from the control Chief of the Air Corps to the tactical commanders.[115]

GHQ Air Force represented the combat arm of the service, while the office of the Air Corps held responsibility for finances, training, and materiel. Neither branch, however, controlled tactical bases, which remained under the control of Army Corps Area commanders. During times of war, GHQ Air Force would be assigned directly to the battlefield commander.

Army Corps commanders, on the whole, did not understand the concept of "strategic" uses of air forces as Spaatz had described. Area commanders expected that GHQ Air Force aircraft were to be used for support of the ground armies during advances against the enemy. This argument between surface forces and air forces was institutionalized with the establishment of the GHQ Air Force.[116]

The dual-command situation was ineffective and inefficient, and, though an improvement over earlier arrangements, was never totally satisfactory to aviation branch leaders. There were, however, some aspects of the restructuring that were definitely superior. Arnold's testimony continued as he explained the true benefits of the restructuring:

> The GHQ Air Force scheme provides:
>
> First: Centralized Control
>
> Second: Uniformity in training and employment

Third: Mobility and the assurance of rapid concentration in any threatened area

Fourth: Equipment and personnel on a wartime footing, permitting

Fifth: Instantaneous deployment the moment war is declared.

Of these concepts the most fundamental are mobility and readiness. All our studies in the theory of modern war lead to the conclusion that air forces will be put into operation at the earliest possible moment.[117]

To those who really understood this concept of airpower, the fact that the GHQ Air Force did not control any Corps Area bases may not have been that important. Both Arnold and Spaatz believed in the offensive nature of airpower. Arnold explained: "Practically speaking, there is no such thing as defensive operations in the air. Our whole concept in the Air Force is offensive: to seek out the enemy; to locate him as early and as far distant from our vital areas as we can; then to carry the fight to him and keep it there. . . . The GHQ Air Force, if properly equipped and trained, constitutes a powerful weapon, ready for immediate use and capable of effective action anywhere within its constantly increasing radius of action."[118]

If the air forces could achieve this type of offensive action, the GHQ Air Force would not even have to worry about the Army Area commanders; they would be busy mobilizing troops and packing rucksacks, while the GHQ Air Force was attacking the enemy far from home. Yet even that issue dissolved in July 1936, when the GHQ Air Force assumed jurisdiction over its own peacetime bases.[119] The Alaska Flight had demonstrated the feasibility of long-range strike operations, but it took the development and procurement of a different airplane, one already on the drawing board, to make the concept practical. Until that time, Arnold's vision for the employment of air forces was simply that: a vision.[120]

○   ○   ○   ○   ○

In January 1936, Arnold returned to Washington. Major General Westover had taken over as chief of the Air Corps in late 1935, after Foulois's quiet retirement from military service.[121] Westover had immediately convinced Gen. Malin Craig, Army chief of staff, that he needed Arnold as his assistant. Craig needed no persuasion, as he was already familiar with Arnold's West Coast performance and reputation.[122] Westover, who had opposed separation from the Army throughout his career, and Arnold, perhaps having learned a lesson about bucking the system at too high a level, agreed that remaining part of the Army held definite advantages for the expanding Air Corps, particularly in the area of logistics and support.[123]

Arnold recalled, "the entire family said good-by, in tears, to March Field."

More than sunny California, he hated leaving his position of operational command, even though he was beginning to feel as though he could do more good for the Air Corps in Washington.[124] But Arnold was to become the assistant chief of the Air Corps and, as such, was placed in direct friendly competition with Andrews's GHQ Air Force. Bee later recalled that March held special memories for her, because it was the last time the Arnold family all lived together under one roof. The children were of age to fly on their own, and they began to leave the nest.[125]

During his first two years back in Washington, Arnold handled a hodge-podge of administrative and public-relations problems. He participated in the restructuring of the Air Corps and the development of the GHQ Air Force system. As Westover's assistant, his views on science, technology, and the Army Air Corps gained nationwide attention, even in the midst of internal Air Corps turbulence.

In January 1936, an Inspector General's study known as the Browning Board recognized the detrimental effect that the dual structure was having on the Air Corps. Col. William S. Browning's panel recommended a consolidation of Air Corps structure that would place the GHQ Air Force under the command of the office of the chief of the Air Corps. Although this recommendation was eventually adopted in March 1939, it was not until June 1941, when the Army Air Forces were officially established, that the situation was finally resolved.[126]

But before the March 1939 restructuring, Arnold chaired a 1936 committee examining how best to create a "balanced air program." There was nothing unusual in his report; in fact, it followed very closely the recommendations made previously by the Drum Board. The numbers for personnel and planes in each report were similar. Surprising today but realistic at that time, the forecast for airplanes totaled 1,399 in 1936, increasing to a meager 2,708 in 1941.[127] Arnold's report primarily attempted to reckon with recovering budgets; no mention was made of scientific research or technological development. Rather, the program's primary concern was purely practical: to save dollars in all areas except purchasing airplanes.

Arnold considered it amazing that despite the rapidly changing global situation, the War Department had done little "clear-cut thinking about American air power." Mussolini's invasion of Ethiopia in 1935, the unveiling of the Luftwaffe in the Spanish Civil War, Adolf Hitler's remilitarization of the Rhineland in 1936, and the Japanese bombing of Shanghai in 1937 all seemed signals of instability and potential future conflict.[128] These events had an impact on Arnold.

By September 1937, General Arnold had modified the conservative approach that his balanced-air-program report had taken. While addressing the Western Aviation Planning Conference, Arnold summarized his philosophy for creating an aeronautical institution in the United States that would be second to none.

Remember that the seed comes first; if you are to reap a harvest of aeronautical development, you must plant the seed called *experimental research*. Install aeronautical branches in your universities; encourage your young men to take up aeronautical engineering. It is a new field but it is likely to prove a very productive one indeed. Spend all the funds you can possibly make available on experimentation and research. Next, do not visualize aviation merely as a collection of airplanes. It is broad and far reaching. It combines manufacture, schools, transportation, airdrome, building and management, air munitions and armaments, metallurgy, mills and mines, finance and banking, and finally, public security—national defense.[129]

Arnold's statement described the evolving technological system of airpower in broad terms, even if he did not make a distinction between empirical versus theoretical research. If the Air Corps had little money for R and D, then perhaps universities and industry could be persuaded to find some. After all, it had been the Guggenheim Fund that had fostered aeronautical departments at several universities almost a decade earlier.[130]

No matter the source, experimental research appeared to be the key to future airpower. Arnold had very cleverly linked Air Corps development to civilian prosperity in the aviation industry, hoping that civilian institutions would pick up research while the Air Corps acquired planes. His ideas reflected Millikan's philosophy—that of bringing the center of aeronautical science in America to Caltech—which had shaped that university since the 1920s. This philosophy, coupled with Arnold's realization that airpower was a complex system of logistics, procurement, ground support bases, and operations, guided his vision for future growth.[131] Arnold's approach to airpower development demonstrated what today is commonly known as the Military-Industrial-Academic complex.[132]

In addition to bolstering industrial and public support for the technological advancement of the Air Corps, Arnold was continually forced to deal with the inherent administrative confusion caused by the establishment of GHQ Air Force the year before. In particular, responsibility for aeronautical research was not well defined between the branches, further slowing his efforts there. Nevertheless, the GHQ Air Force was the first crack in the foundation of the U.S. Army's total control over airpower.[133]

In an effort to spread the word about the potential of airpower, Arnold and Capt. Ira C. Eaker, at that time living at the University of Southern California and taking courses at the school in journalism, published *This Flying Game* in 1936. Arnold actually completed about half of the book while still commanding March Field in 1935. Eaker, a skilled editor, cleaned up the work for publication. As the title implied, the book summarized the many facets of military aviation and included a brief historical review. The authors covered the origins of flight, the most heroic aviation events through the 1930s, airpower strategy, and future concepts for the air weapon. Arnold described the rigors of pilot training and the nature of military airpower by translating his own experience into colorful descriptions for younger readers, whom he saw as potential aviation cadets. The essence of the United States's aviation system was detailed in chapters that described naval air operations and the functions and importance of aircraft maintenance and civil industry.

One of the most striking additions to the work was Arnold's early realization of the valuable contribution and enthusiasm of women fliers in America. He used the most famous contemporary example to encourage other young women to follow aeronautical paths. "Amelia Earhart's exploits," Arnold wrote, "have given her a sure place among the fliers of this generation despite any prejudice against her sex in this hazardous field of endeavor."[134] He tried not to alienate American women, realizing that in the system of airpower that he envisioned, women played an essential role in the factories and support fields. Later, he would enlist women pilots to facilitate the transport of aircraft throughout the United States and in some locations abroad.

The authors also described the standards expected and the qualities possessed by successful military-aviation cadets. Arnold painted a clear picture of desirable qualities for military aviators that, in large measure, have survived a variety of modern social pressures. Once past the physical examination—only one in five applicants qualified—a board of experienced pilots evaluated the candidate to establish whether he was "the flying type." Arnold explained that the board tried to determine if the young man was

> of good moral fiber; whether he is honest, truthful, reliable—whether he possessed the *sine qua non,* courage. Few boys who are effeminate or unmanly get called. Those who are sullen, morose, or antagonistic in personality are generally rejected. The frank, open-faced, pleasant-mannered, serious-minded, cooperatively-inclined boy is the one who is wanted and the one who is selected nine times out of ten.
>
> Any boy who does not possess the characteristics outlined in the preceding paragraphs, who knows in his heart that he is entirely out of step with the ideal flying candidate as pictured here, is simply wasting his time in applying for flying training with Uncle Sam.[135]

Arnold revealed his basic philosophy on employment of airpower within the pages of this work. He advocated the bombing of targets well within the boundaries of hostile territories, reasoning that such bombardments would "have a considerable effect upon the military forces to carry out their plans." He advocated the destruction of railyards, docks, water supplies, bridges, and transportation lines for the enemy's military supplies. To him, the complete effect of this strategy would result in "breaking down the will of the [enemy] people."[136] In essence, Arnold's airpower philosophy was a combination of

Italian theorist Guilio Douhet's morale bombing and Mitchell's strategic-targeting ideas. Arnold envisioned possible uses for both methods, and these resurfaced during his years in command of the Army Air Forces.

Logically, *This Flying Game* concludes by offering some views toward the future of aviation. This last chapter reveals the most about Arnold's early methods for predicting progress for airpower:

> Safe, sure, and sensible prognostications for the future must be based upon events, occurrences, and developments of the past. This is as true in aviation as in any of the older fields of invention or discovery. Too often, during our twenty-four years' experience in air work, the statement has been heard that this or that cannot be done. Perhaps in no other field have the events of to-day made liars out of the prophets of yesterday as completely and rapidly as in the air game. When surmising the future of human flight it is far wiser to predict what may be done than to announce what will not be achieved.[137]

The book even included conjecture about the evolution of aircraft engines from increased potential for propeller-driven craft to "some yet undiscovered power source, untapped or unharnessed," not too far off.

Perhaps the greatest indication that Arnold was convinced about the continued development of airpower into an enormous network of systems—civil and military—was demonstrated by his selection of Donald Douglas as the author of the book's preface. Arnold was cementing the relationship between industry and the military by using his personal friendship with Douglas, one that had developed early in the history of American aviation. Building such relationships was common practice for the ebullient Arnold.

But all did not remain rosy in Arnold's life for long: as was all too frequent an occurrence in these early years of aviation, a tragic aircraft accident claimed the life of Maj. Gen. Oscar Westover on 21 September 1938. The preliminary investigation board concluded that Westover had encountered "a combination of unforseen circumstances and unusual conditions consisting of turbulent air, unusual wind currents from nearby mountains, and convection currents from super-heated concrete pavements which caused a wingtip stall resulting in a left tail spin of about two turns." His proximity to the ground prevented a recovery from this situation. Westover and his passenger, Staff Sergeant Hymes, were killed during the initial impact and incinerated in the ensuing fire. Preliminary findings suggested that local wind conditions rather than pilot error were to blame for the crash.[138] Once again, the stall-and-spin combination had triumphed over human reaction time.

The truth about the events of the ensuing eight days—the days before Arnold gained approval to succeed Westover as chief of the Air Corps—may never be revealed. The weekend of 22–23 September was reserved for grieving. But during the week of 24–28 September, Roosevelt likely met with several advisers in an effort to select the most qualified military leader and political supporter. Arnold's recollections in *Global Mission* describe a "smear campaign" targeting him. Rumors flew of previous exhibitions of drunkenness. Arnold never would discover the origin of these rumors, nor would he try to.[139]

Evidence is largely circumstantial. In late 1936, General Westover waged an Air Corps–wide attack on irresponsible alcohol consumption. Andrews agreed that drinking and flying did not mix, but he was less sure of the approach that Westover had chosen: distribution of drinking-policy letters to each and every GHQ Air Force field officer. "Frankly if I could have discussed the letter in question with you before its issuance I would have advised against it. In spite of its being confidential such matters are bound to leak out at least to the other branches and the general reaction is that things must be pretty bad in the Air Corps if such letters have to be written." Andrews, further, insisted that all such correspondence be immediately destroyed within Westover's staff, and from each and every officer's performance report (201 file).[140]

Two inferences can be made from the publication of the letter and Andrews's response. The most important is that Westover did not perceive Arnold as a drunkard, or he would have removed him as his assistant long before September 1938. Second, it is possible that one of FDR's political enemies had somehow discovered the Westover antidrinking campaign and was shamelessly using it to influence the selection of a different chief of the Air Corps. It is unlikely that the rumor was propagated by a member of the Air Corps itself; none were close enough to Roosevelt to wield such influence. One of FDR's most trusted advisers, Harry Hopkins, knew Arnold. It may have been Hopkins or perhaps Clark Howell who squelched the ploy.

To delineate Arnold's drinking habits during these years is not difficult. He patently denied in his memoirs that he drank "hard liquor," while in his correspondence to Beadle, he freely admitted how many drinks of sherry or port he had consumed at a dinner party.[141] As a service academy graduate raised under the honor code, Arnold would not likely have lied.[142]

But the best proof is the simple fact that Hap Arnold was Westover's assistant chief of the Air Corps. Westover's stance against the overuse of alcohol had been made clear to the entire officer corps. Arnold was not only aware of it, he may even have helped draft the policy, particularly if his past ravings about drunken behavior by officers' wives at Rockwell Field provides any clue as to his own views on the matter. Had General Arnold violated the dictum, there is little doubt that he would have been removed from Westover's service.

Instead, Hap Arnold was selected as the top man in the Air Corps. His experience in Army aviation had prepared him for the tasks that awaited him. On 1 March 1939, the same day that Maj. Gen. Delos C. Emmons replaced

Frank Andrews as GHQ Air Force commander, GHQ Air Force was subordinated to the chief of the Air Corps. From that day, Hap Arnold—operationally experienced under Andrews's GHQ Air Force and administratively experienced under Westover's Air Corps—was in a position to tackle the Air Corps's problems, as he once had told Mr. Howell he could.

9

CHIEF OF THE ARMY AIR CORPS
(1938–41)

When Major General Arnold "shook the stick" and officially took command of the Air Corps on 29 September 1938, many military-aviation projects were under consideration both at Wright Field and at the NACA facility at Langley Field, Virginia: radar, aircraft-windshield deicing, a rocket booster to assist in heavy-aircraft takeoffs, and a host of aircraft and engine design modifications. Many of these projects were related to the four-engine B-17 heavy bomber, brand new but struggling for existence. The plane was an aviation-technology leap in itself.[1] Arnold wasted no time in calling his scientists, "long hairs," to a meeting at the National Academy of Sciences (NAS), under the auspices of the Committee on Air Corps Research, to solve these problems.[2]

It was no surprise that Arnold immediately accelerated Air Corps R and D efforts. In his first message as Air Corps commander, he devoted a paragraph to the subject that reflected his fears concerning advances in foreign airpower technology. "Until quite recently," he stated, "we have had marked superiority in airplanes, engines, and accessories. That superiority is now definitely challenged by recent developments abroad. This means that our experimental development programs must be speeded up."[3] The developments to which Arnold referred did not include the appeasement pact signed at Munich by Neville Chamberlain and Adolf Hitler, though it dominated the news that same day. Rather, his concern involved German developments in aviation. Trusted civilians who had seen the expansion of German industry with their own eyes had kept Arnold informed.[4] From September 1938 until his death in 1950, Hap Arnold kept technological change and its impact upon airpower at the forefront of his command efforts.

Since August 1936, he had advocated a balanced air program. To him, this meant one that supported balance between airplanes, personnel, and bases; not one that emphasized equilibrium in aircraft types (fighters versus bombers). Changes in one of the elements necessarily affected the other two, and without balance between them, inefficiency and budgetary waste resulted. In effect, Arnold believed that a mathematical formula of sorts existed that maximized the utility of airpower. When one part of the formula was lacking, emphasis was logically placed in that area until the formula was once again balanced. The buildup of airpower during his tenure was predicated upon an ever more complex equation of combat crews, airplanes, and base facilities, all of which needed to grow in harmony so as to maximize the potential of available airpower. It was this basic plan that influenced FDR's expansion of the Air Corps in November 1939.[5]

Arnold's increased emphasis on R and D was intended to improve the capability of Air Corps aircraft early in the expansion program.

> The present period in the history of our Air Corps is a trying one for officers and enlisted alike. Everyone must put forth at maximum effort to meet the herculean demands incident to our expansion program. The GHQ Air Force has performed an efficient and commendable task of reorganizing of tactical units and raising to a high level their state of training. This has but served to emphasize the urgent need for more combat and maintenance crews. The air base forces must be greatly increased and in some cases created in order to properly operate and care for the airplanes now being produced as the result of high pressure work on the part of Materiel Division. This necessitates that our Training Center, the Tactical School and the Technical School work at accelerated efficiency, mayhap at longer hours, and increase their output without lowering their present high standards.[6]

Arnold had just left GHQ Air Force as a wing commander, and he spoke with genuine and uninflated authority on GHQ's accomplishments. He also established that training was his top priority for the immediate future of the Air Corps—training of top-notch combat aircrew and excellent aircraft mechanics.

In Arnold's 1936 report, he had noted that "an acute shortage exists in the number of primary training airplanes to train the number of pilots to provide for a balanced program."[7] Logically, he now placed immediate emphasis on solving the training issue, and, after GHQ was subordinated to the commander of Air Corps in March 1939, he had the authority do things his way. This was a situation that did not always please the new GHQ commander, Delos Emmons.

Tooey Spaatz understood Arnold's methods.

There were only a certain number of officers in the Air Corps then [about 2,100], and in building up Hap's program, he had to tear down Emmons' program. In building up the training, he had to tear down the tactical. That's the first thing you have to do. That resulted in arguments and friction between them. Emmons thought Hap was tearing him down too fast. Hap thought that building up the training was more important than building up any particular tactical operations that he might have going on. . . . I think Hap saw that the war was going to be fought eventually over in Europe, and the thing to do was to get personnel into training commands, training centers, and get the production of airplanes going and build up the Air Force. It was just a difference of approach.[8]

Even though the approach was different than the one Emmons might have developed, Spaatz never suggested that anyone but Arnold could have spearheaded the Air Corps from 1938 through the end of World War II.[9]

A close second after training, R and D was given far greater attention than it had received in the past. Arnold's philosophy and a loosening of purse strings increased Air Corps spending to more than $100 million on research alone from July 1940 to July 1941. The "very heavy bomber" program—a program that the Army General Staff had seen little need for in 1938—accounted for $42 million of that total.[10]

Assisting the R and D speeding-up process that Arnold directed, the Guggenheim Aeronautical Laboratory at the California Institute of Technology (GALCIT) and MIT sent representatives to the November NAS meeting. Vannevar Bush and Jerome Hunsaker, both of MIT, grabbed a windshield-de-icing problem for their institution while openly dismissing the rocket-assisted-takeoff program that was later known as JATO, jet-assisted takeoff.

Hunsaker called JATO the "Buck Rogers" job. The first JATO system actually consisted of six eighteen-inch-long rocket motors, not jets, strapped to the underwing of an Army Aercoupe aircraft. The rockets fired for approximately three seconds, boosting the craft to remarkable altitudes.

Bush explained to Robert Millikan and Kármán that he had never understood how "a serious engineer or scientist could play around with rockets."[11] This was actually the prevalent view among scientists at that time. But in a definite reversal of view eighteen months later, Bush, as head of the NACA, offered assistance to Caltech for three separate rocket-assisted programs, two for the Army and one for the Navy.[12] The potential Arnold had realized earlier had finally won formal acceptance from Bush. In recently declassified documents, it is revealed that it was not until Dr. William F. Durand convinced Bush of the project's efficacy that the latter agreed to funding it.[13]

Because of his previous association with Caltech, Arnold knew that GALCIT had already demonstrated some success with rocket technology. The condescending attitude held by the MIT elite did not go over well with Arnold. From this meeting onward, he thought of Bush as less than forward-looking, despite Bush's excellent, even pioneering record in electrical engineering. The case of Vannevar Bush is a classic example of how a talented individual became persona non grata within Arnold's Air Corps. Bush and the institutions he led, concerning specific Air Corps matters, were relegated to less spectacular projects, still requiring concentrated efforts. He was dropped from confidence concerning long-term projects because Arnold did not care for his attitude about the future of jets and rockets.

On the other hand, Millikan and Kármán, representing GALCIT, eagerly accepted the JATO challenge, an attitude that Arnold appreciated and even expected from his longtime associates from California.[14] JATO represented potential funding for the struggling GALCIT Rocket Research Project, established in 1936. This project, also known as GALCIT Project No. 1, was established by Drs. Theodore von Kármán and Frank Malina, and it exists today as the Jet Propulsion Laboratory. It was after his meeting at NAS that Arnold officially began his association with Kármán.

Since his days at March Field, he had seen Kármán as useful in recognizing undeveloped aeronautics technology. Kármán, in complementary fashion, saw the Army Air Corps as a worthy recipient of his services. More important, however, the funding that Arnold made available seemed bottomless and helped Caltech maintain its status as the leading aeronautics university in the country. Kármán was committed to helping the Army but was also dedicated to Caltech, the GALCIT, and Robert Millikan. Nonetheless, this alliance, above all others that Arnold held with scientists and engineers, would prove one of the most significant and engaging collaborations in the development of American airpower. In Kármán, Arnold found the civilian scientist he required as part of his balanced-air-program equation.

The November 1938 NAS meeting was the beginning of Maj. Gen. Hap Arnold's push toward making science and technology a central feature of the Army Air Corps. He even invited General Marshall, then deputy chief of staff, to a luncheon with the visiting scientists. Marshall wondered, "What on earth are you doing with people like that?" Arnold replied that he was "using" their brain power to develop devices "too difficult for the Air Force engineers to develop themselves."[15] He realized that civilian help was the only way to ensure that the Air Corps had the most advanced technology available. He did not much care where the devices came from, only that his Corps benefited from them. By introducing Marshall to this circle of scientists, Arnold garnered support for advanced technology and production R and D from someone who, under Frank Andrews's careful tutelage, already understood the operational importance of airpower. Marshall, who took Malin Craig's place as Army chief of staff in July 1939, became a staunch advocate of the Army Air Forces during World War II, largely due to the airpower education provided by Andrews and Arnold.

Looming war clouds added pressure to all branches of the military, but the Air Corps had the largest burden to carry. The service had to procure not only the weapons of war but also the infrastructure to build them before any real combat preparations could be made. This was no easy task. The airmen's primary weapon was to be the four-engine, long-range Boeing B-17, and it had been canceled in June 1938. Arnold had once called the B-17 "the first real American Air Power. . . . Not just brilliant prophecies, good coastal defense airplanes, or promising techniques; but, for the first time in American history, Air Power that you could put your hand on."[16] In historic importance, he likened the B-17 to the first Wright Military Flyer.[17]

The B-17 was capable of reaching "any part of the enemy country in which the Supreme Commander may wish to destroy important military objectives."[18] According to Arnold, the copilot seat had been added not to work side by side during operations; rather, "it had been installed because the implied range of this airplane suggested that a single pilot would not fly it all the time—[it] showed a new conception of air power."[19] Arnold, Andrews, Spaatz, and many others well understood the important concept of long-range, strategic strikes against the enemy—close-in, tactical strikes in direct support of field forces were secondary in importance, according to unwritten Air Corps doctrine.

Unfortunately the surface forces did not agree, nor did they appear to understand Air Corps philosophy about the employment of airpower and the nature of air force. Procurement of aircraft in 1939 and 1940 was restricted to types designed for direct support of ground troops.[20] Drawing tactical lessons from events in China and Spain, many believed that direct air support for ground troops was the compelling mission for air forces. Air Corps doctrine did not reflect that mission with the same priority, and Arnold continually tried to rectify the misunderstanding by explaining that military air operations consisted of two distinct subdivisions. In September 1937 he had tried to enlighten the Aviation Planning Board: "The first is a member of a combat team, where it supports infantry, artillery and other ground arms. Then, we have the second subdivision called 'Air Force Operations,' where aviation may go far behind the enemy lines, destroy highway bridges, rail centers, manufacturing establishments, and also harass densely populated areas in an effort to break the national will to fight thus forcing Governmental heads to sue for peace."[21]

As far as the Spanish civil war was concerned, Arnold once said, "Anybody who draws any lessons from it, believing that they are equally applicable to two leading world powers in conflict, makes a great mistake. . . . It so happens that no real Air Forces have been engaged there and no Air Force operations on a major scale have been attempted."[22] Arnold, like many airmen, understood the clear differences between strategic bombing and close support of ground armies. The lessons from this conflict did nothing to bolster the case for procurement of long-range bombers: agreeing to use the B-17s would necessarily mean that target numbers of aircraft would not be reached by 1940.

As early as 1937, Arnold had campaigned to expand the aircraft industry's manufacturing infrastructure. "At the present state of the industry," he had adroitly explained, "there is no such thing as a rapid and vast war-time expansion of an airline factory, it simply cannot be done. No first-class aviation factory can double its production out-put of war machines in less than a year."[23] But these words had fallen on deaf ears, until world events dictated a radical change in American foreign policy.

Not only did Arnold seek the advice of scientists, he also gathered information from civilian aviators and industrialists. He had exchanged letters with Charles A. Lindbergh, who was touring Europe in 1938. Lindbergh expressed concern over U.S. lethargy in airplane development: "It seems to me that we should be developing prototypes with a top speed in the vicinity of 500 mph at altitude . . . the trend over here seems to be toward very high speed."[24] This revelation worried Arnold.

In March 1939, Arnold established a special air board to study the problems that Lindbergh had addressed. By April he had convinced Lindbergh to accept an active-duty commission as a member of the study group.[25] This group, known as the Kilner Board, produced a five-year plan for research and development within the Air Corps. The report was shortsighted in many respects, but it did represent the immediate needs of the air arm. Jet propulsion and missiles, for example, were not even mentioned.[26] This latter was surprising, considering that Ezra Kotcher, from the Engineering Division at Wright Field, had submitted a recommendation to the board suggesting that a long-term, transonic-flight research program be initiated at once. To support such a program, gas turbines, rocket-propulsion systems, and high-speed wind tunnels would be essential to the task, as propeller-driven aircraft were incapable of sustained flight at such high speeds, and tunnels were rare.[27]

Another report to Arnold, this from trusted friend and industrialist Larry Bell, suggested that one single German aircraft factory was already producing up to 5,000 aircraft each year, while employing over 70,000 workers. This was superb fodder for American audiences thirsty for reasons to build air forces. Though the numbers were not totally substantiated at that time, they were, in actuality, extremely accurate.[28]

Lindbergh's public impact was immediate but short-lived. In a written recommendation for the NACA by Lindbergh, he gained support for an expanded aeronautical-research facility to be located at Moffett Field, California. The funding was approved on 15 September 1939, the same morning he spoke out against American participation in the European war on three major national radio networks. President Roosevelt had unsuccessfully tried to dissuade him from taking his views directly to the nation.[29]

Lindbergh was a skilled communicator. After his nonstop 1927 flight from New York to Paris, the Guggenheim Fund had invested $100,000 to subsidize a national tour expressly designed to generate support for aviation. By the end of the 1920s, Lindbergh had toured more than eighty cities and influenced millions of Americans. In many respects he had become the American spokesman for aviation.[30] As such, his words carried an inordinate amount of influence. Fearing his effect on public opinion, FDR promised Lindbergh a new cabinet post if he remained silent concerning possible American participation in the European war. Arnold was caught in the middle of the presidential offer, but there was never any doubt in the general's mind that Lindbergh would turn it down and speak his own mind. Arnold was right. Consequently, Lindbergh gave up his commission. But Arnold had already taken to heart his earlier warnings about German aeronautical developments.[31]

Whether Lindbergh, and others as well, had been duped by the Nazis during preplanned factory tours in Germany turned out to be irrelevant. Arnold may have given any firsthand reports from Germany more credibility because of the warning he had received from a German citizen, a self-proclaimed spy, during the 1934 trip to Alaska.[32]

In 1939, while Caltech scientists were working on the JATO problem, Arnold told Kármán of his belief that experimental research was the only way to get and keep American aeronautics ahead of other nations.[33] Arnold wanted to know specifically what type of equipment the Air Corps needed to accelerate the process, and Kármán suggested that a high-speed wind tunnel be built at Wright Field, one operating at 40,000 horsepower. Kármán had earlier suggested the idea to George W. Lewis of the NACA, who refused to consider it. At that time it had been a revolutionary piece of equipment. Arnold immediately found funding for the project, but when George Lewis heard of the Air Corps's attempt to expand its own basic research, he flatly opposed any form of military R and D whatsoever. Further, if there was to be a 20-foot wind tunnel at all, the NACA would build it and would ensure it was designed by the one man who could do the best job.

> "And who is that?" Arnold asked Lewis.
> "Kármán."
> "You're too late. He's designing the wind tunnel for me."[34]

Arnold had zeroed in on Kármán's unique mastery of aeronautics as a tool for the air forces. It was a choice that Lewis unwittingly verified. After the war, Arnold summarized his perceptions on the deficiencies within the NACA.

> It is probable that the NACA, in following its directive to study the "problems of flight," concerned itself overly with the device, with the vehicle of flight. Either the scope of the NACA has been interpreted narrowly, or com-

plimentary subsidization should have been established as fruitful and unexplored fields of research became apparent. The NACA's treatment of the "problems of flight" might be compared to the use of a government subsidy solely for the technical development of the automobile without paying any attention to roads and other complimentary facilities. Those factors which enable the airplane to operate over vast distances or which make it a vital element in the social and economic structure were neglected.[35]

Arnold realized that the NACA, since its creation in 1915, had made vital contributions to aircraft hardware and design. But the organization was doing so without considering how the developments fit into the Air Corps's balanced air program. This was the source of his frustration with the NACA. Airpower was more than simply technologically advanced airplanes; it was the combination of those planes with the infrastructure that turned aircraft into airpower.[36]

By 1939 Arnold's dedication to continuous research, experimentation, and development was more focused, more defined than ever. And he carried that message across the country. His public-awareness campaigns reflected Lindbergh's and Bell's observations and cautions. In January 1939, while speaking to the Society of Automotive Engineers in Detroit, he emphasized that the United States was falling behind in aircraft development and attributed this failing to an inadequate program of scientific research. "All of us in the Army Air Corps," he stated, "realize that America owes its present prestige and standing in the air world in large measure to the money, time, and effort expended in aeronautical experimentation and research. We know that our future supremacy in the air depends on the brains and efforts of our engineers."[37]

During 1939, Arnold supported production R and D and also advocated long-term R and D projects. One initiative, building massive new facilities at Wright Field, was a multiyear project. Additionally, the type of research that Arnold wanted included basic as well as production research. He firmly believed that R and D was an investment. "A few extra million dollars in research and experimental work spent today, tomorrow may bring us dividends in security that no amount of money could buy."[38]

Arnold's official correspondence reflected the same commitment to R and D. In a memorandum to the assistant secretary of war dated 2 March 1939, he vigorously defended proposed funding.

> The work of the large number of aeronautical research agencies in this country should be afforded government support and encouragement only through a single coordinating agency which can determine that the individual and collective effort will be to the best interests of the Government. The NACA is the agency designated by law to carry out basic aeronautical re-

search and its own plant and facilities cannot cover all phases of development. Furthermore, there are many public or semi-public institutions whose students or other research personnel are willing and anxious to perform useful investigation that will contribute to a real advancement of the various branches of aeronautical science.[39]

A member of the NACA Main Committee since becoming chief of the Air Corps, Arnold attended the committee meetings regularly and was familiar with the workings of the group. More important, he was acquainted with the other Main Committee members, who together read like a Who's Who in American aviation. Dr. Vannevar Bush, Orville Wright, Charles Lindbergh, and Harry Guggenheim were all members of the Main Committee in 1939.

Realizing the importance of the technical work being accomplished by the NACA, Arnold established an official liaison between the NACA facilities at Langley Field and the Air Corps Materiel Division at Wright Field. He assigned Maj. Carl F. Greene to the post, in an effort to tighten the relationship between the two organizations.[40] The attempt to consolidate R and D programs was valiant, but time was running short. Conflict in Europe assured that the relationship would never really mature.

The expanding war in Europe dictated a posture of increased readiness for the United States. Even before Germany invaded Poland in September 1939, Arnold realized that to create an effective fighting air force, all American production efforts—requiring massive amounts of labor—would be needed just to build enough aircraft of the designs that were already available.[41] But there was a change in his philosophy after the blitzkrieg crushed Poland and then France.

What had previously been acceptable R and D practice for Arnold—long-term projects for advances in the fundamental research as well as applied or production research—held little promise for immediate payback. The realization that war was coming led him to concentrate almost all R and D efforts on only those projects that would see results in production of training aircraft and combat airplanes to be used as soon as possible against the enemy. Within the Air Corps, fundamental research—basic theoretical aeronautical R and D— would have to take a backseat to the necessities of war. Later, after the war was over, Arnold would be even more convinced that he had made the right decision concerning wartime applied research and aircraft development. "For us to have expended our effort on future weapons to win a war at hand," he wrote General Spaatz at war's end, "would be as stupid as trying to win the next war with outmoded weapons and doctrines."[42]

From September 1939 until the spring of 1944, Arnold directed that the majority of Army aviation R and D efforts be dedicated to near-term improvements in 1939 technologies: the B-17, B-29, fighter aircraft, rocket propulsion, glide bombs, and radar, to name a few. He summed up what would

become his wartime R and D philosophy: "Sacrifice some quality to get sufficient quantity to supply all fighting units. Never follow the mirage, looking for
the perfect airplane, to a point where fighting squadrons are deficient in numbers of fighting planes."[43]

The essence of technological change for the Air Corps involved accepting
and managing a certain amount of risk. The desire for better technology requiring modification and experimentation was overshadowed by the Air
Corps's need for mass production. Arnold realized the polarity and struck a
balance between the need for vast numbers of planes and the desire for better
planes. In the end, a delicate equilibrium was achieved by adherence to his belief in a balanced air program.[44]

During 1939, two factors came to the forefront of Arnold's decision-making process concerning technological development: training and production.
As he explained it to the National Aviation Forum that February: "Please bear
in mind much time is required to build up an air force. It cannot be done
overnight—18 months are required to reach quantity production in planes,
note I said reach—2 years are required to train personnel to make them competent to handle our complicated aircraft. Delay in beginning will make for
undue haste to catch up and frenzied haste makes for waste and extrava-
gance."[45]

Arnold saw a six-month gap between training and production. For the two
systems—aircraft production and aircrew training—to eventually meet,
training was the most urgent priority. Research too had an associated turnaround time, and Arnold believed that the full impact of experimental R and
D was not felt in production "for at least two years."[46] A two-year cycle in aircrew and mechanic training coupled with the lag time for R and D impact dictated the critical outside edge of the development and production cycle.

The apparent ease with which Germany swept into Poland in September
1939 (though many had warned that the country was weak and vulnerable to
invasion) signaled the deterioration of the European military situation. By
May 1940, when Germany quickly overran France and the Low Countries,
FDR had called for a fivefold increase in American aircraft production. Fifty
thousand planes each year seemed a tall order to everyone but Arnold, who
had recommended an even greater number of combat planes despite his staff's
conservative estimates.[47]

Lauris Norstad, a member of Arnold's advisory council, recalled the process
leading to his recommendation. The general had called all his top people together in Washington and urged them: "Gentlemen, here is our opportunity to
tell people in authority and to tell the country what we need. The president has
asked for this figure. I am going to give you until tomorrow morning at 9
o'clock, and you think about how many airplanes we are going to ask for. It
has to be real, but use your imagination. Don't hold yourselves back to restrictions of budgets under which we have been trained in the last few years."[48]

The following morning Arnold announced, "Gentlemen, I am going to call on you to give me your figures. Again, I will tell you, be bold." The first officer suggested an additional squadron at Atlanta, the second asked for a squadron at Oklahoma City, and so on. "Gentlemen, at the outside, even with replacements, this adds up to about 100 planes. To hell with you! I'm going over to the White House now, and do you know what I'm going to tell the President? I am going to tell the President that we need 100,000 airplanes." And according to Norstad, he did.[49]

If FDR's September 1938 aircraft-production plan had truly been the Air Corps's Magna Carta, then the massive expansion that he ordered in 1940 bordered on a de facto Declaration of Independence from the Army—even considering Lend-Lease commitments. Roosevelt, Hopkins, and Marshall had been convinced that the only force that could immediately strike at the heart of the United States's enemies was an air force operating independently from surface forces; tactical forces would be needed later. The "50,000 aircraft" speech acknowledged that the Air Corps would soon operate independently from other military branches at the strategic level.[50] Arnold's suggested number of combat planes would be reached near the end of the war.

Arnold's World War I experiences with aircraft and engine production had convinced him of vast expansion capabilities within American industry, a lesson he did not forget. Apparently FDR, a former assistant secretary of the Navy, had learned a lesson from that war as well. The Wilson administration's policy of neutrality had prevented any serious preparation for war until it had been too late for American industry to gear up for mass production of air weapons. FDR's decision to build planes, and lots of them, was based largely upon the advice of his trusted adviser Harry Hopkins. Hopkins had carefully listened to Arnold and Marshall, who also advocated a buildup in aircraft production, ensuring that American industrial strength would make an impact during the war.

In early January 1939, Arnold had begun his campaign of personal encouragement in the factories, training facilities, and support locations. The spirit behind his enthusiasm was a direct result of the lessons he had learned in the last World War. As he told of that experience, "in the beginning the American aircraft industry had a capacity of less than 100 planes a year. I saw one factory sign a contract eighteen months later to deliver 100 planes a day. . . . The American aircraft industry today is incomparably superior in every regard to the state it had reached even at the close of the last war. . . . So, make no mistake about it, we shall train the mechanics, we shall train the flyers, and we shall build the planes."[51]

Consequently, much of Arnold's time in the months prior to Pearl Harbor and in the early years of American involvement was spent touring factories, arranging training courses for new pilots, establishing bases of operations, haggling over congressional legislation, and encouraging the factory workers he believed were vital to the creation of real American airpower. Arnold personally spent the time touring, because he feared that aircraft production was well behind schedule.

It was not uncommon for him to depart Washington on an Air Corps DC-3, arrive in California early the following day, inspect several aircraft plants and air bases, hop on the plane again, and return to Washington for another full week of work. Gene Beebe, whom Arnold had brought to Washington in November 1938 as his personal pilot and office aide, could hardly keep up. "It wasn't unusual to fly 24 hours with General Arnold. He liked to get away from Washington, and get away fast." [52] Arnold created the frenetic pace himself, but it was because he believed that there was important work to be done. "I always have hope," he scribbled to Bee, "that my next stop will not be as strenuous as the last one." [53] They always were.

Arnold, Beebe, and a few other members of the staff made several of these whirlwind tours to the West Coast, Mexico, and the Northwest. But after Westover's death, Malin Craig had forbidden the chief of the Air Corps from flying without another pilot on board, and only in airplanes with two or more engines. Arnold continued as copilot, giving Beebe a break from the long hours in the air between coasts, and lessening the stress to a degree. [54]

The fall of France in June 1940 eliminated most congressional disagreements about the need for massive expansion of national defense. By the end of June, Arnold and his Air Corps had been given $1.5 billion, with instructions to "get an air force." [55] One hundred million dollars of that budget was dedicated to research alone for the next year. Now the Air Corps had money, but little time. Of the three dominant production factors—labor, money, and time—Arnold insisted that "the most important and indispensable is time. There is no substitute for time. It cannot be bought or improvised. . . . In years gone by we had all the time in the world but no money. Now we have all the money in the world but no time." [56] Echoes of Napoleonic philosophy.

The problem of funding now a memory, the dilemma of expansion stared Arnold directly in the face. The British were already embroiled in preparations for an air battle of a magnitude never yet witnessed in history. They had decided to build a strong defensive air force. It was a decision that may have saved the United Kingdom.

As part of the U.S. solution, Arnold offered a plan to reorganize the Army into three major branches: Service of Supply (later the Army Service Forces), Ground Forces, and Air Forces. Marshall saw exceptional merit in the idea and had his future deputy, Gen. Joseph T. McNarney, enact the new structure, one that formed the basis for Army organization for the remainder of the war. [57] The reorganization may have relieved the problem within the Army, but it never satisfactorily resolved issues within Arnold's organization, a situation that would trouble Arnold throughout the war. Issues concerning air organization were so relentless that Arnold actually attributed part of his physical collapse during the war specifically to them. [58]

By fall 1940, Roosevelt had added several Wall Street bankers and lawyers to Secretary of War Stimson's staff as part of the War Department reorganization. To advise on air matters, respected investment banker Robert A. Lovett, who eventually was named assistant secretary of war for air, became Arnold's alter ego during the massive buildup of the American aircraft industry and air forces. Lovett's November 1940 arrival on the War Department staff occurred well after Air Corps philosophy had been publicly established, mostly by Arnold in those years, during frequent speeches across the country. To Lovett's great credit, he was wise enough to realize his own shortcomings concerning airpower theory, and diligent enough to rectify those before his swearing in as assistant secretary of war for air. His trust in Arnold's direction for the Air Corps was absolute. By the time the United States entered the war, Lovett was one of the Air Corps's most eloquent spokesmen.

Arnold found in Lovett, an unassuming, bald banker with a slight overbite, a man who possessed the qualities in which he was weakest. He found "a partner and teammate of tremendous sympathy, and of calm and hidden force. When I became impatient, intolerant, and would rant around, fully intending to tear the War and Navy departments to pieces, Bob Lovett would know exactly how to handle me. He would say with a quiet smile: 'Hap you're wonderful! How I wish I had your pep and vitality! Now . . . let's get down and be practical.' And I would come back to earth with a bang. I can't imagine a finer man to work with than he was during those tough years from 1940 to the end of 1945."[59] Most of the ideas Lovett supported had been given him by Arnold and the Air Corps staff. Some he expanded, others he modified, but the basics were already well established. Lovett's tact and political savvy balanced Arnold's fervor and aggressiveness. They made a perfect team at the high-command and political level.

The importance of training, R and D, logistics, and supply varied only in degree during the war. Lovett pushed hard for training of pilots and crew in June 1941; Arnold had already established the importance of training programs, back in 1938. By spring 1941 Lovett understood the importance of R and D, a topic that Arnold had openly advocated since he had become assistant chief of the Air Corps. Lovett held off arguing for an independent air force because of logistics and supply issues, just as Arnold had preached since Marshall had become chief of staff. Lovett realized the importance of "complete solidarity of view" between himself and the Air Corps leaders. "Once the competence of the individual had tested, you were accepted by this top band of brothers. In being so accepted, there was none of this division between the civil and the military. It simply did not exist."[60]

Lovett's forte was the delicate creation of functional connections between Stimson, Marshall and Arnold, a skill he put to superior use after taking the oath of office in April 1941. Lovett's banking experience and skill were vital in solving contract issues that developed during the massive buildup of the aircraft industry.[61] His thoughtful temperament turned out to be an excellent balance to the often spontaneous and frequently inspired Arnold. Lovett realized this, and so did Arnold.

Of Arnold, Lovett explained that he "had this quality of profound optimism, of absolute certainty of victory in the future, of dedication to this effective use of air power." He disputed the assertion that Hap Arnold was "an even-tempered man—always angry." Lovett, whose office was adjacent to Arnold's, described him as a "very mercurial" man.

> He responded to emotional stimuli in a very youthful fashion: he would be up one minute, and down in the depths the next. . . . But his attitude toward the future was one of sound belief in it. He was devoted to his family, and did not like people who would tell him that it "couldn't be done." He hated that. . . . If you choose to use an unfortunate word like "vision," he had enough vision to see that we could do with this field things that had up to that time been thought impossible. He had a great deal of imagination, in its proper sense, and he inspired others in the confidence which he felt.[62]

The quiet Lovett was not an outspoken leader. He was a political operator whose efforts smoothed the rough edges between industry and government and, thus, facilitated Arnold's strongest qualities.

The issues that occupied Lovett's days were similar to those that occupied Arnold's days: training schedules, production and legal issues related to Lend-Lease after its passage in March 1941, and recruitment of both officers and enlisted personnel. In large measure, Arnold was the "away team," touring factory after factory across the country, while Lovett defended the Air Corps in Washington. "Hap hated desk work. . . . All the best pilots hated desk work," Lovett recalled.[63]

By early 1941, after one full year of touring factories, engine plants, and training bases, Arnold, now somewhat portly from a rich diet and lack of exercise, was worried. He intimately understood both the politics of Lend-Lease and the technical problems involved in building the needed infrastructure for aircraft production. He had also received reports that the British were ill-using the aircraft that were being sent them—aircraft Arnold would have much rather kept for his own forces.[64] Arnold revealed his deep fears to Major General Andrews, now theater commander of the Panama Canal Zone: "As you know we are leaning over backwards to give everything to the British. Very little is coming to us. . . . Engines are the neck of the bottle more than anything else and England has priority on engines. So, taking everything into consideration, aircraft production insofar as getting airplanes for U.S. units is more or less of a mess, and no matter what we do in this matter there will be no relief for several months in the future. . . . All I can say is that we hope to get planes to everyone—but at this writing it is only a hope."[65]

For General Arnold, R and D, though vital, was not an immediate answer to

American production woes in 1941. Because of his World War I experience with production and development of the Liberty engine, the American version of the DH-4, and his tangential involvement with the Kettering Bug, he had great faith in American industrial power.

It would not be surprising if Arnold laughed out loud when Lovett relayed to him the content of a 4 May 1941 letter from FDR to Stimson. FDR wanted to set production goals at 500 heavy bombers a month. This matter was so urgent that Lovett wanted it to have top priority within the Air Corps.[66] Arnold and others had warned of the danger of meager aircraft production since the end of the last war. More recently, it had been less than three years since the cancellation of the B-17 program mid-stride. This reversal in policy only served to illustrate the volatile nature of politics. To Arnold it was a big, fat "I told you so."

When George Marshall became acting chief of staff in July 1939, he had already been the recipient of an airpower-education program orchestrated by Frank Andrews on the operational end and Hap Arnold on the technical and production end. Marshall, unlike those who had served before him, understood the potential for airpower and was the first chief who acted upon that belief to any great degree. By war's end, Marshall was so airpower-friendly that some airmen referred to him as the Father of the Air Force.[67] Arnold himself admitted, "It is hard to think how there could have been any American Air Force without him."[68] Marshall's influence was crucial to the advancement of the air arm as a striking force throughout World War II.

Marshall was only one part of the solution to the Air Corps's expansion difficulties. Aircraft manufacturers and engine-production companies supported Arnold in a very unusual way: "They got started spending their own money and setting up production," Lovett described, "before the Air Corps got the appropriations from Congress. . . . It takes three to five years between conception and birth of a new aircraft, and they were taking the risk for some months, perhaps a year, until the new Congress came in and gave the money."[69] Arnold's contacts with the industry—Douglas, Lockheed, Curtiss, Boeing, and North American—enabled this unprecedented procedure. As did Lovett, aircraft industrialists trusted Arnold.

Airplane production became the catalyst for American airpower's evolution into a massive technological system by war's end. Until the early years of World War II in Europe, American aircraft industries had still been feeling their way, as had the air forces. The threat of war jolted industry into overdrive. A complete cooperative effort between industry, political forces, the air forces (Army and Navy), military staffs, and the United States's workforce was responsible for the explosion of production that became an enormous part of the "Arsenal of Democracy."

As a result of the 11 March 1941 Lend-Lease Act, Arnold's expertise was needed in Britain to iron out particulars with the Royal Air Force. On 11 April

1941, Arnold crossed the Atlantic on the Pan American Clipper. It was a lengthy journey: "Had dinner at about 10:00 P.M. and then everyone became confused. E.S.T.—Bermuda time—Horta time—Lisbon time—so I don't know what time I did anything." More seriously, Arnold noted that although there was no open talk of war, the British passengers conveyed a "general impression of sadness," the result of the ongoing air war with Germany.[70] Accompanying Arnold was British air minister John C. Slessor, one of those disheartened by the air war.

It was during that trip that Arnold was made aware of the existence a new form of aircraft propulsion: the Whittle turbojet engine. It was not initially the most spectacular of all the Air Corps's scientific and technological research programs, and American jets never flew in combat during World War II. But Arnold's direct involvement in bringing the Whittle jet engine to America illustrated his personal commitment to technology and its application to the American air effort, an effort that immediately linked Whittle's team, Arnold's Air Corps, and Bush's NACA.[71]

But the search for technology was not Arnold's only, even his primary mission. He was to assure the British that Lend-Lease would succeed. Despite the fact that Arnold bemoaned its impact on his air forces, he convinced the RAF staff that Lend-Lease had teeth. Air chief marshal Sir Charles "Peter" Portal, Arnold's RAF counterpart, wrote: "Your presence among us has done more than anything else could have done to encourage us to make 'American help to Britain' a reality in our minds. You have impressed us deeply by your sympathy and understanding of our problems, and by your evident readiness to bear sacrifices in the equipment of your own service in order that ours may have what it requires."[72]

Arnold's constant quest for improved performance, spurred by his knowledge of the jet, forced a confrontation with George W. Lewis, director of aeronautical research at the NACA. John Victory, the NACA's recording secretary, recounted the vitriolic meeting. "Hap," Victory said, at that moment not very happy, wanted to know "why in the name of God we [the Army Air Corps] hadn't got one," by which he meant a 400-plus mph fighter. Lewis replied sardonically, "Because you haven't ordered one."[73] Arnold was furious, and a lengthy argument followed during which Arnold discovered that Lewis was well aware that the technology to build faster planes had existed for some time. Lewis had not suggested building one because it was not the NACA's function to dictate specific military procurement. To Arnold, Lewis was not acting like a true team player.[74] This incident, one that tainted Arnold's personal feelings about Lewis, overshadowed the many successful programs that the NACA as an institution undertook during Arnold's tenure.

Having lost a measure of confidence in the leadership of the NACA, Arnold resorted to other civilian agencies in an effort to capitalize on Whittle's jet engine. It was made available to him by Portal in April 1941. Although the

NACA took steps toward jet-engine development directed by the 1941 Durand Board, formed in March 1941 at Arnold's request, importing the plans and an engine from Britain was the general's personal achievement.[75] The fact that Arnold established the Durand Board before he left for England also demonstrated an ongoing interest in propulsion systems, even before he had been made aware of the Whittle engine.

In September Arnold directed Col. Benjamin J. Chidlaw, chief of the Materiel Command Engineering Branch, to take the plans and create a separate, supersecret production team, including Larry Bell of Bell Aircraft and Donald F. "Truly" Warner of General Electric. GE was selected because of previous work done under the guidance of Sanford Moss: "turbo-supercharging," a process related to the turbojet concept. Both systems used compressors to concentrate airflow (therefore oxygen) and improved engine performance.[76] The project military representative was Col. Ben Chidlaw.

This Bell-GE team was so secret that only fifteen men at Wright Field knew of its existence. The contracts with GE were handwritten and transmitted in person by Arnold's personal liaison, Maj. Donald J. Keirn. Keirn recalled that the first GE contract was for a turboprop that was built in Schenectady, New York, at the same time as the Whittle-engine project was going on at West Lynn, Massachusetts. The three Durand Board engine teams—one at Westinghouse, another sponsored by the NACA, and the GE-turboprop team—were unaware that Arnold had directed Chidlaw to get a jet in the air under absolute secrecy.[77] "Good Mother of God, General Arnold," Chidlaw asked bewildered, "How do you keep the Empire State building a secret?" Sternly, Arnold replied, "You keep it a secret."[78]

Development of the United States' first jet aircraft, the XP-59A, exemplified how Arnold linked technological advancement to American airpower. Once aware of a particular technology, he decided whether it could be applied to Army Air Forces airplanes, thereby improving their combat capability. Some of his decisions concerning technology were flexible. As late as January 1939, for example, he stated that "because of the high efficiency and flexibility of operation of the controllable propeller as it exists today, it will be many years before any means of propulsion, such as rocket or jet propulsion, can be expected on a large scale."[79] But in April 1941, he suddenly changed his mind.

British engine developments revealed during his visit, coupled with the underpinnings of early American turbojet concepts and the promising work done at GALCIT Project No. 1 during 1940, convinced him that jets and rockets held significant potential for his air forces. Arnold always wanted the most advanced capabilities for his airplanes. But after the Nazis strolled into Poland, he expected project results within two years. No later.[80]

Once convinced of a project's efficacy, Arnold gathered trusted scientists, engineers, and officers. Then, using the force of his personality, he directed what he wanted done with the technology. During this phase, he was often personally involved. His teams were given considerable latitude in accomplishing the task and rarely failed to produce results.[81] Some who served on these task forces had private reservations about specified tasks: "You never thought the things he asked you to do were possible," one Douglas Aircraft engineer recalled, "but then you went out and did them."[82] Colonel Chidlaw's XP-59A team was one glittering example of Arnold's leadership in promoting technological change.

A different example of mission accomplishment and dedication to duty began about this same time: the formation of the Women's Airforce Service Pilots (WASPs). The WASP concept was born in late 1941 when Arnold called upon noted aviatrix Jacqueline Cochran to train and utilize American women pilots. With a go-get-'em attitude much like Arnold's, Cochran established her training school at Sweetwater, Texas. "By 1944, over 1,500 women pilots were on active duty with the Army Air Forces. Not only did WASPs ferry planes in the United States, they also flew weather tests and administrative missions, piloted cargo planes, and towed targets for antiaircraft gunnery practice."[83] Although largely accepted by AAF pilots, women fliers would have a tougher time creating social acceptance for their role than the AAF had promoting technological change.

10
COMMANDING GENERAL, ARMY AIR FORCES (1941–44)

Two significant events during the summer of 1941 elevated Arnold's status at both the military and the political advisory levels. Formally, reforms within the War Department resulted in the creation of the Army Air Forces on 20 June 1941. Major General Arnold held the title of deputy chief of staff for air.[1] Informally, as secret preparations were being made by FDR's close adviser Harry Hopkins for the first meeting between the president and prime minister Winston Churchill, it was decided that an American counterpart to the Royal Air Force contingent was required. The glib Arnold was the obvious choice for that job. At the outset of the cooperative Allied effort, he was suddenly and inexorably "in the Big Leagues."[2]

As the Army Air Forces' representative to Argentia (also known as the Atlantic Conference), August 1941, Arnold put to good use his breadth of experience, which now swelled to its final circumference. He earned the trust and respect of both American and British political and military leadership. It was no small benefit that Roosevelt and Churchill were already convinced as to the importance and potential of air force as an immediate response to Nazi advances on the Continent. Argentia meetings were mostly off the record, since the United States was not officially at war with anyone during those months. But plans for war were definitely being made, and both friendships and working relationships were established that became essential after the United States entered the war.[3]

☺   ☺   ☺   ☺   ☺

Arnold arranged to be present as the first Pacific-bound B-17s left California for the Philippine Islands, the place both Marshall and Arnold believed needed

169

these planes the most. As he left for the airfield, Arnold's wife asked when he might return. "When the Japs bomb us," he casually replied. Bee found her husband's comment strange.[4]

Arnold paid a visit to an aluminum plant at Knoxville, Tennessee, on the way West; he was preparing for pending congressional testimony. On the evening of 6 December 1941, Arnold and Beebe landed at Hamilton Field, near San Francisco, just in time to wish the departing bomber crews good luck and send them on their fateful way. The next morning, 7 December, Arnold and his friend Don Douglas spent the day hunting game birds near Bakersfield, California. Upon returning to the rickety cabin that acted as their staging area, Douglas's father, waiting there, came running toward the hunters. He brought the news of the Japanese attack at Pearl Harbor. "Get ready for a long flight," Arnold told Beebe. After a quick trip to San Francisco to check in with the Army commander, Arnold headed directly back to Washington, fulfilling his peculiar promise to Bee.[5]

The flight from California took most of the night and half of the following day. Arnold, Beebe, and an unnamed fighter pilot—recruited at short notice to assist Beebe on the long journey—arrived in Washington at 3:00 P.M. on 8 December. Arnold went directly to his War Department office, while Beebe went home to sleep.[6] By the end of the day, the United States was officially involved in its second worldwide conflagration in less than a quarter century.

Most Sunday mornings after that infamous one, General Eisenhower and other staff officers came to Arnold's office to study global maps. "They were trying to learn the geography of the whole world—refresh their memories. Many little islands, with names that nobody knew, were to become quite important later on."[7] For most military personnel in the Washington area, Sunday became a workday, and Arnold's were long ones. When in his Washington office, he arrived early and did not leave until late at night most days of the week. "His idea of a good time was to work all day in the office, and he'd probably come in from the last conference with the Secretary—in those days it was Mr. Stimson—then, we'd rush out to Bolling Field, jump in a plane, and fly all night."[8] Arnold was responsible for two distinctly different but complementary tasks: building up a combat air force and running a global air war. Restructuring of the Army had generated both the workload Arnold carried and the benefit he enjoyed from unity of command over his air forces.

But General Arnold—now approaching 200 pounds, his face surprisingly chubby—was not the only member of the family who pulled long hours during the war. Hap asked Bee to help run the Air Force Aid Society, formed to assist when tragedy struck young airmen's families. She too worked long days, frequently seven days a week. From these early days of the war until mid-1944, Hap and Bee saw little of each other. And when they were together, they were too tired, too sick, or too distracted to enjoy those moments.

On 21 December, a Sunday afternoon, FDR called together what would become the foundation of his warfighting brain trust for the next five years: Harry Hopkins, Secretary of War Stimson, Secretary of the Navy Knox, Adm. Harold R. Stark, Adm. Ernest J. King, General Marshall, and General Arnold. As Arnold arrived that day he was greeted by a cheerful FDR, who addressed the general as Hap. Flattered and a bit surprised, Arnold told his aide, Gene Beebe, that he was finally "in" with the administration and out from under the cloud of Secretary of the Treasury Morganthau's influential Lend-Lease umbrella.[9] General Arnold became a fully accepted member of the president's staff from that day forward. The need to display a unified American front on issues political and military was imperative now that the United States was in the war—and the British had much greater experience and practice in this particular area. The first wartime Washington conference, Arcadia, was to begin the very next day.

Initially the military members, taken in their entirety, were called the Supreme War Council. It was not until after Arcadia that the term Combined Chiefs of Staff was adopted. On this council, Arnold's primary British contacts were Sir Charles Portal, air chief marshal of the Royal Air Force, and air marshal A. "Bertie" Harris. The topics of discussion were wide-ranging. Enormous, detailed piles of information were briefed and discussed, enabling definite decisions to be made concerning the destruction of "the fighting power of the Germans and Japanese."[10] It was during the formal, combined meetings that overall strategy for the war was decreed.

The Combined Chiefs of Staff decided the military strategy. Working groups then took the grand strategy and turned it into working strategic efforts for each nation's army, navy, and air force. Arnold was a participating member at both the political and military high-command levels and, as such, was directly involved in strategic-level decision-making efforts between Britain and the United States.

His participation in these is most clearly described not by examining each individual conference. Rather, Arnold's participation may be gauged by understanding several fundamental principles that he championed for airpower. The first five may be summarized, broadly, in the following way: the main job of the Army Air Forces was to deliver offensive, daylight, mass-formation bombing flown by exceptionally well-trained crews capable of taking off and landing under any weather conditions.

Secondarily, the Army Air Forces were to support surface operations—directly and indirectly—by attacking close-in targets and by providing air superiority over bomber formations and friendly forces. Aside from actual combat philosophy, Arnold insisted upon maintaining research-and-development programs in order to have the most modern equipment as soon as it was possible to obtain it.

Lastly, Arnold carefully measured his strategic recommendations knowing that "Air power is not made up of airplanes alone. Air power is a composite of airplanes, air crews, maintenance crews, air bases, air supply, and sufficient replacements in both planes and crews to maintain a constant fighting strength, regardless of what losses may be inflicted by the enemy."[11] This principle of a balanced air program had been Arnold's most fundamental since the mid-1930s; now it became the basis for the buildup of the United States's air force. In *Winged Warfare,* a collaborative effort between Arnold and Ira Eaker published in mid-1941, Arnold's "balanced air force" lay at the heart of the chapter "Strategy of Air Force Operations."[12] Named the commanding general of the Army Air Forces in 1942, Arnold made the balanced-air-force program his theme for production, employment, and training. The program served to unify many ongoing efforts nationwide toward one common goal: a balance between personnel, machines, and bases. "As Deputy Chief of Staff I was more of a coordinator of air activities with the rest of the Army than I was building up, but in March of 1942 I became Commanding General of the Army Air Forces and then I had the real task of building up the Air Force."[13]

Despite his convictions concerning the best uses for airpower, Arnold believed that there were occasions during the war when the "political imperative," as insisted upon by the British prime minister and the American president at Arcadia, and the "military imperative"—the principles in which Arnold believed—seemed diametrically opposed. Perhaps the best example of airpower used primarily as a political instrument was the daring raid upon Tokyo led by Lt. Col. Jimmy Doolittle.

Arnold felt that the decision to use Doolittle was a "natural one." He stated that the fearless, technically brilliant officer, the same one he had grounded for stunting back at Rockwell Field some twenty years earlier, "not only could be counted upon to do a task himself if it were humanly possible, but could impart his spirit to others." Jimmy Doolittle, even in the face of accomplishing what Arnold called a "suicidal mission," got things done.[14]

Arnold demonstrated a different kind of courage when he sent Doolittle to Tokyo. The commanding general realized that a failed mission might backfire on the American military and political decision makers. The difficult decision that he made, one that sent friends to possible imprisonment or death and aircraft to inevitable destruction, demonstrated Arnold's understanding of his crews' ability. He possessed the moral strength to sacrifice lives to achieve substantial results, politically or militarily. Arnold trusted Doolittle enough to send him and his airmen on one of the most daring missions ever conceived for military air forces.

The 18 April 1942 raid, though it accomplished little in the way of physical damage, boosted Allied morale in unquantifiable ways. Doolittle's Congressional Medal of Honor spoke not only to his bravery and audacity in leading the raid, but to the political importance of the attack in the eyes of the president.

The mission was made possible only by operating as a joint task force, a force made up of a combination of Army and Navy assets. In this case, the strike force consisted of sixteen Army Air Force B-25 bombers. The transport to the launch site and protection from the enemy were provided by seven Navy ships—the aircraft carrier *Hornet* being the primary player—with Adm. "Bull" Halsey in command of Task Force 16 at sea. Despite all the rivalry between the two services, this mission bridged that gap and demonstrated just what was possible by pooling resources and desire. It was a lesson that was nevertheless ill-used during the war. The mission also exemplified a lesser-known piece of Arnold philosophy: although part of airpower, any group of airplanes, regardless if sea-based or land-based, Army or Navy, was not necessarily air force.[15]

Creation of that air force would take time. Arnold's drive to build the force required new administrative structure and more clearly defined organization. According to Arnold, this was a rather dry topic:

> It is the framework of the structure. It does not possess the interest nor the beauty of the completed habitation—painted, curtains hanging, with pictures on the walls and fires on the hearth. It is likely, for that reason, that it will receive less attention than it merits. Actually, organization, as Clauswitz [*sic*] pointed out, and as Napoleon reiterated, is the most important of all the military functions. . . . One of the most important peacetime functions of the military establishment is the perfection of organization along sound lines. . . . It must never be overlooked in preparations for war. It is the essence of proper national defense.[16]

Much of Arnold's prewar efforts—perhaps a majority of them—had been devoted to perfecting the organizational structure of the rapidly expanding air arm.

Reorganization of the War Department during the war years was complicated, largely administrative in nature, and took an inordinate amount of Arnold's time and effort until January 1945.[17] Even the official Army Air Force historians deferred to a multitude of regulations concerning modifications, rather than try to explain the evolution of the service's organization. Through all the revisions, Arnold's function—from assistant chief of the Air Corps to chief of the Air Corps (in March 1939) to commanding general of the Army Air Forces (in June 1941)—remained fundamentally the same, just expanded in scope as he guided his service through all its ensuing administrative modifications.

Wesley F. Craven and James L. Cate, authors of the seven-volume official history of the Army Air Forces during World War II, described Arnold's and his air staff's official functions as they existed after the major restructuring of the War Department in March 1942. These functions remained in place after that pivotal time.

Actually, the Commanding General, Army Air Forces, as one of the three service representatives on the Joint Chiefs of Staff, functioned on a level parallel to that of the Chief of Staff. As a member of the Combined Chiefs of Staff, he moved at the very highest levels of command in the wartime coalition with Britain. He chose the commanders of the combat air forces, who well understood that he possessed as much power to break them as he had to make them. With the air commanders overseas he communicated regularly, as often as not without reference to formal channels. Controlling the means necessary to implement the operational plans in any theater, he exerted a powerful influence on the development of strategy, tactics, and doctrine wherever AAF units fought. He operated a world-wide system of air transport whose planes moved at his command through all theaters, the commanders of which were denied their traditional prerogative of controlling everything within their area of responsibility. Toward the close of the war, he even exercised direct command of a combat air force—the Twentieth. Throughout the war his staff functioned in a threefold capacity: it superintended the logistical and training establishment of the home front, advised its chief as a member of the high command, and helped him run the air war in whatever part of the world there seemed to be need for attention by Headquarters.[18]

An examination of the organizational charts helps to clarify the Army Air Forces' internal structure as well as the relationship of the AAF to the War Department and the other two major commands under the chief of staff, George Marshall. Additionally, studying the changes in the charts demonstrates, at the highest levels, the massive expansion within the AAF itself (see Appendix 2).

Massive expansion meant massive training efforts—training for pilots, mechanics, bombardiers, navigators, and lots of them. Even while Jimmy Doolittle was assembling his raiders, Arnold was trying to increase the capacity of his basic ground officer schools, those required of each new officer regardless of specialty. He was met with resistance from his staff, particularly the new boss of the Technical Training Command, Maj. Gen. Walter Weaver. Arnold remedied the situation by staging a phone call to Maj. Gen. Millard F. Harmon Jr., at the time stationed at Shreveport, Louisiana, near Louisiana State University (LSU).

After informing the officers in attendance at a staff meeting that the schedule for expanding the officer-training schools was unacceptable, he buzzed Miss Suzie Adkins, his secretary, and loudly ordered her to get Harmon on the phone. She played along. After a few minutes, Adkins interrupted the meeting and connected Arnold to the fictitious Harmon. Arnold spoke into the dead phone line, "How long will it take you to get me LSU? You think you can get it in three or four days? Well that's great!" After hanging up the receiver, he looked over his staff and said, "Gentlemen, you see what you can do when you have the will to do?"

General Weaver excused himself and left immediately for Miami. Two weeks later, basic officer school had opened in Miami, and the Army Air Forces had acquired more than 300 hotels in which to house new officer candidates.[19] It was by methods like this that Arnold forced his will upon his subordinates; he sometimes shamed people into diligence.

To examine each relationship between Arnold, his major commanders, and other subordinate officers is impossible here. However, several close personal and long-term associations must be mentioned. Arnold's most trusted field commander was Tooey Spaatz. Acquainted since 1917, Arnold and Spaatz had served together during several assignments and established an efficient working relationship. Spaatz would assume command of the Army Air Forces upon Arnold's retirement, and he would become the first chief of staff of the independent United States Air Force on 18 September 1947.[20]

Ira C. Eaker, another longtime associate of Arnold's, coauthored three airpower-related books with the general and served as a subordinate commander for him. He admired Arnold, perhaps because Arnold possessed the aggressiveness that he lacked, and he aspired to replace Arnold after World War II. After an excellent bombing-doctrine briefing during a difficult situation at the January 1943 conference at Casablanca, Eaker's personal motivation led him down a path of cautious actions based upon fears of high-level political repercussions both at home and abroad. To some, particularly after he returned to Washington from the Mediterranean theater in the spring of 1945, Eaker appeared manipulative during Arnold's absences from Washington. This was a perception, real or fictitious, that he could not overcome. He reached the position of deputy commanding general of the Army Air Forces with three stars before he retired.[21]

Many American operational commanders played vital roles in the outcome of the global air war. George Kenney, eventually teamed with Douglas MacArthur in the Pacific, remains a legendary story of tact, patience, and assertiveness. Arnold listed him, along with Spaatz and Eaker, as his third most trusted lieutenant—an elite group to be sure.[22]

Haywood S. Hansell and Curtiss E. LeMay exemplified the frequent polarity of command situations. In some, administration and mobilization of resources were required; in others, operational excellence in employment of war-winning weapons took precedence. Jimmy Doolittle spanned the entirety of ranks—from civilian to three-star general—and represented the best and the bravest of tactical commanders, as well as the boldest of operational and strategic commanders near the end of the European bombing campaign.

At the tactical and lower-staff levels, Elwood Quesada, Claire Chennault, Monk Hunter, Orville Anderson, Hugh Knerr, Larry Kuter, Hoyt Vandenberg, and many others served brilliantly. Few of these lower-ranking officers ever penetrated Arnold's personal inner circle, one that consisted of only a few of his most intimate and longtime friends. Necessarily, those who served under General Arnold while still of lower rank had markedly different opinions of him as a man and leader than did Spaatz and Marshall, who knew him on the basis of equivalent rank or longtime friendship. Only Gene Beebe, his pilot, and Bruce Simmons, his driver, were included in Arnold's inner circle by the necessary proximity of their jobs to the general himself.

Nonoperational assignments were of equal importance to Arnold. Commanding the Materiel Division at Wright Field during the war were a parade of officers, some today more well known than others, who held the mantle of the important production and R and D responsibilities for air programs. Although this command changed names several times during the war, its function remained largely unchanged. Wright Field's Materiel Division, by any other name, was the official home of airpower R and D.

Perhaps most responsible for the structure of the Materiel Division was Augustine Warner Robins. He had established the methodology of command from 1935 to 1939, a crucial period in creating the foundations for Army aircraft supply, production, logistics, and R and D. Others followed with significantly shorter tenures: George Brett, Oliver Echols, George Kenney, Arthur Vanaman, Charles Branshaw, Frank Carroll, Benny Meyers, K. B. Wolfe, William S. Knudsen, Hugh Knerr, and, finally, Nate Twining. A few cases of rapid turnover resulted from Arnold's perception that the Materiel Division had a "no-can-do" attitude. Arnold hated that.[23] Other in-and-out tours occurred so that promising young generals could be given combat commands—Kenney and Brett, for example.

Arnold impressed his belief in the importance of scientific knowledge and technological change upon his field commanders, who were directed to use science to best advantage whenever possible. In one wartime case, he wrote to Eighth Air Force commander Ira Eaker, suggesting that he add a science and technology analyst to his staff:

> The more I think of our recent interchange of messages regarding German countermeasures against your bomber formations, the more I am convinced that you should have on your staff a free thinking technical man who is not tied down with current logistics, current modifications, and current procedure in any way. This man's main mission in life should be to sit there and weigh the information received . . . then advise you what action should be taken by you to outsmart the Germans. . . . This technician should also have a staff of two or three more scientists who would help him diagnose German moves and the motives behind them. At this writing, I have nobody in mind at all for this long-haired technical job, but if you think well of the plan I will rake up somebody and send him over to you, and I will also send the assistant scientists to sit there and help him.[24]

The practice of placing civilian scientists on military staffs was not uncommon. Scientists, for example, flew radar missions against submarines while perfecting air-to-surface detection techniques used to defeat German U-boats. This was one of the highest-priority missions of the war, military or political, on land, sea, or air.[25]

The U-boat war is a study in flexibility and guile, at least if one examines it from the German point of view. From the American side, the U-boat war was a near-tragic example of inflexibility and dogmatism. The devastation of commercial shipping that the U-boat caused during 1940 and 1941 was significant.[26] By January 1942, U-boats were beaching themselves like stray whales along the U.S. East Coast. The realization that something needed to be done immediately was clear. The U.S. Navy, despite the lessons available from U-boat performance during the Great War, was unprepared to do battle with these elusive boats. Navy doctrine concentrated on defensive convoy escort rather than on offensive hunter-killer operations. In this regard, the Navy was as doctrinally dogmatic about antisubmarine operations as was the AAF concerning long-range fighter escort later in the war. In time, and after significant loss of life and equipment, both doctrines would evolve to meet unexpectedly effective threats: German U-boats and fighters.[27]

The ultimate resolution and successful counterattack against the U-boat was littered with heated doctrinal debates, jurisdictional arguments, and, finally, major compromises that preserved a fundamental mission for each service: antisubmarine operations for the Navy, and control of all land-based, long-range air assets for the Army Air Forces.[28] This compromise—the Arnold-McNarney-McCain Agreement—was one that Arnold was willing to accept because his Air Forces would have complete control over long-range attack planning and operations against the enemy U-boats. In the eyes of airmen, this was their primary mission.

As part of the AAF's contribution to the antisubmarine campaign, Arnold ordered the formation of the Sea-Search Attack Development Unit (SADU) in May 1942. This team was composed of scientists from MIT and the National Defense Research Committee, with operations personnel from the Navy and the Army Air Forces. Total control of all technical assets having to do with submarine destruction—research and development, production, even some combat execution—fell to this organization. Arnold viewed this specific task with such high priority that he placed the unit directly under his command, eliminating all bureaucratic obstacles to mission accomplishment. Operationally, the SADU was part of First Bomber Command.[29]

Having seen "American-version" radar at Fort Monmouth while still Westover's deputy, Arnold was satisfied with its potential and pushed hard for combat radar capability, but functional units were still in the future.[30] The air battle over Britain during the summer of 1940 only served to reinforce, in Arnold's mind, the importance of radar as part of a complete airpower system. He was so impressed by the heroic performance of the RAF that he dedicated *Winged Warfare* to those "few" airmen: "To the intrepid and courageous flyers of Britain's Royal Air Force, whose matchless exploits in the skies above Europe deserve the praise of the civilized world, this volume is dedicated in admiration and respect."[31]

In April 1942, Dr. Edward L. Bowles, from the MIT Radiation Laboratory, was assigned to the War Department and worked frequently for Arnold as a special radar consultant. Arnold's commitment and Bowles's expertise helped make the SADU an extremely effective—though controversial—unit. In a letter written after the war, Arnold reminded Spaatz of the ultimate impact of SADU and the development of microwave radar: "The use of microwave search radars during the campaign against the submarine was mainly instrumental in ending the menace of the U-boats. Germany had no comparable radar, or any countermeasures against it. In fact, for a long time the Germans were not even aware of what it was that was revealing the position of their subs so frequently."[32] The AAF turned antisubmarine operations over to the Navy in August 1943, after the tide had turned in the Battle of the Atlantic. The Navy continued effective attacks on the U-boat, with greatest effects being delivered by carrier-based aircraft. The role of airpower in World War II, as the antisubmarine campaign demonstrated, was also crucial at sea.

Primarily driven by radar technology, antisubmarine operations became remarkably effective by May 1943. While Arnold authorized many projects besides radar that improved the effectiveness of aircraft during the war, he also pursued innovations in weapons technology. For example, as early as the summer of 1938, he had initiated efforts to rekindle the Liberty Eagle or Kettering Bug.

Between forty and fifty Bugs were in storage, and an assembly-line production plan already existed for the weapon.[33] Arnold secretly called Ket Kettering and William Knudsen, another World War I acquaintance who was now commissioned a lieutenant general in the Army as Air Forces production taskmaster, to discuss the potential of mass-producing the World War I Bug. A relatively inexpensive weapon, many hundreds could be purchased for the price of one B-17 bomber, and built in a fraction of the time. The primary problem was the weapon's limited range. Ket had tinkered with the World War I Bug on and off during the interwar years and made a few technical improvements in the design, but the Cessna GMA-1 Bug still only had an effective range somewhere between 200 and 400 miles. Since the Allies had yet to establish a foothold in Europe, striking directly at Germany from the British mainland was out of the question. The heavy bomber had a much greater effective range, one allowing deep, direct attacks on the Reich. There was little question as to the appropriate course of action, and the Cessna GMA-1 monoplane was shelved.[34]

Other projects, however, did materialize from Arnold's initial inquiries. In the fall of 1939, he had again called upon his old friend Kettering, now vicepresident of General Motors. This time Arnold wanted to develop "glide bombs" to be used in the event of a war. What he described was a device that could be used by the hundreds, dropped miles away from targets, and that might keep his pilots out of the lethal range of enemy flak barrages. Arnold specified that the weapon should glide 1 mile for each 1,000 feet of altitude, carry a sizable amount of high explosives, have a circular error probable of less than half a mile, and cost less than $700 each. Kettering was convinced that it could be done quickly and inexpensively. Interestingly, Arnold's continued efforts at procuring standoff and remote controlled weapons remained a fundamental contradiction to AAF precision-bombing doctrine: technology did not yet allow precision any greater than traditional bombing.[35] At no time was this contradiction more apparent than at the January 1943 Casablanca Conference.

The mechanism responsible for the coordination of Allied efforts such as Torch and Overlord was a series of high-level, combined military and political conferences.[36] As described by Fleet Admiral King: "These international conferences, which are of sufficient duration to allow thorough presentations of matters of mutual interest, make possible on-the-spot decisions not only with respect to strategy and command relationships for combined operations but also with respect to the commitments of each country."[37] The degree of Arnold's contribution to these conferences varied tremendously, from his own and his lieutenants' dominant participation at Casablanca to little if any at Tehran.[38]

Of the Allied summit meetings that Arnold attended as a member of the Joint and Combined Chiefs of Staff—Arcadia, Quebec I and II, Cairo, and Potsdam—the January 1943 meeting at Casablanca was the most important to American airmen. Code-named Symbol, the Casablanca Conference established, among other things, Allied air strategy for defeating the Axis powers. One of the most significant strategic decisions made was to pursue aerial bombardment, in an effort to weaken Nazi industrial might, cripple supply lines, and crush morale.

One of Arnold's personal advisory council members, Col. Jacob Smart, later to plan the gallant raid on the oil fields of Ploesti, recalled: "The American Joint Chiefs of Staff were poorly advised by the White House as to the nature of the conference at Casablanca. . . . They were led to believe that only the principals would meet—that's the President and the P. M.—and as a consequence the Air Staff went completely unprepared."[39] In stark contrast to the American skeleton staff (one including young Lt. Hank Arnold, the general's son, on administrative duty with the Army General Staff), the British delegation included the majority of the Royal Air Force staff and had been transported to Casablanca on a Royal Navy ship assigned specifically for their use.

The size of the British delegation did not pass unnoticed. Even after the forty flying hours and nearly 7,600 flying miles required to reach the destination, Arnold was keen enough to sense an ambush.[40] It was soon confirmed by

Averell Harriman and Harry Hopkins that the RAF and Churchill were going to pressure the AAF to switch from daylight precision to night area bombing. Arnold called for his theater expert, Ira Eaker, who immediately flew to Casablanca from Eighth Air Force headquarters in England. In the meantime Arnold informally discussed the issue of daylight bombing while walking with the prime minister; they spent nearly an hour strolling and discussing the bomber offensive. When Eaker arrived, Arnold essentially "sicced Eaker on the prime minister" to explain why shifting the AAF to night bombing would be a monumental mistake.[41]

Eaker explained that despite British claims to the contrary, night bombing was no less dangerous to aircrew than day bombing. Additionally, American airmen had been trained for precision day attacks, and to transition to night bombing, although not technically as difficult, still required retraining and modification of American bombers. Increased accuracy, though to some seeming more like fiction than fact, might not have been as critical an issue as round-the-clock operations, and these depended upon American bombers. Coupled with the realization that daylight attacks would be instrumental in destroying German day fighters in the air, Churchill was finally convinced of the potential of a combined American-British around-the-clock bombardment campaign.[42]

RAF questions that resulted from Eaker's briefings opened wide the door for the Eighth Air Force commander to solidify the AAF's mission over Europe. Admittedly, AAF efforts during 1942 had not been as impressive as many had hoped. Eaker explained that requirements for air assets during Torch—the invasion of North Africa—had drained resources from the Eighth.[43] He steered away from Lend-Lease issues. Additionally, missions flown were obligated by directive to strike submarine bases and support facilities, not Germany proper. Poor weather and lack of long-range fighter escort were also cited as limiting factors to American operations from Britain.[44] Eaker made it clear that American airpower in Europe had been scattered throughout the theater, thereby precluding concentration of force and unity of command. Eaker's performance at Casablanca was, retrospectively, his finest as an airman and as a general. He changed Churchill's mind, no small achievement, and settled the bombing question once and for all. The AAF was directed to continue daylight precision bombing over Europe.[45]

In the plan finally decided upon, known as the Combined Bomber Offensive, British planes would bomb industrial cities and area targets at night, while American planes would bomb precision targets during the day, and the cycle would continue.[46] No Allied force could reach into Germany or German-held territory but air forces. The often-maligned air arm of 1918 was now the only service "that could even get near a battleground in Western Europe."[47] After Casablanca, Allied air forces were challenged to attack the heart of the enemy. The air forces were handed an independent mission in addition to their ongoing support of theater surface forces; it was a mission that airmen had advocated since the 1920s.[48] At the Casablanca gathering of the "Big Two," plans were finalized for the bombing campaign against the Axis. But in determining the final plan, the American delegation learned several crucial lessons concerning summit preparation and staff work.

Even as Casablanca was Eaker's finest hour, the fact that Arnold sent for him to act as the AAF spokesman for daylight bombing in the face of such adversity demonstrated that Arnold knew his commanders' strengths and used their expertise to achieve AAF objectives. Like a great coach, he used the right players at the right moment in the big game. Arnold realized that Eaker's savvy and experience with ongoing operations made him the most knowledgeable AAF airman on the subject of daylight bombing in practice. In other words, once Arnold realized what was at stake at Casablanca, he loaded the deck. In addition to himself, Spaatz, and Andrews, he added Eaker to counter any British attempts to shift the bombing effort from day to night.[49] Arnold trusted Eaker to win the most important doctrinal argument of the air war, and Eaker came through in a monumental way. Decisions such as these earned Arnold the respect of Allied officers as well as Americans. John Slessor, a future marshal of the RAF, described Arnold's leadership skills as he saw them used during the war:

> He was an intensely likeable person was Hap Arnold, transparently honest, terrifically energetic, given to unorthodox methods and, though shrewd and without many illusions, always with something of a schoolboy naïveté about him. In spite of his white hair and benignly patriarchal appearance, he was a bit of a Peter Pan . . . he had lived through years of frustration which had done nothing to impair his effervescent enthusiasm or his burning faith in the future of airpower. No one could accuse him of being brilliantly clever but he was wise, and had the big man's flair for putting his finger on the really important point.[50]

The resulting Combined Chiefs of Staff directive, 166/1/D, the "Casablanca Directive," established the strategic objectives for the rest of the war, including an independent and sustained mission for the AAF and the RAF. The directive listed the ultimate objective for the bombing offensive originating from the United Kingdom as "the progressive destruction and dislocation of the German military, industrial, and economic system, and the undermining of the morale of the German people to a point where their capacity for armed resistance is fatally weakened." To accomplish this, five specific interim targets were delineated: 1) German submarine construction yards; 2) German aircraft industry; 3) transportation; 4) oil plants; 5) other enemy war industries.[51] The strategic plan added up to this: destroying and disrupting the U-boats while gaining and maintaining air supremacy. Once that had been done, long-range attacks upon German industrial might and civil morale, the primary objective of Allied strategic bombardment, could be accomplished. The cross-channel invasion of Europe could then take place with reasonable assurance of success.

Also at the strategic level, the primacy of defeating the European threat was reinforced. The Pacific theater was essentially relegated to a holding action for AAF assets until massed air forces could be transferred there after the defeat of the Nazi war machine. It appeared likely that the Allied invasion would be delayed until 1944, thus combined airpower assets of the RAF and AAF would fight the Luftwaffe from the air during the rest of 1943 and early 1944. This Combined Bomber Offensive remained conceptual until plans were finalized in May 1943. It was, however, a true air-force operation, the conduct of which was determined by melding two complementary doctrines for application of air force into one, eventually bringing defeat to what was then the most powerful air arm in the world.

After Pearl Harbor, President Franklin D. Roosevelt's determination to use air force to strike at the heart of the Axis powers launched American industry into high gear. Production schemes were developed by Air Corps planners supporting FDR's desire to obtain "complete air ascendancy over the enemy."[52] Arnold, having long before Pearl Harbor recommended to FDR that the United States build more than 100,000 combat aircraft for any potential European war, reacted calmly, with calculation and immediacy. By the time the Army Air Forces were ready to begin bombing deep into Germany, Arnold's orders to his commanders were simple and left no room for misunderstanding. They were to destroy German planes wherever they were found—in the factories, on the ground, or in the air.[53] For the rest of the war, and in concert with Casablanca directives, that was what the AAF did, and, for the most part, Arnold let his operational commanders handle the air war.

Despite the fact that he openly argued in favor of daylight precision bombing doctrine at Casablanca—or used talented subordinates to argue the points for him—Arnold's actions at home spoke louder than many of his words. And as the war continued, his actions toward developing standoff weapons grew more concerted despite protests from his field commanders, who recommended discontinuation of the programs.[54] In spring 1943, Arnold went on a whirlwind tour of his globally deployed forces, with a side trip to China to deliver a letter from FDR to the aging generalissimo Chiang Kai-shek, in which the U.S. president promised continued air support. Upon Arnold's return to Washington, the nature of his command subtly changed.

Organizational issues had often been irksome, but the total production effort that followed Arnold's earlier letters of despair shocked everyone, including Arnold himself. In April 1943, the four-star Arnold wrote to three-star Andrews, by then Marshall's air commander in the European theater, "By God, Andy, after all these years it was almost too much—I don't imagine any of us, even in our most optimistic moments, dreamed that the Air Corps would ever build up the way it has. I know I damn well never did."[55] It was a timely letter.

On 3 May, tragedy struck the Army Air Forces. Frank Andrews died when his B-24 crashed into a cloud-covered mountain in Iceland.[56] The most revered operational commander in the Army Air Forces was gone. At least Andrews had lived to see the beginnings of remarkable successes in wartime aircraft production. Hap Arnold was now the last remaining of the eldest Army air triumvirate. Both Westover and Andrews had, tragically, perished in accidents while piloting their own planes.

Largely due to his leadership, Arnold had won an independent mission for his Air Forces. All that remained was to iron out the details of the execution of the air campaign. This was the purpose of the Trident Conference held in Washington, D.C., that mid-May.[57] It was soon after Arnold's return from his global tour that the first indications of potentially serious health problems surfaced.

Just prior to the Trident Conference, Arnold suffered a painful heart arrhythmia; his heart rate reached 160 beats per minute during the event, and it frightened the otherwise unflappable general. "Maybe within a day or two the medicos will be able to keep the R.P.M. under control," he wrote Marshall on Monday, 10 May.[58] Most disappointing was the fact that he would miss Trident. In fact, Marshall ordered him not to participate. Nonetheless, he was visited at Walter Reed Hospital by several conference participants, including air chief marshal "Peter" Portal, named overall commander of the Combined Bomber Offensive effort.[59]

Despite the advice of his physicians, and after only two weeks' rest, Arnold quickly returned to his fast-paced work schedule. He did take an occasional nap in his private Pentagon office; he had a cot available there. And at least one member of his staff recalled that a wheelchair was tucked away in one of the office closets—a suggestion made by one of the "medicos."[60] Arnold would have none of it, and he did not want anyone else to know about the incident. In this he was largely successful, as even the members of his closest advisory council were unaware of the cause of his May illness.[61] Illness or no, it was time to execute the Combined Bomber Offensive and press the war effort in the Pacific as finalized at the Trident Conference. The cross-channel invasion had been set for 1 May 1944; the invasion clock was ticking.[62]

In preparation for the invasion, the AAF swelled in numbers of machines and personnel; the full weight of the industrial United States was finally mobilized. In 1938, the year Arnold had assumed command of the Army Air Corps, a total of 1,600 officers had been on duty. By March 1944, the Army Air Forces' peak wartime strength had been achieved: 2,411,000 military personnel and, as of October that same year, 422,000 civilians. During World War II, more than 17,000 officers alone were killed while serving in the Army Air Forces. Another 23,000 enlisted personnel and civilians were also killed, while another 80,000 airmen were wounded. In all, during the fighting the Army Air Forces suffered more casualties than the Navy and Marine Corps combined.[63]

In 1939 the Army Air Corps had had 2,100 serviceable aircraft, more than 200 short of the congressionally approved 2,320. From 1940 to 1945, the United States produced a total of 283,230 aircraft, almost 200,000 of them for combat operations. Nearly 23,000 of these were lost or destroyed during combat operations, more than ten times the number of airplanes the Air Corps had possessed in 1938.[64]

This remarkable achievement, made possible by American industrial strength, becomes stunning when one considers that in addition to aircraft, the United States built 10 battleships, 137 aircraft carriers, 349 destroyers, and 203 submarines for the Navy after the Japanese attack on Pearl Harbor. The number of tanks, trucks, armored cars, and bullets grew so large that an accurate accounting is nearly impossible. The industrial effort behind such production, even today, remains difficult to fathom.[65]

General Arnold knew all of the American aircraft builders personally. He spent months visiting their factories during the early years of mobilization and took personal responsibility for checking on the workers, designers, fabricators, and component assemblers across the nation. He and his staff worked long, frequently twenty-hour, workdays. Arnold was driven by his understanding of American industrial capability and capacity, even though most workers and many company presidents could not conceive the totality of the effort. But Arnold believed in American industry and its ability to reach astonishing production goals, even if many industrialists did not. His World War I experience, his time spent at the Army Industrial College, and his command at the Fairfield Air Depot Reservation had instilled within him these convictions.[66]

Jacob Smart, member of Arnold's advisory council, explained the tremendous task Arnold faced in building and equipping an air force. According to Smart, the creation of airpower was accomplished "almost from scratch." He continued:

> The Air Staff was concerned with procurement of materiel and personnel and the building of a management structure that would eventually result in the production of airplanes, personnel to fly them, personnel to maintain them, operate them, transport them from place of manufacture to the theater of operations. We were also concerned with the never-ending problem of developing criteria for meeting competing needs. Such national strategy as we admitted to in those days gave first priority to the European Theater and second priority to the Pacific Theater. But we were constantly faced with the question of, "How much goes to the first priority mission, and how much goes to the second priority mission?" . . . There was competition between the services for personnel and materiel. There was competition for

command positions. It is no exaggeration to say that nobody was completely in charge of anything. Everybody was in charge of everything. . . . It is no wonder that we worked 10, 12, 14 hours a day. In the wintertime, we would arrive at the Pentagon before day light and leave after dark. And many a man never saw the light of day from one day to the other.[67]

Command of forces of this size required centralization. Although it was difficult for many in the Army Air Forces to understand, Arnold realized the crucial importance of unified surface and air command for the cross-channel invasion. Unity of command had been formal Army Air Forces doctrine since the publication of *Field Manual* 100-20, "Command and Employment of Air Power," dated 22 July 1943. Unity of command was not a new concept; rather, it was a long-held principle of war perhaps best understood and utilized by Napoleon. Since before the American Civil War, all West Point cadets had studied his campaigns.

In January 1944, Arnold secretly wrote Gen. Dwight D. "Ike" Eisenhower of his support for the appointment of one supreme commander—air, land, and sea—for the invasion. Arnold's broad view of both the military and political aspects of coalition warfighting was adroit and earned him Ike's respect. "You have always been helpful in my efforts to get these operations functioning on a sound basis and your letter is just additional evidence that you are continuing along the same path. Thank you a lot."[68] Arnold had the ability to know which high-level command battles were worth fighting. Trying to keep command of the air forces away from the supreme commander was not one of those Arnold would have won without tremendous boat rocking. Besides, at the strategic level he had Gen. Carl Tooey Spaatz, Lt. Gen. Jimmy Doolittle, and capable British counterparts such as air chief marshal Portal at Ike's side as airpower advisers.

That same month Arnold took a short trip to California, where he visited his daughter, Lolie, son Bruce, and his newest baby: the Arnold ranch. Bee had purchased the property in Sonoma the year before, and it was her husband's first opportunity to visit what would become his retirement ranch. He was pleased with the land, good soil, wild animals, and potential. He would have constant work while retired. Bruce also surprised him by announcing his engagement to none other than Barbara, the daughter of Arnold's longtime friend and associate Donald Douglas. They would marry the following summer.[69]

As part of the effort to improve AAF punch—delayed somewhat by the massive effort to produce aircraft—Arnold pressed for new aerial weapons. The development of the GB-1 (glide bomb), for example, had been completed, and by spring 1943 it was being dropped against targets in Europe. Although this innovative, simple weapon provided some protection to American airmen, the GB-1 was highly inaccurate. Since the AAF held closely to the doctrine of precision bombing, the erratic GB-1 was finally shelved in May 1944.[70]

The development of the glide-bomb series of weapons (GB-1 through GB-8) included radio-controlled steering, television cameras for aiming, and even a torpedo modification. These sophisticated weapons demonstrated one thing very clearly—General Arnold was not completely sold on precision bombing doctrine as it stood, even after the Casablanca Conference. He was disappointed that the AAF was not achieving his desired level of precision using available resources.

The Kettering/Cessna GMA-1 Bug, although not used operationally, provided technical insight for follow-on remote-controlled bomb projects. For instance, as the air war progressed, B-17 and B-24 bombers began to wear out. These surplus bombers occupied valuable space and, more critically, valuable maintenance time. By late 1943, General Arnold had directed Brig. Gen. Grandison Gardner's Eglin Field engineers to outfit these "Weary Willies" with automatic pilots. The airplanes, both B-17s and B-24s, were then filled with nitrostarch (a form of TNT) or liquid petroleum and remotely flown into enemy targets, such as U-boat construction facilities on the French coast. The explosives were detonated in a manner similar to, but much larger than, the original Kettering Bug.[71]

The operational use of these unpiloted bombers combined with aircraft-dropping glide bombs, mostly GB-4 through GB-8, against German V-1 and V-2 launching sites was called Project Aphrodite. General Spaatz utilized several of these "guided missiles" in August and September 1944 against targets in France. The attacks were largely unsuccessful: the Weary Willies were easily shot down; they suffered mechanical failures; they exploded for no apparent reason. As for the glide bombs, they were far less accurate than was required. The technology behind the Aphrodite mission simply did not work.

The first Aphrodite launch of a Weary B-17 was delayed many times by the unforgiving English weather patterns. Finally, after several false starts, 1st Lt. Fain Pool (pilot) and S.Sgt. Philip Enterline (automatic pilot specialist) began their hazardous mission, this time under relatively clear skies. They were to get their flying bomb into the sky and pointed in the right direction, then jump out, parachuting to safety on English turf. Their B-17, crammed with packages of nitrostarch explosives, was more crowded with only two aboard than with a full crew on a regular combat mission.[72]

Engines were started, but the ground crew was a comfortable mile away from the airplane—just in case. The 32-ton B-17 lumbered to the runway awaiting the appointed 1:45 P.M. takeoff time. At 1:40, Pool taxied his flying bomb into the takeoff position and set the parking break. Just before he advanced the throttles for takeoff, both men heard the frightening scream of the base air-raid siren. Pool realized that the siren signaled the beginning of the mission. The ground crew did not. Expecting the explosive-laden B-17 to vaporize at any second anyway, the few support troops remaining above ground dove headlong into the slit trenches that crisscrossed the airfield for air-raid protection.

The scene was reminiscent of a failed unpiloted-missile test in the fields around Dayton in 1918. The B-17 bomb missed its mark when the autopilot malfunctioned over the target, preventing the mother ship from plunging it directly into the enemy missile site. It missed by more than a mile.

Fortunately, Pool and Enterline survived their parachute jump over the English mainland. The second Aphrodite pilot that day, John Fisher, was not so lucky. His B-17 crashed on top of him only seconds after he had initiated the bailout sequence while still too close to the ground.[73] Aphrodite was clearly a nonprecision system of weapons. Yet Arnold staunchly supported its development even before Germany began to launch V-1 attacks, in the early morning hours of 13 June 1944. Eisenhower then ordered air marshall Arthur Tedder, his air deputy, to get the upper hand on V-1 and V-2, code-named Crossbow, targets at the expense of everything but urgent requirements of the ongoing cross-channel attack. This order seems an overreaction to a threat that Eisenhower himself described only as "very much of a nuisance the last few days."[74] Successful Aphrodite missions would have allowed the AAF to remain within the intent of Ike's orders, but at the same time, flying more Aphrodite missions would not have required the transfer of any additional manned bomber assets away from essential attacks into Germany.[75]

Not only were Willies capable of carrying large amounts of explosives, using them as guided missiles assured that none would remain in American stockpiles, cluttering flight lines with obsolete airplane junk. Arnold remembered the painful Liberty engine lessons from World War I production days. He did not want B-17s or B-24s flying a decade after this war was over, as the DH-4 had done.[76] This was a pipedream, as fewer than twenty aircraft were actually destroyed during Project Aphrodite. In a staff memo, Arnold explained that he did not care whether the Willies were actually radio controlled or just pointed at the enemy and allowed to run out of gas.[77]

Aphrodite missions did provide an opportunity to test new automated-piloting technology in a combat situation. Arnold, apparently not totally discouraged about the project, ordered continued R and D for remotely piloted vehicles until after the end of the war.

Although he had long supported development of nonprecision weapons, in most combat situations, such as those ongoing against Germany, Arnold still preferred manned bombers to Willies. In November 1944, he reminded Spaatz of the salvage rules for damaged aircraft. "The accelerated activities of our fighting forces in all theaters makes it increasingly important that we utilize our material resources to the maximum, not only for the sake of the economy, but also in order that the greatest possible pressure be brought to bear against the enemy."[78] The experienced Arnold realized that to win a war, one side must "try and kill as many men and destroy as much property as you can. If you can get mechanical machines to do this, then you are saving lives at the outset."[79] At this point, though he was willing to try nonprecision methods on occasion, Arnold realized that technology had not surpassed the abilities of manned bombers and could not equal the accuracy or the guile of a bomber in accomplishing the mission.[80]

The importance of Aphrodite was not its impact on the outcome of the war. Arnold had no great hopes for immediate effectiveness of these imprecise weapons. He did, however, insist that improvements in accuracy and destructive power be made as soon as practicable.[81] Aphrodite demonstrated Arnold's willingness to supplement precision-bombing doctrine in an effort to save the lives of American aircrew and deflect political pressure away from his air force, particularly since he was feeling confident that the war in Europe was, essentially, under control by late spring 1944. The British would eventually veto Aphrodite missions, citing possible German retaliation at the imprecise nature of the systems. This made them potential "terror" weapons, an argument that to Arnold and his men seemed hollow.[82]

○   ○   ○   ○   ○

Having established, tested, and validated his command methodology, General Arnold began actively planning for the future of airpower. This involved an organizational problem that Arnold had long been waiting to solve. He pondered which of the many scientific organizations he had been associated with during his career might offer the finest advice concerning future plans for the Army Air Forces.

NACA methodology under George Lewis had left Arnold feeling disappointed, particularly in the field of advanced aircraft research.[83] And although Wright Field had been vital to AAF production research and problem solving, personnel shortages made long-range studies a simple impossibility. Additionally, Arnold said he was irritated with the Materiel Division engineers' no-can-do attitude. Frustrated, he once told a gathering of engineers: "I wish some of you would get in and help me row this boat. I can't do it alone."[84] Arnold often used this approach to stir his troops into action: no one wanted to disappoint General Arnold.

Finally, Arnold was unwilling to request formal assistance from Vannevar Bush, now chief of the Office of Scientific Research and Development (OSRD). Even though this office and its predecessor, the National Defense Research Committee (NDRC), had played a vital role in weapons development during the war, particularly with radar and the atomic bomb, Bush's opinion of the JATO and jet-development programs had dismayed Arnold. He felt that Bush was an excellent electrical engineer but misunderstood his vision. Bush once told Maj. Don Keirn, Arnold's Whittle liaison officer, that the AAF "would be further along with the jet engine had the NDRC been brought into the jet-engine business, but who am I to argue with Hap Arnold."[85] It is likely that Keirn reported this sarcasm directly to Arnold at some point.

Critically, the general and the OSRD chief held widely different views concerning military involvement in R and D. Bush believed that the military should be excluded from any type of research other than production R and D. Arnold was adamant in the belief that long-term R and D also required military input, lest the civilian world determine the development and implementation of airpower doctrine and policy. Their personal differences had likely begun to develop in 1938–39, when Bush held the reins at the NACA and Arnold served on its executive committee. From most accounts, it appeared that they just did not like each other.[86]

Bush, by most accounts, was not an easy man to like. Perhaps the most compelling testimony is offered not by a military man, but by one of Bush's own civilian colleagues, Dr. Edward L. Bowles.

> If you were to look at his recent book . . . you would have to conclude that he pretty much won the second world war and was the Royal Pooh-Bah in damn near everything of importance during his active career. . . . Bush is a complex character, very interesting, paradoxically a good friend, as well as a man whose machinations I have made it my business to escape ever since I matriculated at MIT in 1920 when I suddenly found myself a member of the staff.
>
> If there was anything Bush wanted during the war, it was to sit at the level or right hand of the Joint Chiefs and as part of that prestigious body. He would probably have made the grade had he had the full confidence of Marshall, King and Arnold.[87]

Despite the fact that many of Dr. Bush's ideas were similar to Arnold's during the war years, the friction that developed between these two men was rooted in Bush's views on civilian versus military control of long-term military R and D.[88] In 1942, for instance, Bush recommended the formation of a group to supersede the War Production Board. It would include "research people" having the authority to alter war production plans. This meant, of course, that the military might have to abdicate some measure of control over its doctrine (as reflected in the production decisions made by Bush's scientists). Further, Bush advocated the formation of an independent civilian group of scientists and engineers to screen scientific ideas prior to any military involvement or implementation. "I feel sure," Bush said, "that new and valuable ideas are much more likely to come to fruition if they can develop their formative stages among groups of independent scientists and engineers before being subjected to the rigors of military association."[89] What this meant was that scientists would filter ideas to military planners. In essence, Bush, as the leading scientific adviser to the president, would have had a personal hand in directing military doctrine and planning. But allowing him to wield such power was unacceptable to the Joint Chiefs.

Bush's ideas for control of military R and D were not a secret. In fact, during the war he pressed so hard for acceptance of these ideas that Jerome Hunsaker, his closest working companion from MIT, cautioned him against continued attempts to force the issue of civilian filtering prior to military input. Hunsaker believed that the Army and Navy "would develop resistance of a vigorous nature" to squelch these concepts. To diffuse any possibility of conflict, Hunsaker, after admitting that he did not see how Bush's scheme could work, offered several options for future consideration concerning scientific advice in the decision-making process. "My advice," Hunsaker ultimately wrote to Bush, "is to let this matter rest for the present and not bring it up before your Council until something clear and specific can be presented for discussion."[90] Despite this advice, Bush remained a separatist concerning inputs from military leadership into the path for military R and D. His views effectively prevented him from having any serious impact on the future of Army Air Forces planning in any form. Even his involvement in the development of the atomic bomb did little at the time to alter the doctrine espoused by the Army Air Forces.

By the summer of 1944, after having dealt for five years with short-term research-and-development problems involving available technologies, Arnold had formed strong opinions about the major participants in the American scientific and research communities. Lack of faith in the NACA leadership, exasperation with Wright Field, and the incompatibility of OSRD/NDRC philosophy with Arnold's convictions convinced him that if he was to have an effective long-term plan for the AAF, an independent expert panel was the only answer. He needed freethinking civilian scientists, given initial direction by the AAF. As he had said in different ways on several occasions, the future of American supremacy in the air depended on the brains and efforts of engineers and scientists. The European war was now winding down, with the air war won; the defeat of Japan solidly assured by the rejuvenated U.S. Navy, the success of the Army and Marine island-hopping campaign, and the rapidly building production of the B-29. Arnold turned his thoughts to the distant future. His call to action came in the form of a memo from an old friend and supporter of airpower, Gen. George C. Marshall.

On 26 July 1944, Marshall wrote: "The AAF should now assume responsibility for research, development, and development procurement."[91] The imaginative General Arnold saw an immediate opportunity to act. Many times during the twilight of his career, he would explain the rationale behind his consistent emphasis on forecasting technological changes for the Air Forces. Bernard A. Schriever, Arnold's first chief of the Office of Scientific Liaison in the Pentagon, recalled Arnold's views: "World War I was won by brawn. World War II was won by logistics, and World War III, if it ever comes, will be won by brains."[92] Arnold had already decided that the United States's leading aeronautical scientist, the biggest brain he knew, was Dr. Theodore von Kármán. His trusted associate since the early 1930s, Kármán was the man Arnold needed at the head of the Army Air Forces Long Range Development Program.[93]

Arnold spent a great deal of time in conversation with Robert Millikan in efforts to have Kármán released from his Caltech responsibilities. Kármán had already been a special consultant to the Air Corps and to Arnold. The two had worked together in 1940 at Wright Field, during the construction of the high-speed wind tunnel, and Kármán had participated in the JATO project. Millikan agreed that Kármán had the broad base of knowledge and experience to head such a study. Despite his friendship with Arnold, the prospect of losing the world's leading aeronautics professor to the Pentagon must have disappointed Millikan. But he realized that the Army Air Forces were short on highly competent scientists. He later pointed out that the cooperation that flowed from Caltech to the AAF might not have occurred "had it not been for the fact that you [Arnold] and I have had so many things in common, not only in the last war but in the inter-war period. It has been a very great delight, as well as profit, to me to be able to swap ideas with you and to try to assist in your problems."[94] Arnold's early aviation links were frequently put to excellent use.

By early August 1944, Arnold had successfully "borrowed" Kármán from Caltech and arranged a meeting with the ailing scientist in New York, where he was recovering from recent surgery.[95] On Thursday, 3 August, Arnold cabled Kármán to ask his help. "Have been wanting to see you for some time but have just heard that you are ill." The message continued, "Hope it is nothing serious and am wondering what the chances are of your coming down sometime in the next couple of weeks."[96] Kármán responded on Saturday, 5 August: "Please let me know [at] New York City Westbury Hotel whether my visit first of next week would be agreeable. Please give the time convenient to you. I am also at your disposal at any later date."[97]

Acting with customary swiftness in matters of science and technology, Arnold arranged to meet the professor Monday morning on the tarmac at La Guardia airport, near Kármán's New York hotel.[98] This spared Kármán an uncomfortable trip to Washington and gave Arnold a half-day break from his hectic, brand new Pentagon office—an opportunity he rarely failed to take.[99]

Hap sometimes hated to leave his home on Fort Myer. Though it was spacious for two adults and one high-school-age boy, either Hap or Bee was normally out of town. Hap was continually on the road, attending conferences and visiting factories. Bee, who suffered terribly from hay fever, frequently spent late spring in Nags Head, North Carolina, or at Lake Kezal, Maine, to minimize her symptoms and give her time away from her job.

The family never came together for holidays. Christmas 1943 was quiet, with only Hap, Bee, and David at home. This was not really their fault: Lois had married a hard-drinking Navy pilot in fall 1937, and Hank had gone off to West Point, followed by Bruce, who ended up at Annapolis. Hap would miss Bruce's wedding in June 1944, when he was on the beaches at Normandy. Only such an event could have kept him away: Bruce was marrying Barbara Douglas, and the union symbolized the close personal relationship between Hap's air forces and the Douglas Corporation.

Hank had also married, but both elder sons were soon soon off to war, Hank to Europe and Bruce, by 1944, to the Pacific. David, meanwhile, struggled in a private school in D.C. and would attend West Point, to graduate in 1949. Bee was mostly alone, and this took a gradual toll on her.[100] Yet the meetings and the work schedules continued apace.

✪   ✪   ✪   ✪   ✪

The La Guardia meeting holds a somewhat legendary place in the history of Air Force scientific and technological development. Kármán recalled the details of the meeting, but many of the dates of the events in his later autobiography are inaccurate. Nevertheless, when Arnold's plane arrived, jostled by the rough winds of a passing cold front, Kármán was transported by Army staff car to the end of the runway, where the general joined him after deplaning. Arnold dismissed the military driver and then, in total secrecy, discussed his plans for Kármán and his desires for the forecasting project. Arnold spoke of his concerns about the future of American airpower. How would jet propulsion, radar, rockets, and other gadgets impact that future? "I want you to come to the Pentagon," Arnold suggested, "and gather a group of scientists who will work out a blueprint for air research for the next twenty, thirty, perhaps fifty years."[101] After promising to give all of the orders on Kármán's behalf—the professor insisted on that caveat—Arnold hopped back in his plane, the deal done. Kármán, flattered and excited, was impressed that General Arnold had imagination enough to look far beyond the war. But the timing of Arnold's request was no accident.

Several key elements in wartime operations had been realized, and only after air supremacy had been achieved during the D-day landings was Arnold convinced that Allied victory in Europe was a foregone conclusion. The air war had become brutally routine. More than half the total tonnage of bombs dropped on Germany would fall after D-day.[102] At that point it had become a numbers game, Allied air strength growing daily, while Axis air capability dwindled. The Normandy invasion had been carried out under the umbrella of complete air supremacy.[103] The P-51 had been operating successfully with drop tanks for several months, and results were positive.

The turnaround had only begun in the spring of 1943, while doctrinal disputes were erupting between the Air Corps Tactical School and combat commanders. During the summer of 1943, Arnold and his staff finally ordered that bomber formations be accompanied by fighters during the length of their missions. Arnold was insistent that fighter losses be traded for bomber saves. Not only would this policy get more bombs to the target, but fewer bomber crews would be lost. Once again, even though Arnold himself admitted the near-fatal mistake of waiting to develop the long-range capability of the P-51 and P-47, combat range was the determinant of success. The secondary importance of air superiority as compared with the criticality of strategic bombing in air doctrine also stood in the way of early long-range fighter development.[104]

The issue of long-range fighter escort had been discussed and debated by the AAF Pursuit Board, but the issue of drop tanks had not been discussed. Rather, it was thought, a totally new airplane, some sort of "convoy defender," would be needed. The failure of the Pursuit Board or any one individual to recognize the potential for drop tanks seemed a technological hurdle, not a failure to recognize the need for a long-range escort fighter. Arnold was removed by an ocean from the process; Eaker sat on the board as a member, and Spaatz was in between. None made the linkage between the tanks and adaptability to fighters until some time later.[105]

The XP-59A, on the other hand, was an exceptional program in that it seemed to violate Arnold's general tendency, from late 1939 until mid-1944, to expend R and D efforts only on current and available production equipment. But he believed in the potential capability that might be gained by continuous jet research. A leap ahead, offered by the British transfer of technology, contributed significantly in that area. Arnold envisioned aircraft capable of speeds exceeding 1,000 miles an hour, a notion he inherited from Kármán's work. He completely believed in the future of jets.

Arnold realized, however, that the first jets would not be the production models; he had overshot the technological mark. Instead, he felt it more important to get a jet aircraft flying, and then work on the modifications necessary to make it combat-worthy. In essence, Arnold wanted to make the jet an American production R and D project, not an experimental-test program that would never fly in any significant number. Perhaps he remembered the lesson of Billy Mitchell's Barling Bomber, which had provided vital data and production techniques even though it was an operational failure.[106]

Additionally, Arnold had been able to get a substantial jump on the program by promising the British an improved formula for high-speed, high-temperature turbine blades in return for all available British jet experimental data and an engine. By May 1941, the British had written Dr. Bush at the NACA and asked him to send two engineers to Britain so that the Whittle problem could be straightened out. In a letter from Bush to Arnold on 27 May, Bush volunteered to take over the JATO project from the Air Corps. This was the same project that Bush had once described using science-fiction terms. Bush had only been convinced of the efficacy of the JATO project by Dr. Durand, chair of the NACA Special Committee on Jet Propulsion. Although Durand kept had Bush informed of the general nature of Arnold's programs, there is no evidence that he had informed Bush about the XP-59A until after its first flight.[107]

As it stood, jet aircraft did not have the necessary range to be of much value to the AAF, which would soon be flying missions from England to Germany. Consequently, until the problem of limited range was solved, the production effort was not pushed as hard as that of combat-proven aircraft such as the P-47 and P-51. For this reason, American jets did not contribute directly to World War II victory. In Germany, where required fighter combat range was extremely short, jets made a significant, yet futile, impact on the Allied air campaign.[108]

The super-secret XP-59A, under wraps since its first flight, was revealed to the American public in January 1944. The jet engine was assembled at West Lynn, Massachusetts, under the project title Super-Charger Type No. 1. At Larry Bell's factory, the airframe project received an old program number so as not to arouse any suspicion. The workers themselves were segregated from each other, so that even the members of the team were not totally sure of what they were building.[109]

The plane did not fly until after the United States had entered the war. On 2 October 1942, the Bell XP-59A flew three times. The first two flights were piloted by Bob Stanley, a Bell test pilot and Caltech graduate, and the third by Col. Laurence Craigie, the first military man to fly the American jet plane. Craigie was chief of the Aircraft Projects Branch during development of the XP-59A. In 1944, he became the deputy chief of the Engineering Division of the Air Technical Service Command.[110]

In actuality, the plane had flown for the first time during taxi tests on 30 September 1942 and again on 1 October, but Larry Bell insisted that the first flight was not official until the brass hats were present as witnesses.[111] The internal, Arnold-directed cloak of secrecy was so effective that the NACA general membership had heard only rumors of the technology. Only William Durand himself had been informed of Arnold's Whittle project, but he had been sworn to secrecy. The day the XP-59A flew, he was the only member of the NACA who knew of the existence of the plane. In fact, he was at Muroc, California, the day of the official first flight.[112]

On 7 January 1944, the *Washington Post* carried the inaccurate front-page headline, "U.S. Making Rocket War Plane." The article detailed the events of fifteen months earlier.[113] Colonel Craigie had never revealed his mission even to his wife, who found out about it in January 1944 with the rest of the country. Craigie recalled, "the only project I know of that was more secret was the atomic bomb." The development of the XP-59A was, legitimately, the first Air Force "skunk works" project (much like the F-117 Stealth Fighter of the 1980s). Although little known, the follow-on to the XP-59, the P-80, was also nearing readiness. Recently Laurence Craigie recalled, "If the war would have been going badly in Europe, we might have produced these [P-80s] for combat ops."[114]

Importantly, B-29 production had increased to acceptable combat levels. This long-range heavy bomber was Arnold's Pacific trump card. He had devoted a great deal of personal effort and invested a great deal of personal risk to ensure its development, despite initially severe engine problems.[115] Arnold detailed his involvement in the development of the B-29 after the war, during a House Armed Services Subcommittee investigating the development of the monster B-36 aircraft.

> We knew enough from the B-15, B-17, and B-19 to bring out the B-29. So that the B-29 was a natural development. You couldn't say that I, who was sitting in Washington, and who approved the contract for the B-29, was the guy responsible for the B-29. No matter who was sitting there, the B-29 would have been approved. . . . Long before the B-29 ever had all the bugs out of it . . . long before it ever made that first flight to Manchuria against the Japanese steel mills, the thought came up of the next step. . . . So it was the only normal thing then that I should call together the engineers in Washington and the designers and the scientists and say, "Now listen, this is 1940 . . . we have the B-29 well started. . . . I want you fellows to go out now and think of the next airplane beyond the B-29 . . . something that will go 10,000 miles . . . something that will carry a five-ton bomb load and return to base." It was the only logical thing to do. . . . The bids or requests for designs went out in April 1941. . . . In August we had a big conference to try to see whether there was some way we could push the project because I knew that the war conditions in Europe were such that we might need it. . . . That is the one place where the one man, the individual man, is in the picture . . . he can prod the designers, prod the engineers and prod the manufacturers, and that is what my job was.[116]

Arnold's function then, after initial approval of the project, was to motivate the manufacturers to produce; hence his travel schedule in 1941 and 1942.

Curtis E. LeMay, air general responsible for the successful bombing of the Japanese mainland, later emphasized that the B-29 had not originally been planned for the Pacific theater. "Our B-29 idea came to birth in those days when it appeared that England would go down to defeat, and there'd be no place left to us in the European part of the globe where we might base our planes for future sorties against Axis powers." Further, LeMay described the obstacles Arnold faced while pushing hard for the B-29 production. "B-29s had as many bugs as the entomological department of the Smithsonian Institution. Fast as they got the bugs licked, new ones crawled out from under the cowling. . . . General Arnold had a dozen battles on his hands. He was fighting with the Joint Chiefs for resources; he was struggling to get an organizational setup for air power in that war; he had to rassle against the Army and the Navy every minute."[117]

Only after Arnold was confident that these production and procurement programs were succeeding and operations in Europe had crushed the Luftwaffe did the general return to pre-September 1939 philosophy, once again supporting long-term planning for the future of airpower.[118]

General Arnold and Dr. von Kármán were in "continual conference" after the August 1944 La Guardia encounter. Kármán recalled that he was "more impressed than ever with Arnold's vision," but cautiously so. The professor confided in Millikan that he feared Arnold expected too much from science. Nevertheless, Kármán's was an optimistic caution.[119] Arnold, meanwhile, insisted that Kármán examine everything and let "imagination run wild."[120]

To ensure the accomplishment and excellence of the scientists' crucial task, Arnold imposed no completion deadline, a luxury he later rescinded. He also insisted that Kármán's group travel to all foreign countries, assess their aeronautics programs, and produce a bold final report. He wanted a viable forecast for sustaining future American air supremacy.[121]

Arnold stuck to his modus operandi. Planning for the establishment of the forecasting group itself was totally secret, almost cloak and dagger, just as the LaGuardia meeting had been.[122] As Arnold had secretly given the jet-engine problem to Larry Bell and the GE engine team in 1941, he now gave the critical task of forecasting the requirements for the future of the U.S. Air Force to Kármán and his scientists.

By 23 October, Kármán was so hard at work ironing out the early details of organization that at the other end of the country, his other boss, Robert Millikan, was somewhat distressed that the professor had not communicated his personal status or intentions regarding Caltech from June through September. Millikan's concerns about his gifted professor were abated when Kármán finally telegrammed on 2 October:

> Had several conferences with Arnold: he will see you probably this week. I definitely recommend not to refuse his demand. Consider extremely important working out [here] for him. Program on scientific basis midway between negative attitude to new ideas and overoptimism concerning so called unlimited possibilities of science. Doing this job well also highly important for future of aeronautical research at Caltech. He told me you thought I am the right person. I strongly desire to devote about six months to this job. Feel well recovered but definitely inadvisable for me to plunge into administrative and st[r]enuous duties of ORDCIT [Ordnance, California Institute of Technology] and GALCIT for several months.[123]

This message illustrated that Kármán had had his institution as well as the AAF in mind when he accepted Arnold's offer. Certainly Caltech stood to benefit, both financially and prestigiously, from having the great professor as chairman of the AAF study. Millikan, now placated, realized the potential gains, and by the end of the month he had even authorized other Caltech faculty to participate in the scientists' exploitation of German technology codenamed Operation Lusty (Luftwaffe Secret Technology). Kármán was free to serve the AAF, but the element of potential long-term impact on Caltech and the GALCIT did not pass unnoticed.[124]

This long-term project served to cement the rapidly building interdependence between the Army Air Forces and the academic world. There was no denying that Caltech and Kármán were rewarded by his participation in Arnold's advisory group. Caltech saw continued investment by the Army in meteorology, aeronautics, and rockets over the next three decades. Kármán reaped the rewards of military investment through stock ownership and prestige. Nonetheless, the benefit to the Army Air Forces largely overshadowed these personal and institutional economic issues.[125]

Arnold followed the secret meeting with secret orders, an official written set of instructions dated 7 November 1944. In this letter, Arnold set the boundaries within which the report was to remain. These boundaries were not very restrictive: "Except perhaps to review current techniques and research trends, I am asking you and your associates to divorce yourselves from the present war in order to investigate all the possibilities and desirabilities for postwar and future war's development as respects the AAF. Upon completion of your studies, please then give me a report or guide for recommended future AAF research and development programs."[126]

Initially, Kármán's group was called the AAF Consulting Board for Future Research, but apparently AAFCBFR was too long an acronym even for the Army. The panel was redesignated the Scientific Advisory Group (SAG) on 1 December 1944, by Headquarters Office Instruction 20-76, and it was assigned, as the SADU had been, directly to General Arnold.[127]

Germany's last desperate attempt to end the war was thwarted at the Bulge. This occurred even while the SAG was gathering, anticipating their chance to exploit the work that German scientists had done since the mid-1930s. By January 1945, Kármán's handpicked scientific team of "thirty-one giant brains" had joined him in Washington, where they began executing the monumental forecasting project.

11

GENERAL OF THE ARMY: FIVE STARS FOR AIRPOWER (1944–46)

I n early January 1945, Arnold, having been promoted to five-star general just before Christmas, insisted that Kármán's group throw conservative thinking to the wind. Kármán then reminded the scientists, in his quiet Hungarian-accented, broken English, that they had to deliver on their promises. The younger members of the team found working in the SAG the "equivalent of a semester of grad school each day."[1] Hard work and long hours were essential to the early preparations for the travel that was needed to gather data for the report.

The war years had taken their toll on Hap Arnold. There had been some conjecture that he had suffered from some form of heart disease since 1933, but this is not substantiated by facts. In the early 1920s, Arnold did suffer from acute ulcers that were debilitating enough to keep him from flying planes for a time. He worked himself hard, both physically and mentally, in each military job that he held—sometimes too hard. It was in May 1943 that Arnold had suffered his first documented heart problem.

Most likely the 1943 episode was caused by partial occlusion of coronary arteries and was the first sign of more serious heart problems to come. Many factors contributed to this likelihood—smoking, fatty diet resulting in overweight, high stress associated with the challenges of early flying and high command, and, unknown until his mother's death in 1931, a family history of heart problems. The degeneration of his condition continued until another, more serious blockage occurred early on the morning of 19 January 1945.

Arnold's coronary-artery disease had been responsible for his absence at the Trident Conference in May 1943, and it would preclude his attendance at the Yalta summit in February 1945. His heart condition would keep him from

Orville Wright's funeral in early February 1948, and, ultimately, it would cause his death on 15 January 1950.[2] There was little in the way of medical diagnostic technology to lend assistance during these years, and even less in the way of repairs that were possible to vital internal organs such as the heart.

Roosevelt was on the eve of his fourth and final inauguration when Arnold suffered the major heart attack at his Fort Myer home. Gene Beebe was summoned after the initial emergency call to the Arnolds' family doctor, Lee B. Martin, in Washington. The prognosis was serious. Arnold, it was decided, had suffered a coronary occlusion and needed rest and immediate treatment. Dr. Martin, the same doctor who had treated his 1943 heart problem, cared for him that night. Early the following morning Arnold was transported to Bolling Field and, under Beebe's own careful hand, flown directly to the Army hospital near Coral Gables, Florida.[3]

Beadle joined him there upon her return from California, where she had been visiting Miss Jackie Cochran.[4] Bee's experience at the hospital, which had once been the Biltmore Hotel, was explosive and was the final factor that contributed to her own complete nervous breakdown. Apparently, Bee started an argument with Hap over his "ambitious career" and how it had weakened him over time. Anything that raised Arnold's blood pressure was immediately removed from the hospital room. The attending physician, Dr. Gilbert Marquardt, therefore forbade Bee to spend any time with her husband. Arnold, following strictly the doctor's orders, instructed Bee to go back to Washington. This did not please his wife of thirty-two years.[5] Bee was crushed.

There were other reasons for Bee's somewhat mysterious and unsettling behavior in the face of her husband's dire condition. First, Arnold had earlier "assigned" Bee to serve as the chair for the Air Force Aid Society, an organization that offered assistance and comfort to widowed Air Forces widows and families. It was a job that frequently brought Bee to tears. Her schedule, often seven days a week since Pearl Harbor, and those unfortunates she met were frequently more than she could handle. Her nerves frayed.

One of the Arnolds' most intimate friends, Mary Streett, wife of Gen. Bill Streett of Thirteenth Air Force, recently shed light on Bee's emotional trauma during the last years of the war. "I sometimes felt that she had been an important woman in her own right and I thought that maybe she felt that he had gotten too important for her. . . . Bee had some resentment that Hap was more successful than she was."[6] Bee possessed a European education, came from a high-society background, and was more worldly than most women of her time. Finally, she was facing emotional stresses generated by menopause.[7] These stresses, piled upon the responsibility for David, still at home, finally resulted in a nervous breakdown during February and March 1945.

Bee even accused her husband of having an affair with some unknown woman—which, at that time, was an impossibility. She later admitted that she was terribly overworked. "I had no control of myself at all."[8] Because of the impersonal treatment afforded family members in those days in handling such cases, an emotionally fragile Bee, pushed away by Hap and his doctors, involuntarily helped cause what Mary Streett called "the unpleasantness in Florida."[9]

After the January 1945 attack, Arnold's fast-paced, high-energy life changed forever. He was restricted to his hospital bed, endured blood tests and cardiographs, ate lettuce salads every day, read until bored, and dreamed of "chocolate malted milks and Lady Baltimore cakes—there was no harm in thinking about them." He was told that his heart block was clearing slowly, and that a natural bypass was being formed that would make him as good as new. He was losing excess weight daily, down to 193 from 210 pounds. He was placed on a very strict regimen of graduated exercise and rest, mixed with short flights to different altitudes in an effort to rebuild the strength he had lost. The program appeared to work so well that he promised General Marshall that by early May he would be able to give "far better service than I have been able to during the last two years."[10] The process of cracking open one's chest and performing delicate bypass surgery was still several years away.

During his months in the hospital, the restless Arnold took time to evaluate his life and frequently wrote of his observations and conclusions to a distraught Beadle. Hap Arnold, a five-star general for less than one month, was now restricted to a hospital bed as definitively as any wounded airman. He did not see any staff members, except Beebe, and received no briefings on the conduct of the war—at least not right away. Mostly he read books, including D. S. Freeman's three-volume epic *Lee's Lieutenants*. He also wrote retrospective letters to his family.[11]

Robert Lovett was as furious as he had ever been with Arnold, and it showed in a sarcastic letter to Eaker written at the end of January.

> I have tried ever since I have been here to impress upon Hap the necessity of delegating more and more responsibility and emulating the example of General Marshall in avoiding unnecessary speeches, dinners, and the vast number of engagements which could so easily be declined. In his penitent mood Hap agrees fully but when he begins to feel well again he hops into a plane, makes an inspection at Indianapolis, Louisville, Richmond, a speech that night before the United Bustle and Whistle Manufacturers convention, gets back here at night and then tries to clean up his desk the next day, while attending during the evenings a dinner to a visiting Mexican General, a party for three movie actresses who have come to inaugurate the March of Dimes, a session with the National Geographic Society, and a hearing on the conservation of automobile tires. Worthy as these organizations may be, General Marshall is able to avoid them and I feel that Hap can too.[12]

But Hap Arnold was not like George Marshall. Arnold was like a nickel-cadmium battery—running full power all the time until rapidly losing its charge at the end of its lifetime.

The general described his condition to Lois, his free-spirited daughter, in mechanical terms. "Apparently one of my cylinders blew a gasket and I had to get down here to have an overhaul job done. . . . While I was here they checked my lubrication, ignition, and gasoline system and they said they were working alright."[13] The tone of his letters to Bee were markedly different.

> And then the argument started. It is awfully hard to separate ambition from drive and hard work. In my way I was ambitious and in order to gain my objectives I did drive myself and drive others. . . . I personally feel that the period that has taken the most out of me was the last three years when I was trying to perfect the AAF organization—a period when I needed a Lieutenant who could see the details—carry them out—see the future and make plans to be brought to me for consideration—all these things instead of my having to do them. Had I kept Ira—Tuey [*sic*]—Kenney or men of that character—the AF in the different corners of the world would never have reached their present state of efficiency. Perhaps I was too exacting—perhaps my standards were too high—Had I been satisfied with lower standards I could have gotten along with Stratemeyer [a younger, less-experienced officer] or someone like that—Had I though we never would have had the AF that had the killing instinct to drive through in spite of all obstacles. . . . It is an open question as to when the break started—I knew 2 years ago it was coming—It was just a question as to when and where it would hit me. I knew when you started for the West Coast it was just a matter of days. I did want you to get that trip for I did not see how else you could get a rest and you needed one so badly—As a matter of fact I am not sure that you are in A-1 shape now by any means. . . . I will want you to come down and sit in the sunshine with me—when the doctors don't have to take tests every two hours.[14]

This letter is remarkable for several reasons. It describes Arnold's personal, and frequently intimate, involvement in much of his staff's operations. It reveals his confidence in Eaker, Spaatz, and Kenney, and the importance he placed upon having trusted subordinate commanders in combat positions. The letter also illustrates that Arnold knew he was seriously ill, and that he suspected the same of his wife.

Three days later he wrote another emotional letter, this time after giving more thought to the argument that had triggered Bee's expulsion from his Florida hospital room.

What you said has caused me to do a lot of thinking—you are right—right as you can be. I have been driving—driving myself to the point where I broke—driving others in the office just as hard until they broke—All for a purpose—to build up the finest—the most powerful Air Force this country can produce—All toward bringing this war to an end as soon as possible—So that we can all live natural normal lives. . . . It matters little if I fall by the wayside—if I can not measure up to the standard required for combat officers. All that matters is that I have done the best that I could—I have played my part and have no kick left and if I am cast aside now it is all in the game. To win the war is far more important. . . . I more than anyone—appreciate what you have done for the women and volunteers—for the personal affairs people and thru them to the men overseas and at home. I also know how little credit that any of the girls—you more than any of them have gotten— and yet as I said before the results are immeasurable. . . . You and I have made a fine team. We have traveled together for over 32 years and God willing—we will travel together for many years to come—as a team—each playing his part—no matter what happens now.

Remember—God knows I don't want to continue this life I have been living—I want to be a plain human being—but there is a war to be won and I have apparently been elected to play a part.[15]

More troublesome to him than his heart condition or the fact that General Marshall was soon to be briefed on the severity of the ailment was the deteriorating condition of his relationship with his wife. The tribulations of war and Bee's emotional collapse resulted in the near-end of their relationship of more than three decades.

By mid-February, Arnold was receiving situation briefings at the hospital three times each week. By mid-March, he was feeling better than he had felt in the past two years. But things were not right between Hap and his wife. Bee had asked Hap for a temporary separation.

The roughest week of his recovery was 8–15 March. On the eighth, Arnold wrote that he had hopes that he could say or do something that "will bring us together again." On the ninth his letter read, "We have come down a long road together—we have had our pleasures—our disappointments—our hardships and the satisfaction of having four wonderful children. I can not conceive of traveling the last stretch without you." On Saturday, 10 March: "I still have hopes that we can get together again."[16] Although Bee's letters do not survive, her request for a separation seems clear. But just as quickly as she asked her husband to leave, she once again asked him to stay with her. Her erratic mood swings were a result of the breakdown.

Arnold happily responded to Bee's reconciliation letter: "I am so glad that you have been able to readjust things in your mind and are able to think of continuing the team. . . . I will be back—I promise you—as a considerate husband in two months. I regret more than I can tell that I have fallen down—just when you needed me most."[17] A few days later, in a passionate response to a letter from Bee, Arnold laid bare his heart.

> Let me tell you again that I love you and you are the only woman I ever have loved. I regret that I have caused you so much trouble—so many disappointments—so much grief. I am sorry that I have not measured up to your requirements—especially when you needed me so much. I am sorry that I have been so inconsiderate.
>
> I had to make a decision—follow the doctors' orders or take the normal path and forget my illness and be a normal human being. . . . I suffered too—when I knew I was tearing your heart out. At times I thought of telling all the doctors to go to - - - - and just try—in every way I could to bring you back to me. What is the use of being well if happiness does not come with it? What is the use of being well if the only woman I love is getting farther and farther away from me?
>
> Please have faith in me.[18]

Arnold's heart troubles effectively removed him from the commanding general's chair throughout his rehabilitation period; in effect, his command would never again be as total as it had been before the attack. To the Yalta summit in February 1945, he grudgingly sent Lieutenant General Kuter as a substitute. "I am not sure that Kuter has obtained a stature or the size to fill the bill," he wrote to Bee.[19]

Shortly after Arnold returned to Washington in mid-March 1945, Ira Eaker was reassigned as Arnold's new right-hand man, along with Lt. Gen. Barney Giles. By May, these two men would be running the Army Air Forces. Arnold, at Marshall's behest, had agreed to recall one of his trusted lieutenants to lighten his workload, as he had also promised Bee that he would. Originally Arnold had wanted his eventual replacement, rather than Eaker, to fill the void in Washington. But moving Spaatz away from combat was impractical, and Eaker, though still a bit inexperienced at high-level staff work, would certainly do a fine job now that the war was winding down. Giles was reassigned to the Pacific, a reward of sorts for excellent staff work. Apparently, by the end of March both Giles and Eaker had done well, because Arnold immediately departed Washington for Europe. The trip was intended to be therapeutic: "I expect to live a life of ease and comfort during the next six weeks even though I am in the war theater in Europe," he wrote sister Betty. In reality, it was a victory tour.[20]

During February and March, while Arnold was regaining his strength, Kármán and his assistant director, Dr. Hugh L. Dryden, former head of the National Bureau of Standards, finalized the pending science-and-technology forecast design, attempted to make plans that would accommodate Arnold's request that they visit as many foreign countries as possible, and started the messy process of obtaining security clearances for the scientific team. As one might suspect, establishing this secret organization and planning its itinerary was a paperwork nightmare. After resolving a few security-clearance problems generated by the diversity of the group's members, the Operation Lusty team waited for the liberation of scientific targets on the Continent.

Arnold and his staff were headed for Paris where, by 3 April 1945, they established a base of operations. And, although the staff was "running in all directions," the villa became a haven for the commanding general, who was feeling well rested and stronger each day.[21] While relaxing between short staff briefings, a meeting with Ike and Spaatz, the interrogation of a German Me-262 jet pilot who had defected with an airplane, and evening walks, Arnold managed to arrange a side trip into Germany.[22] The account was recorded by Arnold's colorful speechwriter, Maj. Tom Sheffield, who accompanied the general on the whirlwind tour. April the fifth was a day Sheffield would never forget,

> the day we flew into Germany and saw with our own eyes the terrible destruction our airpower has brought home to the Nazis. . . . Imagine New Haven or any other medium city turned into rubble from end to end . . . where no life stirs because there is no place for life . . . a vast heap of ruin. . . . Now and again a flock of C-47s [transport planes] come back toward France carrying wounded in exchange for the gasoline they have delivered to advancing troops . . . like us . . . unescorted and the General remarks how impossible that would have been a few months ago. . . . The flight back was interesting because we saw not only the same characteristic marks of this war but also the deep zig zag trenches from the last . . . the "War to End All Wars." We saw parts of the Siegfried Line and also the Maginot though they are both hard to see from the air.[23]

Arnold, markedly thinner and tan, even met with his oldest son, Hank, and brought him back to Paris to stay with him as an unofficial aide for a few weeks. Arnold was indeed enjoying himself. "It is a grand change to get away from the merry-go-round of the Pentagon—none of the routine worries."[24] Hank felt compelled to report back to his mother about his father's health, and the report relieved Bee's worries about the trip. "Dad really looks better than he has in years, much more relaxed, and has a better color. He is really enjoying himself and acting more like a tourist than anything. I personally think this trip has done him a world of good. I only wish that he would shove most of his responsibilities off on some of his high paid help."[25]

Hank's last suggestion was good one, and Arnold had already started the process of finding a trusted lieutenant to help him out in Washington after the trip. On 14 April Spaatz and Doolittle visited the general, now sunning on his veranda in Cannes. They spoke of possible changes to the staff after war's end. What they suggested is not recorded (likely an immediate trip back to D.C. followed by retirement), but Arnold did not like their ideas. "We don't agree at all," he wrote to Bee. "I can't see a return to my office until I get a little help there—otherwise I will just wear myself out again."[26] But Spaatz did not give up. He returned on the twentieth with Ira Eaker, this time for a long conference. They discussed "office organization and who I could get in the important places—in time the changes will be complete." These conferences were likely held at the request of Lovett and Marshall. Both feared for Arnold's health and were well aware of his constant tendency to overwork himself.

Arnold had resigned himself to an easier life, for his own sake as well as for Bee's. "As for me," he wrote, "I am still taking all the rest required—9:00 [at night] to 7:30 and 1:00 to 2:45 or 3:00. I can walk up stairs without my heart going haywire. I do walk one two or three miles without any major mishaps."[27] He was never out of the sight of his physician, despite his chipper disposition.

In late April 1945, SAG members departed for Europe to inspect liberated enemy laboratories. Operation Lusty—Kármán called the title "unlikely but pleasant"—fulfilled Arnold's insistence that the SAG travel the world and investigate the most advanced scientific and technological aeronautical information available.[28] Lusty was the code name for a much larger operational exploitation expedition of German technologies by the U.S. Army; the SAG was only one small part, less than ten, of the entire task force, which numbered in the hundreds. Arnold's instructions via his deputy, Lieutenant General Giles, to General Spaatz, the European Allied air commander, were nonetheless clear: "May I ask . . . in view of the importance of this project that you give it your personal attention."[29]

Spaatz, who was already alerted to Arnold's belief in science, did just that. A few months earlier, while en route to Quebec in September 1944, Arnold had informed Spaatz of his conviction concerning the "value and the importance of these long-haired scientists."[30] Arnold had secretly established the SAG as proof of his commitment in this area.

Spaatz's immediate cooperation was vital to the success of the SAG portion of Operation Lusty that began with the group's arrival in Paris on 1 May 1945. Arnold was already headed back to the States, via South America. One member of the Lusty team, H. Guyford Stever, recently noted the critical nature of timing during the Allied advance. Stever recalled that local looting was often a problem, but the Russians were the real concern. More significantly, Stever mentioned that "until this von Kármán mission, we had to piece the enemy's facts together. Now we had the advantage of actually talking to the German scientists and engineers, seeing their laboratories, and hearing them describe their total programs."[31]

Stever's conclusions were echoed by Dr. Hugh Dryden, Kármán's deputy: "I think we found out more about what had been going on in the war in a few days' conversations with some of these key German leaders, than all the running around and digging for drawings and models . . . could bring."[32] Firsthand rather than second or thirdhand information made seeing the German scientific picture much easier. Only after Kármán arrived was the totality of the German scientific effort revealed.

To preserve that scientific picture, the American teams boxed up everything they could and immediately shipped it off to Wright Field. In one location, Navy exploitation teams were the first to arrive after liberation. They quickly boxed up the hardware and technical data in large crates and labeled them "U.S. Navy." Two days later Army teams made it to the same location, whereupon they crated the Navy boxes in larger containers and relabeled them "U.S. Army."[33] Interservice rivalry extended to all rank levels and existed in all career fields, even among scientists. For many reasons, some good and some apparently ridiculous, immediate access to German technical targets was crucial. Spaatz provided the air-transportation capability to meet these requirements.[34] His personal involvement in the early days of the SAG helped strengthen his own understanding of its capabilities during his tour as the first Air Force chief of staff.

Among the most surprising discoveries during the "scientists' invasion" were a jet-powered helicopter built by Doblhoff, swept-back wings hung in high-speed wind tunnels, hidden assembly locations for V-1 and V-2 "vengeance" weapons, and plans for V-3 (intercontinental) rockets. Of greatest interest were thousands of linear feet of data and documents that accompanied these projects. Upon close examination, many of these confirmed the path that American science had already taken. Some, the jet-powered helicopter for instance, were a total surprise.[35]

As the scientists arrived in Europe, Arnold was headed back to the rehabilitation hospital in Miami for a thorough checkup. The trip was somewhat circuitous, as the delegation visited Rio de Janeiro and a few AAF staging bases in Brazil. Bee was relaxing at Nags Head, North Carolina, where she had gone to get away from her own desk job, her hay fever, and other personal responsibilities.[36]

On 8 May 1945, the day victory was declared in Europe, a relaxed Arnold returned to his hospital bed in Miami. This time it was just for follow-up tests and more rest before another combat-theater tour. His next destination was the Pacific. The war was almost over.

While lying in his bed, Arnold turned his attention to the Far East: "I never questioned the wonderful work the Navy had done in the Pacific. In spite of all the obstacles, in spite of many mistakes, their movement across the Pacific was really a magnificent operation."[37] In fact, naval operations had captured necessary bases for the AAF's bombers to use in the offensive against Japan. With-

out these bases—the third element of Arnold's balanced air force program—
there was little that American air force could do against Japan.

After receiving a solid bill of health, in the first week of June Arnold began a
journey west. He delayed briefly in San Francisco so that he could take a trip
north to Sonoma, the location of his retirement ranch.

On 8 June he wrote Bee a detailed accounting of the property. He took pictures of the land and told Miss Adkins to have them developed. He described
the procedures involved in keeping their meat in deep-freeze lockers in town
after slaughter, one of Bee's concerns. Arnold also described the health of the
trees and berry bushes; most were well. "I have ordered 10 tons of feed; 6 of al-
falfa for cows and calves; 4 of oat hay for Duke . . . the cat eats lizards and likes
them . . . the deer are already jumping the fence and getting in the garden."

Bee was completely included in the planning for retirement life: "I have
written Proctor [their attorney] to have the architect here when you and I come
up about the end of the month. . . . I am counting on meeting you here on my
return trip. Bring the plans of the house and anything else that you need to
climb up the hill and spend a couple or three days in this delightful place. . . .
When you meet me here we can write the next chapter."[38]

Arnold then headed to Guam, a trip that took four days from San Francisco.
In 1913, when Arnold and Bee had traveled to the Philippine Islands by transport ship, it had taken three weeks. Transportation technology had lessened
travel time in a way that had changed the world since then. On Saipan, LeMay
and Giles met Arnold at the plane. Later, accompanied by Rosie O'Donnell, a
former member of Arnold's advisory council, he took a tour of the tiny island.
He could hardly believe the scale of the construction that had been accomplished. Later, Arnold had a long meeting with MacArthur.[39] By this time,
LeMay's forces were pounding the Japanese mainland and had already destroyed many of the major cities.

LeMay's success after taking Brig. Gen. Haywood Hansell's place as commanding general of Twenty-first Bomber Command was the result of frustration rather than tactical brilliance. He confided in Arnold that weather had
been their "worst operational enemy," and his first six weeks had seen no
tremendous improvement in bombing accuracy or target destruction over
Hansell's operation. LeMay stated that during those weeks, "we had one vi-
sual shot at a target." It was his frustration with the weather and his knowledge that Arnold, who technically held direct command of the Twenty-first,
demanded results that finally drove the B-29 bombers to low altitudes to accomplish their raids. As LeMay explained, the weather, rather than any pre-
conception about the effectiveness of low-altitude bombing, "was the primary
reason I lowered the altitude for our incendiary attacks."[40] In reality, Hansell,
then LeMay, ran the operation with little input from the recuperating Arnold.

Arnold completed his comprehensive Pacific tour after a long conference with Adm. Chester Nimitz about command organization on and around Guam. He then stopped on Okinawa, where his second son, Bruce, was commanding a gun battery. The two Arnolds met at Bruce's jeep and talked privately for a bit, then posed for photographers and well-wishers. Of the boys, Bruce's mannerisms were most like those of his father. In newsreel footage of their visit, both seem to fidget by kicking dirt with their feet, uncomfortably crossing their arms across their chest, and randomly looking up and down as if afraid to look each other in the eye. General Arnold was noticeably more drawn than in earlier photographs, his uniform hanging loose around his neck and middle. The meeting was documented by a well-publicized photo of the two, and the caption read: "Hi'ya Pop!"[41]

After this enjoyable end to what would be his last trip to the Pacific, Arnold made the long journey back to Washington. Bee could not make the trip west, as originally planned. One more major official tasked remained ahead: Potsdam. But first he was able to spend a few weeks in Washington, finally reunited with Bee in their home.

✪ ✪ ✪ ✪ ✪

In July Arnold was off again to Europe on a rest-and-recuperation trip, this time as the United States's air force representative. After six weeks of traveling throughout the devastated European countryside, Kármán met a cheerfully recovered Arnold in Paris on 13 July 1945, to discuss the scientific team's initial findings. General Arnold, on his way to join President Truman at Potsdam, was in a hurry.[42] He asked the professor to prepare a report summarizing the preliminary discoveries. On 22 August 1945, Kármán submitted his report, *Where We Stand,* satisfying that request.

The carving up of Germany that took place at Potsdam was the political end of a terrible conflict in Europe. All was not work, though, as Arnold drove through Berlin in Hitler's open-top car and slept in the very suite that Heinrich Himmler, S.S. Reichsführer, had once frequented. Arnold was gratified that the brutal war was nearing its now-inevitable end. His letter to Bee reflected the satisfaction of ultimate victory: "The enclosed envelope will probably be a real collectors item some day so you had better keep it. Written on Hitler's stationary—using his seal—sent from Berlin. Note Berlin A.P.O. number on stamp by P.O. Also enclosing a signature by Truman to A.F. day proclamation."[43]

Praise for the Army Air Forces from the new president simply verified what Arnold already knew—air force had played a vital, at times indispensable role in defeating the Axis. But issues of war were still paramount, as the battle still raged in the Pacific. During the conferences in Berlin, the most contested decision between military and political leadership—whether or not to drop the atomic bomb—surfaced only briefly. Best evidence indicates that President

Truman had decided in mid-June to use the atomic bomb against Japanese targets, despite opposition from his Joint Chiefs of Staff.

Although Arnold's views against dropping such weapons were known, he himself was in the Pacific when the final decision was apparently made by Truman. In fact, it appears that Truman gave Ira Eaker, in attendance at the June meeting in Washington, a letter that ordered Spaatz to drop the bomb after the success of the upcoming test was known. Arnold was not involved in the final decision regardless of when it was made; neither were any of the military Chiefs of Staff. Dropping the bomb was a political decision carried out by military forces under military orders. It was the most Clausewitzian act of the war.[44]

Arnold returned from Potsdam worried, but relaxed. He knew what lay ahead for Japan, and, like Marshall, LeMay, Spaatz, and Eaker, he was not happy about it. Arnold waited at home that evening of 5 August 1945, because his direct White House line was many times faster and more accurate than regular phone lines. Bee recalled the home atmosphere the night that Col. Paul Tibbets piloted *Enola Gay* to deliver the most devastating single blow ever dispensed in warfare, both physically and psychologically. Bee recalled, "The night of the atomic bomb, he walked the corridor in that big house, back and forth, waiting for the telephone to ring. In that house, the upstairs library had . . . five different phones, one direct to the White House, and to the Pacific. . . . But the night of that atomic bomb he didn't go to bed, he just walked the floor, and I knew something terrific was happening. But he never gave me any inkling that it was anything so terrific."[45]

❂   ❂   ❂   ❂   ❂

Where We Stand, a summary of the exploitation of German science and technology that Kármán's men had unearthed, became Arnold's trumpet, and he became the herald of airpower. The majority of Arnold's writings, speeches, and letters that discussed technology are laced with the tenets of both the initial and the final Kármán reports. To best understand Arnold's views of technology and science, one must read and comprehend these reports. In his report, Kármán suggested the following "fundamental realities":

1. that aircraft—manned or pilotless—will move with speeds far beyond the velocity of sound.
2. that due to improvements in aerodynamics, propulsion and electronic control, unmanned devices will transport means of destruction to targets at distances up to several thousand miles.
3. that small amounts of explosive material will cause destruction over areas of several square miles.
4. that defense against present-day aircraft will be perfected by target seeking missiles.

5. that only aircraft or missiles moving at extreme speeds will be able to penetrate enemy territory protected by such defenses.
6. that a perfect communication system between fighter command and each individual aircraft will be established.
7. that location and observation of targets, take-off, navigation and landing of aircraft, and communication will be independent of visibility and weather.
8. that fully equipped airborne task forces will be enabled to strike at far distant points and will be supplied by air.[46]

In addition, the report sought to explain why Germany was advanced in some areas and behind in others. Inherent in the title was Kármán's evaluation of U.S. posture in regard to foreign scientific developments. These eight topics and other large sections of the summary appear nearly verbatim in Arnold's final report to the secretary of war, dated 12 November 1945.[47]

For example, German achievements in aeronautics were not attributed to superior scientists; rather, German superiority was due to "very substantial support enjoyed by their research institutions in obtaining expensive research equipment such as large supersonic wind tunnels many years before such equipment was planned in this country."[48] These tunnels supported development in the field of transonic and supersonic wing design, to the point of "practical application." Such ideas were only being discussed in the United States, and this realization was made by none other than Kármán, chief of the leading aeronautics laboratory in the country, the GALCIT.

Kármán added a warning: "We cannot hope to secure air superiority in any future conflict without entering the supersonic speed range." Additionally, the report stated that "the V-2 development was successful not so much because of striking scientific developments as because of an early start, military support, and boldness of execution."[49] An early start, unlimited funding, and bold execution of German scientific plans became a recurring theme throughout the Kármán report.

But there were also areas in which the U.S. held substantial advantage over the Axis. The most glaring of these was in radar development:

> It must be realized that radar is not a facility of attachment which will occasionally be used under bad conditions. Rather, the Air Force of the future will be operated so that radar is the *primary* facility, and visual methods will only occasionally be used. . . . Hence, in an all-weather Air Force, radar must be the universally used tool for bombing, gunfire, navigation, landing, and control. The whole structure of the Air Force, the planning of its operations, its training program, and its organization must be based on this premise. The development and perfection of radar and the techniques for

using it effectively are as important as the development of the jet-propelled plane.[50]

This realization flew in the face of accepted doctrine, but today it appears as the most prescient of all those made during this period. At the time, the Army Air Force's primary doctrine in Europe was that of precision strategic bombing, a position based primarily on the ability to visually acquire the intended target.[51] Kármán also pointed out that the Germans had failed to keep stride with the rest of the world in some areas because "most of the development took place in industrial laboratories . . . but the very brilliant group of German physicists in universities were never called in to participate. Consequently, while engineering design was good, imaginative new thinking was lacking." The professor could always tell where imagination and the element of individual brilliance were missing, whether it was in his students or in notable scientists.

Further, Kármán predicted: "The ability to achieve Air Force operations under all conditions of darkness and weather contributes more than any other single factor to increasing the military effectiveness of the air forces. Hence, any research program designed to overcome the limitations to flight at night and in bad weather will pay big dividends." Realizing that the technology behind radar was rapidly being improved, the professor added a caveat: the Air Force "must be alert in swiftly utilizing any new developments."[52]

By emphasizing radar, Kármán also indirectly assured MIT's future share of military research projects. During the war, it had been the MIT RADLAB that had worked toward American radar excellence. Generally, much as Caltech held the reins of AAF aeronautical science, MIT directed AAF radar programs. In fact, the addition of Dr. Edward Bowles to Arnold's staff in 1943 had linked radar and electronic programs to the AAF, much as Kármán's association with the general had linked aeronautics in earlier years. The rivalry that developed between these schools was more friendly than Caltech's rivalry with the NACA, because both schools held particular expertise in different areas of technological development. And, for the most part, both respected each other's accomplishments.[53]

Radar was but one specific technological device, but *Where We Stand* was broad in its scope. The report addressed the idea of an Air Force school for scientists and engineers, continued relations with the civilian scientific community, and continued cooperation with national agencies concerned with scientific research. It also made more mundane but important suggestions concerning techniques for measurement taking and data collection during experimentation. Perhaps the most interesting recommendation was not directly related to accomplishment of scientific research or development; it concerned problems of organization echoing the report. Kármán wrote Spaatz directly: "It is necessary that the Commanding General of the Air Forces and the Air Staff be advised continuously on the progress of scientific research and development in view of the potentialities of new discoveries and improvements in aerial warfare. A permanent Scientific Advisory Group, consisting of qualified officers and eminent civilian scientific consultants, should be available to the Commanding General, reporting directly to him on novel developments and advising him on the planning of scientific research."[54]

Now anticipating deep budget cuts after war's end, Arnold cabled Kármán, still in Europe, wondering if the report might be finalized by 15 December 1945. To accommodate the general, Kármán canceled an upcoming trip to Japan and sent a few SAG team members to the Orient instead. From October through December, work proceeded at a frenetic pace. After many sleepless nights, Kármán delivered the draft version of the summary report, *Toward New Horizons,* in person to Arnold's desk on 17 December 1945. Eaker and Spaatz later joined Arnold and the professor for a brief introduction to the eighty-page, hard-bound summary volume.[55]

Kármán's synopsis, "Science: The Key to Air Supremacy," introduced the twelve-volume classified report, near 1,200 pages in all.[56] In essence, the work amplified the tenets of the August report, with a few significant additions. Kármán's three-part summary volume addressed the problems associated with "research and development from the point of view of the technical requirements which the Air Forces must meet in order to carry out its task, securing the safety of the nation." The third part of the summary elaborated upon correcting the organizational and administrative problems that had been addressed in *Where We Stand.* Most notable of these elaborations was a plea for government authority to "foster," not "dictate," basic research.[57] This type of long-range, extremely detailed study was the first of its kind ever accomplished in American military history. Along with *Where We Stand,* it was intended to serve as the blueprint for building the United States's air force during the next two decades.

Although this study was critical to Arnold, he did not depend exclusively upon it or upon the SAG for scientific advice. By January 1946, he had allocated $10 million of his military budget to Douglas Aircraft Corporation for a one-year study of future warfare called Project Rand, which blossomed into a three-year, $30 million program. During this first year, a Project Rand mathematician delicately pointed out that not all military problems revolved around math and science. Some problems were best investigated by historians, political scientists, and economists. In 1947, though only 150 were employed there, a "humanities" division was formed at Rand in response to this suggestion. In May 1948, fearing conflict-of-interest questions between the Air Force and Douglas Corporation, the entire division broke away from Douglas, forming the first nonprofit research-and-development corporation in the United States: Rand.[58]

The stated goal for Rand was to provide a "program of study and research on the broad subject of intercontinental warfare."[59] It was to offer long-term, unbiased, thoughtful research to Air Force planners. By 1950, more than 800 men and women were employed in support of that task.[60] In truth, Rand served another purpose in its early days: to act as a counterbalance to Dr. Bush's formulation for the future of American scientific research. Arnold's establishment of Project Rand was the direct result of the general's association with Dr. Edward Bowles, and of industrial as well as familial ties to Donald Douglas. Douglas released the Rand division despite the loss in government revenues, because "it was the right thing to do."[61]

In addition to Project Rand, Arnold had been busy authorizing technology-development programs that looked to the future, particularly in guided missiles. Influenced to act by Kármán's initial report, the general had already believed in the potential of "unpiloted things" for future air forces.[62] Although he had unofficially retired in February, a plan for the April 1946 guided-missile program had been determined and approved during his last months in command of the AAF. A total of $34 million had been allocated to twenty-eight different AAF guided-missile projects.[63]

But Arnold's fears concerning budget cuts were more than accurate. In 1947, the military budget was slashed in typical postwar downsizing, and the guided-missile budget fell from $34 million to $13 million, forcing cancellation of ten programs already under way. Only short-term enterprises that could be completed in minimum time were continued. Of the surviving programs, only one was a long-range, rocket-propelled missile, ICBM-type: the MX-774B, which was under contract to Consolidated Vultee Aircraft Corporation.[64] Thus, although Arnold recognized the need for development in missiles, budget constraints limited Army Air Force programs in this area until the national political climate was once again altered by the advent of the Cold War. In the meantime, the Army and the Navy inherited several of the programs that postwar air forces could ill afford but were still deemed important by the new Joint Chiefs of Staff or the Guided Missiles Committee.[65]

General Arnold was so interested in the possibilities of future airpower development that, based upon Kármán's reports, he offered his personal perceptions of the SAG's importance to Spaatz before he left Washington in February 1946. Spaatz took Arnold's advice to heart and established the Scientific Advisory Board as a permanent group, which met for the first time on 17 June 1946. It was not, however, attached to the commanding general; it had been relegated to the deputy chief of air staff for research and development, Gen. Curtis E. LeMay. Nevertheless, the SAB had survived the end of the war and was established as an organization with the express purpose of providing scientific advice to higher levels of Air Force leadership. The imperfection of the new system would eventually be repaired.

Arnold reminded Spaatz, his eventual successor, that the Air Forces had no great scientists in their ranks. Military R and D labs had stagnated during the war, largely due to increased production requirements and personnel short-ages. Outside civilian help had been required to meet development of aircraft power plants and structural-design problems. Only through civilians had sci-entific and technological potential been realized. Arnold reminded Spaatz: "These men did things that the average Army officer could never have accom-plished. We must not lose these contacts."[66]

The Kármán reports had undeniable and permanent influence upon Arnold. For the rest of his life, he used the ideas contained within the many hundreds of pages to emphasize the importance of pursuing scientific under-standing and applying technological know-how to the U.S. Air Force.

Japan's surrender was met with relief in Washington. Congratulations were offered and small parties were held, but most were too tired to rejoice. General Arnold had decided to retire and tendered his request to General Marshall on 8 November 1945.[67] While at the Potsdam Conference the previous month, Arnold and Dwight D. Eisenhower, the presumed next chief of staff, had se-cretly selected Tooey Spaatz to be the next commanding general of the Army Air Forces.[68]

Beginning in September 1945, the American tradition of massive demobi-lization was once again demonstrated in force. More than 2.4 million people were actively serving in the Army Air Forces. Less than one year later, only 700,000 remained. Arnold left this work to subordinates, while he toured Mexico and South America in an effort to garner support for continued mili-tary cooperation in the coming years. This was a need he had perceived since before the war. But Lovett's warnings about Arnold were right, and the general returned to his Florida hospital bed for a short rest and a scolding after a flare-up in the high altitudes at a few bases in Peru. While Arnold was resting, Harry Hopkins, one of the United States's air force proponents, died of his long-term fight against hemochromatosis—a failed digestive system.[69] Arnold wrote that Hopkins was one of his best friends and "one of the most enthusiastic sup-porters of American Air Power."[70]

The Arnolds left Washington in the last week of February 1946. Spaatz's personal pilot, Robert E. Kimmel, piloted the B-17 from Washington to Sonoma. "Because of General Arnold's poor health, we flew at low alti-tude."[71] By 2 March 1946, Bee and Hap had arrived in California, in the Val-ley of the Moon.

12

HASTEN THE CAISSON
(1946–50)

J ust prior to his departure from Washington for retirement, Arnold, his normally sparkling eyes sagging and tired, his well-receded hair white, wrote a nine-page, single-spaced memorandum to his successor, Gen. Carl Tooey Spaatz. "Herewith are some observations I am passing on to you as a result of my 10 years in Washington. My suggestion is that you read them over carefully by yourself before passing them on to anybody."[1] Included in the memo were suggestions about discipline in a shrinking force, the importance of the air staff, the critical nature of an advisory council, the necessity to dismiss officers who fell short in conduct of their duty, and the need to increase the scientific and technical training within the Army Air Forces themselves. There were also points made about the importance of adequate base housing, extracurricular activities, and support groups for Air Force personnel. Many of these latter topics were new ones for Spaatz, who had spent most of his time in operational rather than administrative commands.

One particularly inflammatory topic that was addressed in the memo was flight pay: "The words 'Flying Pay' are a thorn in the side of ground soldiers, of legislators and many others. We ourselves have probably done much to upset the apple cart by making flying appear so easy, so comfortable and so safe. . . . I am convinced that we should establish at once a system of vocational pay; pay for the work that is being done in the Air Arm, pay for the knowledge that is necessary to accomplish the task. . . . Delete completely increased pay and above everything else, the term 'Flying Pay.'"[2] The divisiveness of this issue had been apparent to Arnold before war's end, but his advice has never been heeded to this day, and the dilemma that Arnold faced still exists.[3]

215

By far the most highly detailed and emphasized section of this memo covered "Scientific Developments." Arnold devoted two full pages to the subject. It is significant to note that throughout the entirety of the lengthy memo, only one individual was mentioned by name: Dr. Theodore von Kármán. No generals, no political figures, no other names at all were considered more vital than Kármán's. This fact represents a striking insight into Arnold's belief in science and its potential for the future of the United States's air force. He went so far as to state clearly that "hereafter, science and research will have the same relative importance as pilot training."[4] Thus, Arnold's commitment to science and technology that had driven many of his decisions during the war—both successes and failures—was passed to Spaatz.

> In view of the type of men he [Kármán] has working with him, I am sure that any research program used as a basis for securing funds that is built around this report, must be accepted. . . . In connection with programs for scientific research and appropriation of funds, in my opinion it is of the utmost importance that there be no administrative obstructions between the officer in charge of these future research problems and programs and the Commanding General of the Army Air Forces. As I visualize it, in time of peace the one man who should have time to think more than anyone else in the whole Air Forces organization, except the young second lieutenants, is the Commanding General, Army Air Forces. Accordingly, he should be able to project himself further into the future than any of the Staff.[5]

Of all advice Arnold offered, emphasis on the potential of scientific research and technological development remained at the forefront of his retirement activities.

For example, just as Arnold was leaving Washington, *National Geographic* magazine published a mammoth article, "Air Power for Peace," that Arnold had written during his final months as commanding general. Fifty-seven pages long, it was the lead piece for the February 1946 issue, and it included thirty-five illustrations, twenty-eight of which were color photographs. Arnold had served on the board of trustees since 1938 and had published articles in the magazine before, but this one was different. It contained views new to the American public, including, for the first time, references to air power in the atomic long-range-missile age.

> While this country must employ all of its physical and moral force in the cause of peace, it must recognize that real security against atomic weapons in the visible future will rest on our ability to take immediate offensive action with overwhelming force. . . . If defenses which can cope with the 3,000 mile-per-hour projectile are developed, we must improve the weapon; be ready to launch projectiles having greater precision with regards to hit-

ting the target, to give them a shorter time of flight, and to make them harder to detect and destroy. . . . This can be done now from long-range bombers, but in the future such missiles may be launched from true space ships, capable of operating outside the earth's atmosphere.[6]

It would be more than a decade before *Sputnik* orbited the earth on 4 October 1957, and Arnold would not be here to witness that event.

Finally, Bee and Hap Arnold arrived at their retirement ranch in Sonoma—such as it was. They had named the ranch El Rancho Feliz, which they translated as Hap's Ranch. Since a literal translation would have been "the happy ranch," this could be another indication that the nickname Hap was short for Happy.[7] Arnold described the ranch to his sister Betty as "a regular tobacco road."[8] It had been left in disrepair by the previous owners and had slowly been rehabilitated by workmen during the final years of the war. On the 41½-acre plot, there existed a spring and adequate potential for well water, rolling hills, good soil, and nearly 20 acres of trees. Initially, the Arnolds had had the old, original farmhouse refurbished and had stocked the farm with chickens and a horse. Arnold had found tenants, Warren and Mary Betts, willing to tend the farm in exchange for room and board. Also before they arrived, the Arnolds had had sixty fruit trees planted, as well as thirty-six grape vines and sixteen berry vines. A road had been constructed from the main highway back to the new house site.[9]

When the Arnolds arrived on 5 March 1946, they were disappointed to find that torrential rains had closed the road to the construction site, and that there was no immediate possibility for reprieve from the weather. Helpless to do anything about the situation, they headed to Southern California for two weeks, where they visited friends and took a side trip to El Paso, Texas, to visit Hap's brother Clifford. They returned to San Francisco for ten more days of relaxation, and then to Sonoma, where the house was nearing completion. By Easter Sunday services, they were moved in and unpacked.[10]

Arnold had always enjoyed a good sermon, particularly around the holidays. "He enjoyed church very much, if he could get a message," Bee recalled. She asked him if "he wanted to join the Baptist church. No, but we used to go to Kenwood to a little community church, and sit on kitchen chairs, and he loved it. One Sunday there would be a Lutheran, another Sunday a Congregationalist, or a Methodist."[11] His basic Baptist upbringing had long ago become too narrow-minded for Arnold; he simply sought a well-preached message. From this and the fact that he worked every Sunday of the war, one might conclude that he was ambivalent toward religion. In reality, Arnold had internalized fundamental Christian beliefs, but he was dubious about the church as an institution. His attitude was perhaps a result of his extremely strict upbringing and the West Point preacher who never excited him while he was a cadet.

Less than two months after the move had been completed, Arnold's lifelong wanderlust once again took hold of him. On 2 June he headed back East for what can best be described as an awards-and-decorations tour coupled with a family visit. He hesitated leaving Bee alone again in the less-than-perfect conditions at the retirement ranch. "Please look at the confusion and troubles at Rancho Feliz as something temporary. We must and will iron out the difficulties. That is the place where we must find peace and contentment. To quote you, 'the place we have been waiting for all these years' . . . without you it will be incomplete. I want to adjust 'me' to make the picture complete and restful to you."[12]

While in Washington he had lunch with his son David Lee, who had just completed his plebe year at West Point and was "riding on high." He visited with his daughter Lois and her husband, Ernie Snowden, and stayed with Mary and Bill Street. He emphasized that while visiting D.C., he made "no entangling alliances with Pentagon inhabitants," one of Bee's fears.[13] This was patently untrue. For the next six months, he acted as a herald in the campaign for a unified air force, a nationwide campaign that only partially succeeded. The topic of his visit with Spaatz and the AAF staff was the "unification bill" that, far from its original form, would eventually separate the Air Force as a service rather than create a national, unified air force.

Arnold was for "real unification" of the air arm. As his son Bruce explained it in 1974, "he wanted to take all the Navy fliers and put them in his Air Force."[14] Arnold believed in total unity of air command, land-based and sea-based. This view, of course, was antagonistic to that of the U.S. Navy, including King, Leahy, and Towers. In retirement, although ultimately unsuccessful in convincing many, Arnold became even more aggressive in pressing his views, both publicly and personally, to high-ranking officials.

The Navy, under the leadership of Adm. John Towers, longtime Arnold friend, was protesting the bill in the strongest terms. Arnold warned Spaatz after returning to Sonoma, emphasizing his views concerning the Navy's intentions and methods.

> I just want to repeat a thought I have told you several times, and that is this: both King and Leahy outlined their thoughts of what the Navy of the future should be—thoughts which conform to those of the present people in power in the Navy—when they said to me, "Hap, if you will let us have your Air Force, with our Marine Ground Force and our Navy, there will be no need for an Army." That was not all wishful thinking on the part of King and Leahy! And it is not all wishful thinking on the part of the Navy itself. Slowly, but surely, they are laying a foundation upon which to build a very fine, rugged "edifice"![15]

The rivalry between air and sea was real. It formed the foundation of the struggle against an independent air force in 1946. The final bill was the direct result of conflicts and compromises between Navy and Army Air Forces leadership, not to mention lessening influence of the hawkish Democratic party in both the House of Representatives and the Senate.[16]

During this trip Arnold received medals from the Panamanian and Chilean embassies, an honorary degree from Harvard, and one from the School of Mines and Technology in Rapid City, South Dakota. He also become an honorary member of an Indian tribe before returning to Hamilton Field on 8 June.[17] These were but a few of the many accolades and hundreds of awards that Arnold earned during a forty-two-year military career.

By mid-July, he was tiring. He wrote Spaatz on 30 July that "leading the life of a General-Farmer is not so simple as it sounds."[18] Most of his difficulties were self-imposed, as they had always been. He realized that he needed administrative help and issued requests for an aide and a driver directly to General Eisenhower and President Truman himself. This request was denied.[19] In addition to his travels and speeches, Arnold was kept busy with his appointment to the California Fish and Game Commission and his writing; he was publishing yet more articles on the importance of science to the United States's air forces.

During the fall of 1946, "Maté" Pool's health began to deteriorate, and Bee spent much of the next two years back East with her family. Arnold continued to travel. In November and December he again flew East. During this trip, he celebrated at a Women Airforce Service Pilots' party, enjoyed a West Point versus Notre Dame football game, and attended a meeting of aircraft industrialists in Cleveland. Arnold may have felt fearless on these trips, because he had just been told by his Sonoma doctor that "as far as my heart was concerned I should live another 20 years."[20] This may also be why Beadle decided to spend so much time with her mother, away from her new Sonoma home. There was one benefit to Bee's absence: the quiet around the ranch gave Arnold ample opportunity to think and write.[21]

One speech-turned-article in particular was published during the ongoing debate over control of the air arm. The work was heavily laced with references to *Where We Stand* and *Toward New Horizons* (the Kármán reports), and both were specifically intended to emphasize the importance of airpower and the differences between air and sea power as demonstrated during the war. Of primary concern during air battles had been speed. After the war, the need for increased speed and range became one of Arnold's strongest arguments for airpower. "Today, with the unprecedented rate of advanced techniques, we are shrinking our time scales so fast that our organizational concepts are lagging pitifully behind. We can no longer afford military organizations whose reaction times are of another order."[22] His obvious slap at the Navy was intentionally used to set up the crux of his talk.

He cut to the quick when he asked: "Are we to build an entire military structure involving ground, sea, and air forces around the existing naval organization, or are we to recognize the Air Forces as a great investment in national security, which has already paid handsome dividends?"[23] Arnold was finally able to say what he had been thinking privately for many years. This speech, with a few editorial modifications and a different title, was published in the international journal *Air Affairs* in December 1946. With news from Spaatz that a compromise between the Air Forces and the Navy had been hammered out, Arnold slowed his pace somewhat. He had decided to take the advice Harry Hopkins had offered from his deathbed—he would write his memoirs.[24]

By April 1947, Arnold had begun writing. "Have just completed page 21 and am on Governors Island with Glenn Curtiss," he wrote to Bee.[25] When he was not writing, he was working the farm. His letters to Bee speak of the condition of his riding horse, Duke; the overdue birth of one of the cows; the status of the flower garden; the condition of the fruit trees. He tried to sell his produce and eggs to local markets, most of the time without success. He often reported on the mischievous activities of his black cocker spaniel, Side-Car.[26]

Arnold had always joked about what damage he might do to any airplanes that came flying over his retirement home. "If one dares fly low over my ranch house, I'll grab a rifle or something and shoot it down!"[27] On 4 April 1947, while Arnold was away, two planes did fly over the valley, dogfighting for more than an hour. Then tragedy struck. The planes collided, severing the tail of one and ruining the landing gear of the other. The tailless plane spun toward the Arnolds' home but missed it, exploding in the southeast pasture. The pilot had parachuted to safety, but remained safe only because Arnold was not there. The other plane returned to an emergency landing at a nearby base. Sgt. Bruce Simmons took matters under control. Arnold's driver during the war, he had moved with his family to the ranch and acted as Arnold's personal helper. He vigorously protected the general and Mrs. Arnold and was loved by the entire Arnold family. Simmons kept the reporters away and assisted in the salvage effort of the plane.[28]

On 18 September 1947, the establishment of the United States Air Force as a separate service drew little attention in the Arnold household. Arnold did, however, manage a trip to Washington the month following the declaration to congratulate the newly independent USAF staff. One particularly distasteful task fell to him during that fall trip. He was asked to testify in an investigation of Gen. Benny Meyers, who had been accused—and was eventually convicted—of embezzlement during the war. Bee recalled that her husband had seen in Meyers "a kindred spirit in getting it done yesterday. . . . I think it hurt Hap, just crushed him."[29] Betrayal of trust was unfamiliar to Arnold, and the Meyers case, stressful and emotional, may have been a contributing factor to his illness that began in December of that year.

In Sonoma, the sixty-one-year-old Arnold returned to his sickbed. This time the difficulty initially appeared to concern his intestinal system. It was complicated by bronchitis and may have included some heart difficulty as well. Regardless the nature of the problem, Arnold was too ill to attend Orville

Wright's funeral in the first week in February 1948. Orville died three days after a heart attack he had suffered on 27 January.[30]

Arnold, on the other hand, recovered fairly quickly, then spending most of 1948 diligently at work on his memoirs. Originally he titled them simply "Hap Arnold's Air Story."[31] Bill Laidlaw, formerly a lieutenant colonel in the Eighth and Ninth Air Forces, had volunteered to ghostwrite for the general, which did not always work out smoothly. In one instance, Arnold took some home-grown vegetables to Laidlaw's place in Boyes Springs, California, where they argued over the book. Simmons recalled that Arnold had one plan for the work, while Laidlaw wanted to emphasize the European war. In disgust, Arnold "slow-gashed" the old Packard he was driving and spattered Laidlaw with dust and cinders. "How do you like that, you SOB?" Arnold shouted out the car window.[32] By June 1948, the pair, still managing to work together, had reached April 1941 and Arnold's trip to England. Arnold hoped to finish by the end of July.[33]

By May 1949, the manuscript finally was largely completed. Laidlaw broke the news that Harper's, the publisher, had lost interest in the book. Nevertheless, they did finally publish it later that year, and without much polishing released it on 21 September 1949. Harper's had turned down Admiral Leahy's autobiography and told Laidlaw that "memoirs have no reader appeal."[34] Arnold was disappointed in the apparent lack of interest in war memoirs, but Bee was little interested in what came to be known around the Arnold house as "The Book."[35] Arnold understood her disinterest; she had experienced it all through his letters for the past two years.

Bee was occupied at her mother's bedside. She saw Hap less frequently than either had hoped for until after Annie Pool died, on the day Hap's book was released. Hap remembered her spirit from their encounter at the dock in Lucerne. "She was always my best relative other than my wife," he consoled Bee.[36] It was time for Bee to come home.

During the fall of 1949, Hap and Bee passed the hours sitting on the porch and watching the antics of the local wildlife. Arnold wrote about the many species that occupied the Valley of the Moon—the evening deer, humming-birds "like fighter planes," quail, raccoon, and circling hawks. He loathed the foxes and skunks that pestered his chickens and fouled the fresh air, as it blew through the valley when the wind was up. Nonetheless, he applauded nature's ability to regenerate itself in the face of greedy game hunters.[37] Arnold and Bee had always loved the outdoors, and they enjoyed their valley immensely. "We loved nature, and so it's funny how many times our thoughts just blended about that," Bee recalled.[38]

On Saturday, 14 January 1950, Simmons drove Arnold to the Sonoma hospital for his heart treatment, an injection of some sort. While he was out, Arnold picked up a set of miniature ribbons that he had custom-ordered for his uniform and sent a telegram to Britannica Publishers urging that the editorial process on his most recent work, a short encyclopedia article on airpower, be accelerated. Arnold knew, as he had in 1945, that he had little time left. "You better hurry up and send me the material before I strike out and the game is called on account of darkness,"[39] Simmons recalled him telegramming. The message struck Simmons as strange, since just the previous Wednesday, Arnold had been given a "five-year warranty" on his heart by his doctor. It turned out to be only five days.

Right up until nearly his last minute, Arnold was still communicating to new members of the national-defense community his belief in the benefits of unified airpower. Four days before he died, he wrote to Louis Johnson, the second secretary of defense:

> Now since most of the smoke is clearing away, and the Department of Defense—from the outside, at least—seems to be running along in a routine manner, I want to congratulate you upon the splendid job you did, with an almost impossible situation confronting you.
>
> In my opinion, without unification, and the economies that go with it, we will never have the power in our Armed Forces which is so essential in this topsy-turvy world.
>
> More power to you! And best of luck![40]

Arnold was totally devoted to the concept of unified airpower, so much so that he ended his autobiography, *Global Mission,* with a stirring, emotional plea for such a force. It was a plea that fell on ears too tired to make real efforts to reorganize the entire Department of Defense.

> Duplications, obsolete construction projects, obsolete techniques and policies, overlapping in the armed services operations and organizations must go by the boards. There is no place for two air forces today any more than there is for two ground forces or two navies. Let us get smart, and, while we have a few years in which to reorganize, do it right. Let us give the people of the United States the best, the most efficient, the most modernly equipped armed forces possible, using as determining factors, our *foreign policy*, and the *capabilities and limitations of our probable enemies* [emphasis in the original].[41]

Arnold's intentions and concepts, meritorious or not, were simply too hard to put into effect so soon after the war and the establishment of a separate Air Force.

✪ ✪ ✪ ✪ ✪

On the Saturday evening of 14 January 1950, the Arnolds were headed for a small anniversary party for Mr. and Mrs. Walter Murphy. Before leaving the ranch, Hap made the unusual request that Bee join him for an evening cocktail in front of the fire; normally he saved his two-drink limit for parties.[42] But on this evening, Hap and Bee sat by the fire together, just as Hap had once said he hoped someday to do, talking over cocktails.

Later, home again after the party, Hap talked with Bee about the release of his book. Despite excellent reviews by General Eisenhower and Jimmy Doolittle, early sales had not met expectations, and it would contribute little income for the Arnolds' retirement. Hap mentioned his disappointment to Bee just before they went to bed.[43] Nevertheless, the general had accomplished a remarkable feat: writing and publishing the story of his life and Army service in only two years. He had passed many hours autographing copies of the work that were sent to him by admirers and old friends.

The morning of 15 January was crisp and cool in the valley. Arnold stirred at 7:00 A.M. and leaned toward Bee, quietly mumbling something inaudible. Then he lay back down in their bed overlooking the Valley of the Moon through the large picture window, and died peacefully at 7:30 A.M., his darling Beadle at his side.[44] He was sixty-three years old.

Arnold's body was flown from Hamilton Field to Washington in a simple pine box with wrought-iron fixtures. Later he was transferred to the metallic casket in which he was put to rest. His body, clad in his seldom-worn Air Force blue uniform, lay in state in an open casket in the National Cathedral Rotunda on 18 and 19 January. The funeral began at 11:00 A.M. on 19 January 1950, planned as a gigantic event. There were to be flyovers by eighty F-84 jet fighters and thirty B-29 bombers; there would then be a "missing man" formation, a tribute to fallen airmen, at the grave site. But terrible weather prevented one of the single greatest flyovers of Washington, D.C., since Arnold himself had ordered thirty-five planes to transit the city during his Morrow Board testimony a quarter century earlier.[45]

Gen. Hap Arnold had many friends in Washington, and probably a few enemies as well. Most attended the ceremony, including the procession of only 5 to 15 miles an hour through the town that Arnold had always claimed he hated. He had once acknowledged his impatient disposition to Spaatz, suggesting that he would someday probably be in a hurry to get the caisson rolling through the gates at Arlington.[46] And if he could have hurried the procession along, he certainly would have: there was no point, he would have said, in taking all this time to bury a broken-down general.

Slowly, somberly, the caisson bearing the dead general, led by an unmounted ceremonial horse (the cavalry's equivalent of the missing-man formation of airplanes) and a royal blue five-star flag, made its way through the main gate of the United States's most hallowed grounds. The procession moved up Roosevelt Drive to the Memorial Amphitheater, where Arnold's flag-draped casket rested during the eulogies, including one by President Truman. Then came the prayers and praises; Arnold had been a Baptist on paper

but had never committed to any one Protestant church. The procession mean-
dered down the hill to Grant Drive, then to the border road for Section 34 of
the cemetery. General Pershing had been buried near Arnold's selected grave
site the previous August, and the perimeter road would eventually bear Pershing's name. By the time the casket reached its destination, a soft snow had
turned into a driving sleet.[47] Near the top of a hill overlooking Washington,
D.C., General of the Air Force Hap Arnold was buried.

The funeral brought the Arnold family together for the first time since they
had departed March Field in 1935. Hank was now a lieutenant colonel, Bruce
a captain, and David a second lieutenant, all in the Army. Lois and her husband, Ernie Snowden, were also in Washington, but she did not attend the funeral. Her grief had overwhelmed her, and she remained sequestered during
the official ceremony.[48]

The Arnold family had never been close. They respected their father very
much, but after their move to March Field in 1931, he had spent less time at
home. He had been the family disciplinarian in their youth, even for Lois, who
got away with more escapades than the boys. As the children grew up, however, their father was away more and more. Regrettably, General Arnold's frequently grueling schedules, long flying exercises and war games, the air mail,
the Alaska Flight, congressional testimony, and factory-inspection tours kept
him apart from his children through many of their teen years.[49]

There were consequences. Lois was afraid to discuss her marriage plans
with her dad, even though she idolized him, because see feared his reaction to
her choice Snowden was a highly decorated Navy fighter pilot who loved to fly,
and he and Arnold got on famously, most of the time.[50] Lois died in 1964.
Hank, even though he had visited his father on occasion during the war, was
not even aware of the Sonoma property until Arnold was near retirement.[51]
Bill Bruce, who often had played practical jokes on his father, seemed closest
to his parents and most like his father in temperament. David was too far separated by age from the rest of the family to mix well until after he had graduated from West Point in 1949. His father, looking frazzled, drawn and thin,
had made it to Dave's wedding following his graduation that year.[52]

After Hap's death, Bee soon assumed the name Arnold—not Grandma or
Bee-Bee or anything else, just Arnold.[53] She lived peacefully at the ranch and
visited the East Coast frequently. She was often asked to represent the Arnold
family at events honoring the general after he died. In 1951, for example, Bee
was the guest of honor along with President Truman at the dedication of the
Arnold Engineering and Development Center (AEDC) in Tullahoma, Tennessee. Today, the AEDC remains the primary high-speed test facility and laboratory used by the USAF. In 1956, Bee Arnold and several other family members attended the dedication of the United States Air Force Academy in
Colorado Springs. The event was to feature the recently formed USAF Thun-
derbirds demonstration team, but one of the young pilots had overimbibed
and the show had to be rescheduled.[54]

Bee died one day after what would have been General Arnold's ninety-second birthday. She was ninety-one. Bruce, called El Bruco by the family, moved into the ranch. Honoring his mother's last request, El Bruco brought John Linton from his 1923 resting place near Philadelphia. He buried his little brother with Bee at Arlington, in the hillside grave next to Hap.[55] Bruce died in 1992 and is buried at Arlington in the same section as his father, as is David, who also died in 1992. Hank died in 1990 and is buried near Sheridan, Wyoming, his retirement home.[56]

Bruce and Barbara's only child, Robert Arnold, runs the ranch. He has even replanted the grapes that once grew there in limited quantities, and he dutifully represents the Arnold family at Air Force events. During the USAF fiftieth-anniversary celebration in Colorado Springs, Robert presented one of General Arnold's five-star flight caps to the United States Air Force Academy for display in the hall that bears the general's name. The cap was carried aboard the space shuttle *Columbia* (STS-78) by Lt. Col. Susan Helms, a 1980 graduate of the Air Force Academy. This flight cap—flown into space, conveyed by a technically trained female Air Force officer who had graduated from an air academy in existence for only four decades—symbolized a few of Arnold's many personal and institutional convictions about the potential for America's air force.

EPILOGUE
"The Spirit of a Man"

On 5 November 1947, Arnold wrote a letter to Lt. Col. LeRoy L. Stefan, who had asked of the general what was required to ensure a successful military career. In the letter, Arnold delineated several fundamental yet indispensable, "generally important requisites" that could be developed and refined by any officer. The first of these was "Basic knowledge: Exact, clear knowledge; not a hazy smattering. This kind of knowledge of the basics of your profession—of every assignment you are given—this is your 'technique'; this constitutes your 'tools.'"[1]

Arnold's entire first year at West Point was an exercise in basic knowledge. A barrage of questions was continually being fired at him, questions such as "Who is the superintendent, Mr. Arnold? Who is the secretary of war, Mr. Arnold?" Plebe year instilled within Arnold, as in all cadets, an understanding of disciplined, military fundamentals. This is not to say that Arnold enjoyed the disciplinary facets of the school—he tolerated them. He often worked around them, as he would throughout his career. As a varsity football player, he also came to realize the importance of play execution and teamwork, both predicated upon the basic knowledge of the game and the team-play book.

As an officer, Arnold concentrated his efforts upon the tasks at hand. He diligently learned the trade of mapping during his assignments in the Philippine Islands; this was a skill that paid unique dividends when he later commanded a global air force during World War II. His career as a pilot drove home the critical nature of complete familiarity with the basics. A slip in any fundamental while in the air often meant serious injury or death. Even the most complete understanding of flight in the early days was not a guarantee of

226

survival. Aeronautics was new science, and phenomena such as accelerated stalls were never fully understood during Arnold's lifetime, as the death toll from air accidents proved.

Arnold's self-imposed grounding after one such accident in 1912 indirectly resulted in an expansion of his basic knowledge beyond that required for operational flying. He learned many of the nuances of General Staff work and rose quickly to the temporary grade of colonel during the Great War. His Washington experience also introduced him to industrialists and scientists who helped him increase his grasp upon aeronautics and aircraft production. A brief tour at the Army Industrial College rounded out his Army education in the field of procurement and production. Understanding the political workings of the War Department served him well when he was recalled to Washington as assistant chief of the Air Corps in 1935.

From his return to Washington until war's end, Arnold applied his cumulative basic knowledge to the task of building aircraft and training airmen to wage a global war. Complete fundamental knowledge could not be gained, however, without much hard work, Arnold's second requisite: "Hard work: unrelenting, hard work. Some persons have a natural capacity for it; others have to develop it. No outstanding success is ever achieved without it."[2]

Arnold's formative years under his father's firm hand had taught the mischievous youth about the nature of a hard life; his years out on the bosque taught him about hard work. Deprived of creature comforts, he and his men thrived while thrashing about in the jungles near Manila and Batangas. Then, during World War I, he kept an inspection schedule that required tremendous physical and mental endurance—but it was war. Personal illness slowed him down only briefly, during his unsuccessful quest to witness combat above the stagnant trenches of Europe. Special missions such as delivering the air mail and the 1934 Alaska Flight tested the limits of Arnold's men and equipment. He reveled in hard work, physical and intellectual.

Eventually, with elevated rank and increased command responsibilities, Arnold's life evolved into one of long hours of General Staff work, less physically strenuous but infinitely more taxing mentally. The consequences of a sedentary, high-pressure career contributed to his illness during World War II, and, eventually, to his death. The first two requisites for success seemed rudimentary, difficult both mentally and physically, yet mechanical in nature. The third was a bit more challenging.

> Vision: The degree of vision depends, naturally, upon the quality of an individual's imagination; yet, one can train himself to look beyond his immediate assignment, to its relation to the next higher echelon of command, and the next, and the next . . . to the highest level or overall sphere of activity of which he can envision its being a part. He can also—if he has the capacity—envision possibilities yet developed: new horizons of activity. This is the

kind of vision that begets enthusiasm; and enthusiasm is the eager, driving force that converts dreams into realities.[3]

The Wright Brothers had once told Arnold: "Nothing is impossible." As early as 1912, and in ever-increasing measure thereafter, he became committed to advancing airpower through the use of science and technology. A study of the technological changes in airplanes and weapons during his career leaves no doubt that he believed in the potential of science; he internalized it. Upon his desk while he was commanding general of the Army Air Forces sat a placard that read: The Difficult We Do Today; The Impossible Takes a Little Longer.[4]

Moreover, Arnold had the unique ability to convince others, even those who said something could not be done, that it could and would be done. Sometimes his methods were harsh: those who failed to produce results were often unceremoniously removed from command. A few times, the projects that he directed were the wrong ones at the wrong time—but he seldom failed to get results from his subordinate commanders and industrial charges. He worked his staff as hard as he worked himself, in order to realize the potential of his imagination.

A tremendous catalyst to this process was his close personal association with American scientific, industrial, and academic communities. At times he placed too much faith in the possibilities of science, and, on more than one occasion, he hung his hopes on pipedream technology. But more often than not, his imaginative ideas were realized.

His retrospective thoughts would even today be considered "outside the box." He wrote, "The principles of yesterday no longer apply. Air travel, air power, air transportation of troops and supplies have changed the whole picture. We must think in terms of tomorrow. We must bear in mind that air power itself can become obsolete.[5]

Of Arnold, Dr. von Kármán once wrote: "You certainly know that I always admired your imagination and judgement, and I believe that you are one of the few men I have met who have the format to have at the same time your feet on the ground and your head over the clouds—even on days when the ceiling is rather high."[6]

In his dedication to scientific knowledge and pursuit of technological advances, Arnold lived on the leading edge of the airfoil. Yet he realized that making decisions about scientific developments and aircraft production required careful thought and was a by-product of experience; he called it "Judgment: not only the judgement that makes quick, correct decisions, but the ability to judge human nature, as well. Putting the right men in the right places—this is an essential in building a strong, successful organization."[7]

Not all of Arnold's decisions were correct, but he could be convinced, by carefully constructed arguments, to change his mind. He trusted his own ability to make decisions, but he also believed in those surrounding him. This belief, founded in decades of practical experience and personal interactions, led him to make judgments that resulted in both triumphs and failures. Representing both sides of the coin were the ultimate success of the B-29 bomber program and the delayed development of long-range escort fighters; and the ultimate poor performance of the XP-59A jet-aircraft and Weary Willy projects.

Arnold's selection of subordinate commanders reflected a similar track record—a combination of success and failure. His trusted lieutenants were frequently given what he considered the most crucial commands. Spaatz, Eaker, Kenney, LeMay, and even Jackie Cochran fell into this category. These commanders were so trusted that Arnold kept them out of Washington to the detriment of his own General Staff needs. He believed that his best belonged in the field, and that is were they were assigned.

When he believed that his selection had proved faulty, he swiftly corrected the perceived mistake. Haywood Hansell, a solid administrator, was replaced by the hard-charging, combat-seasoned LeMay after several months of lukewarm combat results. LeMay, although he initially followed the same path that had resulted in Hansell's dismissal, adapted to poor bombing conditions—more by accident than design. And, with an ever-increasing force of bombers than Hansell's, he incinerated town after Japanese town.

Arnold's close personal relationships with his most trusted commanders helped him decide who his combat commanders would be. However, these relationships did not prevent him from making decisions that he believed would help win the war more quickly. Moving Ira Eaker to the Mediterranean to make room for Spaatz, with whom Eisenhower had worked before and whom he held in high regard, was really not as difficult or agonizing as legend holds. Arnold realized the critical importance of supporting the supreme Allied commander's desires and decisions during one of the most daring operations of the war. In this case, he judged Ike's preference to be more important than any possible negative impact upon his Air Forces.

But Arnold's most prescient judgment—one that he consistently restated during the war years—may have been the one that required him to defer action. To separate the Army Air Forces in the midst of a global conflict would have interfered with many other, more critical, plans and programs that were potential war winners rather than political-agenda fulfillers. Frank Andrews and Hugh Knerr, though well intended, had pursued the idea of an independent air arm at the most inappropriate time imaginable. Arnold's command years ensured that their views were not lost, but rather placed on the back burner. Arnold himself had different views than many about independence as opposed to unification of the United States' air forces—more like Mitchell, less like Andrews. But Arnold's views, more controversial because of the potential impact upon the other services, were not adopted.

A large part of Arnold's time during World War II was spent convincing others, particularly at high levels of military command and political office, that his judgments were correct. He understood the importance of communication skills, from public-relations campaigns to personal conversations with Winston Churchill. "Articulateness: A comparatively overlooked factor, but, nevertheless, a most important one. Many an excellent idea is 'stillborn' because its originator did not have the ability 'to put it across.' Public speaking courses are excellent aids to acquiring this faculty."[8]

Arnold's love affair with publicity began in 1912, when he flew a sack of mail by air to a destination only five miles from his starting point—a remarkable event in those days. He flew his plane in motion pictures, stunting for the real actors. He personally set flying records that were published in the newspapers across the country; he was a celebrity. By the time he reached command, he had rubbed elbows with famous authors, Hollywood personalities, a Nobel laureate, and many Washington politicians. He knew what positive publicity could do for the air arm. During his career he used the popular media—newsreel, books, magazine articles, radio broadcasts, public speeches, and congressional testimony—to swell confidence in airpower when it looked grim, to boost morale when it was low, and to teach those who would listen about the potential of American airpower. He was a skilled speaker and writer. But when he felt that he was not the best one to get the necessary message across, he called upon subordinates who were. The call for Ira Eaker at Casablanca was clearly one of the best examples of Arnold's willingness to use his most qualified people as the voice of the Air Forces.

The ultimate demonstration of Arnold's articulateness was witnessed during the rapid expansion of aircraft factories. His personal involvement was motivational to most of those who worked long, tedious hours on assembly lines. His appearance was also feared by industrial leadership: Arnold had authorized contracts with a handshake and a promise to many of these corporations. In return he expected results—just as he expected results from his field generals. It was Arnold's ability to motivate the hardworking to greater achievements and humiliate the lackadaisical into raising their standards and work ethics that had a tremendous influence upon the United States's ability to produce airplanes—lots of airplanes.

Yet it was his own violation of military procedure that was, in large part, responsible for nearly ending his career on two different occasions: once during the Mitchell trial, and again during his congressional testimony implicating impropriety by a political official in 1940.

Nearly as important as Arnold's motivational skills was his ability to explain airpower to others. One of the most important recipients of his airpower-education course was Robert Lovett, who during the war years acted as airpower's springboard to Harry Hopkins and President Roosevelt. Much credit must also be given to Frank Andrews, who tutored George Marshall before Arnold came to Washington as assistant chief of the Air Corps. Andrews too was a skilled communicator and field general. His untimely demise in

1943 hurt the Air Forces, but at the same time it opened a door for Arnold's ultimate rise to airpower's pinnacle.

Part and parcel with communications skills, almost inexorably so, came

> properly adjusted human relationships. Naturally, this is largely a matter of personality: some persons just naturally get along with people; others, just as naturally, do not. But in the military sphere, if one is going to "get to first base," he must be able to handle men successfully. The study of psychology is undoubtedly a great practical help to those who find the matter of human relationships somewhat difficult; but I have also observed these things help: firmness, plus tolerance; sympathetic understanding of the little man's position and problems, as well as one's understanding of one's relation to the man at the top. Best of all, of course, is the practical application of the Golden Rule—the simplest and best code of ethics as yet devised.[9]

From the president all the way down to most junior enlisted man, Arnold had interpersonal skills that could relax or enrage. He was judicious at high levels of both military and political authority. It was a lesson he had learned and relearned during his early military career. He was forceful and demanding of subordinates. However, despite his often outspoken approach to command, Arnold was also capable of keeping personal feelings out of his professional interactions. His problems with Mason Patrick were never communicated publicly, even while Patrick was in retirement. But Bee knew his feelings; if anything, she was even less willing to share her emotions than he. Arnold told Bee most everything except military secrets, which he guarded with the stubbornness of a military mule. The type of discipline that he displayed in his professional life was consistent during his entire career: rarely did he make a professional argument personal.

In the civilian sphere, Arnold had more experience than any other airman. This was an important factor in the final decision to make him chief of the Air Corps after Westover's crash. He was admired and respected by most industrialists and academics. As Arnold trusted most of his civilian contacts to accomplish particular jobs, they, likewise, trusted him to make good on his contract promises and production orders—which he did, with rare exceptions.

His treatment of subordinates was somewhat different. Arnold expected results from his forces, and there was little room for excuse, as long as adequate supplies and aircraft were available. Arnold decided what was adequate and what was not. Hansell was replaced because he fell short of Arnold's expectations as to what he should have achieved in combat, despite the fact that he had done a superior job of establishing the Twenty-first Bomber Command administratively. Eaker was reassigned because, in addition to a perceived hesitancy to mass forces, Ike had expressed his desire for Spaatz as European air commander. Brett was replaced by Kenney in the Pacific because MacArthur's personality and style demanded it. In no case did Arnold hold a grudge against, or even disparage, the men involved. The Bretts and the Arnolds remained close friends. Each of Arnold's subordinate commanders had strong points, but not all were outstanding combat commanders.

Arnold loved his men. He was known to reassign enlisted troops personally, if he was made aware of family problems or hardships. In one case he found that one of his tool-and-die specialists had to work nights as a custodian just to make ends meet at home. Arnold and Bee gathered boxes of Christmas gifts and food and delivered them to the young airman's door.

He sometimes, in the solitude of his private office, agonized over the deaths of his airmen in combat. Jacob Smart, of the general's advisory council, witnessed him collapse into tears after receiving one particularly deadly raid report. This for Arnold was the side of combat that most others did not see—the agony of command. But more pragmatically, as long as casualties remained below certain predetermined numbers, his decisions to continue raids were both agonizing and simple: the war had to be won.[10]

He loved his wife, Beadle, and no other woman ever had a chance to experience his absolute devotion. He may have written so frequently to her because he felt inadequate as a mate for the young socialite he married in 1913. He was admittedly awkward around her and made overly obvious his romantic approaches throughout his life. He depended upon her advice, notably her suggestion to accept a court-martial rather than resign, as Patrick appeared to desire. But there were untold other occasions. He never understood the subtleties of women—why Bee would rather talk than act, why so much time was required to decide the shape of a cookie. Partly it was this mystery that held his interest for over forty years.

His children initially enjoyed a father who was often home and, lacking the burden of command, seemed happy-go-lucky, a wonderful father. But time chipped away at Arnold's fatherhood. More and more, he was away on duty. His responsibilities soared, and his children, by the time they were in their teens, saw him less and less. The absence of a father figure may have contributed to the boys' abysmal grades. Lois had been a better student, but also a wild one. She had a fierce attachment to her father, until he became wrapped up in military affairs that took much of his time. His inattention to the development of his family was a regret he carried until he died. As Arnold had been raised as a boy—his father working diligently all day every day—he, in the end, raised his own family.

But none of the aforementioned requisites explain more about Arnold himself than the final one:

> Personal integrity: This covers a very wide field. To touch upon one or two—it means, for example, maintaining the courage of one's convictions. By no means should this be confused with *stubborn* thinking. Stubborn thinking is as outmoded as the ox cart. Its exact opposite, resilient thinking, is Today's Must: a man must be able to accommodate his thinking quickly

and accurately to his rapidly changing world; nevertheless, it must be *his* thinking, not someone else's.

Personal integrity also means moral integrity. Regardless of what appear to be some superficial ideas of present-day conduct, fundamentally, today as always, the man who is genuinely respected is the man who keeps his moral integrity sound; who is trustworthy in every respect. To be successful, a man must trust others; and a man cannot trust others, who does not trust himself.[11]

There is no question that Arnold's family upbringing and his West Point years instilled this, his strongest belief. Yet Arnold himself did not trust everyone, and he found it easier not to have dealings with some than to work around his lack of trust in devious ways. But those he did trust enjoyed free and independent authority to accomplish given missions and tasks with relatively little interference from the general. Larry Bell's XP-59A project, Jimmy Doolittle's raid, William Knudsen's efforts in production, LeMay's fire-bombing of Japan, Kármán's study of future technologies, Spaatz's command in any job he ever held, Eaker's eloquent arguments at Casablanca, and Jackie Cochran's administration of the Women Airforce Service Pilots (WASPs) were some of the most well-known illustrations of this fact.

Arnold's personal integrity was sometimes in conflict with military policy or doctrine. His near-obsession with guided-missile weapons and glide bombs ran counter to daylight precision-bombing doctrine. *Precision* was a relative term back then, and most of the unpiloted weapons Arnold pushed for never attained expectations. Although he realized that many of the most technical and highly classified programs were what he called "area-weapons," his personal commitment to their potential outweighed even advice from trusted military associates. Arnold walked a fine line between the potential of science to minimize casualties to his airmen and the realities of time and production. But he stuck with his beliefs.

At home, Arnold could be brutally honest and demanding with his children: "I don't think Dad ever played any favorites; he would whack us all," Hank remembered.[12] He was decidedly less so with his wife. He loved her above all else and was faithful to her always.

In the end, despite his rather descriptive list, Arnold made it perfectly clear that even possessing these requisites could not guarantee success: "When it comes right down to 'brass tacks,' however, in the military field, as well as in other fields, it would seem to be a man's native ability that spells the difference between failure and mediocrity; between mediocrity and success. Two men may work equally hard toward a common goal; one will have just that 'something' the other lacks. That puts him at the top."[13]

And he also realized that he, among a fortunate few, had one quality that could not be learned or taught. Hap Arnold described it as "the intangible, the spirit of a man."[14]

APPENDIX 1
Cadet Record, Career Assignments, and Military Rank Progression

Born: 25 June 1886, Gladwyne, Pa.
Died: 15 January 1950, Sonoma, Calif., age 63.

Cadet Record

All numbers refer to class standing rather than a percentage grade.

Subject	1903–4	1904–5	1905–6	1906–7
overall ranking	82/136	63/119	61/113	66/111
conduct	25	27	21	52
demerits (actual)	45	66	36	105
military/drill		97	70	78
engineering		73		47/62
math	74	49		
English	103	94		
French	98	89		
Spanish		94		
drawing		70	51	
philosophy		66		
chemistry		53		
hygiene		94		
law				100
history				89
gunnery				54
military efficiency				76
deportment & discipline				60

Career Assignments

1 August 1903	entered West Point, the Military Academy
14 June 1907	graduated
5 December 1907	Fort William McKinley, Philippine Islands
9 April 1908	San Mateo, P.I., and various other temporary locations
18 June 1909	en route to U.S. through Asia and Europe
1 October 1909	Governor's Island, N.Y.
20 April 1911	Aviation School, Dayton, Ohio; Simms Station
15 June 1911	College Park, Md. Aviation duty as instructor/ supply officer
25 November 1911	Augusta, Ga. Same duty
15 April 1912	Fort Leavenworth, Kans.
1 May 1912	College Park, Md.
1 July 1912	Connecticut maneuvers
5 August 1912	College Park, Md.
1 October 1912	Fort Riley, Kans. Near-fatal spin
15 November 1912	Washington, D.C. Duty in office of the chief Signal officer
September 1913	Fort Thomas, Ky. Infantry
25 November 1913	en route to P.I.
5 January 1914	Fort William McKinley, P.I. Also Batangas, P.I.
5 January 1916	en route to Madison Barracks, N.Y.
15 March 1916	Madison Barracks, N.Y.
20 May 1916	Aviation School at San Diego, Calif. North Island
5 February 1917	Panama Canal Zone
20 March 1917	Washington, D.C. Assistant executive and executive officer, Air Division, Signal Corps; board control member; assistant director military aeronautics; director of military aeronautics
10 January 1919	Rockwell Field, Coronado, Calif. District supervisor, Western District, Air Service
30 May 1919	Crissy Field, San Francisco. Air officer, Ninth Air Corps Area; also Presidio
17 October 1922	Rockwell Field, Calif. Commanding officer, Air Depot
15 August 1924	Washington, D.C. Student, Army Industrial College
February 1925	graduated AIC, then assigned to the Office of Information, chief Air Corps
March 1926	Marshal Field, Fort Riley, Kans., "exile." Wrote Bill Bruce books
August 1928	Fort Leavenworth, Kans. Student, General Service School

12 June 1929	graduated, then to Fairfield Air Depot, Ohio Commanding officer; chief, Field Service Section, Materiel Division, Air Corps; executive officer, Materiel Division
29 October 1931	en route to March Field, Calif.
26 November 1931	March Field, Calif. Commanding officer
17 January 1936	Washington, D.C. Assistant chief of the Air Corps
21 September 1938	chief of the Air Corps
20 June 1941	chief, Army Air Forces
9 March 1942	commanding general, Army Air Forces; member Joint Chiefs of Staff; member Combined Chiefs of Staff
21 December 1944	General of the Army, five-star rank
9 February 1946	office of the chief of staff
3 March 1946	end tour
30 June 1946	retired with disability (heart problems), forty-three years' service
7 May 1949	General of the Air Force

Military Rank Progression

1 August 1903	cadet
14 June 1907	second lieutenant, Twenty-ninth Infantry
10 April 1913	first lieutenant of Infantry
20 May 1916	captain, Aviation Section, Signal Corps
23 September 1916	captain of Infantry
27 June 1917	major, Aviation Section, Signal Corps
5 August 1917	colonel, temporary, Signal Corps
15 January 1918	major, temporary, Infantry
30 June 1920	captain, permanent grade
1 July 1920	major of Infantry. Transferred to Air Service 11 August 1920
1 February 1931	lieutenant colonel, Air Corps
2 March 1935	brigadier general, temporary, Air Corps (another source: 11 February)
22 September 1938	major general, chief of Air Corps. 30 October, deputy chief of staff Army for Air Matters
15 December 1941	lieutenant general
19 March 1943	General
21 December 1944	General of the Army
30 June 1946	General of the Army (ret.)
7 May 1949	General of the Air Force

APPENDIX 2
Army Air Corps and Air Forces Organizational Charts

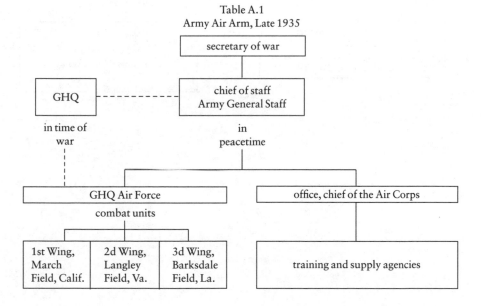

Table A.1
Army Air Arm, Late 1935

Table A.2
Army Air Arm, Late 1940

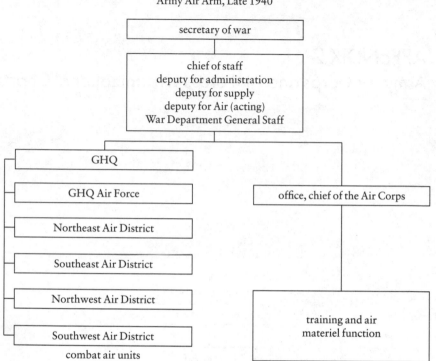

secretary of war

chief of staff
deputy for administration
deputy for supply
deputy for Air (acting)
War Department General Staff

GHQ

GHQ Air Force

Northeast Air District

Southeast Air District

Northwest Air District

Southwest Air District

combat air units

office, chief of the Air Corps

training and air
materiel function

Table A.3
AAF in the Wartime Army

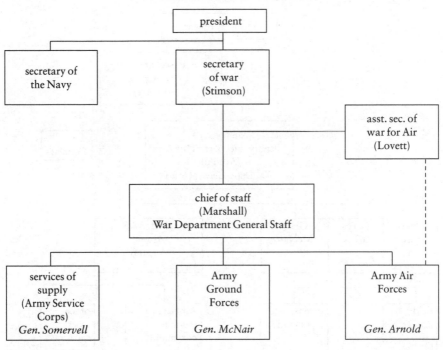

Table A.4
Aviation in Army Organization, Late 1941

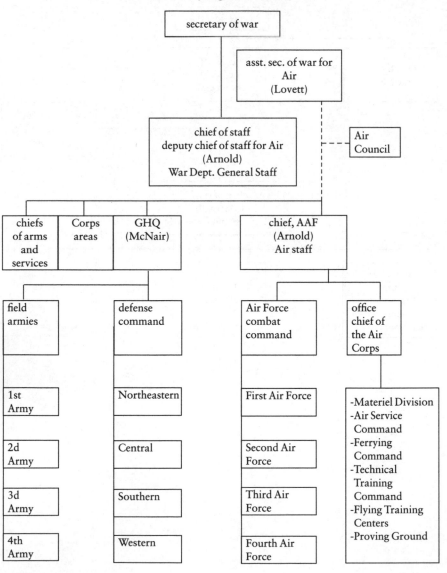

Table A.5
AAF Organization, 29 March 1943

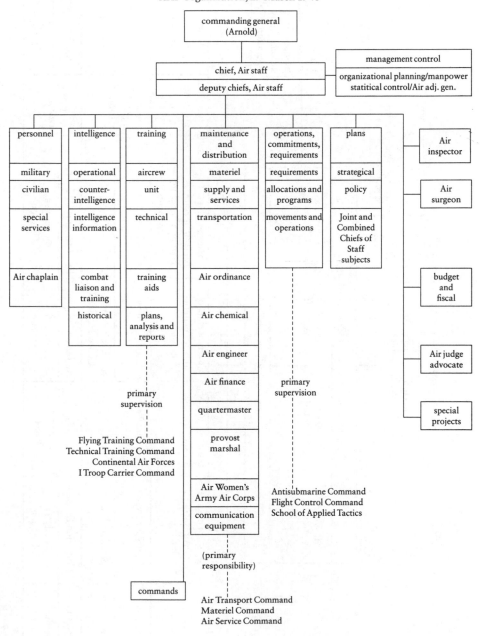

Table A.6
Organization of the Army Air Forces, 1945

commanding general, AAF
Gen. Arnold

advisory council

special consultants

managment control

organizational planning
statistical control
manpower
administrative services
operations analysis

deputy commander, AAF, and chief of staff

deputy chief of Air staff

deputy chief of Air staff

secretary of Air staff

deputy chief of Air staff

deputy chief of Air staff

assistant chief of Air staff personnel

plans and liaison

military personnel

civilian personnel

personnel services

assistant chief of Air staff Intelligence

deputy for targets

operational deputy

Collection Division

Analysis Division

assistant chief of Air staff training

Training Plans and Program Office

Flexible Gunnery Division

assistant chief of Air staff materiel and services

Control Office

Aircraft Resources Control Office

Resources Division

Materiel Division

assistant chief of Air staff operations, commitments, and requirements

adviser for program control

Requirements Division

Commitments Division

assistant chief of Air staff plans

Combined and Joint Staff Division

Logistics Division

Air inspector

Air surgeon

Air finance

judge advocate

legislative services

special projects

Air chaplain	Photographic Division	Unit Training Division	Procurement Division	Weather Division	Operational Plans Division	communications
Air Women's Army Air Corps	Technical Air Intelligence Division		Modification Division	Director Women Pilots Office		flying safety
ground safety	administrative deputy	Individual Training Division	Traffic Division	Bolling Field Liaison office	Postwar Division	asst. for antiaircraft
personal affairs	Historical Division		Air Services Division	AAF's board		information service
provost marshal	counter-intelligence	Training Aids Division	AAF board control office			aeronautical charting
unit personnel	training plans		Air engineer			
	motion-picture services	flight operations	Air chemical officer			
			ordnance officer			
			quartermaster			

all numbered Air Forces, Training Command, Transport Command, Proving Ground Command, Technical Services Command, etc.

Notes

INTRODUCTION

1. Henry Harley Arnold (HHA) to Eleanor Pool Arnold (EPA), 16 June 1944, near Staines, England. Originals in the Robert Arnold collection (RAC), Arnold ranch, Sonoma, California.
2. John Eisenhower, "Strictly Personal," 72. Quoted in Stephen E. Ambrose, *Soldier, General of the Army, President-Elect: 1890–1952* (New York: Simon and Schuster, 1983), 314. See also Dwight D. Eisenhower, *Crusade in Europe* (New York: Doubleday, 1948), 263; and Richard Overy, *Why the Allies Won* (New York: W. W. Norton, 1995), 123–24, 145.
3. Carl "Tooey" Spaatz to HHA, 17 July 1944, "Special Report: Effects of Allied Air Power on the First Month of Overlord Operations, 6 July 1944," RAC. In 1938, Spaatz changed the spelling of his name from Spatz to Spaatz (with two a's) in an effort to rectify pronunciation errors. The correct pronunciation is "Spots." See also Omar N. Bradley, "Effect of Air Power on Military Operations, Western Europe (1945)," Smithsonian Institution, National Air and Space Museum, Ramsey Room, pages 2, 4, 21–22.
4. Omar N. Bradley to HHA, 7 July 1944, Headquarters, First Army, APO 230. Copy in Hap Arnold Murray Green Collection (MGC), USAF Academy Library Special Collections, Colorado Springs. This collection of research by Green is a wealth of information, interviews, documents, and notes taken while the historian prepared a manuscript biography of Arnold during the 1970s. The manuscript, "Hap Arnold: Man in a Hurry," was never completed, and many of the notes must be cross-checked against other primary sources. However, the collection offers much in the study of Arnold. See also Fleet Adm. Ernest J. King, "Second Official Report to the Secretary of the Navy, 1 March 1944 to 1 March 1945," in Walter Millis, ed., *The War Reports of General of the Army George C. Marshall, General of the Army H. H. Arnold, and Fleet Admiral Ernest J. King* (New York: J. B. Lippincott, 1947), 621.
5. Laurence Kuter to Spaatz, 19 July 1944, Spaatz papers, Library of Congress, Washington, D.C. (L/C), Box 15. Kuter joked, "You really should have something laid on for fixing on the spot."
6. Robert E. Kimmel to author, 30 March 1998. Kimmel was Spaatz's primary pilot during much of the war.

247

7. HHA, "Third Report of the Commanding General of the Army Air Forces to the Secretary of War, 12 November 1945," in Millis, ed., *The War Reports*, 455–56.
8. HHA, "Report of Special Board Appointed to Make Up a Balanced Air Program, 5 August 1936" (confidential), U.S. Air Force Historical Research Agency, Maxwell AFB, Ala. (USAF/HRA), 145.93–96.
9. W. G. Kepner, "Air Service, Air Force, and Air Power," *U.S. Air Service* 5, no. 4 (1921): 16–17; and HHA, "Balanced Air Program" (confidential), USAF/HRA, 145.93-96.
10. Henry H. Arnold tombstone, Arlington National Cemetery, square 34, stone 44A.
11. HHA to cadet William Bruce Arnold, 28 March 1943, D.C., RAC. Arnold had been promoted to the rank of general (four stars) on 19 March 1943.

1. HENRY HARLEY ARNOLD

1. Application for membership in Pennsylvania Society Sons of the Revolution. Original application dated 22 January 1898. RAC, Pennsylvania Archives, 2d series, vol. 13, 731.
2. Arnold family history folder, RAC. See also MGC, microfilm roll 1, HHA to Lois Snowden (his daughter), 2 September 1949: "God alone knows where the name 'Alonzo' came from, it is not a family name."
3. Application for Sons of the Revolution, RAC.
4. James M. McPherson, *Battle Cry of Freedom: The Civil War Era* (New York: Oxford University Press, 1988), 485.
5. Mrs. Henry H. Arnold, Columbia University Oral History Interview (CUOHI), 6 May 1959, 21, 22.
6. Mrs. H. H. Arnold, CUOHI, 22. One of the younger family members, R. A. Swartz, insisted that Clifford was favored by their mother, and that Harley had a detached relationship with her in his youth. R. A. Swartz, interviewed by Murray Green, August 1972, MGC, roll 1.
7. Mrs. H. H. Arnold, CUOHI, 21.
8. Arnold family history folder, RAC.
9. *Mennonite*, 15 February 1946. This local paper describes the early moves in Gladwyne; it also explains that the first house became the rectory of St. John the Baptist Vianney Roman Catholic Church. Mrs. Bee Arnold recalled a story about Harley's having once attempted to leap from the roof of the house while holding an umbrella. The ill-conceived test flight resulted in minor injuries to the pilot. From transcript of interview at Arnold ranch, Sonoma, October 1968, MGC, roll 1.
10. General of the Army H. H. Arnold, "Remarks at Lower Merion Township High School, Philadelphia, Pa., 14 February 1946," RAC; see also "Address by Brig. Gen. H. H. Arnold," Gladwyne, Pa., 30 May 1938, RAC; papers of Ira C. Eaker, L/C, Box 38, Arnold speeches, 1937–39 (Eaker papers, L/C, Box 38), 2; Mrs. Barbara Arnold, interview with author, Washington, D.C., 6 April 1995. Mrs. Arnold (now deceased) was the daughter of Donald Douglas and wife of the late William Bruce Arnold, Gen. H. H. Arnold's second son. See also MGC, roll 1.
11. HHA to Eleanor Alexander Pool (EAP), 11 June 1913, RAC.
12. Mrs. H. H. Arnold, interviewed by Murray Green at Arnold ranch, Sonoma, October 1968, transcript in MGC, roll 1. See also Charles Overholster to H. A. Arnold, 3 February 1902, MGC, roll 1.
13. Mrs. H. H. Arnold, CUOHI, 1, 5.
14. Congressman P. Wanger to Dr. H. A. Arnold, 7 October 1901, Norristown, Pa., RAC.
15. HHA, *Global Mission* (draft), 2½; Mrs. H. H. Arnold, CUOHI, 16–17, 19–20.
16. General Henry H. Arnold Collection, Manuscripts Division, Library of Congress (HHA/LC), Box 262A.
17. West Point records, HHA/LC, Box 262A; and Arnold Records, U.S. Military Academy (USMA) Archives, West Point, N.Y.

2. CADET "PEWT" ARNOLD

1. The Newburgh Conspiracy of 1783 was as near a military coup as this country has ever seen. Largely a result of pay disparity for longtime service, the event rattled the foundations of civil control of the military even before the concrete was set. For the interpretations and details of the event and the impact it had on the U.S. military, see Richard H. Kohn's *Eagle and Sword: The Beginnings of the Military Establishment in America* (New York: Free Press, 1975), 17–39, 302–3.
2. *Official Register of the Officers and Graduates of the U.S. Military Academy, West Point* (Official Register), June 1904, 3.
3. *Howitzer*, 1900–1907. Published yearly by New York's Hoskins Press, the cadet yearbook was expensive: a full nine dollars in 1907. The selective use of color plates throughout the book increased the cost of its production, and thus its price.

    I thank Dr. Stephen B. Grove, USMA historian, for his careful evaluation of this chapter. His understanding of West Point traditions and history helped to clarify a few of the foggier areas contained in the early West Point story.
4. *Howitzer*, 1900, 199–209. See also "Pewt's" Military Academy Log Book, United States Air Force Academy Library, Special Collections, Colorado Springs.
5. Much of the background for the descriptive narrative comes from the Columbia University Oral History Interviews' "Reminiscences of Gen. H. H. Arnold's Friends and Family." All interviews were conducted by Dr. Donald Shaughnessy, from 1959 to 1960. The following were particularly useful for this chapter: Col. Benjamin Castle, July 1959, 1–39; Gen. Carl "Tooey" Spaatz, 26 January 1959, 4, 18, 20; Col. Hayden Wagner, 1 August 1959, 1–35; and Mrs. Henry H. Arnold, 6 May 1959. Specifically for this paragraph, Mrs. H. H. Arnold, CUOHI, 7; and Wagner, CUOHI, 3.
6. "List of Cadet Candidates Authorized to Report for Examination at West Point on the 27th Day of July, 1903, Before 8 O'Clock A.M. In War Department Letters and Telegrams Sent Relating to the United States Military Academy, 1867–1904, M2048, USMA Archives, West Point; also Arnold Records, USMA Archives, West Point.
7. Ibid.; and Wagner, CUOHI, 2.
8. Official Register, 1904, 34.
9. Ibid., 18–21; also West Point records, HHA/LC, Box 262A.
10. A number of cadet candidates entered West Point in the later part of July each year to round out the class. These gentlemen faced an intense training period before they were allowed to join the rest of the on-time plebes. Mrs. H. H. Arnold, CUOHI, 17; and Wagner, CUOHI, 2–3.
11. *Howitzer*, 1906, 261; Spaatz, CUOHI, 4.
12. Castle, CUOHI, 8; Wagner, CUOHI, 8. Rumor held that the young man had died from an overingestion of Tabasco sauce at the dining hall, apparently ingested not of his own free will.
13. *Howitzer*, 1907, 40, 306. Picture trying to pull your chin into your neck so that the bottom of the chin touches your Adam's apple. That was the act of dragging in your chin. The more wrinkles produced, the more impressive the effort.
14. Castle, CUOHI, 1–6; *Howitzer*, 1904, 209, see poem "Plebe Days." See also *Howitzer* Advertiser, 1907, 53. This appendix to the 1907 yearbook features a photograph of the proper alignment of a cadet's closet and clothes press.
15. Wagner, CUOHI, 9; the photo is located in the RAC. See also transcription of note in MGC, roll 1.
16. Wagner, CUOHI, 7–9; Castle, CUOHI, 1.
17. Castle, CUOHI, 2–3.
18. Official Register, 1904, 5. First Lieutenant Koehler was promoted to captain the following year. He eventually authored an exercise manual for the entire U.S. Army while a colonel.

Upperclassmen still refer to the entering freshman as beasts until summer encampment, then they become plebes for the rest of the first year. Air Force Academy freshman are commonly called doolies, defined as "that insignificant whose rank is measured in negative units; one whose potential for learning is unlimited; one who will graduate in some time approaching infinity" (*Contrails*, 1977–78). Annapolis freshmen are called swabbies, which is a derogatory reference to those who must swab the decks.

19. Castle, CUOHI, 4.
20. From the modern Doctor Suess character of Christmas fame. More on the grin in Chapter 4.
21. Castle, CUOHI, 4. Height determined your company, tallest in A and F. The average cadet height at that time was near five feet, six inches.
22. *Howitzer*, 1904, 113.
23. Wagner, CUOHI, 5–6.
24. Castle, CUOHI, 1–4. Castle was also a *Howitzer* staff member in 1906–7, which undoubtedly proved helpful in his ability to recall many of these early events with such clarity. Tragically, Castle's son Freddie was killed during World War II. But his heroic combat actions earned him the Congressional Medal of Honor.
25. *Howitzer*, 1907. Official Register, 1904, 34. Castle, CUOHI, 4; and Wagner, CUOHI, 3–4. Castle remembered the ceremony as a bit more full of pomp than did Wagner; in any event, it was short and sweet. See also Arnold Records, USMA Archives, West Point; and Dr. Stephen B. Groves to author, 9 December 1997, West Point.
26. Official Register, 1904, 5. Castle, CUOHI, 5.
27. Wagner, CUOHI, 2–4; Official Register, 1904, 18–21. Depending on whether one adds the fall-backs, the number is around thirty.
28. *Howitzer*, 1905, 119; Wagner, CUOHI, 9.
29. *Howitzer*, 1907, 113.
30. Official Register, 1904, 19; and 1905, 17.
31. Gen. Frank P. Lahm, CUOHI, 1. For academic standings see HHA references in *Biographical Register of the Officers and Graduates of the USMA at West Point New York*, supp. vol. 5, 1900–10; see also Official Register, 1904; and *Howitzer*, 1907. For early Signal Corps aviation history see Rebecca Robbins Raines, *Getting the Message Through: A Branch History of the U.S. Army Signal Corps* (Washington, D.C.: Center for Military History, U.S. Army, 1996), part 4.
32. Wagner, CUOHI, 18.
33. To read the accounts in *Howitzer* (1900–1907) of Army football during these years is a story in its own right. The prose describing the Army-Navy contest in each yearbook contains spectacular drama and description.
34. Castle, CUOHI, 11–17.
35. *Howitzer*, 1904, 214–15; and *Howitzer*, 1906, 264.
36. Official Register, 1904, 34; also Arnold Records, USMA Archives, West Point. Harley Arnold answered the West Point entry form question concerning previous smoking habits in the negative one month prior to the evocation of this privilege.
37. Spaatz, CUOHI, 20.
38. The establishment of nonsmoking areas, and eventually a smoke-free military, is the standard in effect today. Recent medical studies delineating the deleterious effects of secondhand smoke are a large reason for this policy shift.
39. *Howitzer*, 1907, 306. Smokes were hand-rolled in those days. Photographic evidence shows Arnold with cigarettes in hand as late as 1925.
40. Wagner, CUOHI, 24.
41. "Terry's 1904 World's Fair Page," "The Observation Wheel," and "The Liberty Bell." From the 1904 World's Fair Society Newsletters, accessed 15 November 1997.
42. Available through Internet: Terry's 1904 World's Fair Page. A large collection of articles and facts is easily viewed at this home page.

43. J. W. Buel, *Louisiana and the Fair* (St. Louis: World's Progress Publishing Company, 1905), 4, 1,438. Quoted in James J. Horgan, *City of Flight: The History of Aviation in St. Louis* (Gerald, Mo.: Patrice Press, 1984), 62–63.

44. Horgan, *City of Flight,* 59–91. For an eloquent debunking of Whitehead's claim to flight, see Tom D. Crouch, *A Dream of Wings: Americans and the Airplane, 1875–1905* (Washington, D.C.: Smithsonian Institution Press, 1981), 119–26. There is no documentary account of Arnold's visit to the aeronautical exhibit, but since it was one of the major attractions, it is likely that he walked through. Additionally, balloon flying took place every day and was visible throughout the fairgrounds.

45. *Howitzer,* 1906, 98.

46. Ibid., 1904, 115.

47. Wagner, CUOHI, 16.

48. Crouch, *Dream of Wings,* 15.

49. *Howitzer,* 1904, 116.

50. Ibid., 1907, 42. Official Register, 1907, 13.

51. P. S. Michie and F. S. Harlow, *Practical Astronomy* (New York: John Wiley, 1903), title pages and front matter, RAC.

52. Castle, CUOHI, 36–37. The cadet record for the shot put was 37 feet 11 inches, set in 1899; see *Howitzer,* 1907, 185.

53. *Howitzer,* 1905, 121.

54. Ibid., 1907, 159–64.

55. HHA to Mrs. Herbert A. Arnold (mother), "263 days until June," 1905, RAC.

56. *Howitzer,* 1907, 146–64; also West Point records, HHA/LC, Box 262A.

57. *Howitzer,* 1907, 42; also Mrs. H. H. Arnold, CUOHI, 20.

58. Wagner, CUOHI, 19; see also *Howitzer,* 1907, 42, 214. Arnold's photo is nearest the center and next to the drawing of his most famous prank, a fireworks display saluting the class of 1907.

59. *Howitzer,* 1907, 214. The fireworks illuminated a banner that read "1907. . . . Never Again!" This was the unofficial class cheer that had been adopted on the final day of summer encampment in 1906. It was used frequently after that, to signal significant "last-time" events for the class of '07.

60. For accounts of the Hand's activities, see Thomas M. Coffey's, *Hap: The Story of the U.S. Air Force and the Man Who Built It, General Henry H. "Hap" Arnold* (New York: Viking Press, 1982), 20–22. Firsthand accounts can be found in Wagner, CUOHI; and Castle, CUOHI. Photos of the Hand are present in HHA's West Point scrapbook, RAC.

61. Henry Augustus Shute, *The Real Diary of a Real Boy* (Peterborough, N.H.: Noone House, Richard R. Smith Co., reprint 1967), vii–xiii, 3, 6, 13, 19, 25, 33, 35–39, 135–37. See also *Howitzer,* 1907, 61. Some of the lesser pranks that Arnold accomplished were etching initials in glass windows and the guard house wall. L/C, Box 5, Arnold.

62. *Howitzer,* 1943, front inside cover.

63. HHA, *Global Mission* (prepublication proof), RAC, 3. Similarly, many medically qualified members of the cadet wing at the Air Force Academy have attended with the sole purpose of becoming a pilot. The education process was a necessary hurdle to overcome for potential pilots, but was not the singular reason for attending the "Blue Zoo." Patriotism, service history, or simply the tremendous challenge drew other young Americans. This attitude reflects that of H. H. Arnold during his West Point days.

64. Gen. Thomas DeWitt Milling, CUOHI, 58. Lucian K. Truscott Jr., *The Twilight of the U.S. Cavalry: Life in the Old Army, 1917–1942* (Lawrence, Kans.: University Press of Kansas, 1989). Highlights the glories of cavalry life.

65. HHA to Mrs. Herbert Arnold, "108 days till June," 1906, RAC. This letter refers to the 11 February 1906 launch of *l'Alouette,* a small, one-man reconnaissance balloon. Another account of the event may be found in the 10 February 1906 *Army-Navy Journal,* 673.

66. Charles DeForest Chandler and Frank P. Lahm, *How Our Army Grew Wings: Airmen and Aircraft Before 1914* (New York: Ronald Press, 1943), 54–55.
67. HHA's West Point scrapbook, RAC. For journalistic accounts, see *New York Times,* 6 February and 12 February 1906; and *Army-Navy Journal,* 17 February 1906.
68. Mrs. H. H. Arnold, CUOHI, 5–6; Groves to author, 9 December 1997.
69. Wagner, CUOHI, 12; see also *Howitzer,* 1907, for words and music to "Army Blue."
70. Promiscuity held far greater consequences for young ladies in those days than in modern times. Young officers rarely sought to marry a woman who had a reputation as a "harlot." This was detrimental to one's career in the old Army.
71. Mrs. H. H. Arnold, CUOHI, 5–10; Castle, CUOHI, 11–12.
72. *Howitzer,* 1907, 42, 322; Mrs. H. H. Arnold, CUOHI, 1, 5.
73. West Point records, HHA/LC, Box 262A. Specifically, Arnold was "skinned"—put on report—for missing the 3:00 A.M. room inspection and the 4:00 A.M. room inspection, and for "placing banners and notices on the Academy building without authority, about 3:45 A.M."
74. Unpublished comments by Murray Green on D. Copp's *A Few Great Captains* (McLean, Va.: EPM Publications, 1980), RAC; see also Mrs. H. H. Arnold, CUOHI, 5–7. Green's comments originate from many years of Arnold research. His insights are generally accurate, if somewhat inflexible or biased.
75. Mrs. H. H. Arnold, CUOHI, 1–7.
76. Carol Reardon, *Soldiers and Scholars: The U.S. Army and the Uses of Military History, 1865–1920* (Lawrence, Kans.: University Press of Kansas, 1990), particularly part 2 and part 2. See also Russell F. Weigley, "The Elihu Root Reforms and the Progressive Era," in William Geffen, ed., *Command and Commanders in Modern Warfare: The Proceedings of the Second Military History Symposium, USAF Academy, 1968* (Washington, D.C.: Office of Air Force History, 1971), 11–27.
77. Official Register, 1904, academic description.
78. Castle, CUOHI, 36–37.
79. *Howitzer,* 1907, 11–32.
80. Mrs. H. H. Arnold, CUOHI, 17–18.

3. SECOND LIEUTENANT HENRY H. ARNOLD

1. *Howitzer,* 1907, 225. This is not an uncommon feeling for many academy graduates, even in contemporary times. I know this because I was in the USAF Academy Class of 1981. I ended up going back as a history instructor in 1992, much to my own astonishment.
2. HHA, *Global Mission* (draft), 3½.
3. Ibid., 3½.
4. Mrs. H. H. Arnold, CUOHI, 18, 21–23. Later Harley's mother was known to all as Gangy, while Harley's father carried the nickname Daddy Doc.
5. Milling, CUOHI, 7. In the early 1980s, pilot assignments had similar consequences for young airmen. Once assigned to a fighter or bomber, it was nearly impossible to change from one to the other later during a career.
6. HHA, *Global Mission* (draft), 3½–4; Castle, CUOHI, 38–39; and interview with Robert Arnold conducted by author, Sonoma, 1–8 September 1997. Family history was discussed at some length.
7. HHA, *Global Mission* (draft), 4½. Arnold recalled, "We really expected the Japanese to invade the Philippines at any minute." No other Army post at that time held any compelling urgency to prepare for combat. For a fresh academy graduate, this would have been the choice assignment for infantry. See also Castle, CUOHI, 35, 69.
8. Chandler and Lahm, *How Our Army Grew Wings,* 80, n.6; *Pegasus Supplement,* July 1957, "Maj. Gen. George O. Squier"; and Raines, *Getting the Message Through,* 127–33.
9. Castle, CUOHI, 30.

10. Ibid., 34, 40; *Howitzer,* 1907, 52.
11. Castle, CUOHI, 40, 58.
12. Mrs. H. H. Arnold, CUOHI, 10, 11.
13. Castle, CUOHI, 59, 60.
14. Ibid., 55, 56.
15. HHA, *Global Mission* (draft), 4½, 5; HHA to H. A. Arnold ("My dear father"), "In camp 11 miles west of Tarlac," 31 January 1909, RAC. See also Castle, CUOHI, 55; and Mrs. H. H. Arnold, CUOHI, 11.
16. HHA to H. A. Arnold, "In camp 11 miles west of Tarlac," 31 January 1909, RAC.
17. H. A. Arnold to Col. H. L. Scott, 17 January 1908; and Lt. Col. Charles M. Gandy to H. A. Arnold, 8 February 1909, MGC, roll 1, West Point Archives. See also *Howitzer,* 1907, 11, 32, for both Scott's and Gandy's faculty positions.
18. Maj. Gen. F. C. Ainsworth, 14 October 1907, MGC, roll 1, National Archives, RG 94, W-3, 201 Files. This letter was supported by further staff follow-up on 25 November 1907, when Lieutenant Colonel Bell passed a message to Colonel Scott verifying that Arnold was not "S.Q." For background on that "efficient administrator," see Russell F. Weigley, *History of the United States Army* (New York: Macmillan, 1967), 323–39.
19. Gandy to H. A. Arnold, 8 February 1909, MGC, roll 1, West Point Archives.
20. A similar process existed even in the 1980s to determine pilot qualifications for fighter, attack, and reconnaissance (known as FAR qual). Flying-training academic scores, actual flight performance, and a third undefined quality were examined in detail before FAR qual was awarded to a pilot trainee. The final decision usually rested with those instructors with "fighter time" in operational units. This undefined quality equated to the 1907 S.Q. for cavalrymen.
21. HHA to H. A. Arnold, "In camp 11 miles west of Tarlac," 31 January 1909, RAC. It is interesting to note the comparison of natives with a list of indigenous animal life.
22. HHA, *Global Mission* (draft), 4½, 5.
23. Castle, CUOHI, 54.
24. HHA, *Global Mission* (draft), 4½, 5.
25. Ibid., 5.
26. Castle, CUOHI, 39, 55, 56. At the time Arnold's name was added to the list of officers for flight training in 1908, the Signal Corps had just initiated their first contract with the Wright Brothers, calling for only one heavier-than-air flying machine and training for two pilots. When this machine crashed at Fort Myer in 1908, the founding of heavier-than-air flight in the U.S. Army was seriously delayed for almost another year.
27. Signal Corps Specification No. 486, issued 23 December 1907.
28. Tom D. Crouch, *The Bishop's Boys: A Life of Wilbur and Orville* (New York: W. W. Norton, 1989), 375–78.
29. Other members of the selection board were Major Squier, Major Wallace, Lieutenant Lahm, and Lieutenant Foulois. Orville wrote to Wilbur that "everyone seems friendly and the newspapermen are kindly disposed." From Marvin W. McFarland, ed., *The Papers of Wilbur and Orville Wright: Including the Chanute-Wright Letters and Other Papers of Octave Chanute* (New York: McGraw-Hill, 1953), 914–15.
30. Raines, *Getting the Message Through,* 129–31; see also Crouch, *The Bishop's Boys,* 376, 396–99.
31. Castle, CUOHI, 67.
32. HHA, *Global Mission* (draft), 1.
33. Interview with Gay Morris conducted by author, Alexandria, Va., 2 February 1998. Mrs. Morris in the daughter of David Lee Arnold and is Gen. Henry Arnold's granddaughter. Annie Pool, Bee's sister, Lois, and her younger twin brothers, Joe and John, were also there.
34. Eleanor Pool's Berlin diary for 1909, RAC. She and her mother were expecting Harley, but the European mail system let them down. Nonetheless, Harley knew how to reach Mrs.

Pool by letter and by phone, suggesting that he had received this information from home, not from the Pools.

35. Eleanor Pool's Berlin diary for 1909, RAC.
36. Ibid.
37. *New York Times,* 25 July 1909, 1, col 6.
38. HHA, *Global Mission* (draft), 1.
39. HHA, typed manuscript, "Pioneers of the Aerial Trails," n.d., HHA/LC, Box 227.
40. HHA, *Global Mission* (draft), 1½.
41. Ibid., 2.
42. Mrs. H. H. Arnold, 11 March 1970, MGC, roll 1.
43. HHA, *Global Mission* (draft), 5.
44. HHA to Mrs. H. A. Arnold, 16 March 1910, Fort Jay, N.Y., RAC.
45. Mrs. H. H. Arnold, 11 March 1970, MGC, roll 1.
46. "Letters from Billy" (originals in German) in RAC; also Robert Arnold interview with author, 1997.
47. Mrs. H. H. Arnold, 11 March 1970, MGC, roll 1.
48. HHA, *Global Mission* (draft), 5–6; Crouch, *The Bishop's Boys,* 407; and C. R. Roseberry, *Glenn Curtiss: Pioneer of Flight* (Syracuse, N.Y.: Syracuse University Press, 1991, 1972 by Roseberry), 209–10.
49. Crouch, *The Bishop's Boys,* 404–5; and Roseberry, *Glenn Curtiss,* chap. 19.
50. Roseberry, *Glenn Curtiss,* 207–10.
51. Crouch, *The Bishop's Boys,* 406–8.
52. Curtiss collected $2,500 only after filing suit against the committee, who felt that his efforts, although valiant, considering the weather conditions and the fact that he was without his Rheims machine, fell far short of their expectations. See Roseberry, *Glenn Curtiss,* 220–22.
53. Roseberry, *Glenn Curtiss,* 272–79.
54. Crouch, *The Bishop's Boys,* 407–8. Arnold mentions the flight in his own *Bill Bruce and the Pioneer Aviators* (New York: A. L. Burt, 1928), 102.
55. *Global Mission,* 1–21. Arnold just barely failed the ordnance exam with 60 percent (62 percent was required for acceptance). Another researcher has suggested that Arnold knew of his test scores before sending his request for flight duty to the adjutant general. This would mean that Arnold was just trying all his options in some sort of order, placing aviation last.

    In actuality, Arnold had volunteered for flight duty in 1908–9, when Captain Cowan was reassigned to fill training slots. The 7 April 1911 note to the adjutant may have been just an administrative requirement or a reminder that he was still interested. In the end it was Arnold himself who admitted that he was "completely engaged in a project that took all my time. . . . I was trying to get to be a first lieutenant."
56. Milling, CUOHI, 5; Castle, CUOHI, 55.
57. Milling, CUOHI, 3; Brig. Gen. T. DeWitt Milling, "Early Flying Experiences," *Air Power Historian* 3, no. 1 (1956): 93.
58. Chandler and Lahm, *How Our Army Grew Wings,* 193–95. A copy of the order is available in the Pentagon library in the Army General Orders books; also detailed in HHA, *Global Mission,* 15.
59. HHA, *Global Mission* (draft), 6. Library of Congress records indicate different language but the same general idea.

4. "THEY ARE HERE TO LEARN TO FLY"

1. HHA to chief Signal officer, 6 May 1911, Dayton, Ohio, Henry H. Arnold folder, National Air and Space Museum (NASM) Archives. Milling flew the day before, on 2 May. See article by Milling, "Early Flying Experiences," 92–105.

2. Chandler and Lahm, *How Our Army Grew Wings*, 196; Milling, "Early Flying Experiences," 94. Mr. Henry S. Molineau was hired by the Signal Corps in June 1911. He was the only Signal Corps airplane mechanic hired until 1913. The Wrights' factory manager was Mr. Frank Russell.

3. Milling, CUOHI, 9–10.

4. Orville Wright, with an introduction by Fred Kelly, *How We Invented the Airplane* (New York: David McKay, 1953), 52. In Crouch, *The Bishop's Boys*, 245, the Wright brothers were assisted by Charles Taylor. The engine weighed 200 pounds filled with fuel, water, and oil—ready for flight. See also Richard P. Hallion, ed. *The Wright Brothers: Heirs of Prometheus* (Washington, D.C.: Smithsonian Institution Press, 1978), 66.

5. Wilbur Wright to Lt. H. H. Arnold, 10 November 1911, Dayton, Ohio, RAC; see also Milling, CUOHI, 10.

6. Orville Wright, *How We Invented the Airplane*; Crouch, *The Bishop's Boys,* 166–68; Milling, CUOHI, 10–11.

7. HHA, *Global Mission* (draft), 7½.

8. Ibid.; Milling, CUOHI, 10–11.

9. Orville Wright, *How We Invented the Airplane,* 3; Crouch, *The Bishop's Boys,* 166–68.

10. Orville Wright, *How We Invented the Airplane,* 21.

11. Thomas P. Hughes, *American Genesis: A Century of Invention and Technological Enthusiasm* (New York: Penguin Books, 1989), 18, 55–61.

12. Orville Wright, *How We Invented the Airplane,* 32–35; Milling, CUOHI, 24.

13. Dik A. Daso, *Architects of American Air Supremacy: General Hap Arnold and Dr. Theodore von Kármán* (Maxwell AFB, Ala.: Air University Press, 1997). See also Peter L. Jakab, *Visions of a Flying Machine* (Washington, D.C.: Smithsonian Institution Press, 1990); and interview with Tom Crouch conducted by author, Washington, D.C., 12 January 1998. It was a combination of pure empiricism, scientific methodology, and the ability to deal with scientific chaos (random uncertainty) that came to define American scientific research and development throughout the twentieth century, particularly in the field of aeronautics.

14. Milling, "Early Flying Experiences," 96.

15. Ibid., 95; also Milling, CUOHI, 15, 21; and Wright Company to Lt. Henry H. Arnold, 2 March 1912, Dayton, Ohio, Wright papers, L/C, Box 9, Arnold folder (Wright papers, L/C).

16. Milling, "Early Flying Experiences," 96.

17. Chandler and Lahm, *How Our Army Grew Wings,* 207; Milling, CUOHI, 13–16.

18. Milling, "Early Flying Experiences," 95.

19. HHA, *Global Mission* (draft), 8; Milling, CUOHI, 13.

20. Milling, "Early Flying Experiences," 95; HHA, *Global Mission* (draft), 7½; Crouch, *The Bishop's Boys,* 436–37.

21. Limited discussion is offered on the Curtiss school, as Arnold was not one of his students. The Curtiss-trained pilots eventually merged with the Wright-trained pilots at College Park, Maryland, in June 1911. For an explanation of the Curtiss aircraft flying characteristics see, Milling, CUOHI, 16–18, 30.

22. HHA, *Global Mission* (draft), 8½.

23. Milling, CUOHI, 11.

24. During my flying career, an accident somewhere always seemed to add a new checklist.

25. Crouch, *The Bishop's Boys,* 11, 427.

26. 1911 Arnold and Welsh flight reports, RAC.

27. Milling CUOHI, 20.

28. Ibid., 22.

29. Flying log, 3–13 May 1911, and HHA to chief Signal officer, 13 May 1911, Dayton, Ohio,

NASM Archives, Henry H. Arnold folder. Orville's thoughts are described in Milling, CUOHI, 22.

30. HHA to chief Signal officer, 20 May, 27 May, 4 June, and 10 June 1911, USAF/HRA 168.655-2, located in "Misc. Correspondence of Col. E. L. Jones."

31. HHA to H. A. Arnold, 2 July 1911, Army and Navy Club, Washington, D.C., RAC; and HHA, *Global Mission* (draft), 12. See also Chandler and Lahm, *How Our Army Grew Wings*, 198; and Raines, *Getting the Message Through*, 132. The provisional "aero company" organized at Fort Sam in April was disbanded 10 May 1911, after the fatal crash that killed Lt. G. E. M. Kelly. Kelly AFB in San Antonio still bears his name.

32. HHA to H. A. Arnold, 2 July 1911, RAC.

33. Chandler and Lahm, *How Our Army Grew Wings*, 196; Milling, CUOHI, 29.

34. Chandler and Lahm, *How Our Army Grew Wings*, 196–98; Milling, CUOHI, 27–28.

35. Chandler and Lahm, *How Our Army Grew Wings*, 199.

36. Orville Wright to HHA, 18 November 1911, Wright papers, L/C.

37. Milling, CUOHI, 28.

38. A copy of the news article resides at in NASM Archives, Arnold folder.

39. HHA to Mrs. H. A. Arnold, 20 July 1911, Army and Navy Club, Washington, D.C., RAC. Tommy Milling remembered that the headlines were the result of a tendency to sensationalize any flying event that occurred. Almost any flight was headline news and was generally exaggerated in its difficulty, but less so in its danger.

40. HHA to Mrs. H. A. Arnold, 20 July 1911, RAC; also recounted in *Global Mission* (draft) 12; and Chandler and Lahm, *How Our Army Grew Wings*, 200–201.

41. "Aero Mail-Carrying Begins at New York," *Aero: America's Aviation Weekly*, 30 September 1911, 1. A difficult source to locate, copies of this are kept at the NASM Library.

42. Israel Ludlow, "The Aeroplane and the Motion Picture Camera, *Aeronautics* 10 (January 1912): 13.

43. Chandler and Lahm, *How Our Army Grew Wings*, 214.

44. HHA to Orville Wright, 6 November 1911, College Park, Md., Wright papers, L/C.

45. Ibid.; see also Chandler and Lahm, *How Our Army Grew Wings*, 206–7; Milling, "Early Flying Experiences," 97–98; and Milling, CUOHI, 33.

46. HHA, *Global Mission* (draft), 14½.

47. Milling, "Early Flying Experiences," 101; Milling, CUOHI, 34–36, 69.

48. Wilbur Wright to HHA, 10 November 1911, Dayton, Ohio, RAC. To test the engine performance, the machine was placed in a closed shed and the motor turned on. Propeller revolutions were measured just as the water in the radiator began to boil over (caused by no forward motion to cool the water). As long as the resultant number was between 410 and 440 per minute, the engine passed the test. Less than 410 indicated that the engine was "palpably in need of attention." Several repetitions of the test were required to ensure correct results. The American tendency toward empiricism in science was readily apparent in these instructions. This letter also was the first documented "Caution, Warning, or Note" pertaining to a particular airplane. Today's military flight manuals are loaded with similar admonishments pertaining to safe operation of aircraft.

49. HHA to Orville Wright, 19 November 1911, Army and Navy Club, Washington, D.C., Wright papers, L/C. Further clarification of testing measurements and load capacity were also discussed.

50. Today's modern fighter aircraft use afterburner in exactly the way Arnold described—during takeoff and climb, and to maintain control at slow maneuvering speeds. Additionally, during combat scenarios, afterburner is utilized to gain rapid advantage in altitude or speed over that of an adversary. The combat uses for airplanes were not thoroughly understood in 1911, but the need for more powerful engines to improve performance has been one of the many driving forces in aircraft development.

51. A description of the Model C and a diagram are located in McFarland, ed. *The Papers of Wilbur and Orville Wright,* 1,200–1; see also Milling, CUOHI, 38–39.
52. Orville Wright to Mr. Arnold, 18 November 1911, Dayton, Ohio, Wright papers, L/C.
53. Chandler and Lahm, *How Our Army Grew Wings,* 211; Milling, "Early Flying Experiences," 96.
54. Milling, CUOHI, 32.
55. HHA to "Folks at Home," 20 December 1911, Augusta, Ga., RAC.
56. Chandler and Lahm, *How Our Army Grew Wings,* 211–16.
57. HHA to Orville Wright, 24 February 1912, Augusta, Ga., Wright papers, L/C.
58. Wright Company to Lt. Henry H. Arnold, 2 March 1912, Dayton, Ohio, Wright papers, L/C.
59. Today's "technical orders" and "block" system of aircraft production and improvement are the latest evolution of what began as trial by fire and life-or-death reaction to early mechanical shortcomings.
60. HHA/LC, Box 3; HHA, *Global Mission* (draft), 14; and Chandler and Lahm, *How Our Army Grew Wings,* 215–16.
61. Chandler and Lahm, *How Our Army Grew Wings,* 209–10.
62. Ibid., 210.
63. Requisition requirements for airplanes, 1912. Original in RAC. See also Raines, *Getting the Message Through,* 133.
64. HHA, *Global Mission* (draft), 11; Wilbur's father wrote of his son that he possessed "unfailing intellect, imperturbable temper, great self-reliance and as great modesty, seeing the right clearly, pursuing it steadfastly," for all of his forty-five years. From Milton Wright's diary, 30 May 1912, as quoted in Crouch, *The Bishop's Boys,* 449.
65. HHA, *Global Mission* (draft), 10⅓x.
66. HHA to Betty (sister), 5 June 1912, Dayton, Ohio, RAC.
67. Milling, "Early Flying Experiences," 101.
68. HHA, *Global Mission* (draft), 8: "All those early aviators knew more than they could tell anybody." Arnold recalled that much remained unexplained about flying.
69. HHA to H. A. Arnold, 22 August 1912, College Park, Md., RAC.
70. Ibid.; Milling, CUOHI, 46. The story is told from the family-legend perspective in Bruce Arnold's manuscript, "My Dad Hap," RAC. After "ahoying" two fishermen, Arnold asked for help getting back to shore.

    "Am I close enough to shore that you can pull me in," he called with effort.

    "Y'ain't fah," one fisherman answered. "Practically on Plymouth Rock!"

    "Well, why don't you come in and rescue me?" called Pop.

    "Person fool enough to git in one of them things don't deserve to be rescued," the fisherman answered.

    "I guess he's right," thought Pop, as he quietly floated out with the tide.

Of course, Lieutenant Kirtland was never mentioned by Bruce in the story, the real version of which took place in less than perfect weather.
71. HHA, *Global Mission* (draft), 15½.
72. HHA to Mr. Wright, 2 September 1912, College Park, Wright papers, L/C.
73. Ibid.
74. Ibid.
75. HHA to H. A. Arnold, 22 August 1912, College Park, RAC; see also *Howitzer,* 1907, 89.
76. HHA to EAP, 22 June 1913, Washington, D.C., RAC.
77. Ibid.
78. HHA to EAP, 20 June 1913, MGC. Arnold loved to have fun, and a drink was never out of the question in his early career. His father had been rather strict about the use of alcohol and did not even permit it at Harley and Bee's wedding, a decision he later wished he had modi-

fied to allow champagne. Tommy Milling, Arnold's best man for the affair and a fellow pilot, smuggled some liquor up from the Pools' cellar during the reception anyway. It was interesting that after the war, Arnold and Bee were both subjects of a Pabst Beer ad that showed them at their ranch in the Sonoma Valley.

79. HHA to H. A. Arnold, 31 October 1912, Fort Riley, Kans., RAC.
80. HHA to commanding officer Chandler, Signal Corps Aviation School, 6 November 1912, Fort Riley, Kans., USAF/HRA, 168.65-38. Also in Arnold, *Global Mission* (draft), 15½–16.
81. HHA to commanding officer, Signal Corps Aviation School, 6 November 1912.
82. Milling, "Early Flying Experiences," 102.
83. A photographer was on hand during the maneuvers that day and documented both the take-off and the return to the landing zone of Arnold's plane. Sadly, the photographer had just taken his picture before the landing attempt was made. Had he waited a few more seconds, valuable evidence might yet exist today of the actual flight conditions of the craft. The original photos are in RAC.
84. Milling, "Early Flying Experiences," 102. Orville Wright had experienced similar events with whirlwinds that "were so violent that the machine turned clear around with me in spite [of] all I could do with the rudders." Orville Wright to Capt. Charles DeForest Chandler, 16 November 1912, Dayton, Ohio, in McFarland, ed. *The Papers of Wilbur and Orville Wright* 1,050–51.
85. Even today, aspiring young pilots practice accelerated stalls in the basic phases of flight training. Fatal accidents resulting from pilots pulling too hard on the control stick are most common in the landing pattern, when speeds are slower than in normal flight to accommodate landing. Pulling hard on the stick while slowing can overtax the lift capability of the aircraft wing, and a stalled condition can be immediately induced. This is what happened to Arnold.
86. HHA, *Global Mission* (draft), 15½.
87. Orville Wright to Israel Ludlow, 24 December 1912, Dayton, Ohio, in McFarland, ed. *The Papers of Wilbur and Orville Wright,* 1,052–53.
88. Milling, CUOHI, 57.
89. HHA to commanding officer, Signal Corps Aviation School, 6 November 1912. Arnold was not alone in his request to be relieved: several others requested transfer back to their land-based careers.
90. Milling, CUOHI, 57. "Everybody expected to be killed. That's absolutely true!" said Milling.
91. HHA, second lieutenant, to commanding officer, Signal Corps Aviation School, 6 November 1912. The first portion of the letter describes the progress being made with the various airplanes at Fort Riley. Observation techniques and a number of engine problems were discussed. Arnold's disclosure of the near-accident occurred at the end of the report, in a straightforward paragraph of explanation. HHA/LC, Box 3 and Box 222; HHA, *Global Mission* (draft), 16–16½. See also see National Archives, RG 94, W-3, 201 Files.

5. "A CUSHION-CHAIR OFFICER"

1. HHA to EAP, 19 July 1913, Washington D.C., RAC.
2. "The Men and the Machines, 1913–1915," *Air Power Historian* 3, no. 3 (1956): 173–75; Crouch, *The Bishop's Boys,* 463–67.
3. Crouch, *The Bishop's Boys,* 458.
4. Orville Wright to HHA, 30 January 1913, Dayton, Ohio, RAC; also in Wright papers, L/C; and in McFarland, ed. *The Papers of Wilbur and Orville Wright,* 1,057–58.
5. As an Air Force USAF T-38 instructor pilot, I found the cause of these fatal crashes fairly

clear upon examination. All USAF pilots today practice accelerated stalls in every aircraft they fly, and at regular intervals. Practice in the techniques involved in recognizing the stall and recovering appropriately has saved many lives in the past fifty years. Nonetheless, one of the leading causes of aircraft accidents remains the accelerated stall and the failure to recognize or recover from the condition before ejection or ground impact.

6. HHA to EAP, 2 June 1913, RAC.

7. Eleanor Pool's Berlin diary, 3 January 1912, RAC.

8. Ibid., 6, 8 January 1912.

9. HHA to Mrs. Herbert Arnold, 11 January 1913, Dayton, Ohio, RAC.

10. Mrs. H. H. Arnold, CUOHI, 22–24.

11. Raines, *Getting the Message Through,* 133–35.

12. Juliette A. Hennessy, *The United States Air Arm: April 1861 to April 1917* (Washington, D.C.: Office of Air Force History, 1985), 108.

13. HHA to EAP, 28 June 1913, Washington, D.C., RAC. Many staff officers feel exactly the same way today, as they try to meet short suspenses on time-critical projects, such as preparing senior staff for congressional testimony.

14. HHA to EAP, 26, 28, 30 June 1913, Washington, D.C., RAC; HHA, *Global Mission* (draft), 16½; "The Men and the Machines, 1913–1915," 172 (on funding see 178); Maurer Maurer, ed., *The U.S. Air Service in World War I* (Washington: Office of Air Force History, 1978–79), vol. 2, 12–13, 19–20; Raines, *Getting the Message Through,* 134.

15. HHA to EAP, 22 June 1913, and various other dates in June, Washington, D.C., RAC.

16. HHA, *Global Mission* (draft), 14.

17. HHA to EAP, 6 June 1913, Washington D.C., RAC. Having closed the doors on three active-duty flying units for the USAF, I know there are mixed emotions when the event is finally over. The joys of flying combined with memories of lost comrades make a sober tonic. Unfortunately feelings, unlike mathematical formulas, do not cancel out; they simply peak in opposite directions.

18. Clark G. Reynolds, *Admiral John H. Towers: The Struggle for Naval Air Supremacy* (Annapolis: Naval Institute Press, 1991), 44. Photographs of the business sign show the company name as Curtis, with one s. HHA to EAP, 19 July 1913, Washington D.C., RAC. From mid-June until early August 1913, Arnold made repeated daily trips to the Annapolis Engineering Center. In many instances engines had not arrived, were not assembled, or could not be started for testing. By the end of August Arnold was pretty much fed up with the Navy's engine plant, Curtiss's engines, and production testing in general. HHA to EAP, 13 June–31 July 1913, Washington and Annapolis, RAC.

19. Reynolds, *Admiral John H. Towers,* 66–67; see also HHA, *Global Mission* (draft), 8½.

20. Milling, CUOHI, 57.

21. Reynolds, *Admiral John H. Towers,* 290.

22. HHA to EAP, 4 June 1913, Washington, D.C., RAC.

23. Ibid., 14 August 1913.

24. Mrs. H. H. Arnold, CUOHI, 89–90.

25. As in France while viewing the first plane to have flown across the English Channel, Arnold wondered about possibilities for the future of airplanes.

26. HHA to EAP, 18 June 1913, Washington, D.C., RAC.

27. Ibid., 26 June 1913: "Dear Bee, You did not accept me with any rapidity. In fact you were rather slow and made me nervous and impatient waiting for you to answer."

28. HHA to EAP, 1 June 1913, Washington, D.C., RAC.

29. HHA to "My Dear Bee," 1 June 1913, RAC.

30. HHA to EAP, 4 June 1913, Washington D.C., RAC: "There always was more or less sentiment surrounding our relationship . . . something that has been getting stronger within me ever since—I do not know when. . . . Perhaps on the ships in League Island Navy Yard in

June 1907." This was just after his West Point graduation, while he was visiting Ardmore, Pennsylvania.

31. Currently, the entirety of these letters not found in the Library of Congress are in the RAC.

32. HHA to EAP, 17 June 1913, Washington, D.C., RAC. The term *running around* had a different connotation in 1913 than it does in modern times. Arnold was referring to his propensity to remain an active attendee at club dances and dinners.

33. HHA to EAP, 17 June 1913, Washington, D.C., RAC.

34. Eleanor Pool's Berlin diary, January 1912, RAC. There exists circumstantial photographic evidence that Arnold smoked during his retirement years. However, those who knew him well from the mid-1920s onward swore that they never saw him with a "smoke" in his hand.

35. HHA to EAP, 16 August 1913, Washington, D.C., RAC.

36. Ibid., 13 July 1913; also various letters from June through August 1913, Washington D.C., RAC. The exchange of letters, almost funny if it hadn't gone on so long, finally resulted in the determination of a 10 September wedding. It was a perfect example of the uncertainty of Army life, and it appeared to bother Harley more than it did Bee.

37. HHA to EAP, 1 June 1913, Washington, D.C., RAC.

38. Ibid., 16 June 1913.

39. Ibid., 27 August 1913.

40. Ibid., 26 June, 28 August 1913.

41. Ibid., 29 July 1913.

42. Ibid., 4 August 1913.

43. Ibid., 5 August 1913.

44. Ibid., 14 August 1913. The next day he admitted to Bee that he thought he might turn out be a jealous husband. Later letters show him to be politely demanding but never jealous.

45. HHA to EAP, 18 August 1913, Times Square Station, N.Y., RAC.

46. HHA to EAP, 22 June 1913, Washington, D.C., RAC.

47. Ibid., 6 August 1913.

48. HHA to "My Dear Bee," 2 June, 4 June, 9 June 1913, Washington, D.C., RAC.

49. HHA to EAP, 10 June 1913, Washington D.C., RAC.

50. Ibid., 28 July 1913.

51. Ibid., 22 July 1913.

52. Ibid., 12 July 1913.

53. Ibid., 8 July 1913.

54. Interview with Dr. Robert Alvus conducted by author, Fairfax, Va. Dr. Alvus is a cardiac surgeon at Fairfax Hospital. Today many physicians believe that continual fluctuations in weight can contribute to heart disease as well as other maladies. The combination of a fat-filled diet, smoking, lack of regular exercise, and a contained temperament set Arnold on a gradual but unexplored road to medical troubles later in life.

55. HHA to EAP, 14 July 1913, Ogle Hall, Annapolis, Md., RAC.

56. HHA to EAP, 23 August 1913, Burgess Plant, RAC.

57. HHA to EAP, 18, 28 June 1913, Washington, D.C., RAC.

58. Ibid., 5 August 1913.

59. HHA to EAP, 24 August 1913, Marblehead, Mass., RAC.

60. Henry H. Arnold, General of the Air Force (ret.), interviewed by T. A. Boyd, El Rancho Feliz, Sonoma, 19 October 1949, transcript in MGC. See also Milling, "Early Flying Experiences," 98. Milling describes early inquiries about the European LeRohne motor, for example.

61. HHA to EAP, 11 August 1913, Washington, D.C., RAC.

62. Crouch, *The Bishop's Boys*, 461.

63. HHA to EAP, 23, 24 August 1913, Washington, D.C., RAC.

64. HHA to Mr. Wright, 27 January 1913, Wright papers, L/C. The sand test was accomplished by flipping the aircraft over and loading the wings with sand until the wing spars began to crack. Thus aircraft strength was determined by inverted sand weight that simulated the forces of lift on the wings themselves.
65. HHA to Mr. Wright, 1 February 1913; HHA to O. Wright, 23 February 1913; HHA to Mr. Wright, 15 March 1913, Wright papers, L/C. Orville tried to reassure Arnold that the scout ship was the "easiest machine that we build. Its high speed in landing is its only drawback. It is a very strong machine and has a larger factor of safety than any of the other models." O. Wright to HHA, 22 March 1913.
66. Mr. Wright to HHA, 6 May 1913, Wright papers, L/C. Arnold once wrote to Bee that "I never could give myself a very high mark when it came to solving complex problems at a distance." 22 July 1913, Washington, D.C., RAC.
67. "The Men and the Machines, 1913–1915," 173–75; also in HHA, *Global Mission* (draft), 16.
68. HHA to EAP, 28 July 1913, Washington, D.C., RAC.
69. Mrs. H. H. Arnold, CUOHI, 13; also HHA to EAP, 12 June 1913, Washington, D.C., RAC. Harley was astonished by the large number of invitees.
70. Mrs. H. H. Arnold, CUOHI, 13; and HHA, *Global Mission*, 43–45. There is no reference to the wedding other than this: "Eleanor Pool and I intended to be married in September. . . ." It seems peculiar to omit such an event in his life unless it was *really* an embarrassing affair.
71. Mrs. H. H. Arnold, CUOHI, 13–14.
72. Ibid., 13–15.
73. Ibid., 15–16.
74. HHA to EAP, 29 August 1913, Washington, D.C., RAC.
75. Mrs. H. H. Arnold, CUOHI, 23–25. Bee received violets from her men in Berlin. She knew they were interested when the violets arrived.
76. Mrs. H. H. Arnold, CUOHI, 25.
77. Bee's Berlin diary describes the tragic death of one of her friend's infant children. "It was a fearful shock," as she described the event in her entry of 1 January 1912.
78. HHA to EPA, 26 January 1914, Batangas, RAC; also various other letters from field locations near Batangas.
79. HHA to EPA, 23 February 1914, Corregidor, RAC.
80. Herbert A. Arnold to "My Dear Children," 16 February 1914, Ardmore, RAC.
81. HHA to EPA, 28 January 1914, "same place," RAC; Mrs. H. H. Arnold, CUOHI, 28.
82. Thomas Parrish, *Roosevelt and Marshall: Partners in Politics and War* (New York: William Morrow, 1989), 72.
83. "Dashing" Milling to "Pewt" Arnold, 25 January 1914, American Embassy, Paris, RAC.
84. Ibid.
85. Mrs. H. H. Arnold, CUOHI, 32–33; HHA to EPA, 3 May 1915, "in Camp," RAC.
86. EPA to "Maté" (Mother, Annie Pool), 10 February 1915, Fort William McKinley, Philippines, RAC.
87. Emphasis in original. Maté to EPA, 18 November 1914, Ardmore, RAC.
88. Mrs. H. H. Arnold, CUOHI, 34.
89. Ibid., 33.
90. See Alfred F. Hurley's *Billy Mitchell: Crusader for Air Power* (Bloomington: Indiana University Press, 1964), chap. 1.
91. Mrs. H. H. Arnold, CUOHI, 35. In fact, it was Dargue who flew with Arnold on his first flight in four years at North Island in November 1916.
92. Arnold always believed that Mitchell had called him back into aviation; see HHA, *Global Mission* (draft), 17.
93. Mrs. H. H. Arnold, CUOHI, 35.

6. CAPTAIN TO COLONEL

1. HHA to EPA, 9 May 1915, Fort William McKinley, RAC.
2. HHA to EPA, 25 August 1915, Batangas, RAC. There are some references to the German advances against Russia in a 19 August 1915 letter, HHA to EPA, RAC.
3. Several letters discussing the war were written between Harley and his mother, father, brother, and wife before the United States entered the conflict on 6 April 1917. Since Arnold's father and brother were members of the National Guard, topics centered around their training and mission. Because Bee had some health problems associated with childbirth, Harley tried not to burden her with detailed discussions about war. While in Batangas, he frequently dined with his colonel, and after a family dinner, he and the colonel would have "a long talk on the war." Undated letter written on Saturday (either 21 or 28 August 1915), HHA to EPA, RAC. The familiar scene from the movie *Titanic* (1997) that depicts the men excusing themselves from the dinner table to smoke cigars, drink brandy, and argue politics was perhaps more a reality in those days.
4. The Air Force has endured competition for command throughout its short history. In the early days, the rift was between young pilots and ranking Army officers without flying experience. Approaching World War II the chasm widened, between bomber pilots who ran the war and fighter pilots who, by and large, did not. Nearing the Vietnam era, the tables were reversed, and fighter pilots led the USAF in most command billets. Today the schisms continue, but they are developing between those with operational space-systems experience (satellites, space lift, even space weapons) and those who are bound by the earth's atmosphere. The struggle for command appears to have shifted over time, based upon the relative importance of prevailing USAF doctrine and, to a certain extent, the relative amount of dollars spent on procurement of specific systems. For an interesting examination of this topic, see Mike Worden's *Rise of the Fighter Generals: The Problem of Air Force Leadership, 1945–1982* (Maxwell AFB, Ala.: Air University Press, 1998).
5. The term *Aviation Section* referred to the portion of the Signal Corps to which all aviation personnel were assigned. Within the office of the chief Signal officer, the subdivision that dealt with aviation matters was known as the Aeronautical Division. In 1917 that entity became the Air Division; in 1918 it was redesignated the Air Service Division. Succinctly described in Raines, *Getting the Message Through,* 202.
6. Raines, *Getting the Message Through,* 165–66.
7. HHA to EPA, 30 March 1916, Madison Barracks, N.Y., RAC; HHA, *Global Mission* (draft) 13.
8. HHA to EPA, 17 February 1917, Ardmore, RAC.
9. HHA, "Outline of History: Aviation Section, Signal Corps and Division of Military Aeronautics, April 1917–October 1918," 2, USAF/HRA, 168.65011-4: "National Advisory Committee of [*sic*] Aeronautics that had for its purpose study of technical problems of flight—also Aviation Committee on Council of National Defense. Both advisory only, and of no actual value in development."
10. Roger E. Bilstein, *Orders of Magnitude: A History of the NACA and NASA, 1950–1990* (Washington, D.C.: National Aeronautics and Space Administration), 1–15; Howard S. Wolko, *In the Cause of Flight: Technologists of Aeronautics and Astronautics* (Washington, D.C.: Smithsonian Institution Press, 1981), 18; Robert F. Futrell, *Ideas, Concepts, and Doctrine: Basic Thinking in the United States Air Force, 1907–1960* (Maxwell AFB, Ala.: Air University Press, 1989), vol. 1, 19; Wesley Frank Craven and James Lea Cate, eds., *The Army Air Forces in World War II* (Chicago: University of Chicago Press, 1948), vol 1, 7; and Maurer, ed., *U.S. Air Service in World War I,* vol. 2, 75–89. The Air Service sent a few ill-prepared planes with Pershing as aerial observers. Before long many of them were destroyed due to crashes, and there were several casualties.

11. Raines, *Getting the Message Through,* 147–53.
12. HHA/LC, Box 3, folder 13; see also Murray Green, "Hap Arnold: Man in a Hurry," chap. 7, p. 6, MGC.
13. Mrs. H. H. Arnold, CUOHI, 35.
14. Ibid., 37; HHA, *Global Mission,* 17½.
15. HHA, "The History of Rockwell Field," 1923, 81, RAC; Mrs. H. H. Arnold, CUOHI, 38–39.
16. Corey Ford, draft article, no title, ca. 1945, RAC. The pilot was likely Dargue.
17. HHA to EPA, 6 February 1917, Washington, D.C., RAC.
18. Ibid., ca. 6 February 1917; see also HHA, "Outline of History," USAF/HRA, 168.65011-4.
19. HHA to EPA, 13 February 1917, Washington, D.C, RAC.
20. Ibid., 15 February 1917.
21. HHA to EPA, 19 February 1917, New York, N.Y., RAC.
22. HHA to EPA, 26 March 1917, Canal Zone, RAC.
23. Ibid., 18 March 1917.
24. Ibid., 20 March 1917.
25. Mrs. H. H. Arnold, CUOHI, 36–37. In 1928 Lahm refused to accept Arnold under his command in San Antonio, following Arnold's Command and General Staff School tour. Instead Arnold ended up at Fairfield Air Depot in Ohio. This twist of fate, although not one of Arnold's top choices of duty, proved critical to his understanding of the Army's system of research and development in regards to technological advances, and it unwittingly contributed to his growing base of knowledge concerning the procurement and development of airpower.
26. EPA to HHA, 14 March 1917, Coronado, Calif., RAC.
27. HHA to EPA, 3 March 1917, Canal Zone, RAC.
28. Ibid., 26 March 1917. Interestingly, Arnold begged Bee to find a few "technical books" covering the ongoing war in Europe. He had loaned several to General Edwards, who was thirsty for more. HHA to EPA, 23 March 1917, Canal Zone, RAC.
29. HHA to EPA, 3 March 1917, Canal Zone, RAC; HHA, Global Mission (draft), 17½. Arnold toured the isthmus in the general's car. On the trip he met up with Captain Cowan, who had earlier recruited him into the flying business, and John Rogers, a naval lieutenant who had gone through the Wright flight school with Arnold and Milling in 1911 and was now stationed in Panama.
30. HIIA to EPA, 5 September 1917, Washington, D.C., RAC. "Well we are Colonels at last to date from August 15—what do you know about that." He wrote to Bee, in Ardmore, about the festivities: "I invited all the bunch up to celebrate the promotion and found all our gin and vermouth gone. When I went south there was two full bottles of gin and two of vermouth. Evidently some one [among the hired help] likes our gin." One of those promoted to colonel who was younger than Arnold was E. Gorrell, the historian for the Allied Expeditionary Forces in Europe.
31. Green, "Hap Arnold: Man in a Hurry," chap. 8, p. 1, MGC.
32. Hurley, *Billy Mitchell,* 27; Raines, *Getting the Message Through,* 191.
33. E. S. Gorrell and Phil Carroll, "Colonel Raynal Cawthorne Bolling," *U.S. Air Service* (March 1920): 18.
34. Irving B. Holley Jr., *Ideas and Weapons, Exploitation of the Aerial Weapon by the United States during World War I: A Study in the Relationship of Technological Advance, Military Doctrine, and the Development of Weapons* (New York: Yale University Press, 1953), chap. 3.
35. Raines, *Getting the Message Through,* 194; see also "Raynal C. Bolling," Bolling Commission Report, ca. 1918, Pentagon Library.
36. HHA/LC, Box 3, folder 13, Washington Service Diary, 1917–1918.

37. HHA, "Outline of History," USAF/HRA, 168.65011-4.
38. On 20 May 1918, President Wilson issued an executive order separating aviation from the Signal Corps. This resulted in the creation of two newly independent organizations within the War Department: the Division of Military Aeronautics and the Bureau of Aircraft Production. Each was under direct control of the secretary of war, Newton Baker.
39. Green, "Hap Arnold: Man in a Hurry," chap. 8, p. 8–9, MGC.
40. Order 300-3, 1 August 1917, RAC. This travel order reflected the itinerary for the whirlwind midwestern visit. Several newspaper articles covered the visit. Headlines included the following: "Officers Here for Inspection at Camp Kelly, Will Solve Problems"; "Interest in Aviation Board's Visit." RAC.
41. Mrs. H. H. Arnold, CUOHI, 43–45. Some of these reasons included shortages of skilled labor and machine tools, new designs that required new assembly processes, and finer materials than those required for automobile manufacture.
42. Walter J. Boyne, *De Havilland DH-4: From Flaming Coffin to Living Legend* (Washington, D.C.: Smithsonian Institution Press, 1984), 26–33.
43. HHA, "Airplanes, Less Engines, Including Propellers and Airplane Parachutes: A Study Prepared by the Air Service, 1922," RAC. This fifteen-page report summarizes Arnold's survey results of industrialists after the war. It covers the many shortfalls of aircraft production during World War I.
44. HHA to EPA, 13 August 1917, Rantoul, Ill., RAC. Today an inspection team would travel by air between most locations. In 1917, transport by plane was considered to unreliable for time-critical missions, particularly when several inspectors were involved. The chances of cross-country breakdowns was still rather high. Additionally, many team members were not pilots and would have to act as passengers. Air transport had a long way to go.
45. HHA to EPA, 11 August 1917, New Orleans, RAC. Later, at a World War II conference in Quebec, Arnold displayed uneasiness with interracial dancing during a show attended by the top brass. His discomfort with racial issues was typical for that day: see David Irving's *War Between the Generals* (New York: Congdon and Lattès, 1981), 297.
46. HHA to EPA, 31 October to 2 November 1918 (hospital diary), England, RAC. Later Arnold would be much more complimentary of the French women. "There are no 'flat tires' over here. People say that the American Army refurnished the Parisian women with the clothes they had lost during the war."
47. HHA to Jerome C. Hunsaker, 27 September 1917, Washington, D.C., NASM Archives, Arnold folder.
48. Green, "Hap Arnold: Man in a Hurry," chap. 8, p. 21, MGC.
49. The B. J. Arnold Report, USAF Historical Research Agency, Maxwell AFB, Ala., K289.9201-1, K205.1104-4; copy also held at the Air University Library, 623.451W253B (microfilm). This report summarizes all of the Army Air Corps's guided-missile programs from 1917 through the 1940s.
50. B. J. Arnold Report.
51. USAF Museum, Wright-Patterson AFB, Dayton, Ohio, Kettering Bug folder. Many photos are included, as well as many of the original documents that described the weapon and its construction. Additional information on the Bug is located in the B. J. Arnold Report. Fewer than ten successful tests were accomplished in 1918.
52. HHA, *Global Mission* (draft), 27–28; Hughes, *American Genesis*, 130–34; Glenn Infield, "Hap Arnold's WW I Buzz Bomb," May 1974, NASM Archives, Bug folder. A short summary of early unpiloted-missile programs can be found in Kenneth P. Werrell's *The Evolution of the Cruise Missile* (Maxwell AFB, Ala.: Air University Press, 1985), chap 1. At about the same time as the Dayton test, a similar incident occurred during a test of a European unguided missile.
53. HHA, *Global Mission* (draft), 27½.

54. Ibid., 27–28; B. J. Arnold Report. Some accounts, including one of my own, have suggested that Arnold was the pilot pulled from the chase car. Further research shows this to be unlikely: the dates between the test flight and Arnold's departure for England are too close together. It is most plausible that Arnold was not even in attendance at the second test, but had already headed back to Washington to plead his case to go to Europe. Another pilot in a flight suit aided the deception at the second test. See Dik Daso, "The Kettering Bug," *MHQ* 10, no. 4 (1998): 44–45.

55. The team members are listed in the B. J. Arnold Report. See also *Global Mission* (draft), 27–28.

56. HHA/LC, World War I Diary.

57. Flying Bomb records at the USAF/HRA clearly show that Arnold believed the accuracy of these weapons would improve. Yet he was willing, at this early date, to experiment with them, even to the point of using them in combat.

58. B. J. Arnold Report, Flying Bomb records. On the Kenly memo Arnold's initials, HHA, indicate him as the author.

59. HHA, *Global Mission* (draft), 30.

60. The severity of Arnold's illness on the way to Europe can be deduced from his letters home to Bee, during October and November 1918, RAC. The exact dates of his journey are noted in his official order book, RAC. Arnold's "World War I Trip Diary" also mentions the illness, H. H. Arnold papers, L/C; see also HHA to EPA, 11 October 1918, New York, RAC.

61. HHA to EPA, 11, 12 October 1918, New York, RAC.

62. Mrs. H. H. Arnold, CUOHI, 47.

63. Ibid., 14 October 1918. See also David R. Mets, *Master of Airpower: General Carl A. Spaatz* (Novato, Calif.: Presidio Press, 1988), 104.

64. HHA to EPA, 15 October 1918, New York, RAC.

65. HHA to EPA, 24 October 1918, "in port," RAC.

66. Arnold's order book, certified departure for France, 17 October 1918, aboard HMS *Olympic*, RAC; HHA to EPA, 16 October 1918, New York, RAC; HHA to EPA, 24 October 1918, "in port," RAC. See also Flint O. Dupre, *Hap Arnold: Architect of American Air Power* (New York: Macmillan, 1972), 40–41. Rube Fleet later became the president of Consolidated Aircraft Company and helped the World War II B-24 bomber production program to success.

67. HHA to EPA, 26 October 1918 (hospital diary), England, RAC.

68. Mrs H. H. Arnold, CUOHI, 41. According to Bee, Arnold told that story for the rest of his life. At the time it must have made quite an impression. The account is less severe in *Global Mission*.

69. HHA to EPA, 2 to 4 November 1918, London and Paris, RAC. Other news was that Milling assumed command of the First Army Air assets; Peebles died suddenly of the flu; Jimmy Dickey was killed in action; Foulois was so ill he had to take a rest in the south.

70. HHA to EPA, 6 November 1918, Chaumont, France, RAC.

71. HHA to EPA, 9 November 1918, Ligney, France, RAC.

72. HHA to EPA, 14 November 1918, Souilly, France, RAC.

73. Ibid., 14 November 1918.

74. Ibid., 14 November 1918. In a 17 November letter, Arnold spoke of the condition of returning prisoners who told tales of the retreating German army: "They are a sorry looking sight."

75. HHA to EPA, 14 November 1918, Souilly, France, RAC.

76. Arnold was aware that he was no "war scarred veteran," but his career apparently never suffered from lack of combat medals. Wartime medals had been one of his goals in the first place.

77. Mrs. H. H. Arnold, CUOHI, 42. HHA to EPA, 14 November 1918, Souilly, France, RAC.

78. HHA, *Global Mission* (draft), 23½.
79. Maurer, ed., *U.S. Air Service in World War I*, 88; see also HHA, *Global Mission* (draft), 23½.
80. The original report is located in the historical archives at the Presidio, Calif. A copy exists at the Arnold ranch, RAC.
81. HHA, *Global Mission* (draft), 25½.
82. HHA, "Airplanes, Less Engines," 1–2, RAC.
83. Ibid.
84. Ibid., 3. Problems ranged from the original DH-4 propeller design, which provided less than one-inch ground clearance when the airplane rotated for takeoff, to the installation of devices in production models that, found to be unserviceable in practice, were later removed from the airplane.
85. I am indebted to Dr. Irving B. Holley Jr. for his comments on this section of the book. His personal experience and many years of research in this area greatly aided my understanding of the issues involved.
86. HHA, "Airplanes, Less Engines," 4, RAC.
87. Ibid., 5. The other factors were competent management, complete equipment (tools and machinery), floor space, cooperation between designers and manufacturers, raw and fabricated materials that met specifications, and skilled labor.
88. HHA, "Airplanes, Less Engines," 7, RAC.
89. Ibid., exhibit B, final page.
90. Ibid., 7, 8.
91. Hurley, *Billy Mitchell*, 36–37.
92. HHA, *Global Mission* (draft), 36; for a summary of the postwar happenings, see also James P. Tate, *The Army and Its Air Corps: Army Policy Toward Aviation, 1919–1941* (Maxwell AFB, Ala.: Air University Press, 1998), 6.
93. HHA, *Global Mission* (draft), 32½–33½.
94. Mrs. H. H. Arnold, CUOHI, 45; *Global Mission* (draft), 32–33.

7. INTERWAR YEARS

1. Arthur Sweetser, *The American Air Service: A Record of Its Problems, Its Difficulties, Its Failures, and Its Final Achievements* (New York: D. Appleton, 1919), 256. See also the more available Maurer Maurer, *Aviation in the U.S. Army, 1919–1939* (Washington, D.C.: Office of Air Force History, 1987), 3–15.
2. Mets, *Master of Airpower*, 1–38; and Richard G. Davis, *Carl A. Spaatz and the Air War in Europe* (Washington, D.C.: Center for Air Force History, 1993), 3–35.
3. HHA/LC, photo albums; also Maurer, *Aviation in the U.S. Army*, 17–19.
4. Maurer, *Aviation in the U.S. Army*, 44–46.
5. HHA, *Global Mission* (draft), 32–36. Carroll V. Glines, *Jimmy Doolittle: Master of the Calculated Risk* (New York: Van Nostrand Reinhold, 1972), 37–38. For an excellent tribute to Jimmy Doolittle, see the winter 1993 issue of *Air Power History*, dedicated to the life of the aviation pioneer.
6. Ira C. Eaker, CUOHI, 24 July 1959, 1.
7. James Parton, *"Air Force Spoken Here": General Ira C. Eaker and the Command of the Air* (Bethesda, Md.: Adler and Adler, 1986), 31–34; Eaker, CUOHI.
8. Henry H. Arnold and Ira C. Eaker, *This Flying Game* (New York: Funk and Wagnalls, 1936); Arnold and Eaker, *Winged Warfare* (New York: Harper and Brothers, 1941); *Arnold and Eaker, Army Flyer* (Harper and Brothers, 1942).
9. Mets, *Master of Airpower*, 40–43.
10. Special Order 152, 30 June 1919, RAC. On 20 May 1919, Arnold's aviation rating was

upgraded from Junior Military Aviator to Military Aviator, a new descriptor. Special Order 144-0, RAC.

11. Maurer, *Aviation in the U.S. Army*, 131–33; see also Erwin N. Thompson, *Defender of the Gate: The Presidio of San Francisco, a History from 1846 to 1995* (San Francisco: Golden Gate National Recreation Area, California National Park Service, 1997), 685.

12. Special Order 143-0, 30 June 1920; Special Order 169-0, 1 July 1920, RAC.

13. HHA, *Global Mission* (draft), 35½–36. The official orders revoking Arnold's wartime commission to full colonel still exist at the Arnold ranch.

14. Maurer, *Aviation in the U.S. Army*, 135.

15. HHA, *Global Mission* (draft), 33; also Maurer, *Aviation in the U.S. Army*, 138.

16. Mitchell to HHA, 29 June 1919, telegram, RAC; Special Order 283, 6 December 1919, RAC; Special Order 114, 14 May 1920, RAC.

17. HHA, "History of Rockwell Field," 109, RAC; Maurer, *Aviation in the U.S. Army*, 106–8.

18. HHA to HAA, 4 July 1922, Presidio, Calif., RAC.

19. Special Orders 212 and 181, 3 October and 5 September 1922, RAC; HHA, *Global Mission* (draft), 38½. Recently, since the discovery that gastric ulcers are caused by specific forms of bacterial infections, treatment has become remarkably successful.

20. John Linton Arnold birth announcement, 11 August 1921, 7¼ pounds, RAC.

21. Mrs. H. H. Arnold, CUOHI, 48.

22. Donald Douglas, CUOHI, 20 March 1959, 55.

23. The medical effect of alcohol on the blood is a proven fact today, but it might have raised eyebrows when used as an explanation for drinking in the late 1930s.

24. Quoted in Green, "Hap Arnold: Man in a Hurry," chap. 10, p. 11, MGC.

25. HHA, *Global Mission* (draft), 41½.

26. "Barling Bomber: Army's Super Plane," *U.S. Air Service* 8, no. 8 (1923): 15–19; "Initial Flight of the Barling Bomber," *U.S. Air Service* 8, no. 9 (1923): 17.

27. "Barling Bomber," 15–19. Picture this process something like the reverse of today's 747 landing gear that touches rear wheels first, then shifts the weight of landing forward to the second set of wheels.

28. "Initial Flight of the Barling Bomber," 17.

29. HHA, *Global Mission* (draft), 39½, 46½.

30. Advertisements in *U.S. Air Service* 8, nos. 8 and 11.

31. HHA, *Global Mission* (draft), 46.

32. HHA, "History of Rockwell Field," 112–14; Maurer, *Aviation in the U.S. Army*, 183.

33. HHA, memo to Rockwell Air Intermediate Depot personnel, 21 December 1923, RAC.

34. Mrs. H. H. Arnold, CUOHI, 51.

35. HHA to EPA: several letters during June 1924 chronicle the surgery and early recovery period. The specific problem is not discussed, but Arnold's reference to "those troubles" leads one to believe that the surgery might have been related to childbirth. It was not a tubal ligation or a hysterectomy.

36. Mrs. H. H. Arnold, CUOHI, 48; HHA to EPA, 2 June 1924, Coronado, Calif., RAC; HHA to EPA, 31 May 1924 (among others), Coronado, RAC. In this letter, Harley implored Bee to "get cured of your ailments or your imagination and come back feeling like your old self again if it takes three months or longer." The implication is clearly that Bee's mental health was questioned by her husband, almost to the point of frustration. Bee Arnold, at her own request, would eventually be buried with John Linton in Arlington National Cemetery. Son William Bruce had his ashes exhumed from Philadelphia and transferred to Washington for the internment when she died in 1978.

37. HHA to EPA, 6 June 1924, Coronado, RAC; and Maurer, *Aviation in the U.S. Army*, 137. To escape the children, Arnold relaxed by playing golf—frequently hitting in the low eighties.

38. Maj. Gen. Mason Patrick to HHA, 10 June 1924, RAC.
39. Patrick's commendation for HHA's 201 File, RAC.
40. Mrs. H. H. Arnold, CUOHI, 51. Additionally, Betty had become employed out in California, and word reached Bee that she was to assist Harley with the move. This may have added to Bee's determined effort to return to Coronado just for the move.
41. HHA to EPA, 16 June 1924, Coronado, RAC. Certainly, although it was admirable of him to spend time with the children, Arnold's report to Beadle following the 4 July 1924 celebration left her uneasy. "Quite a fourth of July. No casualties." HHA to EPA, 5 July 1924, Coronado, RAC.
42. HHA to EPA, 21 June 1924, Coronado, RAC.
43. Ibid., 12 July 1924.
44. Ibid.
45. HHA, "History of Rockwell Field," RAC.
46. "Industrial College of the Armed Forces, 1924–1949," twenty-fifth anniversary pamphlet, 25 February 1949. Copy on file at Special Collections, National Defense University Library, Washington, D.C.
47. HHA to EPA, 9 September 1924, Washington, D.C., RAC.
48. Maurer, *Aviation in the U.S. Army*, 186.
49. EPA to Mother Pool, 16 March 1924, Los Angeles, Calif., RAC.
50. HHA to EPA, 9 September 1924, Washington, D.C., RAC. Some authors have mistakenly included H. H. Arnold as a member of the "Around the World Flight." This is an error. Lt. Leslie Arnold, an alternate pilot, joined the mission midstream, replacing a pilot who became ill. The error was likely the result of a nondescript publicity poster that featured photos of the aviators titled by their ranks and last names only.
51. "Industrial College of the Armed Forces."
52. HHA/LC, Box 3, folder 17; HHA, *Global Mission* (draft), 41.
53. Douglas, CUOHI, 54, and many other references point to a special relationship between these two men.
54. HHA, "Performance of Future Airplanes," *U.S. Air Service* 10, no. 7 (1925): 17–19. The next few paragraphs are based upon this article.
55. HHA, "Performance of Future Airplanes," 18.
56. Ibid.
57. Ibid., 19.
58. William Mitchell to J. K. Montgomery, 11 February 1926, Washington, D.C., J. K. Montgomery papers, University of South Carolina.
59. HHA, "Hap Arnold's Air Story" (unpublished manuscript, later edited and revised into *Global Mission*), RAC. This quote was deleted by Arnold's editor.
60. Eaker never testified. He was the assistant legal officer, and propriety precluded such direct participation. Arnold, Spaatz, and Eaker did, however, meet each night before they expected to testify and reviewed what they might say, covering pertinent facts about the Air Service that would bolster Mitchell's testimony. See Hurley, *Billy Mitchell*, chap. 6.
61. Maurer, *Aviation in the U.S. Army*, 73–74. Interestingly, Arnold had pointed out the futility of predictions on aircraft performance beyond five years in his July 1925 article "Performance of Future Airplanes." His conclusions in terms of time frame were similar to the results reached by the Morrow Board. Technological advances made forecasts for production ventures of minimal value.
62. HHA, *Global Mission*, (draft), 43; Mrs. H. H. Arnold, CUOHI, 52–58.
63. Mrs. H. H. Arnold, CUOHI, 53–55; HHA, *Global Mission* (draft), 44.
64. Mrs. H. H. Arnold, CUOHI, 53.
65. Ibid., 55–56, 61. There was no love lost between the two families after the Mitchell trial and Arnold's admonishment had passed. Mrs. Arnold was particularly clear concerning her

feelings about General Patrick: "I think General Patrick was little bit jealous . . . because he didn't have the entree to senate meetings and things. . . . I think both the Patricks felt a little bit outside of it."

66. HHA, *Global Mission* (draft), 44; Special Order 52, 4 March 1926, RAC.
67. Douglas, CUOHI, 67.
68. HHA to EPA, 14 May 1927, Fort Sam Houston, Tex., RAC.
69. For an excellent summary of the Guggenheim contributions to American aviation, see Richard P. Hallion, *Legacy of Flight: The Guggenheim Contribution to American Aviation* (Seattle: University of Washington Press, 1977).
70. Interview with Richard P. Hallion conducted by author for *New World Vistas*, Bolling AFB, Washington, D.C., 28 August 1995. *New World Vistas: Air and Space Power for the 21st Century* (Washington, D.C.: USAF Scientific Advisory Board, 1995), a 1995 Air Force science and technology forecast, was completed 15 December 1995. See also Paul A. Hanle, *Bringing Aerodynamics to America* (Cambridge, Mass.: MIT Press, 1982), chap. 2. Hanle details Millikan's quest for Guggenheim funds.
71. Hallion, *Legacy of Flight*, 46–53; Doolittle oral interview, 26 September 1971. For an excellent summary of Millikan's influence at Caltech, see Dr. Judith Goldstein's *Millikan's School: A History of the California Institute of Technology* (New York: W. W. Norton, 1991).
72. Michael H. Gorn's *The Universal Man: Theodore von Kármán's Life in Aeronautics* (Washington, D.C.: Smithsonian Institution Press, 1992) points out that Prandtl's popularity in the United States was largely the result of the wide range of publicity that Göttingen had received in America. Kármán, at this point in his career, was not universally known, except to aeronautical scientists throughout the world. See Hanle, *Bringing Aerodynamics to America*, chap. 5, for a detailed discussion of Prandtl and his methodology. Chap. 6 focuses on the differences and the interaction between Prandtl and Kármán. Hanle's primary-source research is excellent. For the differences between the two scientists, see particularly p. 65.
73. *The Guggenheim Aeronautical Laboratory of the California Institute of Technology (GALCIT): The First Twenty-Five Years* (Pasadena, Calif.: Caltech, 1954); see also Gorn, *Universal Man*, 39–40, 56; and Theodore von Kármán with Lee Edson, *The Wind and Beyond: Theodore von Kármán, Pioneer in Aviation and Pathfinder in Space* (Boston: Little, Brown, 1967), 124.
74. Robert H. Kargon, *The Rise of Robert Millikan: Portrait of a Life in American Science* (Ithaca, N.Y.: Cornell University Press, 1982), 119; Kármán and Edson, *Wind and Beyond*, 151.
75. Henry H. Arnold, *Airmen and Aircraft: An Introduction to Aeronautics* (New York: Ronald Press Company, 1976). Inscription at RAC.
76. Letter from John W. Huston to author, 22 February 1996. See HHA, *Global Mission* (draft), 44–48; Hurley, *Billy Mitchell*, 100–105; Mrs. H. H. Arnold, CUOHI, 64–65.
77. Brig. Gen. E. E. Booth to chief of the Air Corps, 17 December 1926, Fort Riley, Kans., RAC.
78. HHA, *Global Mission* (draft), 44½.
79. HHA to EPA, 19 March 1927, San Antonio, Tex., RAC.
80. Mrs. H. H. Arnold, CUOHI, 64–65.
81. HHA to Clifford H. Arnold, 15 March 1927, Fort Riley, Kans., RAC.
82. Ibid.
83. Arnold testimony can be found in the Andrews papers, L/C, Box 16. The actual number of flyable aircraft was not exactly known. But there were few combat-worthy planes.
84. Green, "Hap Arnold: Man in a Hurry," chap. 12, 6–12, MGC.
85. Mrs. H. H. Arnold, CUOHI, 55–56.
86. Quoted in Green, "Hap Arnold: Man in a Hurry," chap. 12, p. 15–15a, MGC, from Arnold's 201 file in the National Archives.

87. Green, "Hap Arnold: Man in a Hurry," chap 14, p. 1, MGC.
88. *New York Times,* 23–30 July, 1927; also Douglas, CUOHI, 65.
89. HHA to EPA, 6 June 1927, Wilbur Wright Field, Ohio, RAC.
90. HHA to John K. Montgomery, 15, 24 July 1927, John K. Montgomery papers, typed manuscript, Caroliniana Library, University of South Carolina, Columbia; also HHA, *Global Mission* (draft), 44½–47½.
91. Wayne Biddle, *Barons of the Sky* (New York: Henry Holt, 1991), 156.
92. HHA to Montgomery, 24 July 1927, J. K. Montgomery papers, University of South Carolina. Montgomery would later surface during the air-mail controversy in 1934. His Latin American airline had made a bid to carry the mail throughout South America but did not win the contract, even though their bid was lower than the one issued the contract. Montgomery's lawsuit was one of those that resulted in the cancellation of air-mail contracts by Postmaster General Farley in 1934.
93. Montgomery to HHA, 27 July 1927, J. K. Montgomery papers, University of South Carolina. Included in this letter are the specifics of the salary and perks offered to Arnold: the presidency of Pan Am; $8,000 per year; 300 shares of B stock (voting shares) and 1,200 more if he stayed with the company. It is unclear whether the 300 shares were intended to be delivered even had Arnold not stayed with the company. In any case, he did not accept this tempting offer. See also Green, "Hap Arnold: Man in a Hurry," chap. 12, p. 6, MGC.
94. HHA, *Global Mission* (draft), 44½.
95. Coffey, *Hap,* 126.
96. At some point in a military pilot's career—for some sooner, some later—the decision to quit the flying game arises. Whether this is to leave service or take a non-flying job on the General Staff, or a position as an academic instructor or liaison with another non-flying service, it is one of the most difficult decisions for a military pilot to make. Arnold may not have been ready to give up the excitement of military flying.
97. Arnold papers, Billy Bruce folders, L/C. See also David K. Vaughan, "Hap Arnold's Bill Bruce Books," *Air Power History* 40, no. 4 (1993): 43–49.
98. Gay Morris interview with author, 1998. The manuscripts are no longer available, having been destroyed or misplaced during one of son David's moves. See also Green, "Hap Arnold: Man in a Hurry," chap. 13, p. 24, MGC.
99. Special Order 135, 9 June 1926, "Presidential Air Mail Service," RAC. Arnold papers, Billy Bruce folders; Vaughan, "Hap Arnold's Bill Bruce Books."
100. Special Order 159, 5 September 1928, and Special Order 131, 6 June 1929, RAC; also Maurer, *Aviation in the U.S. Army,* 102, 200; and Hurley, *Billy Mitchell,* 104. Fechet and Arnold were more than just casual friends. Fechet had an affection for the Arnold children, particularly little Lois. Arnold relayed the following message to Lolie: "Gen. Fechet says that if he can he will come back to Fort Riley and visit her and that there are few girls that he would travel over a thousand miles to see." HHA to EPA, 16 May 1927, Fort Sam Houston, Tex., RAC.
101. Green, "Hap Arnold: Man in a Hurry," chap. 14, p. 1, MGC.

8. INTERWAR YEARS, COMMAND EXPERIENCE

1. Lois E. Walker and Shelby E. Wickam, *From Huffman Prairie to the Moon: The History of Wright-Patterson Air Force Base* (Dayton, Ohio: Air Force Logistics Command, 1986), 59–61, 79, 149. The complete and detailed story of the evolution of today's Wright-Patterson Air Force Base is told in this work. During the 1920s and 1930s, several name changes and consolidations of adjacent areas occurred, thereby confusing the issue between McCook Field, Wilbur Wright Field, North Field, and the Fairfield Depot. The complex known as Wright-Patterson was not officially created until 1 July 1931. For more details on the life of

A. W. Robins, see William Head, *Every Inch a Soldier: Augustine Warner Robins and the Building of U.S. Airpower* (College Station, Tex.: Texas A and M University Press, 1995).

2. Walker and Wickam, *From Huffman Prairie to the Moon,* 80–82.

3. Address of Brig. Gen. H. H. Arnold, assistant chief of the Air Corps, at the Western Aviation Planning Conference, 23 September 1937, USAF/HRA, 168.3952-119.

4. Walker and Wickam, *From Huffman Prairie to the Moon,* 59–61, 149.

5. Gardner W. Carr, "Organization and Activities of Engineering Division of the Army Air Service," *U.S. Air Service* 6, no. 6 (1922): 9–12.

6. Carr, "Organization and Activities of Engineering Division of the Army Air Service," *U.S. Air Service* 7, no. 1 (1922): 22.

7. Ibid., 22–27. The "type" chart is reproduced in Walker and Wickam, *From Huffman Prairie to the Moon,* 190.

8. Carr, "Organization and Activities of Engineering Division of the Army Air Service," *U.S. Air Service* 7, no. 2 (1922): 27.

9. Ibid.

10. Ibid.

11. James R. Hansen, *Engineer in Charge: A History of the Langley Aeronautical Laboratory, 1917–1958* (Washington, D.C.: National Aeronautics and Space Administration, 1987), 4–6.

12. Ibid., 7–8.

13. Ibid., 8–9.

14. Carr, "Organization and Activities of Engineering Division of the Army Air Service," *U.S. Air Service* 7, no. 2 (1922): 27; see also Alex Roland, *Model Research: The National Advisory Committee for Aeronautics, 1915–1958* (Washington: National Air and Space Administration, 1985).

15. Walker and Wickam, *From Huffman Prairie to the Moon,* 197–99. The hangar story that follows has been substantiated by the boyhood buddy of Wright Brothers' biographer Tom D. Crouch, name tk, who lived at Wright Field at the time. Crouch recounted his friend's story, which featured an unauthorized excursion into the hangar that had housed the burned-out Barling and many other useless airplanes.

16. William Bruce Arnold, "My Dad Hap," RAC. The story that follows is taken from this manuscript. The reader will note that there is enough evidence from other sources to substantiate this event. Tom Crouch interview with author, 1998.

17. HHA, *Global Mission* (draft), 39½, 46–46½.

18. Col. H. H. Arnold Jr. (ret.), interviewed by Murray Green, Sheridan, Wyoming, 29–30 August 1972, transcript in MGC, roll 25. See also Walker and Wickam, *Huffman Prairie,* 218–19. Arnold appeared to be getting used to the system during these two years. He directed projects on flame suppression from engine exhausts and contrail dissipation; the intent of both was to make American aircraft less visible to enemy gunners. Maj. Gen. Donald J. Keirn (ret.), interviewed by Murray Green, Delaplane, Virginia, 25 September 1970, transcript in MGC, roll 31.

19. Douglas, CUOHI, 65–67. "The depression that started in 1929 didn't affect us at all, actually," Douglas recalled.

20. Many of Arnold's letters contained instructions for deposits of monthly checks in the savings and loan. Mrs. H. H. Arnold, CUOHI, 80–81. The Arnolds' entire education fund was wiped out. See also Pool family genealogy, RAC.

21. HHA to "Father and Mother," 17 April 1930, Mather Field, Calif., RAC; HHA to EPA, 19 January 1931, Ardmore, RAC; EPA to Dr. Arnold, 18 January 1931, Fairfield, Ohio, RAC.

22. The evolution of Arnold's nickname has erroneously been explained by many authors in many different, albeit plausible, ways. The evidence, however, is clearly seen by examining his personal letters. At no time before his mother's death does he sign a letter using "Hap,"

nor does Bee ever address him as Hap until 1931. During courtship, Bee addressed Harley as Billikens, Sunny Jim, and, finally, Sunny. Arnold addressed Bee as BB and then Beadle.

23. HHA, *Global Mission* (draft), 47.

24. Special Order 234, 6 October 1931, RAC.

25. Spaatz, CUOHI, 35–36; Mrs. H. H. Arnold, CUOHI, 89.

26. H. W. Bowman, interviewed by Murray Green, 23 August 1969, transcript in MGC, roll 26. Bowman flew several of Millikan's experimental missions. His task was to orbit a particular area with a 500-pound lead ball at various altitudes up to 21,000 feet. Bowman felt certain that Millikan had introduced Arnold to Kármán at Caltech. See also HHA, *Global Mission* (draft), 50–50½; and Mrs. H. H. Arnold, CUOHI, 89. Mrs. Arnold was well acquainted with Millikan, who frequently visited the Arnold home at March Field. See Kargon, *The Rise of Robert Millikan*, for a fair description of the Karl Compton challenge.

27. HHA, "Hap Arnold's Air Story," 108–108a, RAC. In the published book, his editor changed the word *ancestor* to *dress rehearsal* for the Berlin Airlift. HHA, *Global Mission* (draft), 48.

28. Department of the Interior press release, 13 February 1934, Death Valley National Monument, Calif., RAC; see also HHA, *Global Mission*, 50–50½; and James T. Patterson, "New Deal" Grolier Online, 15 May 1998, gi.grolier.com/presidents/ea/side/newdeal.html.

29. Robert E. Sherwood, *Roosevelt and Hopkins: An Intimate History* (New York: Harper and Brothers, 1948), 52: Harry Hopkins's ultimate argument for the Civil Works Administration was that "Hunger is not debatable." Arnold and Hopkins thought much alike. See also HHA, *Global Mission* (draft), 50½–51.

30. Diary of Herbert A. Arnold, January–September 1933, RAC; Mrs. H. H. Arnold, CUOHI, 81–82; H. H. Arnold Jr. and William Bruce Arnold, interviewed by Murray Green, Sheridan, Wyo., and Sonoma, Calif., MGC.

31. Mrs. H. H. Arnold, CUOHI, 91–92.

32. Diary of Herbert A. Arnold, January–September 1933, RAC. In one instance, just ten days after a major earthquake had done significant damage in Los Angeles, Compton, Santa Anna, and Palm Beach, Arnold got more than 300 airplanes in the air for an aerial review.

33. Spaatz, CUOHI, 33.

34. Ibid.

35. HHA, Global Mission (draft), 48–51½; Spaatz, CUOHI, 33–37.

36. Diary of Herbert A. Arnold, January–September 1933, RAC.

37. Spaatz, CUOHI, 36.

38. Ibid., 36–37.

39. Ibid.

40. James A. Farley, *Jim Farley's Story: The Roosevelt Years* (New York: McGraw-Hill, 1948), 46. See Benjamin S. Kelsey's *The Dragon's Teeth?* (Washington, D.C.: Smithsonian Institution Press, 1982), 38–39. Kelsey explained that Alabama senator Hugo Black had chaired the investigation of alleged impropriety. He concluded that "small operators had been discriminated against and big companies had been favored." This conclusion seems valid if one considers correspondence in the J. K. Montgomery papers, University of South Carolina. Montgomery, the same man who had offered Arnold the presidency of Pan Am in 1927 and since 1928 had been the owner of a small airline company, had issued the low bid for a few Latin American mail routes and was not issued the contract. He filed suit against the government.

41. HHA to EPA, 12 and 13 March, 8 May 1934, Salt Lake City, Utah, RAC.

42. For an excellent and concise examination of the air-mail operation, see John F. Shiner, *Foulois and the U.S. Army Air Corps, 1931–1935* (Washington, D.C.: Office of Air Force History, 1983), 125–49; see also Maurer, *Aviation in the U.S. Army,* 299–317.

43. HHA to EPA, 20 February 1934, Salt Lake City, RAC.

44. Foulois instruction to Zone commanders, quoted in Shiner, *Foulois and the U.S. Army Air Corps,* 136.
45. HHA to EPA, 2 March 1934, Salt Lake City, RAC. Two days later, Arnold told Bee that he expected to be in Salt Lake for at least two more months. He asked her to come and visit him there. In April, she did.
46. HHA to EPA, 7 and 11 March 1934, Salt Lake City, RAC.
47. HHA, *Global Mission* (draft), 50½–51½.
48. HHA to EPA, 11 March 1934, Salt Lake City, RAC. Two days later, he wrote in total frustration, "The total absence of reports telling of our successful operations, of the mail runs completed, of the mail carried, of the long hours our pilots have flown over the routes. . . ."
49. HHA to EPA, 11 March 1934, Salt Lake City, RAC.
50. Ibid., 12 and 13 March, 8 May 1934.
51. Ibid., 20 March 1934. Bee visited Hap in Salt Lake during early April. Apparently, despite terrible weather, the couple spent the hours becoming reacquainted. Hap wrote on 5 April, "Well sweetie, I had a wonderful time while you were here and we had our second honeymoon." Later, on 8 April: "I *miss you* a lot. The bed hasn't broken down yet."
52. HHA to EPA, 9 April 1934, Salt Lake City, RAC.
53. Ibid., 5 April 1934. Hap met with Will Rogers during this week, and he described the conditions under which the Air Corps was flying. Rogers had earlier written about the situation in one of his columns in Kansas City; in Shiner, *Foulois and the U.S. Army Air Corps,* 134.
54. HHA, *Global Mission* (draft), 52½.
55. Shiner, *Foulois and the U.S. Army Air Corps,* 148–49; Maurer, *Aviation in the U.S. Army,* 317.
56. HHA to EPA, 19 March 1934, Salt Lake City, RAC.
57. Shiner, *Foulois and the U.S. Army Air Corps,* 148.
58. Kelsey, *The Dragon's Teeth,* 39. In an interview conducted by the author, Washington, D.C., 9 October 1995, Gen. Bernard Schriever (ret.) adamantly insisted that flying the mail in 1934 assured American preparedness for the production efforts of World War II. He had been flying for the airlines in the poor weather northwest and was one of the few experienced pilots flying the poor-weather routes.
59. Shiner, *Foulois and the U.S. Army Air Corps,* 126.
60. HHA to EPA, 12 April 1934, Salt Lake City, RAC.
61. Irving B. Holley, *Buying Aircraft: Matériel Procurement for the Army Air Forces* (Washington, D.C.: Center of Military History, United States Army, 1964, reprint 1989),118–21. Holley's work remains the definitive study of procurement issues and policy for the Army's air forces.
62. Holley, *Buying Aircraft,* 119–21.
63. HHA to EPA, 14 November 1934, Washington, D.C., RAC. Arnold was in D.C. to testify before the Howell Commission.
64. HHA to EPA, 19 April 1934, Salt Lake City, RAC.
65. Ibid., 20 April 1934.
66. Ibid., probably 12 May 1934.
67. Ibid., 8 May 1934. In this letter, Arnold also mentioned that one of his pilots was refusing an assignment to Dayton after the mail operation was over. "I don't blame him a bit," was Hap's comment. His distaste for Wright Field remained.
68. HHA, *Global Mission* (draft), 48–51½.
69. Hugh J. Knerr, "Washington to Alaska and Back: Memories of the 1934 U.S. Air Corps Test Flight," *Aerospace Historian,* March 1972, 20.
70. *Howitzer,* 1907. Oscar Westover was short by fate, and muscular from a cadet career as a gymnast and track star. "Tubby" was not derogatory.
71. HHA to EPA, 28 June 1934, Wright Field, RAC.

72. Ibid., 26 June 1934.
73. Ibid., 6 July 1934.
74. Knerr, "Washington to Alaska and Back," 20–21.
75. HHA to EPA, 10 July 1934, Wright Field, RAC.
76. Ibid., 2, 4, 6, 7, and 8 July 1934.
77. Ibid., 15 July 1934. Arnold championed what the modern Air Force calls the dedicated-crew-chief program.
78. HHA to EPA, 16 July 1934, Wright Field, RAC.
79. Ibid., 18 July 1934.
80. HHA's Alaska diary, 18 July–9 September 1934, RAC.
81. Ibid.; HHA to EPA, 21 and 22 July 1934, Edmonton, Alberta, Canada, RAC.
82. HHA to EPA, 22 July 1934, Edmonton, RAC.
83. HHA to EPA, 23 July 1934, Whitehorse, Yukon Territory, RAC.
84. Ibid.
85. HHA to EPA, 24 July 1934, Fairbanks, Alaska, RAC.
86. HHA to EPA, 17 August 1934, Seattle, Wash., RAC
87. HHA to EPA, 3 August 1934, Anchorage, Alaska, RAC. For some unknown reason, Arnold allowed an inexperienced B-10 pilot to take one of the birds out on a flight. The pilot ended up in Cook's Bay, and the B-10 was swamped in twenty to forty feet of icy water. Remarkably, the other crews were able to save the plane and drain the water from the fuselage. After more than one full week of work on the airplane, it cranked up on the first try and flew the rest of the way to Washington, much to Arnold's relief.
88. Knerr, "Washington to Alaska and Back," 20–24.
89. HHA's Alaska diary, RAC; HHA to EPA, 4 August 1934, Fairbanks, Alaska, RAC.
90. HHA's Alaska diary, RAC.
91. HHA, Global Mission (draft), 53.
92. Ibid., 53–53½, 60½–61.
93. HHA's Alaska diary, RAC; Maurer, Aviation in the U.S. Army, 354.
94. HHA's Alaska diary, RAC; HHA to EPA, 14 November 1934, Washington, D.C., RAC. Arnold used the 18,000-mile figure to argue for the award of the Distinguished Flying Cross to all the members of the mission. That request was never honored.
95. In early 1970, historian Murray Green showed Knerr documentary evidence of Arnold's attempts to pry DFCs out of the Army's decorations people. Knerr apparently still felt he had been cheated out of the DFC. He had done most of the preparation for the Alaska flight before Arnold's arrival in Dayton, he explained to Green. The inch-thick file is located in the RAC.
96. Knerr, "Washington to Alaska and Back," 20–24. Knerr's recollections of the flight, published in 1972, revealed his perceptions of his own contribution to the success of the mission. He wrote: "I had charge of all preparations for the flight. . . . I had to see that crews were trained to handle the B-10s. . . . I found the airplane sitting on the steep beach at the end of the water [No. 145]." All of these statements were true, but the reality of the situation was that nobody actually accomplished anything individually for the mission—it was a team effort. Knerr's article included three specific jabs at Hap Arnold's conduct of the mission, two concerning his navigation skills and one holding him responsible for the ditching of tail No. 145 in Cooks Inlet (every aircraft has a unique identification number displayed on its tail). Though responsibility for the accident should indeed be given to Arnold, Knerr did not add that on the test mission he had led to Dallas, one of his planes had not made it due to mechanical problems. It had been forced to land short of the destination. Nevertheless, Knerr and his men had received high praise for the Dallas flight.
97. HHA to EPA, 14 November 1934, Washington, D.C., RAC; John H. Scrivner, "Maj. Gen. Orvil A. Anderson," Air Force Magazine, June 1979, 103–5. The balloon ascent was Explorer I, 28 July 1934, before the completion of the Alaska Flight.

98. Maurer, *Aviation in the U.S. Army,* 322.
99. HHA to EPA, 8 November 1934, Washington, D.C., RAC.
100. Ibid.
101. HHA to EPA, 8 and 14 November 1934, Washington, D.C., RAC.
102. Ibid., 14 November 1934.
103. Ibid. There is no documentary evidence that Howell had talked to FDR about Arnold during this period. But Howell and FDR were well acquainted and spoke often. It is possible that Howell arranged the meeting between Arnold and FDR, as a preliminary step to push Arnold as a future chief of the Air Corps.
104. Interview with William Rees Sears conducted by author, Tucson, Ariz., 8 July 1995. After Clark Millikan, Robert Millikan's son, joined the faculty at Caltech, Kármán differentiated between the two by calling Robert Old Millikan—to everyone but Old Millikan himself. Dr. Sears, a friend of Kármán's, was also his student and then colleague. He was one of only a few who called the professor by his informal name, Todor. For an excellent summary of the Guggenheim influence, see Hallion, *Legacy of Flight.*
105. For a more detailed discussion of Kármán's association with Arnold and the Air Force, see my *Architects of American Air Supremacy: Gen. Hap Arnold and Dr. Theodore von Kármán* (Maxwell AFB, Ala.: Air University Press, 1997).
106. Theodore von Kármán, oral interview, 27 January 1960, conducted by D. Shaughnessy, USAF Academy Oral History Interviews, USAF Academy, Colo.; Gorn, *Universal Man,* 81. Also in NBC newsreel covering the Rose Garden ceremony where Kármán was given the first Medal of Science by President Kennedy, January 1963. Kármán reminisced about Arnold and his inquisitive nature back in the early days.

    Arnold's flight logs carefully document his trips to California while he was at Fairfield Depot. From 27 December 1929 through 4 January 1930, Arnold was in the Los Angeles area on an inspection tour. From 18 February through 7 March 1930, he visited a variety of locations in Southern California. After a brief trip north, Arnold returned to the L.A. area from 24 to 29 March. During these trips, there was ample opportunity for him to have visited Caltech and Robert Millikan. Although Kármán did not visit Caltech until the first week in April 1930, later trips allowed him and Arnold to meet. A copy of these logs is located in both the HHA/LC and the USAF Museum, Wright-Patterson AFB, Dayton, Ohio, Arnold folder. The fact that Kármán ranked Arnold as a major would seem to date their initial meetings to before 1 February 1931, when Arnold was promoted to lieutenant colonel.
107. "Daniel Guggenheim Founds School of Aeronautics," *U.S. Air Service* 10, no. 7 (1925): 36.
108. Daniel Guggenheim, "Aeronautical Engineering Offers Most Promising Future," *U.S. Air Service* (February 1927), 26.
109. Some historians of technology also use Corrthe term *metasystem.*
110. Gorn, *Universal Man,* 116, 158.
111. Holley, *Buying Aircraft,* 119–21.
112. Frank Andrews to HHA, 4 January 1935, Washington, D.C., F. M. Andrews papers, L/C, Box 1, Corr. "A."
113. Spaatz, CUOHI, 40–41. Nearly all of the oral histories and most written histories suggest that Arnold and Andrews had a tremendous working relationship. Each recognized the other's strengths: Arnold was the administrator and builder, Andrews the operator and equipment user.
114. Spaatz, CUOHI, 44.
115. "Remarks made by Brig. Gen. Hap Arnold to the Sub-committee on War Department Expenditures of the House Appropriations Committee at March Field," 13 September 1935, 450.01-1, vol. 2, 1941, appendix to Fourth AF Historical Study, USAF/HRA.
116. The U.S. Army and the USAF still ruthlessly debate the appropriate application of the

United States' air forces. While stationed at the Pentagon, I witnessed both productive and counterproductive discussions between the services concerning the application of airpower. In the end, the arguments concerning application of forces—whether to provide tactical, operational, or strategic effects in support of the theater commander—have remained largely unchanged from 1935 to 1999.

117. "Remarks made by Brig. Gen. Hap Arnold to the Sub-committee on War Department Expenditures."

118. Ibid. In today's Air Force, the "radius of action" has approached only the limits of the crew aboard. Refueling and ever-more efficient engines have expanded the radius to every inch of the globe.

119. Maurer, *Aviation in the U.S. Army,* 340.

120. "Remarks made by Brig. Gen. Hap Arnold to the Sub-committee on War Department Expenditures."

121. Shiner, *Foulois and the U.S. Army Air Corps,* 171–92, 254–55.

122. Maj. Gen. Malin Craig to Lieutenant Colonel Arnold, 20 January 1935, the Presidio, RAC.

123. HHA, *Global Mission* (draft), 58–59.

124. HHA, Global Mission, 152–53. Herman S. Wolk, *Planning and Organizing the Post War Air Force, 1943–1947* (Washington, D.C.: Office of Air Force History, 1984), 12–15.

125. Mrs. H. H. Arnold, CUOHI, 82.

126. Maurer, *Aviation in the U.S. Army,* 341.

127. HHA, "Balanced Air Program" (confidential), USAF/HRA, 145.93-96. See also Wolk, *Planning and Organizing the Post War Air Force,* 12–20.

128. HHA, *Global Mission* (draft), 56½.

129. Address of Brig. Gen. H. H. Arnold, assistant chief of the Air Corps, at the Western Aviation Planning Conference, 23 September 1937, USAF/HRA, 168.3952-119. Emphasis in the original. This belief in research may have been the result of earlier association with Dr. Robert Millikan. In 1934, Millikan had warned military officials through the executive Scientific Advisory Board, established in the summer of 1933, that "research is a peacetime thing and . . . moves too slowly to be done after you get into trouble." Quoted in Michael S. Sherry, *Preparing for the Next War: American Plans for Postwar Defense, 1941–1945* (New Haven, Conn.: Yale University Press), 123.

130. Hallion's *Legacy of Flight* summarizes the entire story of the Guggenheim influence on the early years of American aviation.

131. In another speech, "Air Lessons from Current Wars," an address before the Bond Club, Philadelphia, 25 March 1938, Arnold emphasized the foundations of airpower as not just planes, but also "the number of flyers, mechanics, and skilled artisans available . . . and the size and character of the ground establishments we lump under the general name 'air bases.'" Eaker papers, L/C, Box 38.

132. Michael S. Sherry, *The Rise of American Air Power: The Creation of Armageddon* (New Haven, Conn.: Yale University Press, 1987), 200–201.

133. Maurer, *Aviation in the U.S. Army,* 319–43.

134. Arnold and Eaker, *This Flying Game,* 37. Openness to women pilots and other female contributions to the aeronautics field is evident throughout the work.

135. Arnold and Eaker, *This Flying Game,* 110.

136. Ibid., 128–29.

137. Ibid., 250.

138. Preliminary accident report, General Westover, chief of the Air Corps, 21 September 1938, Andrews papers, L/C, Box 7, Open Corr., Oscar Westover.

139. HHA, *Global Mission* (draft), 62.

140. Andrews to Westover (draft), n.d. (after 25 November 1936), Andrews papers, L/C, Box 7, Open Corr., Oscar Westover.

141. HHA, *Global Mission* (draft), 62. Many letters to Bee, even from Alaska in 1934, mention that Arnold had taken a swill of port. None mention hard liquor of any kind. In those days, "to take a drink" usually meant hard liquor, the legacy of Prohibition still young. This cultural phenomenon might best be understood when compared with today's language. For example, in the 1990s the phrase "having sex" holds a variety of meanings, while in the 1930s, it meant only one thing. While in 1930s, "having a drink" normally referred only to hard liquor, a 1990s interpretation generally includes all alcoholic beverages.

   Some have attributed Hugh Knerr with spreading this rumor, but there is no concrete evidence supporting that contention. It is also true that Knerr held no affection for Arnold, calling him the Old Slicker. Historian Murray Green has pointed to FDR's press secretary, Steve Early, and his military adviser, Col. Edwin M. "Pa" Watson, as the two most likely responsible for the rumors in Washington concerning Arnold's drinking habits. He agrees that it was Hopkins who probably saved Arnold's reputation with FDR.

142. Even today, the honor code is held in high regard by academy graduates. There is no doubt, however, that in 1907 the West Point honor code was respected and followed to far greater extent than it might be in today's society.

9. CHIEF OF THE ARMY AIR CORPS

1. HHA to Oscar Westover, 18 May 1937, MGC, L/C, Box 55. For a list of the NACA projects, see the NACA Executive Meeting Minutes, National Archives Annex, College Park; see also Robert van der Linden, "The Struggle for the Long-Range Heavy Bomber: The United States Air Corps, 1934–1939," master's thesis, George Washington University, 1981. "Shaking the stick" is how a pilot takes control from another pilot in command of an aircraft in flight.
2. Gorn, *Universal Man,* 84; Ira C. Eaker, oral interview, 19 October 1978, USAF Academy Oral History Interviews, USAF Academy, Colo.
3. Major General Arnold, chief of the Air Corps, "A Message from the Chief to the Corps," 30 September 1938, NASM Archives, Henry H. Arnold folder. This message was Arnold's first as chief following Westover's death.
4. HHA, *Global Mission* (draft), 61.
5. Tate, *The Army and Its Air Corps,* 170–71.
6. HHA, "A Message from the Chief to the Corps," 30 September 1938.
7. HHA, "Balanced Air Program" (confidential), USAF/HRA, 145.93-96.
8. Spaatz, CUOHI, 41–42.
9. Ibid.
10. Craven and Cate, *Army Air Forces in World War II,* vol. 6, 13.
11. Kármán and Edson, *Wind and Beyond,* 243; see also Kármán oral interview, USAF Academy, 2.
12. Bush to HHA, 27 May 1941, Washington, D.C., Navy Building, HHA/LC, Arnold papers, classified folder (declassified for this work by NASA).
13. Durand to Bush, 10 May 1941, HHA/LC (declassified for this work by NASA).
14. There are detailed accounts of this meeting in the Robert Millikan Collection, L/C, 9.15, roll 10. In a letter from Max Mason to HHA, 5 January 1939, Mason summed up the results of the NAS meeting of the "long hairs." Mason chaired the committee; diesel-engine problems were studied by "Boss" Kettering; rain and snow static went to F. Jewett; and alloy development was left to commercial interests. See also Roland, *Model Research,* vol. 2, 428. Hunsaker had just returned to the NACA after having been off the committee roster for nearly fifteen years. See interview with Dr. Ivan Getting conducted by author, Washington, D.C., 9 November 1994. Dr. Getting was one of the original members of the Scientific Advisory Group. He was a radar specialist at the MIT Radiation Laboratory (RADLAB) until his selection for the SAG in 1944.

15. HHA, *Global Mission* (draft), 59–60; see Sherry, *The Rise of American Air Power*, 186–88.
16. HHA, *Global Mission* (draft), 55½.
17. Ibid., 56.
18. "Remarks of Brig. Gen. H. H. Arnold at the Convention of the Air Corps Reserve Officers, Dayton, Ohio," 15 September 1938, USAF/HRA, 168.3952-119.
19. HHA, *Global Mission* (draft), 56.
20. Van der Linden, "The Struggle for the Long-Range Heavy Bomber," 125–30.
21. Address of Brig. Gen. H. H. Arnold, assistant chief of Air Corps, U.S. Army, before the Bond Club, Philadelphia, Pa., 25 March 1938, Eaker papers, L/C, Box 38, 4.
22. Ibid., 5. Eaker verified that Arnold and his staff reviewed intelligence reports on the air battles of the Spanish Civil War. One of Arnold's 1938 speeches covered that war in great detail and concentrated on the uses of airpower.
23. Address of Brig. Gen. H. H. Arnold, assistant chief of the Air Corps, at the Western Aviation Planning Conference, 23 September 1937, USAF/HRA, 168.3952-119, 10.
24. Charles A. Lindbergh to HHA, 29 November 1938, USAF/HRA, 168.65-40.
25. Charles A. Lindbergh, *The Wartime Journals of Charles A. Lindbergh* (New York: Harcourt Brace Jovanovich, 1970), 184–85.
26. Craven and Cate, *Army Air Forces in World War II*, vol. 6, 178–80.
27. James O. Young, *Meeting the Challenge of Supersonic Flight* (Edwards AFB, Calif.: Air Force Flight Test Center History Office, 1997), 3. In a March 1944 *Air Force* magazine article, "Our Jet Propelled Fighter" (6–8, 64), Ezra Kotcher described the differences between jet and rocket propulsion.
28. "Remarks of Brig. Gen. H. H. Arnold at the Convention of the Air Corps Reserve Officers," 4; and "Performance and Development Trends in Military Aircraft and Accessories," speech given by Maj. Gen. H. H. Arnold before the Society of Automotive Engineers, Detroit, Michigan, 11 January 1939, 15–16, USAF/HRA, 168.3952-119. For German statistics, see Edward L. Homze, *Arming the Luftwaffe: The Reich Air Ministry and the German Aircraft Industry, 1919–1939* (Lincoln, Nebr.: University of Nebraska Press, 1976), 159, 190.
29. Lindbergh, *Wartime Journals*, 256–58.
30. Leonard S. Reich, "From the *Spirit of St. Louis* to the SST: Charles Lindbergh, Technology, and Environment," *Technology and Culture* 36, no. 2 (1995): 365–67; see also Robert E. Herzstein, *Roosevelt and Hitler: Prelude to War.* New York: Paragon House, 1989, 226–31; and Jeffery S. Underwood, *The Wings of Democracy: The Influence of Air Power on the Roosevelt Administration, 1933–1941* (College Station, Tex.: Texas A and M University Press, 1991), 111.
31. Charles A. Lindbergh, *Autobiography of Values* (New York: Harcourt Brace Jovanovich, 1976), 190–92; also Lindberg, *Wartime Journals*, 256–58.
32. HHA, *Global Mission* (draft), 53.
33. The idea of scientific superiority was a constant theme in the years before Pearl Harbor and was exemplified in many of the speeches Arnold gave in 1938, 1939, and 1940. As an example, see "Performance and Development Trends in Military Aircraft and Accessories," speech given by Maj. Gen. H. H. Arnold before the Society of Automotive Engineers, Detroit, Michigan, 11 January 1939.
34. Kármán and Edson, *Wind and Beyond*, 226.
35. HHA, "Science and Air Power," *Air Affairs*, December 1946, 193.
36. Address of Brig. Gen. H. H. Arnold, assistant chief of Air Corps, U.S. Army, before the Bond Club, Philadelphia, Pa., 25 March 1938, Eaker papers, L/C, Box 38, 4.
37. "Performance and Development Trends in Military Aircraft and Accessories," speech given by Maj. Gen. H. H. Arnold before the Society of Automotive Engineers, Detroit, Michigan, 11 January 1939, 15–16.

38. Ibid., 16. In this section, Arnold quoted from a speech given by Louis Johnson, assistant secretary of war. Arnold apparently helped to write the speech.
39. HHA to the assistant secretary of war, 2 March 1939, USAF/HRA, 167.8-33.
40. NACA letterhead, 1938, Kármán Collection; and NACA Executive Meeting Minutes, National Archives Annex, College Park. Arnold served on the executive (main) committee from October 1938 to April 1946.
41. In an 11 May 1939 speech at the Air Corps Tactical School, Arnold outlined the delicate balance required between training, production, and basing to maintain an effective force.
42. HHA to Spaatz, 9 November 1946, at St. Francis College, Spaatz papers, L/C, Box 256. Arnold's detailed comments are in response to a news article that was critical of Air Force leadership during the war. Arnold feared that the hostile tone might influence funding in the Congress, and he warned Spaatz to read it carefully.
43. Arnold and Eaker, *Winged Warfare,* 239.
44. Holley, *Buying Aircraft,* 22–26. In Holley's account, Arnold exchanged letters with the Materiel Division in March 1939 and discussed the issue of mass production and design changes. Holley wrote: "If a manufacturer introduces major design changes in each successive aircraft turned out, efficient production in the sense of large-quantity fabrication by repetitive machine process is patently impossible. Fluid design changes and a high rate of production are mutually exclusive."
45. Address of Brig. Gen. H. H. Arnold, chief of the Air Corps, U.S. Army, before the National Aviation Forum, Washington, D.C., 20 February 1939, Eaker papers, L/C, Box 38, 6.
46. Address of Maj. Gen. H. H. Arnold at the Army Industrial College, Washington, D.C., 24 February 1940, USAF/HRA, 168.3952-119, 2.
47. FDR, "Fifty Thousand Airplanes," message to a joint session of Congress, 16 May 1940. Reprinted in Eugene M. Emme's, *The Impact of Airpower: National Security and World Politics* (Princeton, N.J.: D. Van Nostrand, 1959), 69–72.
48. Gen. Lauris Norstad, USAF/OHI, K239.0512-1116, Maxwell AFB, Ala., USAF/HRA.
49. Ibid. By 1944, the United States was producing more than 120,000 airplanes per year. It is unclear whether Arnold intended to fight the war with 100,000 airplanes, or whether he meant that number as a yearly target. Nonetheless, the number was relayed to FDR.
50. HHA, *Global Mission* (draft), 56½.
51. HHA, "The New Army Air Force," typed manuscript, for *Army Magazine,* 29 July 1940, USAF/HRA, 168.3952-122, 1939–40. For a more detailed look at the lessons that might have been learned after the First World War, see Holley, *Ideas and Weapons,* chap. 9.
52. Brig. Gen. Eugene H. Beebe, interviewed by Murray Green, Long Beach, Calif., 1 October 1969, transcript in MGC, roll 26, page 3.
53. HHA to EPA, 12 December 1939, Portland, Oreg., RAC.
54. Beebe, 1 October 1969, MGC, roll 26, pages 3, 7.
55. Quoted in Craven and Cate, *Army Air Forces in World War II,* vol. 6, 13.
56. HHA, "Men Fly, Not Planes," 20 July 1940, USAF/HRA, 168.3952-122.
57. Craven and Cate, *Army Air Forces in World War II,* vol. 6, 26–32.
58. HHA to EPA, March and April 1945, Miami, Fla., RAC.
59. HHA, *Global Mission* (draft), 71. The published version of *Global Mission* omits the reference to Lovett individually and mentions only the Stimson, Marshall, Lovett team.
60. Robert A. Lovett, 1–15 January 1959, CUOHI, 12. Such a relationship between the secretary of the Air Force and the Air Force chief of staff has been rare in the short history of the service. Although neither Lovett nor Arnold were officially the secretary or chief of staff, they acted as such from 1940 until 1945.
61. Jonathan Foster Fanton, "Robert A. Lovett: The War Years," Ph.D. dissertation, Yale University (Ann Arbor, Mich.: University Microfilm International, 1978). The summary of Lovett's contribution is detailed, but the work lacks comparison to the preexisting condi-

tions and philosophy that were prevalent in the Air Corps prior to Lovett's arrival as air secretary. Because of this, the dissertation tends to credit Lovett with the creation of ideas rather than simply the support of ideas that already existed.

62. Lovett, CUOHI, 14, 19.
63. Ibid., 20–21.
64. Beebe, 1 October 1969, MGC.
65. HHA to Andrews, 22 January 1941, Andrews papers, L/C, Box 1, Corr. "A."
66. Fanton, "Robert A. Lovett: The War Years," 62.
67. Beebe, 1 October 1969, MGC, roll 26, page 16.
68. HHA, *Global Mission* (draft), 71.
69. Lovett, CUOHI, 18. Orders from France and Britain also bolstered industrial confidence.
70. HHA to EPA, 11 April 1941 (Good Friday), en route to London, RAC. A passenger list was included with this letter, as well as a personal telegram of greeting from Juan Trippe, Pan Am president.
71. Durand to Bush, 10 May 1941, and Bush to HHA, 27 May 1941, HHA/LC (declassified for this work by NASA). The story of why the United States did not develop the jet engine earlier may be traced to the nation's tendency toward utilitarian uses for science. The story, a fascinating study in the evolution of American science, is expertly covered in Edward W. Constant II's *The Origins of the Turbojet Revolution* (Baltimore: Johns Hopkins University Press, 1980). For the nuts and bolts of the Air Corps's delay, see Irving B. Holley, "Jet Lag in the Army Air Corps," in Harry R. Borowski, ed., *Military Planning in the Twentieth Century: Proceedings of the Eleventh Military History Symposium, USAF Academy, 1984* (Washington, D.C.: Office of Air Force History, 1986), 123–54.
72. Charles Portal to HHA, 23 April 1941, London, RAC.
73. John F. Victory, oral interview no. 210A, October 1962, USAF Academy Oral History Interviews, USAF Academy, Colo. Victory was the first employee of the NACA in 1915 and served as secretary throughout the period of this study.
74. Victory, oral interview, USAF Academy. Essentially Lewis sat at his desk in Washington and strictly adhered to the "advisory mission" of NACA. It was rare that the NACA offered to expedite research or offer data without first being asked by the Army Air Corps. Arnold certainly saw this attitude as an obstacle to rapidly expanding the size and balanced capability of the air arm. See Hugh L. Dryden, USAF/HRA, K146.34-41, 23. Dr. Dryden substantiates the basis of the 500-mph story.
75. Bush to Hunsaker, 10 March 1941, Bush papers, L/C, Box 53, Hunsaker folder. It is not clear whether Arnold asked for the formation of these engine committees based upon requests from Wright Field and Ezra Kotcher, but it seems that there must have been some type of impetus to start the research, since the committee was formed before Arnold's trip to England in April.
76. Maj. Gen. Frank Carroll, interviewed by Murray Green, Boulder, Colo., 1 September 1971, transcript in MGC, roll 12. See also James O. Young, "Riding England's Coattails: The U.S. Army Air Forces and the Turbojet Revolution," typed manuscript (photocopy), Edwards AFB, Calif.: Air Force Flight Test Center History Office, 1995.
77. Maj. Gen. Donald J. Keirn, interviewed by Murray Green, Delaplane, Va., 25 September 1970, transcript in MGC, roll l2. Keirn proves that there were two separate engine projects at General Electric at the same time. See Roland, *Model Research,* for Durand Committee discussion; see also Walker and Wickam, *From Huffman Prairie to the Moon,* 254.
78. Gen. Benjamin Chidlaw, interviewed by Murray Green, Colorado Springs, 12 December 1969, transcript in MGC, roll 12. The question of why the United States was so late entering the jet age is expertly examined in Constant, *Origins of the Turbojet Revolution,* 150–75 in particular. He cites the American tradition of empiricism as the reason that "radical" technologies were not produced before they were in more theoretically oriented countries, such as Germany and England.

The NACA and Wright Field, since the mid-1920s, anyway, had succumbed to the lure of utility above the necessity of theoretical understanding. Kármán, trained in the German style, would ensure that Air Force research never entirely followed the same path.

79. "Performance and Development Trends in Military Aircraft and Accessories," speech given by Maj. Gen. H. H. Arnold before the Society of Automotive Engineers, Detroit, Michigan, 11 January 1939, 14.
80. Young, "Riding England's Coattails," 12.
81. Laurence S. Kuter, "How Hap Built the AAF," *Air Force Magazine,* September 1973, 88–93.
82. F. W. Conant, 20 March 1959, CUOHI. Conant worked for Donald Douglas during this period.
83. HHA, speech to last WASP graduating class, 7 December 1944, RAC. See also HHA, *Global Mission* (draft), 130½.

10. COMMANDING GENERAL, ARMY AIR FORCES

1. Craven and Cate, *Army Air Forces in World War II,* vol. 1, 115.
2. Ibid., vol. 6, 24–25. In an undated letter, Arnold called the trip to Placentia Bay his first experience in the big leagues. See also Coffey, *Hap,* 220.
3. HHA, *Global Mission* (draft), 100.
4. Mrs. H. H. Arnold, MCG, 22 August 1970, 7. In this interview Bee also said, "Hap knew something." What she meant by that was never explained, but it does raise the question of what the high-level staffs really knew about Japanese fleet movement at this stage of the war.
5. Beebe, 1 October 1969, MGC, roll 26, pages 1–2.
6. Ibid., 2–3.
7. Ibid., 29.
8. Ibid., 7, pt. 2.
9. Ibid.; HHA, *Global Mission* (draft), 100. In an unofficial form of Lend- Lease, it had been secretary of the treasury Henry Morganthau's insistence on allowing a Frenchman to fly an Air Corps experimental airplane before the United States had actually entered the war that almost resulted in another exile from Washington—to Guam, this time. Arnold recounts the unpleasant experience in *Global Mission.*
10. HHA, *Global Mission* (draft), 102½–3.
11. Ibid., 105½–6.
12. Arnold and Eaker, *Winged Warfare,* 140–65.
13. Testimony of Gen. H. H. Arnold before a House Armed Service Subcommittee relative to the B-36 type aircraft, 19 August 1949, San Francisco, RAC.
14. James H. Doolittle with Carroll V. Glines, *I Could Never Be So Lucky Again* (New York: Bantam Books, 1991), 230–88. The best account of the planning and execution of the raid is found in this autobiography. See also HHA, *Global Mission* (draft), 109–109½.
15. The Doolittle raid did not follow any precision-bombing doctrine, nor was it intended to do so. The purpose of the raid was to fulfill political desires. This attack was one directed against Japanese morale and, as such, it violated the Army Air Forces' policy of attacking military-industrial targets. The removal of Norden bombsights from the B-25s to protect the secret technology was another tangential indicator of the real purpose of such a mission. The Norden sight allowed the greatest precision then possible during high-altitude bombing. It included wind drift and other variables in its computating. On the other hand, the strategic impact of the raid, despite the fact that it violated doctrine, was undeniable.
16. Arnold and Eaker, *Winged Warfare,* 104–5. Although it is unlikely that Napoleon ever "reiterated" anything that Clausewitz wrote, the quote is well intended to make a point about the importance of structure and organization.
17. HHA to EPA, 5 February 1945, Miami, Fla., RAC.

18. Craven and Cate, *Army Air Forces in World War II,* vol. 6, 28–29. This section of the official history contains the best overall discussion of the evolution of the AAF administrative staff during the war, and it should be consulted as a starting point by any student interested in the institutional evolution of the Air Force.

19. HHA, *Global Mission* (draft), 106½–7. In Craven and Cate, *Army Air Forces in World War II,* vol. 6, 152–53, Weaver is said to have remarked, "the best hotel room is none too good for the American soldier." This quote originated some months after his initial staff meeting with General Arnold.

20. Ira C. Eaker, "Memories of Six Air Chiefs," *Aerospace Historian,* December 1973, 188–96.

21. Beebe, 1 October 1969, MGC; Parton, *"Air Force Spoken Here."*

22. HHA to EPA, March 1945, Miami, Fla., RAC.

23. Lt. Gen. Donald L. Putt, oral interview by James C. Hasdorff, Atherton, Calif., 1–3 April 1974, USAF Academy Oral History Interviews, 24; see also Head, *Every Inch a Soldier.*

24. HHA to Eaker, 8 August 43, Eaker papers, L/C, Box 50. This philosophy carried over into his directions to Kármán's mission in the fall of 1944; HHA to Eaker, 16 October 43, Eaker papers, L/C, Box 50. In this letter, Arnold offered direct instructions on how to fly formations, as well as on fuse settings, bomb sizes, and targeting.

25. Williamson Murray, "The Air War in Europe," 1998, 23.

26. For charting the exploits of the U-boats, as well as an overview of merchant ships sent to the bottom of the Atlantic Ocean and the Gulf of Mexico, see Craven and Cate, *Army Air Forces in World War II,* vol. 1, 516–17.

27. Craven and Cate, *Army Air Forces in World War II,* vol. 1, 514–19; see also Nathan Miller, *War at Sea: A Naval History of World War II* (New York: Scribners, 1995).

28. Craven and Cate, *Army Air Forces in World War II,* vol. 1, 519. The antisubmarine story is covered in two locations in Craven and Cate: vol. 1, chap. 15, 515–53; and vol. 2, chap. 12, 377–411.

29. Craven and Cate, *Army Air Forces in World War II,* vol. 1, 550.

30. The multi-cavity magnetron that made shortwave radar practical was a British invention.

31. Arnold and Eaker, *Winged Warfare,* dedication.

32. HHA to Spaatz, 9 November 1946, Spaatz papers, L/C, Box 256. Stimson diaries, 1 April 1942, in MGC, roll 12, documents Bowles's assignment as special consultant. Spaatz to HHA, 1 September 1944, and HHA to Spaatz, 12 September 1944, MGC, roll 12; HHA to Westover, 18 May 1937, MGC, roll 12.

33. The Bion Arnold Report, "F. B." at USAF/HRA, microfilm, Maxwell AFB, Ala.

34. "Glide Bombs," USAF/HRA, 202.4-1, V.7, 1941–1945. Interestingly, Elmer Sperry and Charles Kettering had argued over who had officially invented the Bug during their first collaboration. Sperry's working relationship with "Ket" deteriorated until Sperry finally quit the project in 1919.

35. "Glide Bombs," USAF/HRA, 202.4-1, V.7, 1941–1945. This folder contains a variety of documents covering all aspects of the GB-1 thru GB-8 program.

36. Conferences listed by their most common code names, places, and dates.

Argentia	Placentia Bay	August 1941
Arcadia	D.C.	December 1941–January 1942
Symbol	Casablanca	January 1943
Trident	D.C.	May 1943 (Arnold not there: heart attack)
Quadrant	Quebec	August 1943
Sextant	Cairo	November–December 1943
Eureka	Tehran	November 1943
Octagon	Quebec	September 1944
Argonaut	Yalta	February 1945 (Arnold not there: heart attack)
Terminal	Potsdam	July–August 1945

For a detailed examination of Argentia, see Theodore A. Wilson, *The First Summit: Roo-*

sevelt and Churchill at Placentia Bay, 1941 (Lawrence, Kans.: University Press of Kansas, rev. ed., 1991). For Potsdam, see Charles L. Mee Jr., *Meeting at Potsdam* (New York: M. Evans, 1975).

37. Adm. Ernest J. King, "Second Official Report to the Secretary of the Navy, 1 March 1944 to 1 March 1945," in Millis, ed., *The War Reports,* 571.

38. Arnold's trip diaries, available at the L/C and at the USAF Academy Library, shed some personal insight on the proceedings.

39. Interview with Gen. Jacob E. Smart conducted by author, Arlington, Va., 31 May 1997. General Smart recently published his personal recollections of the meeting in an article, "The Casablanca Conference, January 1943," *Air Power History* 46, no. 3: 36–43.

40. HHA to EPA, 16 January 1943, Casablanca, RAC.

41. Jacob E. Smart interview with author, 1997; see also HHA, *Global Mission* (draft), 144½.

42. Craven and Cate, *Army Air Forces in World War II,* vol. 2, 301–2. This section contains a clear discussion of "The Casablanca Directive"; see 274–307.

43. For Torch Operations, see George F. Howe, *Northwest Africa: Seizing the Initiative in the West* (Washington, D.C.: Center of Military History, United States Army, 1991).

44. Craven and Cate, *Army Air Forces in World War II,* vol. 2, 302–3.

45. HHA, *Global Mission* (draft), 145; see also Parton, *"Air Force Spoken Here,"* 222.

46. Craven and Cate, *Army Air Forces in World War II,* vol. 2, 278.

47. Ibid., vol. 6, 21.

48. The Air Corps Tactical School has been teaching the concept of strategic bombardment since the mid-1930s. This doctrine was the manifestation of several airpower theorists. See Peter R. Faber, "Interwar U.S. Army Aviation and the Air Corps Tactical School: Incubators of American Airpower," in Phillip Meilinger, ed., *The Paths of Heaven: The Evolution of Airpower Theory* (Maxwell AFB, Ala.: Air University Press, 1997), 183–238. Even as early as 1921, Major Kilner had written about strategic air operations in *U.S. Air Service* magazine.

49. HHA to EPA, 18 January 1943, Casablanca, RAC. In this letter, Arnold told Bee that he and Tuey shared a room, and that he and Andrews had conferred during the conference concerning important topics.

50. Sir John Slessor, *The Central Blue: The Autobiography of Sir John Slessor, Marshal of the RAF* (New York: Frederick A. Praeger, 1957), 326.

51. Craven and Cate, *Army Air Forces in World War II,* vol. 2, 305.

52. Memo from FDR to George Marshall, 24 August 1942, cited in Craven and Cate, *Army Air Forces in World War II,* vol. 2, 277.

53. Craven and Cate, *Army Air Forces in World War II,* vol. 3, xxviii. There are many occasions in speeches and memos in which Arnold, in various terms, voiced this order.

54. "Glide Bombs," USAF/HRA, 202.4-1, V.7, 1941–1945.

55. HHA to Andrews, 29 March 1943, Andrews papers, L/C, Box 1, Corr. "A." For a brief summary of Andrews's career, see DeWitt S. Copp's "Frank M. Andrews: Marshall's Airman," in John L. Frisbee, ed., *Makers of the United States Air Force* (Washington, D.C.: Office of Air Force History, 1987), 43–72.

56. Copp, "Frank M. Andrews: Marshall's Airman," 43.

57. Craven and Cate, *Army Air Forces in World War II,* vol. 2, 307.

58. HHA to Marshall, 10 May 1943, Washington, D.C., RAC.

59. HHA, *Global Mission* (draft), 163.

60. HHA to Marshall, 10 May 1943, Washington, D.C., RAC.

61. Jacob E. Smart interview with author, 1997.

62. Craven and Cate, *Army Air Forces in World War II,* vol. 2, 373.

63. Richard P. Hallion interview with author, 1995. At the time of the interview, Dr. Hallion was the official Air Force historian.

64. Craven and Cate, *Army Air Forces in World War II,* vol. 6, 32–33.

65. The facts in this paragraph have been compiled from a number of references: Craven and Cate, *Army Air Forces in World War II*, vol. 6, 32–33; Maurer, *Aviation in the U.S. Army*, 436–37; and John Ellis, *Brute Force: Allied Strategy and Tactics in the Second World War* (New York: Viking Press, 1990), which includes numerous charts and tables throughout the work.

66. The aircraft industry, at Donald Douglas's behest, assembled a book of photographs, each personalized for General Arnold, after the successful end to the war. All major aircraft builders were included at their own request. RAC.

67. Jacob Smart, AFOHI, 48.

68. A. D. Chandler, ed. *The Papers of Dwight David Eisenhower: The War Years,* vol. 3 (Baltimore: Johns Hopkins University Press, 1970), 1,677.

69. Coffey, *Hap,* 527–28. From personal letters.

70. HHA to Kettering, 3 November 1939, reprinted in MGC, folder 6.38. This letter marked the beginning of controllable missile development that included powered and nonpowered bombs and missiles of all kinds. See HHA to Spaatz, n.d., in MGC, from Spaatz papers, L/C, Box 8, record MM: "Obviously, this is an area weapon," Arnold wrote. See also memo from Brig. Gen. Oscar Anderson to George Stratemeyer, 2 April 1943, in MGC, Arnold papers, Box 137; Craven and Cate, *Army Air Forces in World War II,* vol. 6, 253–62; and "Glide Bombs," USAF/HRA, 202.4-1, V.7, 1941–1945.

71. "Glide Bombs," USAF/HRA, 202.4-1, V.7, 1941–1945.

72. Jack Olsen, *Aphrodite: Desperate Mission* (New York: G. P. Putnam's Sons, 1970), 96–101.

73. Aphrodite File, USAF/HRA, 527.431A-21, V.2, 1944–1945; Olsen, *Aphrodite,* 96–101. Also killed in an Aphrodite aircraft was Lt. Joseph Kennedy. His was one that just vaporized in midair for no apparent reason. See Hank Searls, *The Lost Prince: Young Joe, The Forgotten Kennedy* (New York: World Publishing Company, 1969).

74. DDE to GCM, 19 June 1944, and DDE to Arthur W. Tedder, 18 June 1944, in Chandler, ed. *The Papers of Dwight David Eisenhower*, vol. 3, 1,933 1,936.

75. "Glide Bombs," USAF/HRA, 202.4-1, V.7, 1941–1945.

76. Lt. Gen. Henry Viccellio, interviewed by Murray Green, San Antonio, Tex., 13 May 1970, transcript in MGC, roll 36; HHA to Kenney, 25 October 1944, L/C; HHA's war diary, October 1944–December 1945, L/C. For a summary of Crossbow and Allied countermeasures, see Craven and Cate, *Army Air Forces in World War II,* vol. 3, 525–46.

77. Lt. Gen. Fred Dean, interviewed by Murray Green, Hilton Head, S.C., 20 February 1973, transcript in MGC, roll 12; HHA to Spaatz, 22 November 1944, reprinted in MGC, roll 12.

78. Arnold staff memo, 2 November 1944, HHA/LC, Arnold papers, Box 44; HHA to Spaatz, 22 November 1944, MGC, roll 12. Weary Willy aircraft were flown to the enemy battle lines, then the pilot transferred control to a "mother" control airplane and bailed out in friendly territory. Willy Orphan was totally radio-controlled and was remotely launched and guided into enemy territory, sometimes from a mother ship that followed it to enemy territory. Aphrodite was also totally radio controlled, normally from the ground.

79. HHA, Bowles, Ridenour, phone transcript, 9 August 1944, MGC, roll 12.

80. The circular error probable (CEP) for bombs dropped in World War II during American daylight missions was 3,200 feet for a 2,000-pound bomb. During Desert Storm, CEP for the same size bomb using precision guidance was 3 meters for more than 80 percent of the bombs dropped. Richard P. Hallion interview with author, 1995.

81. "Glide Bombs," USAF/HRA, 202.4-1, V.7, 1941–1945.

82. Spaatz to Doolittle, 27 January 1945, Aphrodite File, USAF/HRA, 527.431A, V.1, 1944.

83. Roland, *Model Research,* 192. Arnold did not give up on NACA altogether. In 1944 he pressured Donald Marr Nelson to push the construction of the Jet Engine Facility in Cleveland, Ohio. This facility became the test center for engines that Arnold had once kept secret

from the NACA in earlier years. Ironically the facility was named after George Lewis, the research director whom Arnold and Kármán distrusted.

84. Grandison Gardner, 9 March 1959, CUOHI, 11–13, 33. Gardner refers to Arnold's hesitation to use Wright Field engineers for important projects. Tactical research was even taken away from Wright Field and moved to Eglin AFB under command of Gardner for this very reason. See also Putt, oral interview, USAF Academy.

85. Maj. Gen. Donald J. Keirn, 25 September 1970, MGC, roll 12.

86. Several of the original scientists on the Scientific Advisory Group suggested that Arnold and Bush never got along.

87. Edward L. Bowles to Murray Green, 11 August 1971, Wellesley Hills, Mass., MGC.

88. Vannevar Bush, "Organization of Defense Research," as sent to Harry Hopkins, 3 March 1941, Bush papers, L/C, General Correspondence, Box 51, H. Hopkins folder. Vannevar Bush had been involved in conflicts with the military services before. Specifically, he had butted heads with naval Vice Adm. Harold G. Bowen and, in that case, had forced Bowen's removal from his position. Harvey M. Saplosky, *Science and the Navy: The History of the Office of Naval Research* (Princeton, N.J.: Princeton University Press, 1990), 17–18.

89. Vannevar Bush, "Research and the War Effort," speech to the American Institute of Electrical Engineers, New York, 26 January 1943, Bush papers, L/C, General Correspondence, Box 174.

90. Jerome Hunsaker to Vannevar Bush, 24 March 1942, Bush Papers, General Correspondence, Box 53.

91. Marshall to HHA and Gen. Brehon B. Somervell, Army Services of Supply commander, 26 July 1944, MGC, roll 12.

92. Gen. Bernard Schriever interview with author, 1994.

93. Ivan Getting interview with author, 1994. Dr. Getting believed that Arnold had consulted Dr. Edward Bowles before deciding upon Kármán to head the SAG. Arnold respected Bowles's opinion and had been impressed by his work on the SADU. He trusted his views on the direction for science and technology for the Air Force.

94. Dr. Robert Millikan to HHA, 5 September 1945, MGC, roll 12.

95. Kármán medical records, folder 152.3, Caltech Archives, Beckman Center, Pasadena, Calif.; William Rees Sears interview with author, 1995; F. W. Thomas to Kármán, 19 May 1944, folder 73.6, Caltech Archives; C. Millikan to Kármán, 18 July 1944, folder 73.6, Caltech Archives; R. Millikan to HHA, 3 August 1944, folder 16.19, Millikan Collection, Caltech Archives. Additionally see Kármán and Edson, *Wind and Beyond*, 267–70; Kármán, oral interview, Indiana University special collections; HHA, *Global Mission*, 532; and Thomas A. Sturm, *The USAF Scientific Advisory Board: Its First Twenty Years, 1944–1964* (Washington, D.C.: USAF Historical Division Liaison Office, 1967), 3–4.

   In May 1944, Kármán had been advised that surgery was required for a nagging stomach ailment (he called it a carcinoma in his autobiography). The trouble had evidently started in the summer of 1941, and he visited the Mayo Clinic. By mid-July 1944, the surgery had been completed and Kármán was recuperating at the Westbury Hotel, New York City. He felt well enough to ask Clark Millikan for information on continuing programs at the GALCIT. According to Dr. Robert Millikan, Kármán was supposed to be at a "sanitarium" near Bolton Landing, Lake George, New York, for a month's recuperation, but he was never there for more than two weeks at a time.

96. Telegram from HHA to Theodore von Kármán, 4 August 1944, Lake George, N.Y., HHA/LC, Kármán folder. Arnold's secretaries addressed Kármán as Carmen, Professor Kármán, or Mr. Kármán.

97. Radiogram from Theodore von Kármán to HHA, 5 August 1944, HHA/LC, Kármán folder.

98. Arnold's office log, normally full each day he was in Washington, was mysteriously void on

7 August. Normally, on days when Arnold was unavailable, Ms. Adkins made annotations as to who came to visit and why. This Monday, nothing was entered in the log. This evidence supports the conclusion that Arnold had taken a secret trip to meet with the professor on 7 August.

99. Beebe, 1 October 1969, MGC. It was obviously sometime in early August that Arnold met with Kármán to discuss the foundations of the Scientific Advisory Group, not in September, as has generally been thought.

This exchange is significant for two reasons. First, Kármán's response indicates that he was well enough to meet Arnold at any time after Sunday, 6 August 1944, and that he had, in fact, planned a visit to Washington during the coming week. Secondly, from 5 August on, Kármán was in New York City at the Westbury Hotel. This address change was underlined on the radiogram received by Arnold's office.

All accounts refer to a cool, windy day at the airport on the date of the meeting. Weather reports in the *New York Times* show that a cold front passed LaGuardia on the eve of 6 August (national weather service maps from *New York Times*). It appears that Arnold wasted no time in acting on Kármán's reply. Early Monday, the temperature was a cool 73 degrees. In fact, it was front-page news as a welcome break from a sweltering heatwave. Tuesday, 8 August, it was even cooler—70 degrees in the morning—but got warmer during the day. The winds were not as strong that day, either. Arnold likely just picked up and flew to LaGuardia to meet with Kármán; it would have meant only a morning out of the office. Although other frontal passages occurred in September, Arnold was on his way to Maine by the ninth to celebrate his anniversary with Bee, before departing for Octagon in Quebec, 11–16 September. There is no mention of the LaGuardia meeting in Arnold's Octagon trip log. It is true that Kármán's autobiography, *The Wind and Beyond,* specifically states that he met Arnold in September, p. 268. The same page specifically states that he moved to Washington in December, yet Kármán wrote a letter to William Sears addressed from Washington, D.C., on 30 September 1944. Twenty years after the fact, a few months may not have been too important.

100. Coffey, *Hap.* Much of Coffey's personal correspondence is quoted in his book, but none is available to researchers. Much has been substantiated by still-living Arnold family members.

101. Kármán and Edson, *Wind and Beyond,* 268. Also see weather analysis in the previous note.

102. Overy, *Why the Allies Won,* 124–25. Includes a brief summary of the tonnage dropped over Germany.

103. Stephen E. Ambrose, *The Supreme Commander: The War Years of General Dwight D. Eisenhower* (New York: Doubleday, 1969), 314.

104. Stephen L. McFarland and Wesley P. Newton, *To Command the Sky: The Battle for Air Superiority over Germany, 1942–1944* (Washington, D.C.: Smithsonian Institution Press, 1991), 113–15, 139–40.

105. Davis, *Carl A. Spaatz and the Air War in Europe,* 63–64.

106. Testimony of Gen. H. H. Arnold before a House Armed Service Subcommittee relative to the B-36 type aircraft, 19 August 1949, San Francisco, RAC.

107. Durand to Bush, 10 May 1941, and Bush to HHA, 27 May 1941, HHA/LC classified folder (declassified for this work by NASA).

108. Brig. Gen. Godfrey McHugh, interviewed by Murray Green, Washington, D.C., 21 April 1970, transcript in MGC, roll 33; Colonel Lyon to HHA, September 1941, in MGC, HHA/LC, Box 43; Maj. Gen. Frank Carroll, 1 September 1971, MGC, roll 12. In HHA interview with T. A. Boyd, range emerged as a major factor in determining which weapons or aircraft to build. The problems for Germany, at least in home defense, did not involve worries about range. See also Daniel Ford, "Gentlemen, I Give You the Whittle Engine," *Air and Space,* October–November 1992, 88–98.

109. Lt. Gen. Laurence Craigie (USAF, ret.), interviewed by Murray Green, Burbank, Calif., 19 August 1970, transcript in MGC, roll 12. Additional information on the Whittle can be found in the HHA/LC, Box 47. Walt Bonney, representing Bell Aircraft Corporation, was tasked to answer a flood of calls after the *Washington Post* story was released on 7 January 1944. In his press release, he emphasized the total secrecy of the project beginning in September 1941. Bonney did write a brief history of jet propulsion to placate the mass inquiries, but the secret nature of jet propulsion was protected. Walt Bonney, Bell Aircraft Corporation, 11 January 1944, NASM Archives, Jet Propulsion folder. Arnold's "Second Report of the Commanding General of the Army Air Forces to the Secretary of War," 27 February 1945, USAF/HRA, 168.03, tells the story from his perspective: "Never has a plane been built in this country under greater secrecy," 76. See also Young, "Riding England's Coattails"; and Kotcher, "Our Jet Propelled Fighter," 6–8, 64.

110. Walker and Wickam, *From Huffman Prairie to the Moon,* 254.

111. Craigie, 19 August 1970, MGC, roll 12. Gen. Franklin Carroll (USAF, ret.), interviewed by Murray Green, 1 September 1972, MGC, roll 26. In *Army Air Forces in World War II,* Craven and Cate mistakenly state that Craigie was first to fly the jet. See also Ford, "Gentlemen, I Give You the Whittle Engine."

112. Bilstein, *Orders of Magnitude,* 31–48; Roland, *Model Research,* 191–92; Dryden, CUOHI.

113. *Washington Post,* 7 January 1944, 1.

114. L. Craigie, interviewed for Wingspan Network, Washington, D.C., shown 20 June 98.

115. Curtis E. LeMay with MacKinlay Kantor, *Mission with LeMay: My Story* (Garden City: Doubleday, 1965), 321–24.

116. Testimony of Gen. H. H. Arnold before a House Armed Service Subcommittee relative to the B-36 type aircraft, 19 August 1949, San Francisco, RAC. For an excellent summary of the early history of the B-29 Superfortress, see Kenneth P. Werrell's *Blankets of Fire: U.S. Bombers Over Japan During World War II* (Washington, D.C.: Smithsonian Institution Press, 1996), 56–83.

117. LeMay with Kantor, *Mission with LeMay,* 321–22.

118. Craven and Cate, *Army Air Forces in World War II,* vol. 6, 218–19.

119. Kármán and Edson, *Wind and Beyond,* 267–68. Millikan to Knudsen, 3 October 1944, Robert Millikan papers, Caltech Archives.

120. HHA to Spaatz, 6 December 1945, and HHA to Eaker, 22 May 1945, MGC, roll 12; Craven and Cate, *Army Air Forces in World War II,* vol. 6, 234; Sturm, *The USAF Scientific Advisory Board,* 37.

121. HHA, *Global Mission* (draft), 196; reinforced by a cable sent to Spaatz after the war was nearing completion, 15 April 1945, MGC.

122. On 25 October, in a reply to a letter from Lt. Gen. George Kenney concerning future planning, Hap detailed more than thirty specific actions pertaining to aircraft production and design, but he did not mention the Kármán project that had already been initiated. Hap added only a brief clue in a postscript: "There is still more that is being prepared now but will not be actuated until the Post-War Period." On 9 November 1944, Hap Arnold spoke to the NACA Aeronautical Research Laboratory, where he cryptically told the gathering of scientists and engineers that when the AAF got stuck in a development problem or when looking toward the future of aeronautics, "normally we go to the NACA and ask you people to do that work for us." But Arnold would not go to the NACA this time.

123. Kármán to Millikan, 2 October 1944, folder 20.28, Caltech Archives.

124. Brig. Gen. F. O. Carroll, chief, Engineering Division, Wright Field, to R. Millikan, 12 September 1944, confirmation on 29 September via Western Union, folder 16.19, Millikan Collection, Caltech Archives.

125. In reality it was these very issues, particularly the element of private profit arising from military investment, that defined the Military-Industrial (and also Academic) Complex that

Aerojet General represented. Although it was not until two decades later that the term was officially used for the first time, the existence of the Military-Industrial complex as early as the 1940s was undeniable.

126. HHA to Kármán, 7 November 1944, Washington, D.C., U.S. Air Force Scientific Advisory Board, Pentagon (USAF/SB), 1944–45 file.

127. Kármán's first report for the SAG, 23 November 1944, USAF/SB; Gorn, *Universal Man,* 99–100; HHA to Kármán, 7 November 1944, USAF/SB.

11. GENERAL OF THE ARMY

1. Kármán, oral interview, Indiana University; and T. F. Walkowicz, "Von Kármán's Singular Contributions to Aerospace Power," *Air Force Magazine,* May 1981, 60–61; Gorn, *Universal Man,* 47.

2. Interview with Dr. Robert Alvus conducted by author, Fairfax, Va., 29 June 1998. Dr. Alvus is a coronary surgeon in the Washington, D.C., area and a retired Army officer. Diagnostic techniques in the 1940s were simple, and family history, diet, habits, and lifestyle were not considered. Addtionally, there was very little equipment capable of pinpointing specificities of the disease. It is difficult to pinpoint precisely the dates for Arnold's heart problems. His concern about how any serious malady might affect his career prevented official documentation of the events.

3. Beebe, 12 August 1970, MGC, roll 26, page 51; Mrs. H. H. Arnold, 22 August 1970, MGC, pages 18–19. The Air Forces' surgeon general, Dr. Dave Grant, also visited Arnold that first night, but Lee Martin was the acting physician.

4. Mrs. H. H. Arnold, 22 August 1970, MGC, page 18.

5. Beebe, 12 August 1970, MGC, roll 26, pages 53–55; see also Mrs. H. H. Arnold, 11 March 1970, MGC, page 2.

6. Interview with Mrs. Mary Streett conducted by author, Arlington, Va., 21 May 1997.

7. Ibid.

8. Mrs. H. H. Arnold, 11 March 1970, MGC, pages 2–6.

9. Mrs. Mary Streett interview with author, 1997.

10. HHA to EPA, 2 and 6 February 1945, Miami, Fla., RAC; HHA to Marshall, 22 March 1945, Miami, Fla., RAC.

11. HHA to EPA, 5 February 1945, Miami, Fla.

12. Lovett to Eaker, 28 January 1945, Eaker papers, L/C.

13. HHA to Lois Snowden, 22 February 1945, MGC.

14. HHA to EPA, 5 February 1945, Miami, Fla., RAC.

15. Ibid., 8 February 1945.

16. Ibid., 8, 9, 10 March 1945.

17. Ibid., 12 March 1945. Arnold's letters were carried back and forth to Washington daily by official courier.

18. HHA to EPA, 14 March 1945, Miami, Fla., RAC.

19. Ibid., 8 February 1945.

20. HHA to Betty, 31 March 1945, Washington, D.C., RAC; Parton, *"Air Force Spoken Here,"* 432–33.

21. HHA to EPA, 3 April 1945, Paris, RAC.

22. Ibid., 4 April 1945.

23. Ibid., 5 April 1945. Sheffields remarks were included in Hap's letter home.

24. HHA to EPA, 6, 11 April 1945, Paris, RAC. Additionally, Hank Pool, Bee's nephew, met up with the Arnolds in Paris. General Arnold gave the boys fifty dollars and sent them out on the town, a pleasure they both enjoyed.

25. Hank Arnold to EPA, 6 April 1945, Paris, RAC.

26. HHA to EPA, 14 April 1945, Cannes, RAC.

27. Ibid., 20 April 1945.

28. Kármán, oral interview, USAF Academy; interview with Chester Hasert conducted by author, National Academy of Sciences, Washington D.C., 10 November 1994; also Operation Lusty folder, USAF/HRA. Arnold's heart attack in mid-January did not interfere with the operation of the SAG. He had already given them their marching orders before he was taken ill. He spent the next few months in Florida recuperating, before the SAG investigated European scientific laboratories.

29. Giles to Spaatz, 19 April 1945, folder 90.2, Caltech Archives; Kármán and Edson, *Wind and Beyond*, 272; Gorn, *Universal Man*, 103–5; and Kármán, oral interview, USAF Academy.

30. In a reply to an earlier letter praising radar developments, Arnold wrote to Spaatz on 12 September 1944, affirming his trust in scientists, MGC, roll 12.

31. Interview with H. Guyford Stever conducted by author, Washington, D.C., 18 May 1995.

32. Dryden, CUOHI, 24.

33. Interview with Homer Joe Stewart conducted by author, Palo Alto, Calif., 21 July 1995.

34. H. Guyford Stever interview with author, 1995. Dr. Stever was working with the British RADLAB as part of the MIT exchange team when Lusty operations began. He was attached to Kármán's group in the place of Dr. L. DuBridge, who was unavailable. Stever was chairman of the SAB from 1962 to 1964 and is also a former presidential science adviser.

35. H. Guyford Stever interview with author, 1995; and Richard P. Hallion interview with author, 1995. See also MGC, roll 12, summary of memo from Kármán to HHA, 30 July 1945, documenting the group's travels to that point.

36. HHA to EPA, 1 May 1945, Pernambuco, Brazil, RAC.

37. HHA, *Global Mission* (draft), 197½–98.

38. HHA to EPA, 8 June 1945, Sobre Vista, Calif., RAC.

39. HHA to EPA, 13 and 17 June 1945, Saipan, RAC.

40. Curtis F. LeMay to HHA, 5 April 1945, Twenty-first Bomber Command HQ, LeMay papers, Box 11, Official Correspondence, L/C. Flexibility is vital in any military success, whether it be intentional or accidental.

41. Official AAF newsreel footage from June 1945, RAC; HHA, *Global Mission* (draft), 208½.

42. Mee, *Meeting at Potsdam*, 85. Arnold's letters home substantiate the dates in Paris.

43. HHA to EPA, 14 July 1945, Potsdam, RAC.

44. Gar Alperovitz, *The Decision to Use the Atomic Bomb, and the Architecture of an American Myth* (New York: Alfred A. Knopf, 1995), parts 5 and 6; see also Mee, *Meeting at Potsdam*, 85; and HHA, *Global Mission*, 219½–20. Arnold deferred targeting decisions and readiness reports to Spaatz, his Pacific commander.

45. Mrs. H. H. Arnold, 22 August 1970, MGC, page 7.

46. Theodore von Kármán, *Where We Stand: First Report to General of the Army H. H. Arnold on Long Range Research Problems of the Air Forces with a Review of German Plans and Developments,* typed manuscript (Wright-Patterson Air Force Base, Ohio: Air Force Materiel Command History Office, 22 August 1945), 1–2. Sturm has summarized the early efforts of the SAG in *The USAF Scientific Advisory Board,* which includes the evolution and decline of the group through 1964. Alan Gropman has nicely summarized the report itself in "Air Force Planning and the Technology Development Planning Process in the Post–World War II Air Force: The First Decade, 1945–1955," in Borowski, ed., *Military Planning in the Twentieth Century,* 154–230.

47. HHA, "Third Report of the Commanding General of the Army Air Forces to the Secretary of War," 12 November 1945, in Millis, ed., *The War Reports,* 462.

48. Kármán, *Where We Stand,* 5.

49. Ibid., 8, 12, 21.

50. Ibid., 75–76.
51. Maj. Gen. Haywood Hansell Jr. to author, 4 October 1979. Although the AAF did accomplish a limited number of area bombing missions in Europe, these were supplemental to precision attacks in almost every case. American doctrine had been clearly spelled out at the Air Corps Tactical School since 1935 as "the full-blown theory of high-level, daylight precision bombardment of pinpoint targets." Eighth Air Force Commander Lt. Gen. Ira C. Eaker was a 1936 ACTS graduate. Robert T. Finney, *History of the Air Corps Tactical School, 1920–1940* (Washington: Center for Air Force History, 1992), 68–70. For an excellent summary of the report, see *The United States Strategic Bombing Surveys, Summary Volume, 30 September 1945* (reprinted by Maxwell AFB: Air University Press, 1987), 34–39.
52. Finney, *History of the Air Corps Tactical School,* 77–79, 83.
53. Jack H. Nunn, "MIT: A University's Contribution to National Defense," *Military Affairs,* October 1979, 120–25. Nunn emphasized a long relationship that MIT carried on with the Navy, also in the radar and aeronautics field. Dr. Ivan Getting, a member of the MIT RADLAB during these years, says that the rivalry is today overplayed. In the 1930s and '40s, travel between East and West in the United States was time-consuming and inconvenient. MIT and Caltech were separated by distance, not by philosophy. Dr. Ivan Getting interview with author, 1994.
54. Theodore von Kármán to Carl A. Spaatz, 9 January 1946, SAB, Pentagon, Washington, D.C., 1946 file.
55. HHA's office logs for December 1945, MGC and HHA/LC; see also Kármán and Edson, *Wind and Beyond,* 290; and Gorn, *Universal Man,* 113–14.
56. Theodore von Kármán, "Science: The Key to Air Supremacy," in *Toward New Horizons* (Washington, D.C.: Scientific Advisory Group, 15 December 1945), 1.3.
57. Kármán, *Toward New Horizons.* Although future attempts were made to repeat the forecast, none made such a monumental impact on the structure or the vision of the U.S. Air Force. The originals of the Kármán report are located in both the Arnold and Spaatz papers in the L/C, as well as at the Air Force Materiel Command Archives at Wright-Patterson AFB, Ohio.
58. A. E. Raymond, 18 March 1959, CUOHI. The actual decision to give Douglas $10 million was made during a meeting in California in which Ted Conant, Donald Douglas, Edward Bowles, and General Arnold were present. See Futrell, *Ideas, Concepts, and Doctrine,* 478; Kármán and Edson, *Wind and Beyond,* 302; Holley, "Jet Lag in the Army Air Corps," in Borowski, ed., *Military Planning in the Twentieth Century,* 167–73. The Ford Foundation began contributing funds for Rand projects in 1948. By 1959, Advanced Research Projects Agency and NASA were also linked to Rand projects. By the mid-1970s, Rand was working on projects for state, local, and private organizations, the Air Force being only a small part of the organization represented by the Rand Project Air Force division. Gen. Lauris Norstad believed that Dr. Edward Bowles had a great deal of influence over Arnold's decision to form Rand. Norstad, interviewed by Murray Green, 15 July 1969, MGC, roll 12.
59. "An Introduction to Project Air Force" (Santa Monica, Calif.: Rand Publication CP-77, June 1990), 1–3.
60. Dr. Courtland Perkins, "Impromptu Remarks Given at the National Academy of Sciences," 10 November 1994, on the occasion of the fiftieth anniversary of the SAB (transcript). Differentiated from the SAB, Rand produced studies and research papers, while the SAB gave direct advice to the Air Force chief of staff. This role was eventually expanded to include the secretary of the Air Force as well.
61. Martin J. Collins, "Internalizing the Civilian: Rand and the Air Force in the Early Cold War," typed manuscript. speech given at the 1993 Annual Society for the History of Technology Meeting; interview with Mrs. Barbara Arnold conducted by author, Washington, D.C., 6 April 1995 (Arnold's son William Bruce married Barbara Douglas); Mr. Robert Arnold to author, 8 April 1999.

62. Described in Futrell, *Ideas, Concepts, Doctrine*, 205, 262 n.68. Arnold frequently referred to missiles as unpiloted craft; the term ICBM had not yet been officially coined.
63. Jacob Neufeld, *Ballistic Missiles in the United States Air Force, 1945–1960* (Washington, D.C.: Office of Air Force History, 1990), 26–27; Futrell, *Ideas, Concepts, and Doctrine*, 239.
64. Neufeld, *Ballistic Missiles*, 28–33, 239; see also Max Rosenberg, *The Air Force and the National Guided Missile Program, 1944–1950* (Washington, D.C.: USAF Historical Division Liaison Office, June 1964), 75–85.
65. Neufeld, *Ballistic Missiles*, 50–56; Dr. I. B. Holley to author, 1 October 1998.
66. HHA to Spaatz, 6 December 1945, MGC, roll 12.
67. HHA to Marshall, 8 November 1945, Washington, D.C., copy in RAC.
68. HHA, *Global Mission* (draft), 216.
69. Sherwood, *Roosevelt and Hopkins*, 931.
70. HHA, *Global Mission* (draft), 223½.
71. Robert E. Kimmel to author, 30 March 1998.

12. HASTEN THE CAISSON

1. HHA to General Spaatz, 6 December 1945, Washington, D.C., copy located in MGC, files 0.00 and 8.99.
2. HHA to General Spaatz, 6 December 1945, Washington, D.C., MGC, roll 12.
3. The issue of flight pay is still alive and well in the modern Air Force. Most recently, pilots for certain critical airplanes were offered bonuses as incentive to remain in military service. The bonus program of the 1980s and 1990s, directed by Congress and implemented by the USAF, has been a dreadful failure. Evidence indicates that forcing young Air Force pilots to choose to accept the aviation bonus (and an additional commitment of years' service) actually forces them out of service rather than allow them to defer a career make-or-break decision. Other divisive issues that have surfaced in the 1990s have been the decision concerning who is authorized to wear leather flying jackets and who is entitled to increased flight pay across the board.
4. HHA to General Spaatz, 6 December 1945, Washington, D.C., MGC.
5. Ibid.
6. HHA, "Air Power for Peace," *National Geographic*, February 1946, 137–94. Arnold also published a chapter titled "Air Force in the Atomic Age" in Dexter Masters and Katharine Way, eds., *One World or None* (New York: McGraw-Hill, 1946). This book consolidated in one volume the views of notables such as Hans Bethe, Leo Szilard, Irving Langmuir, and Robert Oppenheimer concerning the nature of nuclear war.
7. The nickname was not used until after Hap's mother passed away in 1931. See Chapter 8.
8. HHA to Betty, 1 May 1946, Sonoma, Calif., RAC.
9. Ibid.; Mrs. H. H. Arnold, 22 August 1970, MGC, page 6; Mr. Robert Arnold to author, 8 April 1999.
10. HHA to Betty, 1 May 1946, Sonoma, Calif., RAC; Mrs. H. H. Arnold, 11 March 1970, MGC. Bee's account dates their arrival to 2 March 1946. In any event, it was the first week in March.
11. Mrs. H. H. Arnold, 22 August 1970, MGC, page 27.
12. HHA to EPA, 3 June 1946, Bolling AFB, Washington, D.C., RAC; HHA to EPA, 4 June 1946, Newburg, N.Y., RAC.
13. HHA to EPA, 3 June 1946, Bolling AFB, Washington, D.C., RAC.
14. William Bruce Arnold, interviewed by Murray Green at Arnold ranch, Sonoma, 17 August 1974, transcript in MGC, roll 25, page 18.
15. HHA to Spaatz, 6 August 1946, Hamilton Field, Calif., RAC.
16. The rivalry between these services is alive and well, albeit shrouded by a mask of coopera-

tion and unity of purpose. One need look no further than the battle over the Navy's FA-18EF and the Air Force's F-22 fighter to realize that today, national interests are not being served as a result of the compromises made more than fifty years ago.

17. HHA to EPA, 2 June 1946, Hamilton Field, RAC.
18. HHA to Spaatz, 30 July, 1946, Hamilton Field, Spaatz papers, L/C, Box 256, "Chief of Staff."
19. Eisenhower to HHA, 2 July 1946, Washington, D.C., Spaatz papers, L/C, Box 256, "Chief of Staff"; and HHA to Truman, 11 July 1946, Hamilton Field, Spaatz papers, L/C, Box 256, "Chief of Staff."
20. HHA to EPA, 30 October 1946, Sonoma, RAC.
21. HHA, *Global Mission* (draft), 224½–25.
22. HHA, "The Past Predicts the Future," talk given at the I.A.S. Summer Meeting, 19 July 1946, MGC, Edward Bowles folder.
23. HHA, "The Past Predicts the Future."
24. Spaatz to HHA, 5 February 1947, Washington, D.C., Spaatz papers, L/C, Box 256, "Chief of Staff."
25. HHA to EPA, 2 April 1947, Sonoma, RAC.
26. HHA to EPA, various letters in 1946 and 1947, RAC.
27. HHA, *Global Mission* (draft), 224½.
28. HHA to EPA, 5 April 1947, Sonoma, RAC.
29. Mrs. H. H. Arnold, 11 March 1970, MGC, pages 18–19.
30. Message from Stuart Symington and Spaatz to HHA, 18 September 1947, Washington, D.C., and Spaatz to HHA, 28 January 1948, Spaatz papers, L/C, Box 256, "Chief of Staff." See also Crouch, *The Bishop's Boys,* 524.
31. This title is evident on the early drafts of the manuscript located at the Arnold ranch, RAC.
32. Bruce Simmons, oral interview, 7 October 1969, Lusby, Md., USAF Academy Oral History Interviews, USAF Academy, Colo. (copy at RAC), 11.
33. HHA to EPA, 1 and 6 June 1948, Sonoma, RAC.
34. Ibid., 29 May 1949; also HHA to Betty, 13 September 1949, Sonoma, RAC.
35. All family members interviewed (Barbara Arnold, Gay Morris, and Robert Arnold) called *Global Mission* "the book." It was a family joke that has survived the years.
36. HHA to EPA, 21 September 1949, Sonoma, RAC.
37. HHA, "Wildlife in and Near the Valley of the Moon," *National Geographic,* March 1950, 400–14.
38. Mrs. H. H. Arnold, 11 March 1970, MGC, 12.
39. Simmons, oral interview, USAF Academy (copy at RAC), 11.
40. HHA to Honorable Louis Johnson, Secretary of Defense, 11 January 1950, Hamilton, Calif., RAC.
41. HHA, *Global Mission* (draft), 227.
42. Mrs. H. H. Arnold, 11 March 1970, MGC, 15.
43. Ibid.
44. Air Force official announcement, 15 January 1950, RAC.
45. "Defense Chiefs Meet Plane Bringing Body of Arnold Here," *Evening Star,* Washington, D.C., 18 January 1950, A-6. Copy of article located at the National Defense University Archives, Fort Leslie McNair, Washington, D.C., Arnold folder.
46. HHA to Carl A. Spaatz, 19 August 1942, Washington, D.C., MGC.
47. HHA, funeral file, RAC. Newsreel footage and hundreds of newspapers chronicled the funeral in the 20 January editions. The *Washington Post*'s cover story was Arnold's funeral. Over time, Arlington caretakers have planted trees and grasses throughout the cemetery, and their choice for the tree planted immediately beside the now root-covered grave reflects a tremendous irony: a fifty-foot-tall Japanese zelkova tree provides shade to those at rest on that hill.

48. There is no pictorial record that includes Lois at the funeral.
49. HHA to EPA, 8 February 1945, RAC.
50. Lois Arnold to EPA, November 1937, RAC. Lois and Ernie's courtship was remarkably short—six weeks—and Lolie was sure that her father would not approve of her engagement. Ernie's letters often discuss the war and combat, and they show a tremendous concern for the general and Mrs. Arnold.
51. Col. H. H. Arnold Jr., 29–30 August 1972, MGC, roll 25.
52. Unlabeled newspaper articles covering Dave's wedding, RAC.
53. Gay Morris interview with author, 1998.
54. Unlabeled newspaper article on Arnold Engineering and Development Center dedication and United States Air Force Academy dedication, RAC.
55. Robert Arnold interview with author, 1997; "Eleanor P. Arnold, Widow of Air Hero," *Washington Post*, 29 June 1978, obituaries. John Linton Arnold's tombstone is etched on the backside of his mother's stone.
56. Arlington National Cemetery, Section 34. Bruce and Barbara are now buried together in the traditional Arlington style—one headstone—Bruce on one side, Barbara, who died in 1997, on the other.

EPILOGUE

1. HHA to Stefan, 5 November 1947, Air University Library.
2. Ibid.
3. Ibid. "New horizons" is undoubtedly a reference to the scientific study *Toward New Horizons,* which was accomplished by the Scientific Advisory Group in December 1945.
4. Ira C. Eaker, "Memories of Six Chiefs," *Aerospace Historian,* December 1973, 188–96.
5. HHA, *Global Mission* (draft), 227. The last sentence was not added until after the final draft and only appears in the published book on p. 615. Although not yet realized, the U.S. Air Force today is transitioning to an air-and-space force whose ultimate destiny is a space-and-air force. See the official Air Force mission statements since 1996.
6. Theodore von Kármán to HHA, 7 December 1949, folder 1.24, Caltech Archives.
7. HHA to Stefan, 5 November 1947, Air University Library.
8. Ibid.
9. Ibid.
10. Gen. Jacob Smart interview with author, 1997.
11. HHA to Stefan, 5 November 1947, Air University Library.
12. Col. H. H. Arnold, interviewed by Murray Green at Sheridan, Wyoming, 30 August 1973, MGC, roll 25.
13. HHA to Stefan, 5 November 1947, Air University Library.
14. Ibid. There are tens of letters from individuals who, essentially, suggest that Arnold not only was right about the "intangible," but that he had whatever the "intangible" quality was as well. Lauris Norstad referred to Arnold as a "man of spirit—of the spirit." Norstad, USAF/OHI, K239.0512-1116, Maxwell AFB, Ala., USAF/HRA, 553. Others too had many of these characteristics, but Spaatz, Eaker, Marshall, Doolittle, Lovett, Truman, Eisenhower, Millikan, Kármán, and many others echoed Norstad's assessment that Arnold had some unique quality, an intangible trait that was put to use at just the right time. To quote them all would certainly create the appearance of professional hero worship. Yet these letters do exist; they are genuine, and most are handwritten and appear quite sincere.

SELECTED BIBLIOGRAPHY

ABBREVIATIONS USED

CUOHI	Columbia University Oral History Interview
HHA/LC	Arnold Papers, Library of Congress
L/C	Library of Congress
MGC	Hap Arnold Murray Green Collection, USAF Academy Library Special Collections, Colorado Springs
NA	National Archives
NASM	National Air and Space Museum
RAC	Robert Arnold Collection
USAF/HRA	U.S. Air Force Historical Research Agency

MANUSCRIPTS AND ARCHIVAL MATERIAL

Robert Arnold Collection, Sonoma, Calif.
Located at the Arnold ranch is the collection of letters from Hap Arnold to his wife, Bee, as well as paintings, awards, correspondence, and miscellaneous memorabilia. The personal nature of this book is largely the result of access to these valuable letters and artifacts.

California Institute of Technology, Institute Archives, Pasadena, Calif.
Theodore von Kármán Collection
Papers of Robert A. Millikan

Jet Propulsion Laboratory Archives, Pasadena, Calif.
Various papers covering the early days of the GALCIT were used from this archive.

Library of Congress, Manuscript Division, Washington, D.C.
Papers of Frank M. Andrews, Henry Harley Arnold, Vannevar Bush, Ira C. Eaker, Curtis E. LeMay, Robert A. Millikan, William "Billy" Mitchell, Carl Andrew Spaatz, and Orville and Wilbur Wright.

National Defense University Archives, Washington, D.C.
H. H. Arnold Collection

Harry S. Truman Library, Independence, Mo.
Papers of Harry S. Truman

University of South Carolina, Caroliniana Library, Columbia, S.C.
Papers of John K. Montgomery

U.S. Air Force Historical Research Agency, Maxwell AFB, Ala.

U.S. Air Force Academy Library, Special Collections, Colorado Springs
"Pewt" Arnold's Military Academy Log Book; "Hap" Arnold, Murray Green Collection;
    papers of Maj. Gen. Haywood S. Hansell, Gen. Laurence S. Kuter, John F. Victory, and
    Theodore von Kármán.

U.S. Air Force Museum, Wright-Patterson AFB, Ohio
Kettering Bug folder
Papers of Henry H. Arnold
Ercoupe folder

U.S. Military Academy Library, West Point, N.Y.
A variety of sources were used to piece together Arnold's cadet life; the Official Register and the
    Howitzer were most helpful.

U.S. Air Force Scientific Advisory Board, Washington, D.C.
Early SAG files contain many organizational documents that are missing in other locations.

U.S. National Archives and Records Administration

NATIONAL ARCHIVES, WASHINGTON, D.C.

Record Group 18: office of the chief of the Air Corps
Record Group 94: W-3 and 201 files

NATIONAL ARCHIVES, COLLEGE PARK, MD.

Record Group 255: NACA Executive Committee meeting minutes
Record Group 111: H. H. Arnold photo collection

NASM Archives, Washington, D.C.
Folders of H. H. Arnold, Vannevar Bush, Max Munk, Ludwig Prandtl, Theodore von Kármán;
    Jet Engines, General and 1920–45; George W. Lewis Collection.

NASM Archives, Silver Hill, Md.
Papers of Jerome Clarke Hunsaker
A microfiche copy of the Kármán papers are located here.

ADMINISTRATIVE HISTORIES AND REPORTS

Arnold, H. H. "First Report of the Commanding General of the Army Air Forces to the Secre-
    tary of War." 4 January 1944. In Walter Millis, ed., *The War Reports of General of the Army*

George C. Marshall, General of the Army H. H. Arnold, and Fleet Admiral Ernest J. King. New York: J. B. Lippincott, 1947.

———. "Second Report of the Commanding General of the Army Air Forces to the Secretary of War." 27 February 1945. In Millis, ed., *The War Reports.*

———. "Third Report of the Commanding General of the Army Air Forces to the Secretary of War." 12 November 1945. In Millis, ed., *The War Reports.*

Bush, Vannevar. *Science: The Endless Frontier.* Washington, D.C.: U.S. Government Printing Office, 1945.

"Case History of Whittle Engine." Historical Study No. 93, Air Force Logistical Command History Office, n.d.

Craven, Wesley Frank, and James Lea Cate, eds. *The Army Air Forces in World War II,* 7 vols. Chicago: University of Chicago Press, 1955. Reprinted by Office of Air Force History, 1985.

Maurer, Maurer, ed. *The U.S. Air Service in World War I,* 4 vols. Washington, D.C.: Office of Air Force History, 1978–79.

New World Vistas: Air and Space Power for the 21st Century, ancillary vol. Washington, D.C.: USAF Scientific Advisory Board, 1995.

Rand Corporation: The First Fifteen Years. Santa Monica, Calif.: Rand, 1963.

"United States Air Force Scientific Advisory Board 50th Anniversary, 1944–1994, Commemorative History, November 9–10, 1994." Washington, D.C.: USAF/SAB, 1994.

Von Kármán, Theodore. *Where We Stand: First Report to General of the Army H. H. Arnold on Long Range Research Problems of the Air Forces with a Review of German Plans and Developments.* Original manuscript held at Wright-Patterson Air Force Base, Ohio: Air Force Materiel Command History Office, 22 August 1945.

———. "Science: The Key to Air Supremacy." Vol. 1 of 13-vol. government report. Executive summary from *Toward New Horizons,* 15 December 1945. Published by the SAG in limited numbers; originals held at Wright-Patterson Wright-Patterson Air Force Base, Ohio.

MEMOIRS, BIOGRAPHIES, AND PUBLISHED PERSONAL PAPERS

Ambrose, Stephen E. *The Supreme Commander: The War Years of General Dwight D. Eisenhower.* New York: Doubleday, 1969.

Arnold, Henry H. *Global Mission.* New York: Harper and Brothers, 1949. Various drafts of this work are available in the L/C in the Arnold papers and are valuable to review. Citations used in this work are from the page proofs of the printed book, rather than from any one of the three original manuscripts.

———. *Airmen and Aircraft: An Introduction to Aeronautics.* New York: Ronald Press, 1926.

———. *Bill Bruce and the Pioneer Aviators.* New York: A. L. Burt, 1928.

———. *Bill Bruce, the Flying Cadet.* New York: A. L. Burt, 1928.

———. *Bill Bruce Becomes an Ace.* New York: A. L. Burt, 1928.

———. *Bill Bruce on Border Patrol.* New York: A. L. Burt, 1928.

———. *Bill Bruce on Forest Patrol.* New York: A. L. Burt, 1928.

———. *Bill Bruce in the Trans-Continental Race.* New York: A. L. Burt, 1928.

Arnold, Henry H., and Ira C. Eaker. *Army Flyer.* New York: Harper and Brothers, 1942.

———. *Winged Warfare.* New York: Harper and Brothers, 1941.

———. *This Flying Game.* New York: Funk and Wagnalls, 1936.

Bush, Vannevar. *Modern Arms and Free Men: A Discussion of the Role of Science in Preserving Democracy.* New York: Simon and Schuster, 1949.

Chandler, A. D., ed. *The Papers of Dwight David Eisenhower: The War Years,* 5 vols. Baltimore: Johns Hopkins University Press, 1970.

Chandler, Charles DeForest, and Frank P. Lahm, *How Our Army Grew Wings: Airmen and Aircraft Before 1914.* New York: Ronald Press, 1943.

Coffey, Thomas M. *Hap: The Story of the U.S. Air Force and the Man who Built It, General Henry H. "Hap" Arnold.* New York: Viking Press, 1982.

Crouch, Tom D. *The Bishop's Boys: A Life of Wilbur and Orville.* New York: W. W. Norton, 1989.

Daso, Dik A. *Architects of American Air Supremacy: Gen. Hap Arnold and Dr. Theodore von Kármán.* Maxwell AFB, Ala.: Air University Press, 1997.

Davis, Richard G. *Carl A. Spaatz and the Air War in Europe.* Washington, D.C.: Center for Air Force History, 1993.

Doolittle, James H., with Carroll V. Glines. *I Could Never Be So Lucky Again.* New York: Bantam Books, 1991.

Dupre, Flint O. *Hap Arnold: Architect of American Air Power.* New York: MacMillan, 1972.

Eisenhower, Dwight D. *Crusade in Europe.* New York: Doubleday, 1948.

Farley, James A. *Jim Farley's Story: The Roosevelt Years.* New York: McGraw-Hill, 1948.

Frisbee, John L., ed. *Makers of the United States Air Force.* Washington, D.C.: Office of Air Force History, 1987.

Glines, Carroll V. *Jimmy Doolittle: Master of the Calculated Risk.* New York: Van Nostrand Reinhold, 1972.

Golley, John. *Whittle: The True Story.* Washington, D.C.: Smithsonian Institution Press, 1987.

Goodstein, Judith R. *Millikan's School: A History of the California Institute of Technology.* New York: W. W. Norton, 1991.

Gorn, Michael H. *The Universal Man: Theodore von Kármán's Life in Aeronautics.* Washington, D.C.: Smithsonian Institution Press, 1992.

Griffith, Thomas E. *MacArthur's Airman: General George C. Kenney and the War in the South Pacific.* Lawrence, Kans.: University Press of Kansas, 1998.

Hallion, Richard P., ed. *The Wright Brothers: Heirs of Prometheus.* Washington, D.C.: Smithsonian Institution Press, 1978.

Hanle, Paul A. *Bringing Aerodynamics to America.* Cambridge, Mass.: MIT Press, 1982.

Head, William. *Every Inch a Soldier: Augustine Warner Robins and the Building of U.S. Airpower.* College Station, Tex.: Texas A and M University Press, 1995.

Horgan, James J. *City of Flight: The History of Aviation in St. Louis.* Gerald, Mo: Patrice Press, 1984.

Hughes, Thomas Alexander. *Over Lord: General Pete Quesada and the Triumph of Tactical Air Power in World War II.* New York: Free Press, 1995.

Hurley, Alfred F. *Billy Mitchell: Crusader for Air Power.* Bloomington, Ind.: Indiana University Press, 1964.

Kargon, Robert H. *The Rise of Robert Millikan: Portrait of a Life in American Science.* Ithaca, N.Y.: Cornell University Press, 1982.

Kenney, George C. *General Kenney Reports.* New York: Duell, Sloan, and Pearce, 1949; reprint, Washington, D.C.: Air Force History and Museums Program, 1997.

LeMay, Curtis E., with MacKinlay Kantor. *Mission with LeMay: My Story.* Garden City, N.Y.: Doubleday, 1965.

Leslie, Stuart W. *Boss Kettering.* New York: Columbia University Press, 1983.

Lindbergh, Charles A. *Autobiography of Values.* New York: Harcourt Brace Jovanovich, 1976.

————. *The Wartime Journals of Charles A. Lindbergh.* New York: Harcourt Brace Jovanovich, 1970.

McFarland, Marvin W., ed. *The Papers of Wilbur and Orville Wright: Including the Chanute-Wright Letters and Other Papers of Octave Chanute.* New York: McGraw-Hill, 1953.

Meilinger, Phillip S. *Hoyt S. Vandenberg: The Life of a General.* Bloomington, Ind.: Indiana University Press, 1989.

Mets, David R. *Master of Airpower: General Carl A. Spaatz.* Novato, Calif.: Presidio Press, 1988.

Mitchell, William. *Memoirs of World War I: From Start to Finish of Our Greatest War.* New York: Random House, 1960.

Parton, James. *"Air Force Spoken Here": General Ira C. Eaker and the Command of the Air.* Bethesda, Md.: Adler and Adler, 1986.

Pogue, Forrest C. *George C. Marshall: Ordeal and Hope, 1939–1942.* New York: Viking Press, 1966.

———. *George C. Marshall: Organizer of Victory, 1943–1945.* New York: Viking Press, 1973.

Reynolds, Clark, G. *Admiral John H. Towers: The Struggle for Naval Air Supremacy.* Annapolis, Md.: Naval Institute Press, 1991.

Roseberry, C. R. *Glenn Curtiss: Pioneer of Flight.* Syracuse, N.Y.: Syracuse University Press, 1991.

Sherwood, Robert E. *Roosevelt and Hopkins: An Intimate History.* New York: Harper and Brothers, 1948.

Shiner. John F. *Foulois and the U.S. Army Air Corps, 1931–1935.* Washington, D.C.: Office of Air Force History, 1983.

Von Kármán, Theodore, with Lee Edson. *The Wind and Beyond: Theodore von Kármán, Pioneer in Aviation and Pathfinder in Space.* Boston: Little, Brown, 1967.

Whittle, Frank. *Jet: The Story of a Pioneer.* London: Frederick Muller, 1953.

Wright, Orville, with an introduction by Fred Kelly. *How We Invented the Airplane.* New York: David McKay, 1953.

MONOGRAPHS AND OTHER SECONDARY SOURCES

Alperovitz, Gar. *The Decision to Use the Bomb, and the Architecture of an American Myth.* New York: Alfred A. Knopf, 1995.

Ambrose, Stephen E. *Soldier, General of the Army, President-Elect: 1890–1952.* New York: Simon and Schuster, 1983.

Bilstein, Roger E. *Orders of Magnitude: A History of the NACA and NASA, 1915–1990.* Washington, D.C.: National Aeronautics and Space Administration, 1989.

Borden, Norman E., Jr. *The Air Mail Emergency: 1934.* Freeport, Maine: Bond Wheelwright, 1968.

Borowski, Harry R., ed. *Military Planning in the Twentieth Century: Proceedings of the Eleventh Military History Symposium, USAF Academy, 1984.* Washington, D.C.: Office of Air Force History, 1986.

Boyne, Walter J. *De Havilland DH-4: From Flaming Coffin to Living Legend.* Washington, D.C.: Smithsonian Institution Press, 1984.

Coffman, Edward M. *The War to End All Wars: The American Military Experience in World War I.* New York: Oxford University Press, 1968; reprint Madison, Wis.: University of Wisconsin Press, 1986.

Constant, Edward W., II. *The Origins of the Turbojet Revolution.* Baltimore: Johns Hopkins University Press, 1980.

Corn, Joseph J. *The Winged Gospel: America's Romance with Aviation, 1900–1950.* New York: Oxford University Press, 1983.

Crouch, Tom D. *A Dream of Wings: Americans and the Airplane, 1875–1905.* Washington: Smithsonian Institution Press, 1981.

Dastrup, Boyd L. *The U.S. Army Command and General Staff College: A Centennial History.* Manhattan, Kans.: Sunflower University Press, 1982.

Ellis, John. *Brute Force: Allied Strategy and Tactics in the Second World War.* New York: Viking Press, 1990.

Emme, Eugene M. *The Impact of Airpower: National Security and World Politics.* Princeton, N.J.: D. Van Nostrand, 1959.

Finney, Robert T. *History of the Air Corps Tactical School, 1920–1940.* Washington: Center for Air Force History, 1992.

Futrell, Robert F. *Ideas, Concepts, and Doctrine: Basic Thinking in the United States Air Force, 1907–1960,* 2 vols. Maxwell AFB, Ala.: Air University Press, 1989.

Geffen, William, ed., *Command and Commanders in Modern Warfare: The Proceedings of the Second Military History Symposium, USAF Academy, 1968.* Washington, D.C.: Office of Air Force History, 1971.

Gorn, Michael H. *Harnessing the Genie: Science and Technology Forecasting for the Air Force, 1944–1986.* Washington: Office of Air Force History, 1988.

Greer, Thomas H. *The Development of Air Doctrine in the Army Air Arm, 1917–1941.* Maxwell AFB, Ala.: Historical Division, Research Studies Institute, Air University, 1955.

Hallion, Richard P. *Legacy of Flight: The Guggenheim Contribution to American Aviation.* Seattle: University of Washington Press, 1977.

Hansell, Haywood S., Jr. *The Air Plan That Defeated Hitler.* Atlanta, Ga.: Higgins-McArthur, 1972.

Hansen, James R. *Engineer in Charge: A History of the Langley Aeronautical Laboratory, 1917–1958.* Washington, D.C.: National Aeronautics and Space Administration, 1987.

Hennessy, Juliette A. *The United States Air Arm: April 1861 to April 1917.* Washington, D.C.: Office of Air Force History, 1985.

Herzstein, Robert E. *Roosevelt and Hitler: Prelude to War.* New York: Paragon House, 1989.

Holley, Irving B., Jr. *Ideas and Weapons, Exploitation of the Aerial Weapon by the United States during World War I: A Study in the Relationship of Technological Advance, Military Doctrine, and the Development of Weapons.* New York: Yale University Press, Washington, D.C., 1953.

———. *Buying Aircraft: Matériel Procurement for the Army Air Forces.* Washington, D.C.: Center of Military History, United States Army, 1964.

Homze, Edward L. *Arming the Luftwaffe: The Reich Air Ministry and the German Aircraft Industry, 1919–1939.* Lincoln, Nebr.: University of Nebraska Press, 1976.

Howe, George F. *Northwest Africa: Seizing the Initiative in the West.* Washington, D.C.: Center of Military History, United States Army, 1991.

The *Howitzer: The Yearbook of the United States Military Academy Corps of Cadets.* West Point, N.Y.: USMA Printing Office, 1903–7.

Hughes, Thomas P. *American Genesis: A Century of Invention and Technological Enthusiasm.* New York: Penguin Books, 1989.

Hurley, Alfred F., And Robert C. Ehrhart, eds. *Air Power and Warfare: The Proceedings of the Eighth Military History Symposium, United States Air Force Academy, 18–20 October 1978.* Washington, D.C.: Office of Air Force History, 1979.

Jakab, Peter L. *Visions of a Flying Machine.* Washington, D.C.: Smithsonian Institution Press, 1990.

Kelsey, Benjamin S. *The Dragon's Teeth?* Washington, D.C.: Smithsonian Institution Press, 1982.

Kennett, Lee. *The First Air War, 1914–1918.* New York: Free Press, 1991.

Kohn, Richard H. *Eagle and Sword: The Beginnings of the Military Establishment in America.* New York: Free Press, 1975.

Loosbrock, John L. and Richard M. Skinner. *The Wild Blue: The Story of American Airpower.* New York: G. P. Putnam's Sons, 1946 through 1960.

MacIsaac, David. *Strategic Bombing in World War II.* New York: Garland Publishing, 1976.

Maurer, Maurer. *Aviation in the U.S. Army, 1919–1939.* Washington, D.C.: Office of Air Force History, 1987.

McPherson, James M. *Battle Cry of Freedom: The Civil War Era.* New York: Oxford University Press, 1988.

Mee, Charles L., Jr. *Meeting at Potsdam.* New York: M. Evans, 1975.

Meilinger, Phillip S., ed. *The Paths of Heaven: The Evolution of Airpower Theory.* Maxwell AFB, Ala.: Air University Press, 1997.

Miller, Nathan. *War at Sea: A Naval History of World War II.* New York: Scribners, 1995.

Morrow, John H., Jr. *The Great War in the Air: Military Aviation from 1909 to 1921.* Washington, D.C.: Smithsonian Institution Press, 1993.

Neufeld, Jacob. *Ballistic Missiles in the United States Air Force, 1945–1960.* Washington, D.C.: Office of Air Force History, 1990.

Olsen, Jack. *Aphrodite: Desperate Mission.* New York: G. P. Putnam's Sons, 1970.

Overy, R. J. *The Air War, 1939–1945.* New York: Stein and Day, 1981.

———. *Why the Allies Won.* New York: W. W. Norton, 1995.

Parrish, Thomas. *Roosevelt and Marshall: Partners in Politics and War.* New York: William Morrow, 1989.

Raines, Rebecca Robbins. *Getting the Message Through: A Branch History of the U.S. Army Signal Corps.* Washington, D.C.: Center for Military History, U.S. Army, 1996.

Reardon, Carol. *Soldiers and Scholars: The U.S. Army and the Uses of Military History, 1865–1920.* Lawrence, Kans.: University Press of Kansas, 1990.

Roland, Alex. *Model Research: The National Advisory Committee for Aeronautics, 1915–1958,* 2 vols. Washington: National Air and Space Administration, 1985.

Sapolsky, Harvey M. *Science and the Navy: The History of the Office of Naval Research.* Princeton, N.J.: Princeton University Press, 1990.

Schaffer, Ronald. *Wings of Judgment: American Bombing in World War II.* New York: Oxford University Press, 1985.

Searls, Hank. *The Lost Prince: Young Joe, The Forgotten Kennedy.* New York: World Publishing Company, 1969.

Sherry, Michael S. *Preparing for the Next War: America Plans for Postwar Defense, 1941–1945.* New Haven, Conn.: Yale University Press, 1977.

———. *The Rise of American Air Power: The Creation of Armageddon.* New Haven, Conn.: Yale University Press, 1987.

Shute, Henry Augustus. *The Real Diary of a Real Boy.* Peterborough, N.H.: Noone House, Richard R. Smith Co., ca. 1900; reprint 1967.

Smith, Merritt Roe, ed. *Military Enterprise and Technological Change: Perspectives on the American Experience.* Cambridge, Mass.: MIT Press, 1985.

Smith, Perry McCoy. *The Air Force Plans for Peace, 1943–1945.* Baltimore: Johns Hopkins University Press, 1970.

Sturm, Thomas A. *The USAF Scientific Advisory Board: Its First Twenty Years, 1944–1964.* Washington, D.C.: USAF Historical Division Liaison Office, 1967.

Sweetser, Arthur. *The American Air Service: A Record of Its Problems, Its Difficulties, Its Failures, and Its Final Achievements.* New York: D. Appleton, 1919.

Tate, James P. *The Army and Its Air Corps: Army Policy Toward Aviation, 1919–1941.* Maxwell AFB, Ala.: Air University Press, 1998.

Thompson, Erwin N. *Defender of the Gate: The Presidio of San Francisco, a History from 1846 to 1995.* San Francisco: Golden Gate National Recreation Area, California National Park Service, 1997.

Truscott, Lucian K., Jr. *The Twilight of the U.S. Cavalry: Life in the Old Army, 1917–1942.* Lawrence, Kans.: University Press of Kansas, 1989.

Underwood, Jeffery S. *The Wings of Democracy: The Influence of Air Power on the Roosevelt Administration, 1933–1941.* College Station, Tex.: Texas A and M University Press, 1991.

Walker, Lois E., and Shelby E. Wickam. *From Huffman Prairie to the Moon: The History of Wright-Patterson Air Force Base*. Dayton, Ohio: Air Force Logistics Command, 1986.

Weigley, Russell F. *History of the United States Army*. New York: Macmillan, 1967.

Werrell, Kenneth P. *Blankets of Fire: U.S. Bombers over Japan During World War II*. Washington, D.C.: Smithsonian Institution Press, 1996.

———. *The Evolution of the Cruise Missile*. Maxwell AFB, Ala.: Air University Press, 1985.

Wilson, Theodore A. *The First Summit: Roosevelt and Churchill at Placentia Bay, 1941*. Lawrence, Kans.: University Press of Kansas, rev. ed., 1991.

Wolk, Herman S. *Planning and Organizing the Post War Air Force, 1943–1947*. Washington, D.C.: Office of Air Force History, 1984.

Wolko, Howard S. *In the Cause of Flight: Technologists of Aeronautics and Astronautics*. Washington, D.C.: Smithsonian Institution Press, 1981.

Worden, Mike. *Rise of the Fighter Generals: The Problem of Air Force Leadership, 1945–1982*. Maxwell AFB, Ala.: Air University Press, 1998.

Wright, Monte D., and Lawrence J. Paszek, eds. *Science, Technology, and Warfare: The Proceedings of the Third Military History Symposium, United States Air Force Academy, 8–9 May 1969*. Washington, D.C.: Office of Air Force History, 1970.

Young, James O. *Meeting the Challenge of Supersonic Flight*. Edwards AFB, Calif.: Air Force Flight Test Center History Office, 1997.

———, ed. *Supersonic Symposium: The Men of Mach One*. Edwards AFB, Calif.: Air Force Flight Test Center History Office, 1990.

ARTICLES

Primary

Arnold, Henry H. "Air Force in the Atomic Age," in Dexter Masters and Katharine Way, eds., *One World or None*. New York: McGraw-Hill, 1946.

———. "Science and Air Power." *Air Affairs*, December 1946, 184–95.

———. "Air Power for Peace." *National Geographic*, February 1946, 137–94.

———. "Tomorrow," in James H. Straubel, ed. *Air Force Diary: 111 Stories from the Official Service Journal of the USAAF*. New York: Simon and Schuster, 1947.

———. "Tradition Can't Win Wars." *Collier's*, 15 October 1949, 13, 65–66.

———. "Performance of Future Airplanes." *U.S. Air Service* (July 1925).

"Barling Bomber: Army's Super Plane." *U.S. Air Service* 8, no. 8 (1923): 15–19.

Carr, Gardner W. "Organization and Activities of Engineering Division of the Army Air Service." *U.S. Air Service* 6, no. 6 (1922): 9–12.

Eaker, Ira C. "Memories of Six Air Chiefs." *Aerospace Historian*, December 1973, 188–96.

Gorrell, E. S., and Phil Carroll, "Colonel Raynal Cawthorne Bolling." *U.S. Air Service* (March 1920): 18.

"Initial Flight of the Barling Bomber." *U.S. Air Service* 8, no. 9 (1923): 17.

Kepner, W. G. "Air Service, Air Force, and Air Power." *U.S. Air Service* 5, no. 4 (1921): 16–17.

Knerr, Hugh J. "Washington to Alaska and Back: Memories of the 1934 U.S. Air Corps Test Flight." *Aerospace Historian*, March 1972, 20.

Kotcher, Ezra. "Our Jet Propelled Fighter." *Air Force*, March 1944, 6–8, 64.

Kuter, Laurence S. "The General vs. The Establishment: Gen. H. H. Arnold and the Air Staff. "*Aerospace Historian* (September 1973): 185–89.

———. "How Hap Built the AAF," *Air Force Magazine*, September 1973, 88–93.

Milling, Brig. Gen. T. DeWitt. "Early Flying Experiences," *Air Power Historian* 3, no. 1 (1956): 93.

Mitchell, William, Col. "Lawrence Sperry and the Aerial Torpedo." *U.S. Air Service* 1 (January 1926).

Von Kármán, Theodore. The Next Fifty Years." *Interavia* 10, no.1 (1955): 20–21.

Walkowicz, T. F. "Von Kármán's Singular Contributions to American Aerospace Power." *Air Force Magazine,* May 1981, 60–61.

———. "USAF Scientific Advisory Board: Hap's Brain Child." *Air Force Magazine,* June 1955.

Whittle, Frank. "The Birth of the Jet Engine in Britain," in W. J. Boyne and D. S. Lopez, eds., *The Jet Age: Forty Years of Jet Aviation.* Washington, D.C.: Smithsonian Institution Press, 1979.

Secondary

"An Introduction to Project Air Force." Santa Monica, Calif.: Rand Publication CP-77, June 1990, 1–3.

Collins, Martin J. "Internalizing the Civilian: Rand and the Air Force in the Early Cold War." Speech given at the 1993 Annual Society for the History of Technology Meeting.

Ford, Daniel. "Gentlemen, I Give You the Whittle Engine." *Air and Space,* October–November 1992, 88–98.

Grier, Peter. "New World Vistas." *Air Force* 79, no. 3 (1996): 20–25.

"Daniel Guggenheim Founds School of Aeronautics," *U.S. Air Service* 10, no. 7 (1925): 36.

Hall, R. Cargill. "Shaping the Course of Aeronautics, Rocketry, and Astronautics: Theodore von Kármán, 1881–1963." *Journal of Aerospace Sciences* 26, no. 4 (1978): 369–86.

———. "Theodore von Kármán, 1881–1963." *Aerospace Historian* (Winter 1981): 252–58.

Hallion, Richard P. "Pioneer of Flight: Doolittle As Aviation Technologist." *Air Power History* 40, no. 4 (1993): 9–15.

Hunley, J. D. "The Enigma of Robert H. Goddard." *Technology and Culture* 36, no. 2 (1995): 327–50.

Nunn, Jack H. "MIT: A University's Contribution to National Defense." *Military Affairs,* October 1979, 120–25.

Reich, Leonard S. "From the *Spirit of St. Louis* to the SST: Charles Lindbergh, Technology, and Environment," *Technology and Culture* 36, no. 2 (1995): 351–93.

Roland, Alex. "Science, Technology, and War." *Technology and Culture* supplement to vol. 36, no. 2 (1995): S83–S99.

Schaffer, Ronald. "American Military Ethics in World War II: The Bombing of German Cities." *Journal of American History* 67, no. 2 (1980): 318–34.

Scrivner, John H. "Maj. Gen. Orvil A. Anderson," *Air Force Magazine,* June 1979, 103–5.

Shiner, John F. "The Air Corps, the Navy, and Coast Defense, 1919–1941." *Military Affairs,* October 1981, 113–20.

"The Men and the Machines, 1913–1915." *Air Power Historian* 3, no. 3 (1956): 173–75.

Vaughan, David K. "Hap Arnold's Bill Bruce Books." *Air Power History* 40, no. 4 (1993): 43–49.

LETTERS TO AUTHOR

Ira C. Eaker, 1 October 1979, 7 December 1979
Murray Green, 18 November 1993, 9 February 1994, 20 June 1994
Stephen B. Groves, 9 December 1997
Haywood Hansell, 4 October 1979, 9 December 1979
I. B. Holley Jr., 1 October 1998
John W. Huston, 13 December 1993, 19 August 1994, 22 February 1996
Robert E. Kimmel, 30 March 1998

INTERVIEWS BY AUTHOR

Dr. Robert Alvus, 29 June 1998
Mrs. Barbara Arnold, 6 April 1995
Mr. Robert Arnold, 14–16 July 1995

Tom Crouch, 6 February 1998
Dr. Ivan Getting, 9 November 1994
Dr. Richard P. Hallion, 28 August 1995
Mr. Chester Hasert, 9 November 1994
Ms. Gay Morris, 2 February 1998
Gen. Bernard A. Schriever (ret.), 9 November 1995, 12 March 1996
Dr. William Rees Sears, 8 July 1995
Bruce Simmons, 7 May 1997
Gen. Jacob E. Smart, 31 May 1997
Dr. H. Guyford Stever, 18 May 1995
Dr. Homer Joe Stewart, 21 July 1995
Mrs. Mary Streett, 21 May 1997

USAF ACADEMY ORAL HISTORY INTERVIEWS

Lt. Gen. Ira C. Eaker, 19 October 1978
John F. Victory, No. 210A, October 1962
Dr. Theodore von Kármán, No. 212, 27 January 1960

MURRAY GREEN COLLECTION INTERVIEWS

General of the Air Force H. H. Arnold, by T. A. Boyd, 19 October 1949
Col. H. H. Arnold Jr. (ret.), 29–30 August 1972
Mrs. H. H. Arnold, October 1968, 22 August 1972
William B. Arnold, 17 August 1974
Gen. Eugene Beebe, 1 October 1969
Brig. Gen. H. W. Bowman, 23 August 1969
Maj. Gen. Franklin Carroll, 1 September 1971
Gen. Benjamin Chidlaw, 12 December 1969
Lt. Gen. Laurence Craigie, 19 August 1970
Lt. Gen. Fred Dean, 20 February 1973
Maj. Gen. Donald J. Keirn (ret.), 25 September 1970
Bruce Simmons, 7 October 1969
R. A. Swartz, August 1972
Lt. Gen. Henry Viccellio, 13 May 1970

COLUMBIA UNIVERSITY ORAL HISTORY INTERVIEW PROGRAM (CUOHI)

Reminiscences of Friends and Family of Gen. Henry Hap Arnold (used with permission)
Mrs. H. H. Arnold
Gen. Eugene Beebe
Col. Benjamin Castle
F. W. Conant
Donald Douglas
Hugh L. Dryden
Gen. Grandison Gardner
Maj. Gen. Frank P. Lahm
Robert A. Lovett
Thomas D. Milling
A. E. Raymond
Gen. Carl A. Spaatz

AIR FORCE HISTORICAL RESEARCH AGENCY ORAL HISTORY INTERVIEWS, OTHERS

Gen. Laurence Craigie, interviewed on Wingspan Network, 20 June 1998
Hugh Knerr, K239.0512-616, 1012
Lauris Norstad, K239.0512-1116, 1473
Lt. Gen. Donald L. Putt, K239.0512-724
Theodore von Kármán, K146.34-59
Theodore von Kármán, interviewed by Shirley Thomas, tape, January 1960.

UNPUBLISHED PAPERS

Dryden, Hugh L. "Memorial Ceremony for Theodore von Kármán, 1881–1963." Memorial proceedings. USAF Academy Special Collections.
Fanton, Jonathan Foster. "Robert A. Lovett: The War Years," Ph.D. dissertation, Yale University. Ann Arbor, Mich.: University Microfilm International, 1978.
Komons, Nick A. "Science and the Air Force: A History of the Air Force Office of Scientific Research." Arlington, Va.: Historical Division, Office of Information, Office of Aerospace Research, 1966.
Murray, Williamson. "The Air War in Europe." 1998.
Van der Linden, Robert. "The Struggle for the Long-Range Heavy Bomber: The United States Air Corps, 1934–1939," master's thesis, George Washington University, 1981.
Young, James O. "Riding England's Coattails: The U.S. Army Air Forces and the Turbojet Revolution." TMs (photocopy). Edwards AFB, Calif.: Air Force Flight Test Center History Office, 1995.

Index

A

accelerated stalls, airplane flight characteristic, 58, 62
Adkins, Suzie, 174, 207
advisory council, 160, 215, 232
aerial torpedos. *See* bugs
Aero Club of America, 28, 57
Aeronatical Board, 37
Ainsworth, Fred C., 36
Air Corps, U.S. Army, 113–14, 122, 151
Air Corps Materiel Division, Wright Field, 176, 188
airfields, 88, 101
Air Force Aid Society, 199
air mail, carried by the Air Corps (1934), 130–35
airpower terminology defined, 4–5; as megasystem, 142, 146, 148
Air Service, U.S. Army, 101, 103
air supremacy, 1, 192, 196
Alaska flight, 135–41, 144, 227
Allen, James, 34, 57, 60
American Expeditionary Force (AEF), 95
Anderson, Orville, 175
Andrews, Frank M., 140, 142, 149–50, 154–55, 164, 181–83, 230
Aphrodite. *See* Project Aphrodite
appropriations, aviation, 63–64, 82, 101, 133, 143, 162, 165, 213

Arcadia Conference, 171, 179
Argentia Conference, 169
Arlington National Cemetery, 223–24
Army Air Forces, 169, 174, 208
Army Industrial College, 110–11, 119, 184, 227
Arnold, Ann Louis Harley ("Lou") (mother), 8–9, 31, 126, 198
Arnold, Bion J., 91
Arnold, Clifford Hood ("Cliff") (brother), 9, 96, 116, 217
Arnold, David Lee (son), 116, 192, 199, 218, 224–25
Arnold, Eleanor ("Bee" and "Beadle") (wife), 29–30, 38, 40, 60, 42, 65, 79, 124, 125–27, 134, 145, 149, 192; childbirth, 85, 92, 116; emotional challenges, 199–200; menopause, 199; miscarriage, 76; physical problems, 78, 107, 191, 206; pregnancy, 75–76, 82
Arnold, Henry H., Jr. ("Hank") (son), 83, 179, 192, 204, 224–25
Arnold, Henry Harley ("Hap"): airpower, 4–5, 171–72; animals and pets, 207, 217, 220–221; athletic nature, 17, 20–21, 25–26, 109, 226; books and articles, 115, 119, 146, 148, 172, 216, 219, 221–22; cavalry and horsemanship, 21, 24, 27–28, 33, 58; coronary artery disease, 71, 183, 198; courtship, 28, 30, 39, 41,

Arnold, Henry Harley ("Hap")(*cont.*)
66–67; daily work habits, 71, 88–89,
162, 170, 173, 183–84, 200, 205, 227;
death of, 221–23; drinking and alcohol,
27, 67, 109, 149; eating habits, 71, 198;
elements of career success, 226–33; expectations of subordinates, 107, 172;
family history, 7–12, 119, 129; fate, 65,
131; flying experiences, 46–50, 56, 58–
59, 82, 147; funeral of, 223–24; hard
work and, 227–28; heart attacks, 162,
198–203, 214, 219, 221, 222; humor,
24, 67–68; hunting, 35–36, 138, 170;
immaturity, 30, 31, 117; impatience, 69–
70, 163, 223; integrity, 232–33; love and
affection, 30, 41, 69–70, 75–76, 93–94,
203, 233; marital problems, 67, 109,
118, 202–4, 218; nickname, 27, 51, 126;
physical description, 17, 39, 109, 125,
170, 181, 200, 204, 208, 215; politics,
80, 113, 131–32, 172; positive attitude
and drive, 113–14, 141, 148, 164, 174–
75, 181, 228–29; R and D, 125, 127,
146, 151, 153–54, 158–60, 164–65,
171, 187–90, 197, 212, 214, 216; race
and ethnicity, 89; religion, 61, 217,
223–24; safety, 73, 131–33; secondary
schooling, 10–11; self-characterization,
40, 68; shyness, 29, 67; smoking habits,
21, 27, 67, 198; staff experience, 84,
117, 140, 164, 201, 227; stress, 71, 75,
133, 198; stunt pilot, 51, 230; technology, 3, 52, 146, 151, 154, 160, 166–68,
176, 191, 196, 209, 215, 227–28; temper, 36, 134–35; treatment of Bee, 76,
78, 201–2, 221, 232; treatment of
children, 108–9, 224–25, 232–33;
treatment of subordinates, 136, 220,
228–33; ulcers, 104–5; use of profanity, 26, 31; wedding, 67–68,
74–75
Arnold, Herbert Alonzo ("Daddy Doc")
(father), 7–9, 31–32, 36, 40, 63, 75,
126, 129
Arnold, Isaac Johnson (brother), 10
Arnold, John Linton (son), 105–6, 108–9,
225
Arnold, Lois ("Lolie") (daughter), 78, 89,
185, 192, 218, 224
Arnold, Robert (grandson), xvii, 225
Arnold, Sophia Elizabeth ("Betty") (sister),
9, 39, 63, 66, 74, 203, 217

Arnold, Thomas Herbert ("Tommy")
(brother), 9, 31
Arnold, William Bruce ("Bill Bruce") (son),
92, 124, 185, 192, 208, 218, 224–25
Arnold Engineering and Development Cen-
ter (AEDC), 224
Arnold-McNarney-McCain Agreement,
177
"Arsenal of Democracy," 165
atomic bomb, 188, 194, 208, 209
Atwood, Harry, 50
Aviation Planning Board, 155

B

B-10, 134–35, 136, 141
B-17, 151, 155–56, 159, 165, 169, 186
B-2, 127–28
B-24, 186
B-25, 173
B-29, 159, 190, 195, 223, 229
B-36, 195
Baker, Newton D., 80, 102
Baker Board, 142
Balanced Air Program, 145, 152, 154, 158,
172, 207
balloons, 28, 83, 140
Barnes farm, Augusta, Georgia, 52–54
Batangas, Philippes, 76
Battle of Britain, 162, 177
Battle of the Atlantic, 178
"beast barracks," 14
Beck, Paul, 50, 54
Beebe, Eugene, 162, 170–71, 176, 199
Bell, Larry, 118, 156, 167, 194, 197
Benet-Mercier machine gun, 51
Bennett International Balloon Race (Paris,
1906), 20
Berlin, Germany, 40, 208
Billingsley, William D., 65
Bishop, Harry, 82
Black, Hugo L., 134
Black Hand, 26–27, 31
Bleriot, Louis, 39, 72, 77
Bolling, Raynal C., 86
Bolling Commission, 86
Bolling Field, 170
Booth, Ewing J. ("Barney"), 115
border patrol, Mexico, 104
Bosque, 35, 77
Bowles, Edward, 3, 178, 189, 211, 213
Bradley, Omar N., 2

Brett, George, 176
Browning Board, 145
Bucknell College, 12
bugs (flying bombs), 87, 90–93, 165, 178, 186. *See also* glide bomb
Burgess, W. Starling, 72
Burgess Company, 72
Burgess-Wright "tractor" seaplane, 55
Burwell, Harvey S., 102
Bush, Vannevar, 3, 153–54, 159, 166, 188–90, 193, 213

C

Cairo Conference, 179
California Fish and Game Commission, 219
California Institute of Technology (Caltech), 4, 92, 115, 127–28, 141–42, 146, 153, 157, 191, 196–97, 211
Call, Loren H., 70
Carr, Gardner W., 122
Casablanca Conference, 175, 179–81, 186
Castle, Frederick C., 34, 37
Chamberlain, Neville, 151
Chandler, C. DeForrest, 49, 51, 77
Chennault, Claire, 175
Chidlaw, Benjamin, 167–68
Churchill, Winston, ix, 2, 169, 180
Civil Conservation Corps (CCC), 128–29
Civil Works Administration (CWA), 128
Cochran, Jacqueline, 168, 199
College Park, Maryland, 49–51, 54–55, 57, 64
Columbia space shuttle (STS-78), 225
Combined Bomber Offensive (CBO), 180, 182–83
Combined Chiefs of Staff, 171, 179
Command and General Staff College, Fort Leavenworth, 34
Committee on Air Corps Research, 151
Compton, Karl, 127
Coolidge, Calvin, 112–14, 119
Cowan, Arthur S., 37, 42, 85
Craig, Malin, 130, 140, 144, 154, 162
Craigie, Laurence, 194
Curtiss, Glenn, 41–42

D

Dargue, Herbert A., 77–81
Davidson, F. Trubee, 114

Davis, Dwight, 114
Dawson, Wiley Evans ("Wobley"), 34
Dayton Engineering Laboratories Company, 92
D-day, 2, 192
Death Valley, California, 128
Deeds, Edward A., 88
Delco Company. *See* Dayton Engineering Laboratories Company
DeMille, Cecil B., 102
Dern, George H., 139
DH-4, 86, 96–98, 102–4, 107, 115, 120, 124, 165, 187
doctrine, air, 54–55, 57, 66, 100, 112, 128, 138, 144, 146–48, 155, 179–80, 186–93, 207, 209, 211, 216–17, 219, 222, 233
Doolittle, James H. ("Jimmy"), 102, 105, 172, 185, 204, 223
Douglas, Barbara, 185
Douglas, Donald, 3, 111, 117–18, 141, 148, 170, 185, 213
Douglas Aircraft Corporation, 212
Douglas World Cruiser, 110
Drum, Hugh A., 139
Drum Board, 142, 145
Dryden, Hugh L., 203, 205
Durand, William F., 153, 193–94
Durand Board, 167

E

Eaker, Ira C., 102, 105, 146, 175–76, 180–81, 200–1, 203, 205, 209
Earhart, Amelia, 147
Echols, Oliver, 176
Edwards, Clarence, 84
Eglin Air Force Base, Florida, 91
Eisenhower, Dwight D. ("Ike"), 1, 170, 185, 214, 219, 223
Eisenhower, John, 1
El Aquario, 136
El Rancho Feliz, 185, 207, 217
Emmons, Delos, 149, 153
Engineering Division, McCook Field, 122–23
engines, aircraft, 45, 52, 56, 61–62, 64–65, 77, 80, 96–97, 110, 112, 148, 161, 164–65, 167, 195
experimentation, aeronautic, 45–46, 51, 97, 123, 146, 158–59
Explorer I, 140

F

Fairbanks, Alaska, 135, 137
Fairfield Air Depot, Ohio, 120–27, 184
Farley, James A. (postmaster general), 130, 133
fatalities, aviation, 37–38, 55, 71, 104, 130, 148, 183–84, 187, 227
FB. *See* bugs
Fechet, James E., 119
Field Manual *100-20,* 185
fighter escort, 180, 193, 229
First Wing GHQ Air Force, 127–30
Fleet, Reuben, 94
"Flight Around the World" (1924), 110
flying bombs. *See* bugs
Fogleman, Ronald R., xvi, xix
Ford, Henry, 3, 91
Forest Fire Patrol, 103
Fort Jay, Governors Island, New York, 38, 40, 44
Fort Leavenworth, Kansas, 34, 115, 119–20
Fort McKinley, Philippines, 34–35, 76, 79
Fort Myer, Virginia, 34, 37, 57, 191
Fort Riley, Kansas, 57–60, 114–15, 117, 119, 140
Fort Thomas, Kentucky, 69, 74
Foulois, Benjamin D., 76, 122, 130–31, 134–35, 142

G

Gandy, Charles, 36
Gardner, Grandison, 186
General Electric (GE), 167
General Headquarters (GHQ), Air Force, 127, 142–46, 149–50, 152
Germany, aeronautical developments, 156–57, 205–6
Giles, Barney, 203, 205
Glassford, William A., 83–84, 104
glide bomb, 159, 178–79, 185–86
Global Mission (Hap Arnold), 127, 149, 219, 222–23
GMA-1 Bug, 178
Goering, Hermann, 139
Gorrell, Edward, 96
Graham, Harry, 70
Grant, Ulysses S., 18, 41
Great Depression (1924), 122, 126

Greene, Carl F., 159
Guggenheim, Daniel, 114–15, 141
Guggenheim, Harry, 115, 159
Guggenheim Aeronautical Laboratory, California Institute of Technology (GAL-CIT), 141, 153–54, 167, 196–97, 210
Guggenheim Fund, 114, 141–42, 146, 157

H

Halsey, William F., Jr. ("Bull"), 173
Hamilton Field, California, 130, 170
Hansell, Haywood S., Jr., 175, 207
Harmon, Millard F., 174
Harriman, Averell, 180
Harris, Air Marshal A. ("Bertie"), 171
Hay, James, 78
Hazlehurst, L. W., Jr., 55
Hickam, Horace, 131, 133, 140
Himmler, Heinrich, 208
Hitler, Adolph, 145, 151
Hollywood, California, 129
Hopkins, Harry L., 128–29, 149, 161, 169, 171, 180, 214, 220, 230
House Resolution 28728, 63
Howell Commission, 140, 142, 149–50
Hudson, Henry, 41
Huffman Prarie, Ohio, 23
Hunsaker, Jerome C., 85, 151, 190
Hunter, Frank ("Monk"), 95, 130, 175

I

Infantry, U.S. Army, 32, 43, 73
Ismay, Gen. Hastings, ix

J

Jefferson, Thomas, 13
jet-assisted takeoff (JATO), 153–54, 157, 188, 191, 193
jet propulsion, 193–94, 206, 211
JN-2, 81
JN-3, 81, 115
JN-4, 86
Johnson, Louis, 222
Joint Chiefs of Staff, 209
Jones, Byron Q., 82, 131–33, 140
Jouett, Jack, 118
Juliets, 15–16

K

Kármán, Theodore von, xii, 115, 141–42, 154, 157, 191–92, 197–98, 205–6, 208, 210–12, 214, 216, 219, 228
Keirn, Donald J., 167, 188
Kenly, William L., 89–90, 92
Kenney, George C., 175–176, 201
Kettering, Charles ("Ket"), 3, 91, 178
Kettering Flying Bug, 119, 178, 186
Kilner Board, 156
King, Ernest J., 2, 171, 179
Kirtland, Roy C., 50, 55
Kitty Hawk, North Carolina, 18
Knerr, Hugh, 135–36, 139, 175–76
Knudsen, William, 176, 178
Koehler, Herman J., 17, 21
Kotcher, Ezra, 156
Krick, Irving, 141
Kuter, Laurence, 175, 203

L

La Guardia Airport, New York, 191–92, 196
Lahm, Frank P., 20, 28, 85
Laidlaw, Bill, 221
Leahy, William D., 2
Lee, Robert E., 18
LeMay, Curtis E., 175, 195, 207
Lend-Lease Act, 164–66, 180
LePere aircraft, 104
Levée, Charles, 28
Lewis, Isaac N., 51
Lewis, George W., 157, 166, 187
Liberty Eagle (bug), 178
Liberty Engine, 88, 165, 187
Liggett, Hunter, 99
Lindbergh, Charles A., 156–57, 159
Lower Merion High School, 10
Lovett, Robert A., 163–65, 200, 205, 214, 230
Ludlow, Israel, 51, 59
Luftwaffe (German air force), 2, 139, 145, 182
Lusitania, 80
Luzon, Philippines, 35

M

MacArthur, Douglas, 127, 133–34, 139, 175, 207

Mackay Trophy, 57, 135, 139
"Magna Carta" for Air Corps, 161
Malina, Frank, 154
March Field, California, 127, 130, 142, 144
Marquardt, Dr. Gilbert, 199
Marshall, Gen. George C., 2, 77, 154, 161–62, 165, 169, 171, 176, 183, 190, 200, 203, 205, 214, 230
Marshall, Lily, 77
Martin, Glenn L., 134
Martin, Dr. Lee B., 199
Massachusetts Institute of Technology (MIT), 88, 127, 153–54, 177–78, 190, 211
McCook Field, Ohio, 106, 110, 122–23
McNarney, Joseph T., 130, 162
mechanics, aircraft, 80, 127, 137
Mennonite, 8
Menoher, Charles T., 99, 103
Meyers, Bennett E., 220
Military-Industrial-Academic complex, 141–42, 146, 228
Millikan, Robert A., 4, 91, 115, 127–28, 141–42, 146, 153–54, 191, 196–97
Milling, Thomas D., 33, 43–45, 49, 51, 55, 57–58, 65, 72, 74, 77, 98
Mills, Albert L., 18
missiles: guided, 213, 217, 233; unguided, 90
Mitchell, William ("Billy"), xv, 28, 86, 95, 98–100, 102, 104–5, 112, 119, 124; court martial, 112, 114–16, 230
Molineau, Henry S., 80
Montgomery, John L., 112, 118
Morgenthau, Henry, Jr., 171
Morrow Board, 113–16
Moss, Sanford, 167
Muroc Air Base, California, 194

N

napalm, xii
Napoleonic philosophy, 162
National Academy of Sciences, 151
National Advisory Committee for Aeronautics (NACA), 81, 123–24, 151, 156–59, 166–67, 188–89, 190, 193–94, 211
National Aeronautics and Space Administration (NASA), 124
National Air and Space Museum (NASM), xviii

National Bureau of Standards, 203
National Defense Act (1916), 82
National Defense Research Committee (NDRC), 177, 188, 190
NBL-1 (Barling Bomber), 106, 124–25, 193
Nelson, Eric, 110
Newburgh Conspiracy, 13
New Deal, 128–29
Nimitz, Chester, 208
Norstadt, Lauris, 160
North Island, California, 79–80
Northrop, Jack, 118

O

O'Donnell, Rosie, 207
Office of Scientific Liaison, 190
Office of Scientific Research and Development (OSRD), 188–90
Olympic, 94
Operation Lusty (Luftwaffe Sercret Technology), 197, 204–5
Ostfriesland, 105
Overlord, 179, 183

P

P-47, 193, 194
P-51, 192–94
Panama Canal Zone, 72, 83, 164
Pan Am Airlines, 118
Paris, France, 204, 208
Patrick, Mason M., 94, 108, 111–19, 134–35, 231
Pearl Harbor, Hawaii, 170, 182
Penrose, Boies, 33
performance, aircraft, 46–48, 73, 81, 112
Pershing, Gen. John J., 35, 81, 86, 92–93, 104, 108, 224
Philippine Islands, 33–34, 75–78, 169, 207
Pickford, Mary, 101
Ploesti Raid, 179
political correctness, xv
Pool, Annie Alexander (Bee's mother), 10–11, 38, 221
Pool, Eleanor. *See* Arnold, Eleanor
Pool, Lois (Bee's sister), 74
Portal, Sir Charles ("Peter"), 166, 171, 183, 185

Post, Henry B., 61
Potsdam Conference, 179, 208–9
Prandtl, Ludwig, 141
Pratt, William V., 121, 127, 140
Presidio, California (Crissy Field), 102
production, aircraft, 72, 87–88, 90, 96–98, 106, 111, 120, 156, 160–62, 165, 183–84, 195, 230
Project Aphrodite, 186–88, 229
Project RAND, 212–13
public relations, Hap Arnold's use of, 133, 137, 145, 158, 230

Q

Quebec Conference, 179, 205
Quesada, Elwood R., 175
Quimby, Harriet, 50

R

radar, 159, 176–78, 188, 210–11
Radiation Laboratory, Massachusetts Institute of Technology (RADLAB), 211
radio, 122–23, 135, 137
"Real Diary of a Real Boy" (Shute), 27
refueling, in air, 107
Ribot Cable, 86
rivalry, Army-Navy, 21, 26, 64–65, 85, 104, 112, 136, 173, 196, 206, 218–20
Robins, Augustine Warner, 121, 176
rockets, 153, 159
Rockwell, Lewis C., 56, 70, 130
Rockwell Field, California, 82, 99, 101, 107, 129, 149, 172
Roosevelt, Franklin D., 128, 140, 149, 152, 156–57, 163, 165, 169–71, 182, 199, 230
Roosevelt, Theodore ("Teddy"), 22
Root, Elihu, 30
Royal Air Force (RAF), 165–66, 169, 177–79, 182
Royce, Ralph, 140

S

Sands, Alfred L. P., 58–59
Savannah River, Georgia, 53
Schriever, Bernard, 190
Scientific Advisory Board (1945), 213

Scientific Advisory Group (1944), 197–98, 205–6, 212
Scott, Frank, 55
Scott, H. L., 36
Scott, Riley E., 51
Scriven, George P., 60, 63, 65, 73
Sea-Search Attack Development Unit (SADU), 177–78
Selfridge, Thomas, 37
Sheffield, Thomas, 204
Shute, Henry A., 27
Signal Corps, Aeronautical Division, 37, 42, 73, 78, 81
Simmons, Bruce, 176, 220
Simms Station, Ohio, 43–44
Slessor, Air Marshal John C., 166, 181
Smart, Jacob, 179, 184
Smith, Lowell, 110
Snowden, Ernie (son-in-law), 192, 218
Somervell, Brehon B., 241
Spaatz, Carl A. ("Tooey"), 2, 15, 101, 103, 105, 112, 129–30, 142, 144, 152–53, 155, 159, 175–78, 181, 185, 201–6, 211–15, 218
Spanish civil war, 155
Sperry, Elmer, 84, 91
Sperry, Lawrence, 84
S.Q. (special-qualification status), 36
Squier, George O., 34, 83, 89, 93
St. Louis World's Fair, 22
Stefen, LeRoy L., 226
Stever, H. Guyford, 205
Stimson, Henry L., 163, 165, 171
strategic bombing, 106–7, 143, 155, 171, 180, 193, 204, 206
Stratemeyer, George E., 201
Streett, Mary, 199, 218
Supreme War Council, 171

T

Taft, William Howard, 33, 36
Task Force 16, 173
technological development, 90–94, 96, 106–7, 112, 120, 122–25, 129, 133–34, 141, 179, 186, 203, 207, 211, 216; civilian specific, 56–57, 118, 142
Tedder, Air Marshal Sir Arthur, 187
Tokyo Raid, 172
Torch, North Africa, 179–80
Toward New Horizons, 212

Towers, John H., 64, 218
training, 89, 143, 152, 160, 163, 174, 227
Trident Conference, 183
Truman, Harry S., 208–9, 219, 224
Twenty-first Bomber Command, 207
Twining, Nathan, 176

U

U-boat warfare, 87, 177–78, 181
unification of airpower, 185, 218, 222, 229
United States Air Force Academy (USAFA), 14, 224–25
U.S. Military Academy. *See* West Point
U.S. Naval Academy, 14, 64

V

V-1 buzz bomb, 2, 187, 206
V-2 vengeance rocket, 187, 206, 210
Valley of the Moon, 214, 221–23
Vandenberg, Hoyt S., 175
Victory, John, 106

W

Wagner, Hayden, 10, 18, 23
Wanger, Irving P., 11, 33
Warner, Donald F. ("Truly"), 167
War Production Board, 189
Washington, D.C., 70, 83, 88, 110, 140, 145, 170, 224
Washington, George, 29
Weary Willy. *See* Project Aphrodite
Weaver, Walter, 174–75
Welsh, Art L. ("Al"), 48, 55
Westover, Oscar, 131, 135, 144, 148–50, 162, 183
West Point (U.S. Military Academy), xvii, 1, 11–31, 118, 218–19, 226, 233
Where We Stand, 208–12
Whitehead, Gustav, 23
Whittle, Frank, 193
Whittle jet engine, 166–67, 188
Wills, C. H., 91
Wilson, Woodrow, 80, 86, 161
wind tunnels, 46, 141, 157, 206, 210
Winged Warfare (Hap Arnold and Eaker), 172, 177
Women Airforce Service Pilots (WASP), 168, 219

Wood, Leonard, 74, 85
World War I, 94–99, 227
Wright, Milton, 44
Wright, Orville, 37–38, 55, 59, 62–63, 73, 91, 159, 198–99, 220–21. *See also* Wright Brothers
Wright, Wilbur, 23, 41–42, 55. *See also* Wright Brothers
Wright Brothers, 3, 18, 23, 34, 44, 46, 48, 72, 106, 228
Wright Field, Ohio, 122–29, 137, 151, 156, 167, 176, 188, 190–91, 206
Wright Flyer, 38, 42–43
Wright Glider, 45
Wright Military Flyer, 38, 41, 52, 155
Wright Model B, 44–46, 49, 52, 70
Wright Model C, 52, 55–57, 59, 61–63

X

XNBL-1. *See* NBL-1
XP-59A, 167–68, 193–94, 229

Y

Yalta Conference, 198
YB-10, 134–40

Z

Zimmermann Telegram, 87

192—